PENNY NICHOLS

FOR DYLAN

PENNY NICHOLS © 2019 REED, MEANS, & WIEGLE.

ISBN: 978-1-60309-448-1   23 22 21 20 19   5 4 3 2 1

SPECIAL THANKS TO MARY SHELLEY AND WILLIAM SHAKESPEARE FOR THE DIALOGUE ASSIST.

PUBLISHED BY TOP SHELF PRODUCTIONS, PO BOX 1282, MARIETTA, GA 30061-1282, USA. TOP SHELF PRODUCTIONS IS AN IMPRINT OF IDW PUBLISHING, A DIVISION OF IDEA AND DESIGN WORKS, LLC. OFFICES: 2765 TRUXTUN ROAD, SAN DIEGO, CA 92106. TOP SHELF PRODUCTIONS®, THE TOP SHELF LOGO, IDEA AND DESIGN WORKS®, AND THE IDW LOGO ARE REGISTERED TRADEMARKS OF IDEA AND DESIGN WORKS, LLC. ALL RIGHTS RESERVED. WITH THE EXCEPTION OF SMALL EXCERPTS OF ARTWORK USED FOR REVIEW PURPOSES, NONE OF THE CONTENTS OF THIS PUBLICATION MAY BE REPRINTED WITHOUT THE PERMISSION OF IDW PUBLISHING. IDW PUBLISHING DOES NOT READ OR ACCEPT UNSOLICITED SUBMISSIONS OF IDEAS, STORIES OR ARTWORK.

PRINTED IN KOREA.

EDITOR-IN-CHIEF: CHRIS STAROS.

DESIGNED BY GILBERTO LAZCANO.

VISIT OUR ONLINE CATALOG AT TOPSHELFCOMIX.COM.

PENNY NICHOLS

WRITTEN BY MK REED & GREG MEANS
ART BY MATT WIEGLE

CHAPTER ONE

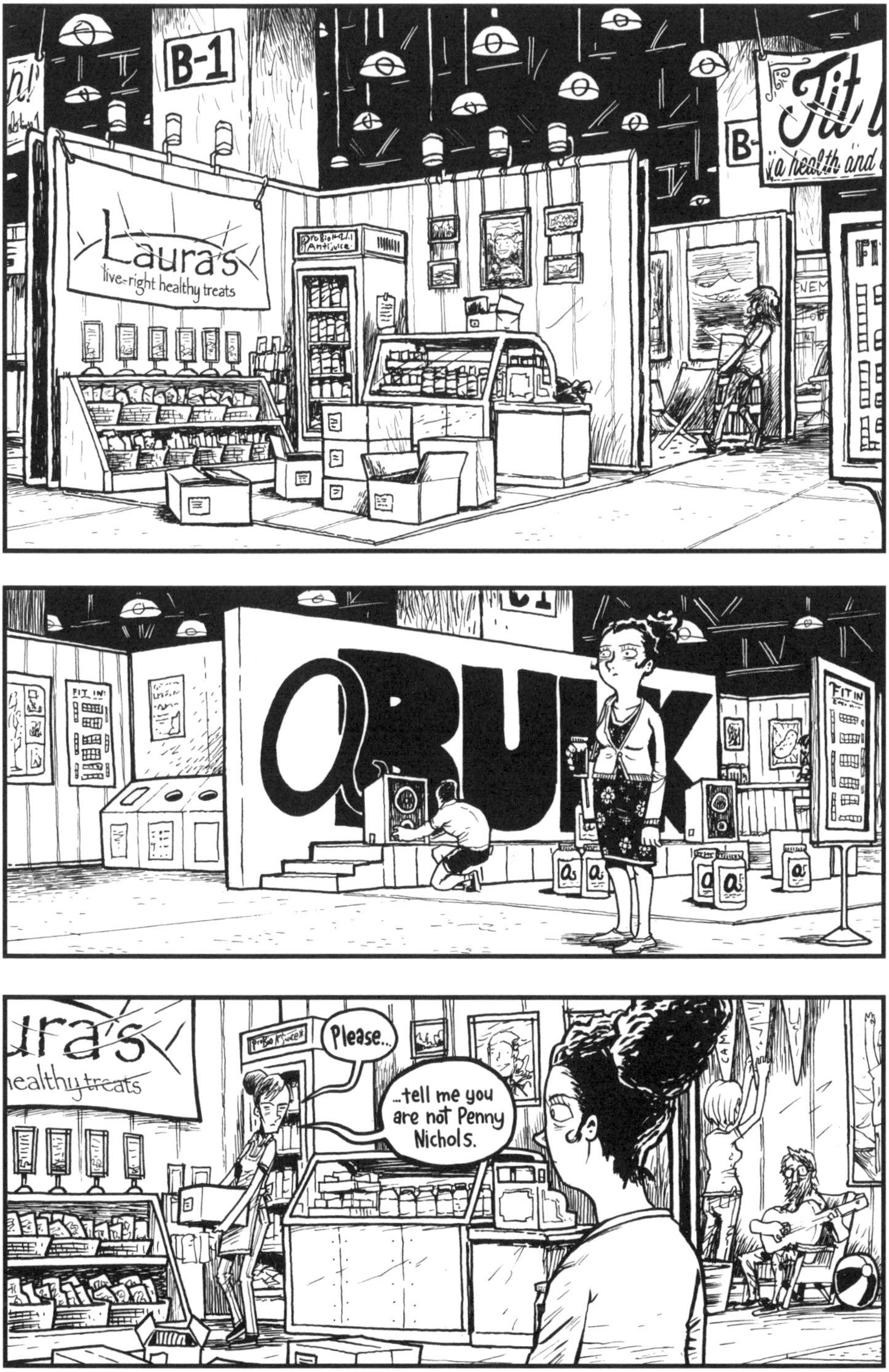
B-1
Laura's
live-right healthy treats
FIT IN!
Please...
...tell me you are not Penny Nichols.

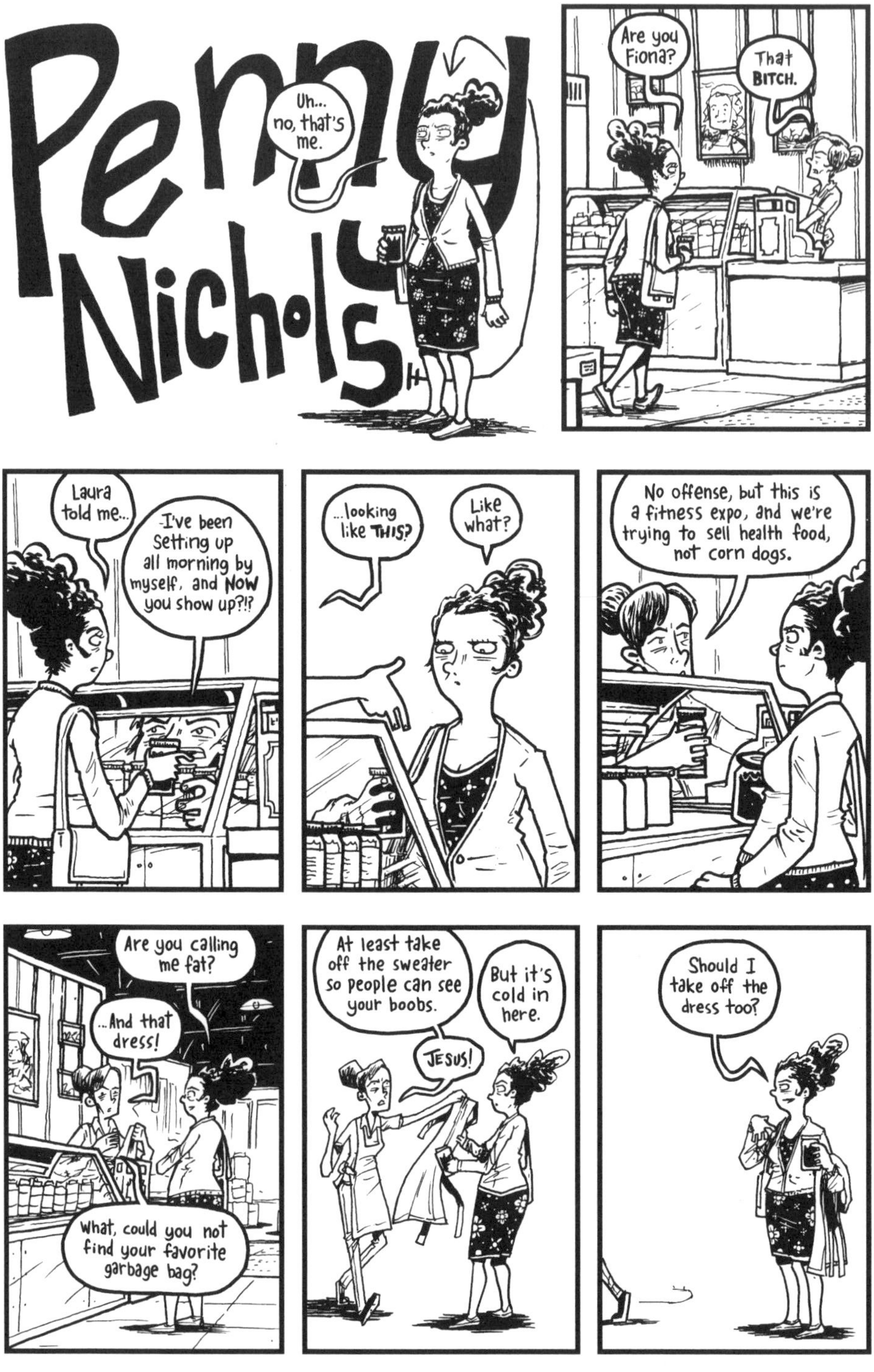
Penny Nichols
Uh... no, that's me.
Are you Fiona?
That BITCH.
Laura told me...
I've been setting up all morning by myself, and NOW you show up?!?
...looking like THIS?
Like what?
No offense, but this is a fitness expo, and we're trying to sell health food, not corn dogs.
Are you calling me fat?
...And that dress!
What, could you not find your favorite garbage bag?
At least take off the sweater so people can see your boobs.
But it's cold in here.
JESUS!
Should I take off the dress too?

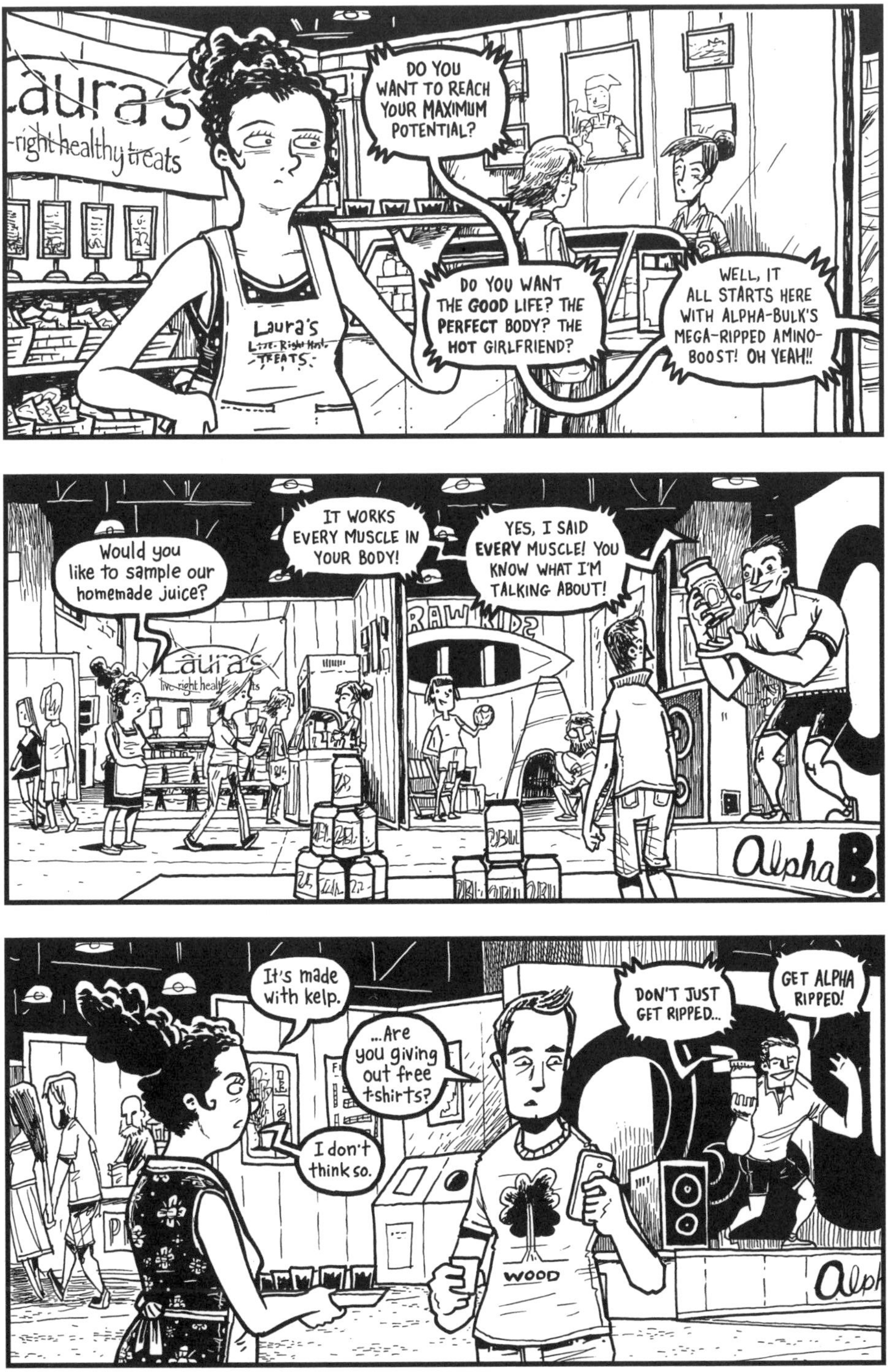
Laura's
right healthy treats
DO YOU WANT TO REACH YOUR MAXIMUM POTENTIAL?
DO YOU WANT THE GOOD LIFE? THE PERFECT BODY? THE HOT GIRLFRIEND?
WELL, IT ALL STARTS HERE WITH ALPHA-BULK'S MEGA-RIPPED AMINO-BOOST! OH YEAH!!
Laura's
TREATS
Would you like to sample our homemade juice?
IT WORKS EVERY MUSCLE IN YOUR BODY!
YES, I SAID EVERY MUSCLE! YOU KNOW WHAT I'M TALKING ABOUT!
Laura's
AlphaB
It's made with kelp.
...Are you giving out free t-shirts?
I don't think so.
DON'T JUST GET RIPPED...
GET ALPHA RIPPED!
WOOD

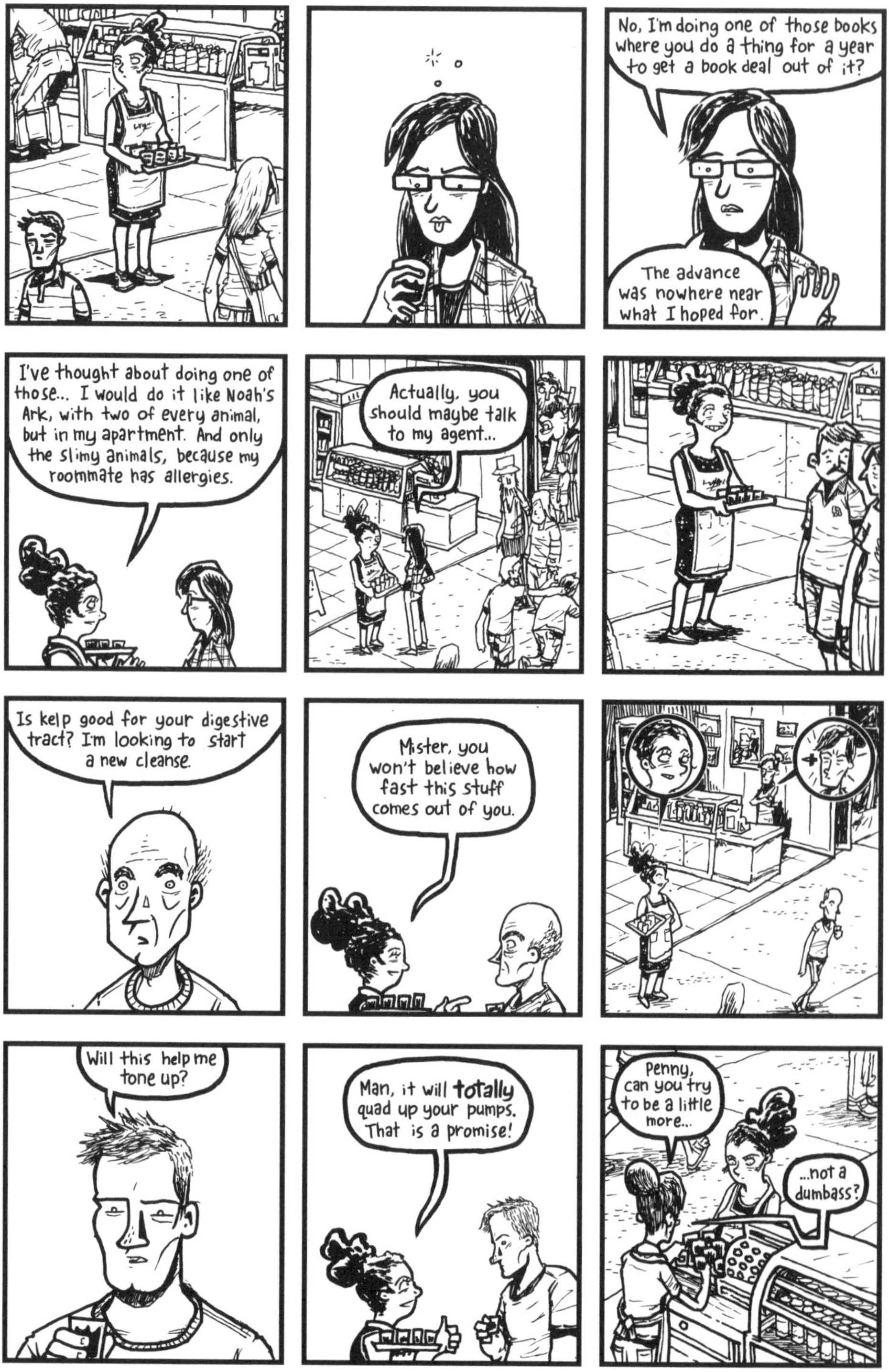
No, I'm doing one of those books where you do a thing for a year to get a book deal out of it?
The advance was nowhere near what I hoped for.
I've thought about doing one of those... I would do it like Noah's Ark, with two of every animal, but in my apartment. And only the slimy animals, because my roommate has allergies.
Actually, you should maybe talk to my agent...
Is kelp good for your digestive tract? I'm looking to start a new cleanse.
Mister, you won't believe how fast this stuff comes out of you.
Will this help me tone up?
Man, it will **totally** quad up your pumps. That is a promise!
Penny, can you try to be a little more...
...not a dumbass?

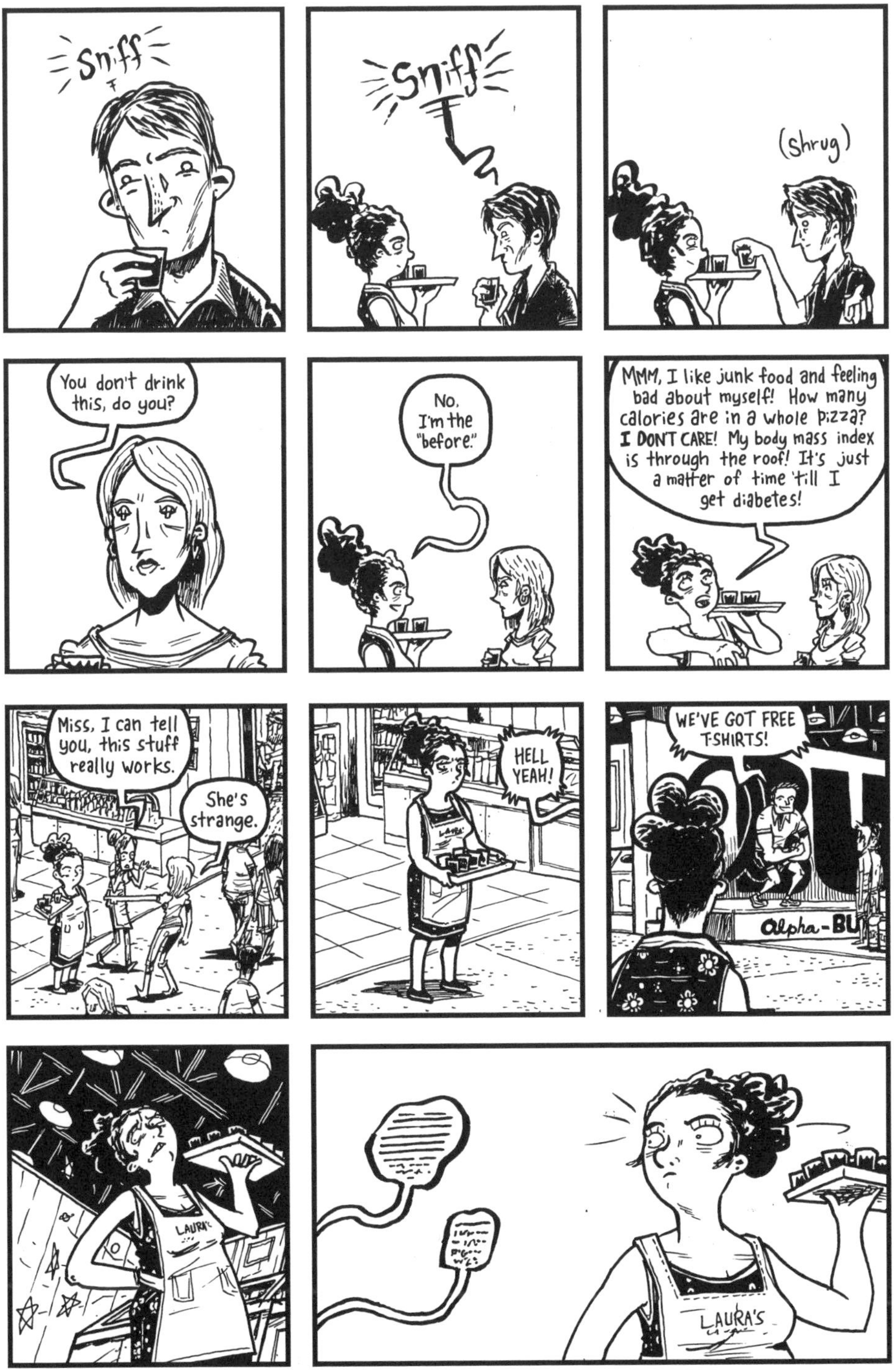
Sniff
Sniff
(shrug)
You don't drink this, do you?
No. I'm the "before."
MMM, I like junk food and feeling bad about myself! How many calories are in a whole pizza? I DON'T CARE! My body mass index is through the roof! It's just a matter of time 'till I get diabetes!
Miss, I can tell you, this stuff really works.
She's strange.
HELL YEAH!
WE'VE GOT FREE T-SHIRTS!
Alpha-BU
LAURA'S
LAURA'S

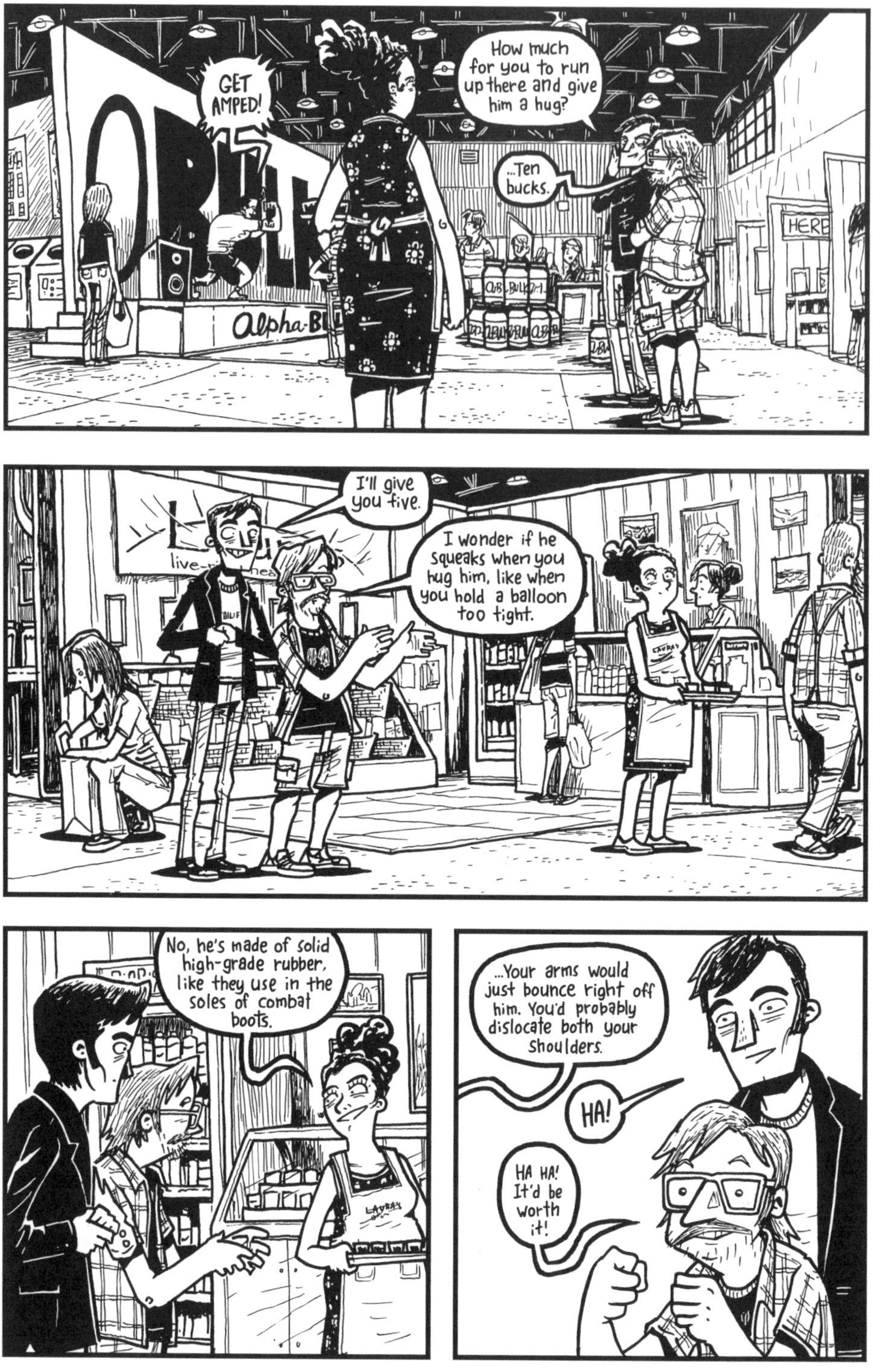
GET AMPED!
How much for you to run up there and give him a hug?
...Ten bucks.
HERE
alpha-BU
I'll give you five.
I wonder if he squeaks when you hug him, like when you hold a balloon too tight.
No, he's made of solid high-grade rubber, like they use in the soles of combat boots.
...Your arms would just bounce right off him. You'd probably dislocate both your shoulders.
HA!
HA HA! It'd be worth it!

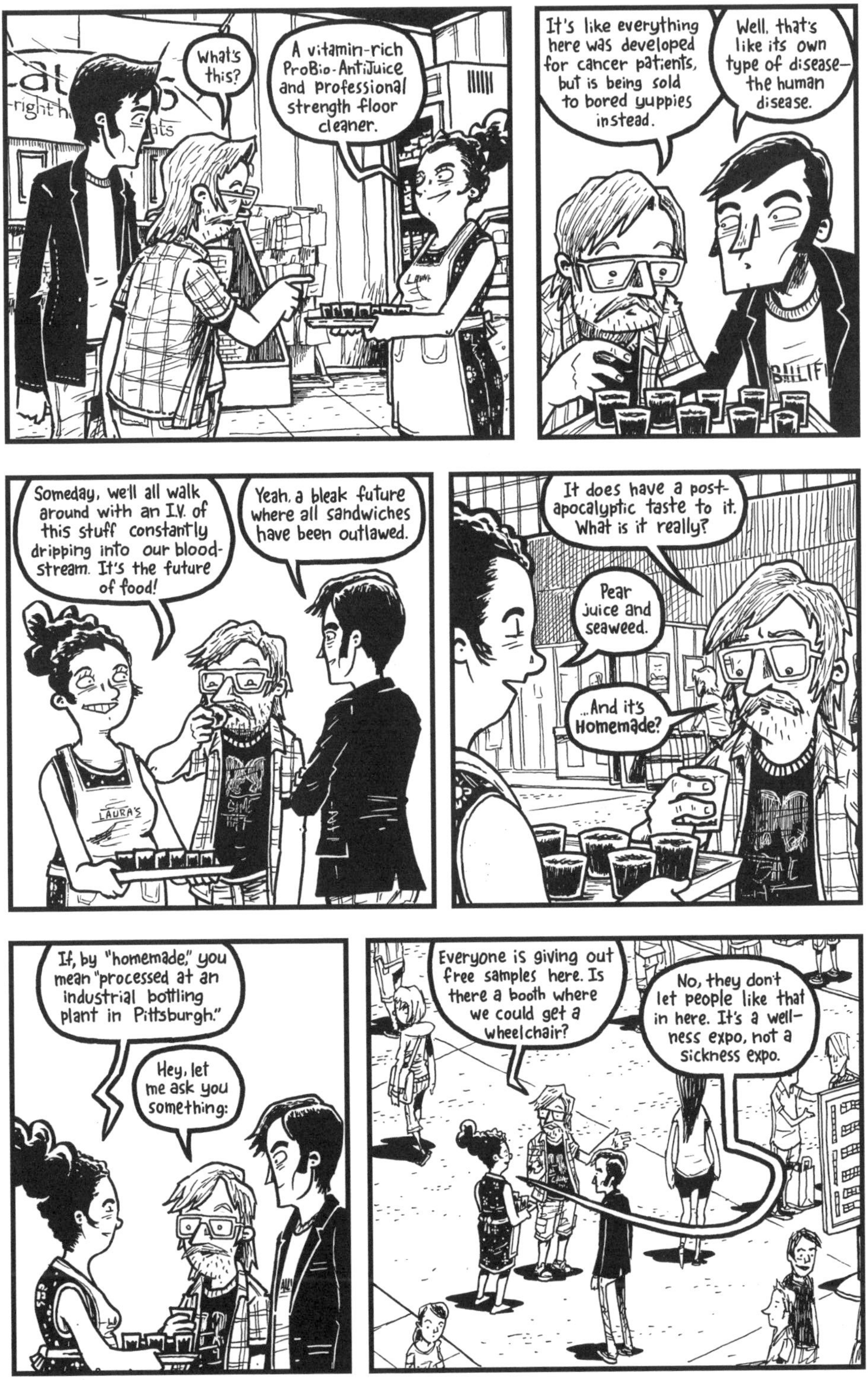
What's this?
A vitamin-rich ProBio-AntiJuice and professional strength floor cleaner.
It's like everything here was developed for cancer patients, but is being sold to bored yuppies instead.
Well, that's like its own type of disease— the human disease.
Someday, we'll all walk around with an I.V. of this stuff constantly dripping into our blood-stream. It's the future of food!
Yeah, a bleak future where all sandwiches have been outlawed.
LAURA'S
It does have a post-apocalyptic taste to it. What is it really?
Pear juice and seaweed.
...And it's Homemade?
If, by "homemade," you mean "processed at an industrial bottling plant in Pittsburgh."
Hey, let me ask you something:
Everyone is giving out free samples here. Is there a booth where we could get a wheelchair?
No, they don't let people like that in here. It's a well-ness expo, not a sickness expo.

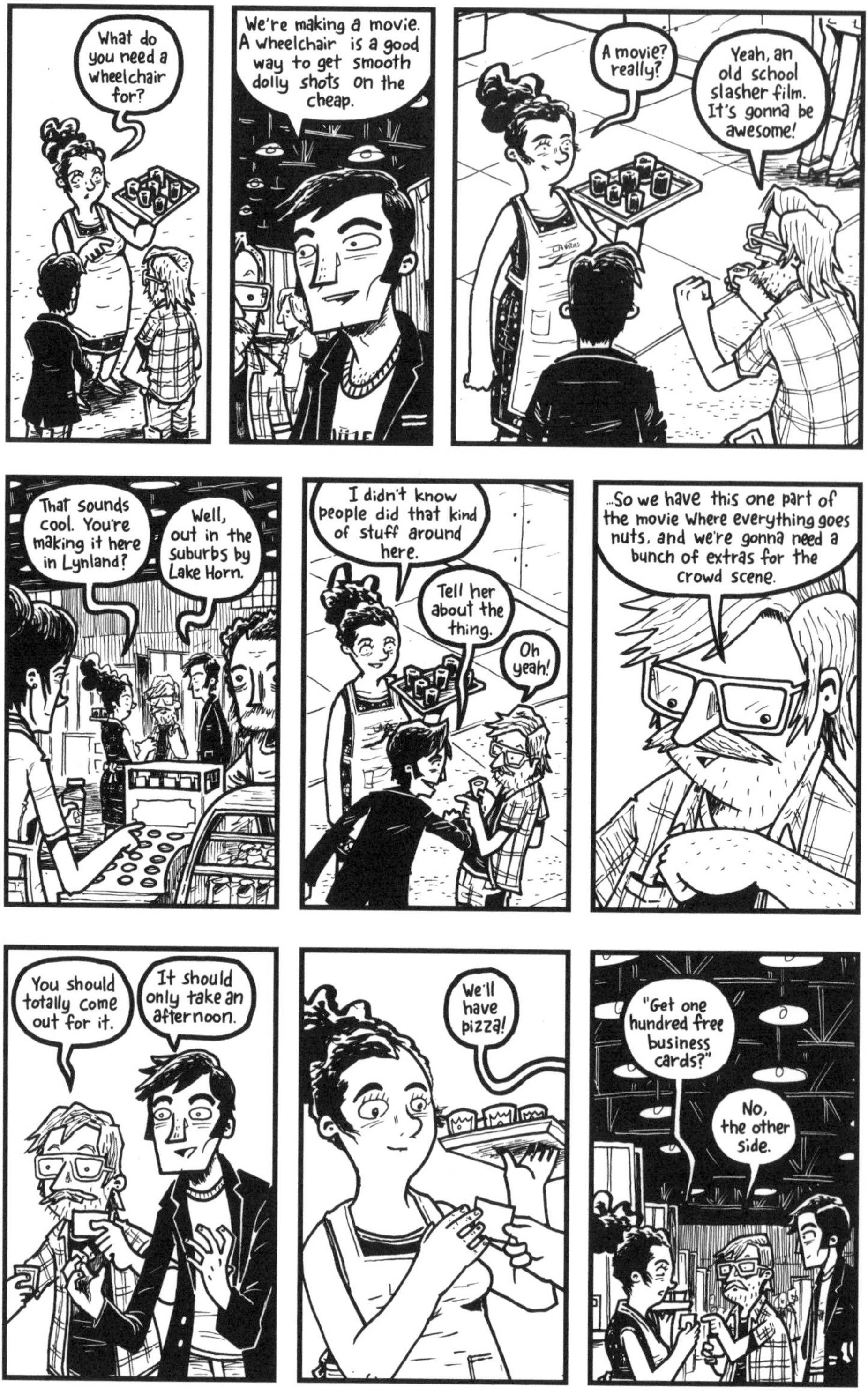
What do you need a wheelchair for?
We're making a movie. A wheelchair is a good way to get smooth dolly shots on the cheap.
A movie? really?
Yeah, an old school slasher film. It's gonna be awesome!
That sounds cool. You're making it here in Lynland?
Well, out in the suburbs by Lake Horn.
I didn't know people did that kind of stuff around here.
Tell her about the thing.
Oh yeah!
...So we have this one part of the movie where everything goes nuts, and we're gonna need a bunch of extras for the crowd scene.
You should totally come out for it.
It should only take an afternoon.
We'll have pizza!
"Get one hundred free business cards?"
No, the other side.

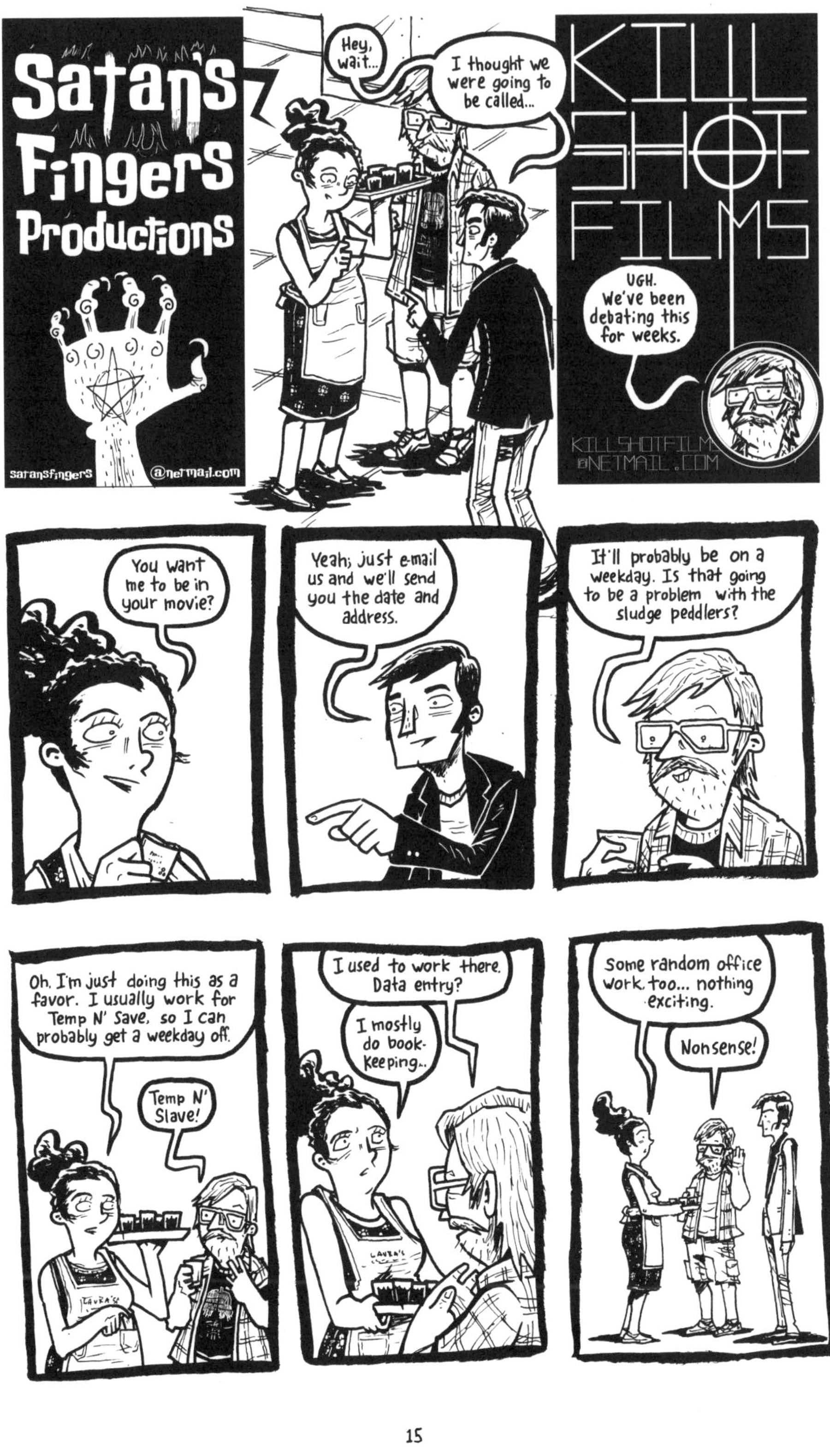
Satan's Fingers Productions
satansfingers @netmail.com
Hey, wait...
I thought we were going to be called...
KILL SHOT FILMS
UGH. We've been debating this for weeks.
KILLSHOTFILMS @NETMAIL.COM
You want me to be in your movie?
Yeah; just e-mail us and we'll send you the date and address.
It'll probably be on a weekday. Is that going to be a problem with the sludge peddlers?
Oh. I'm just doing this as a favor. I usually work for Temp N' Save, so I can probably get a weekday off.
Temp N' Slave!
I used to work there. Data entry?
I mostly do book-keeping...
Some random office work, too... nothing exciting.
Nonsense!

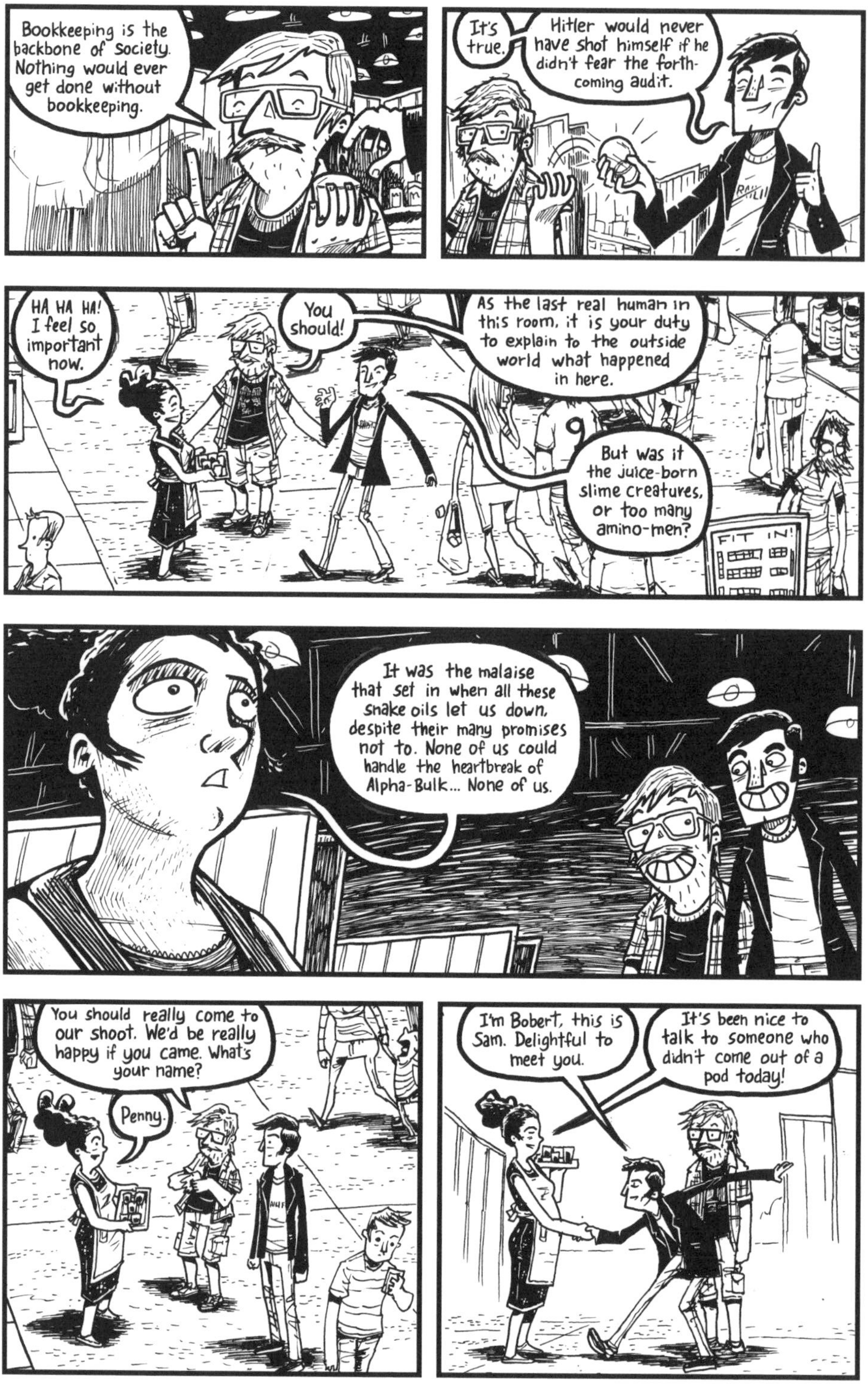

Bookkeeping is the backbone of society. Nothing would ever get done without bookkeeping.
It's true.
Hitler would never have shot himself if he didn't fear the forth-coming audit.
HA HA HA! I feel so important now.
You should!
As the last real human in this room, it is your duty to explain to the outside world what happened in here.
But was it the juice-born slime creatures, or too many amino-men?
FIT IN!
It was the malaise that set in when all these snake oils let us down, despite their many promises not to. None of us could handle the heartbreak of Alpha-Bulk... None of us.
You should really come to our shoot. We'd be really happy if you came. What's your name?
Penny.
I'm Bobert, this is Sam. Delightful to meet you.
It's been nice to talk to someone who didn't come out of a pod today!

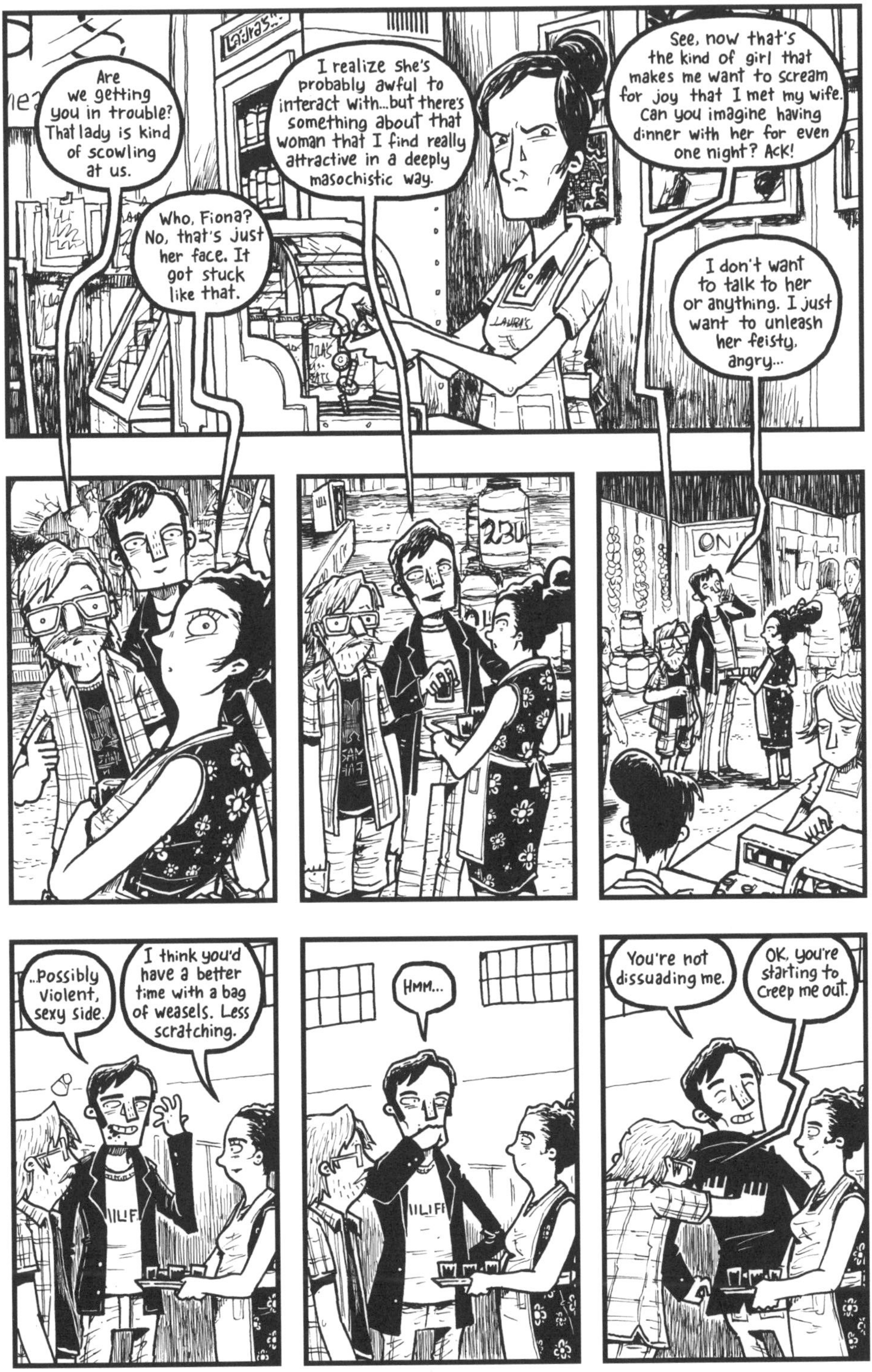

Are we getting you in trouble? That lady is kind of scowling at us.
Who, Fiona? No, that's just her face. It got stuck like that.
I realize she's probably awful to interact with...but there's something about that woman that I find really attractive in a deeply masochistic way.
See, now that's the kind of girl that makes me want to scream for joy that I met my wife. Can you imagine having dinner with her for even one night? Ack!
I don't want to talk to her or anything. I just want to unleash her feisty, angry...
..Possibly violent, sexy side.
I think you'd have a better time with a bag of weasels. Less scratching.
HMM...
You're not dissuading me.
OK, you're starting to creep me out.

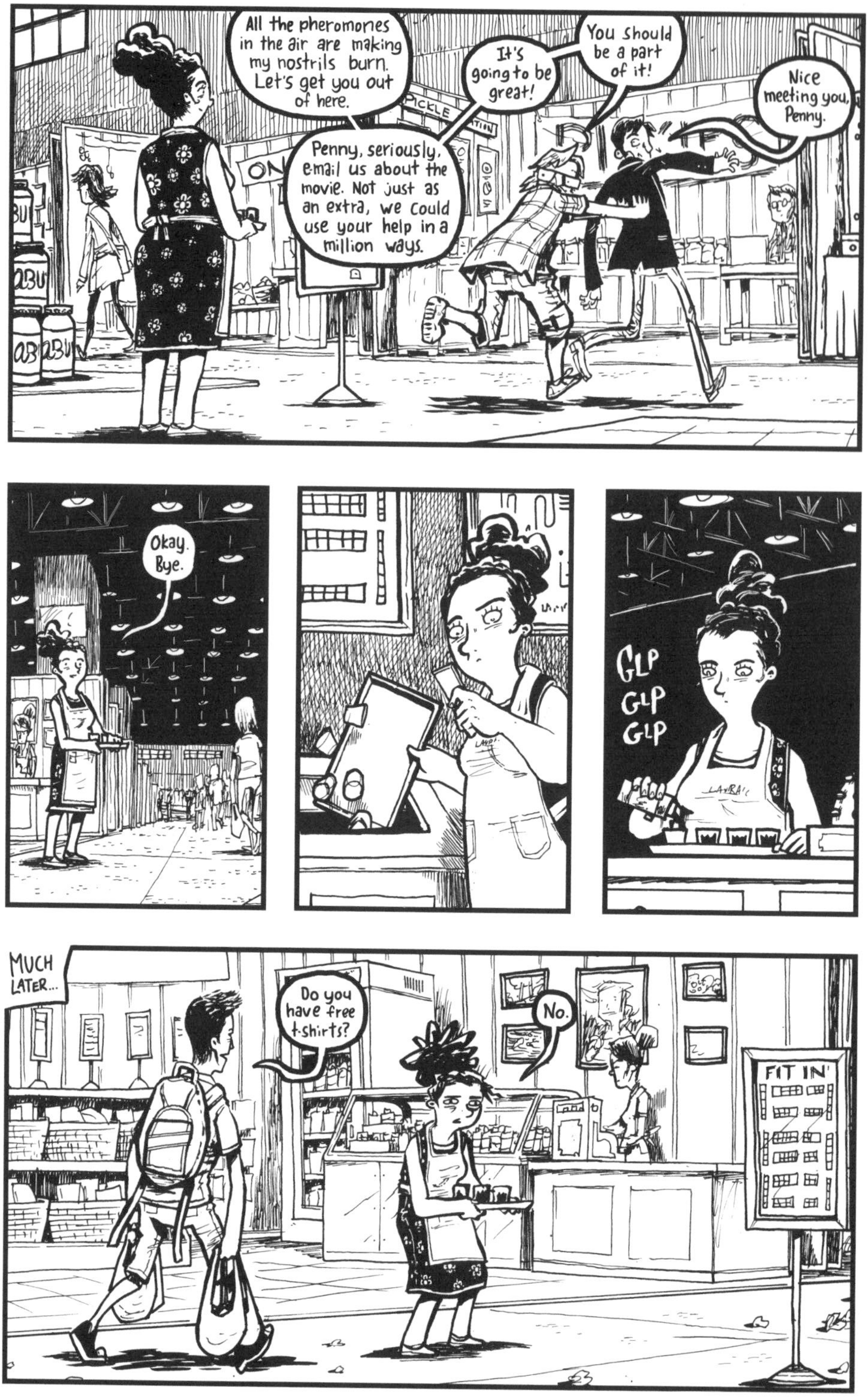
All the pheromones in the air are making my nostrils burn. Let's get you out of here.
Penny, seriously, e-mail us about the movie. Not just as an extra, we could use your help in a million ways.
It's going to be great!
You should be a part of it!
Nice meeting you, Penny.
Okay. Bye.
GLP
GLP
GLP
MUCH LATER...
Do you have free t-shirts?
No.
FIT IN'

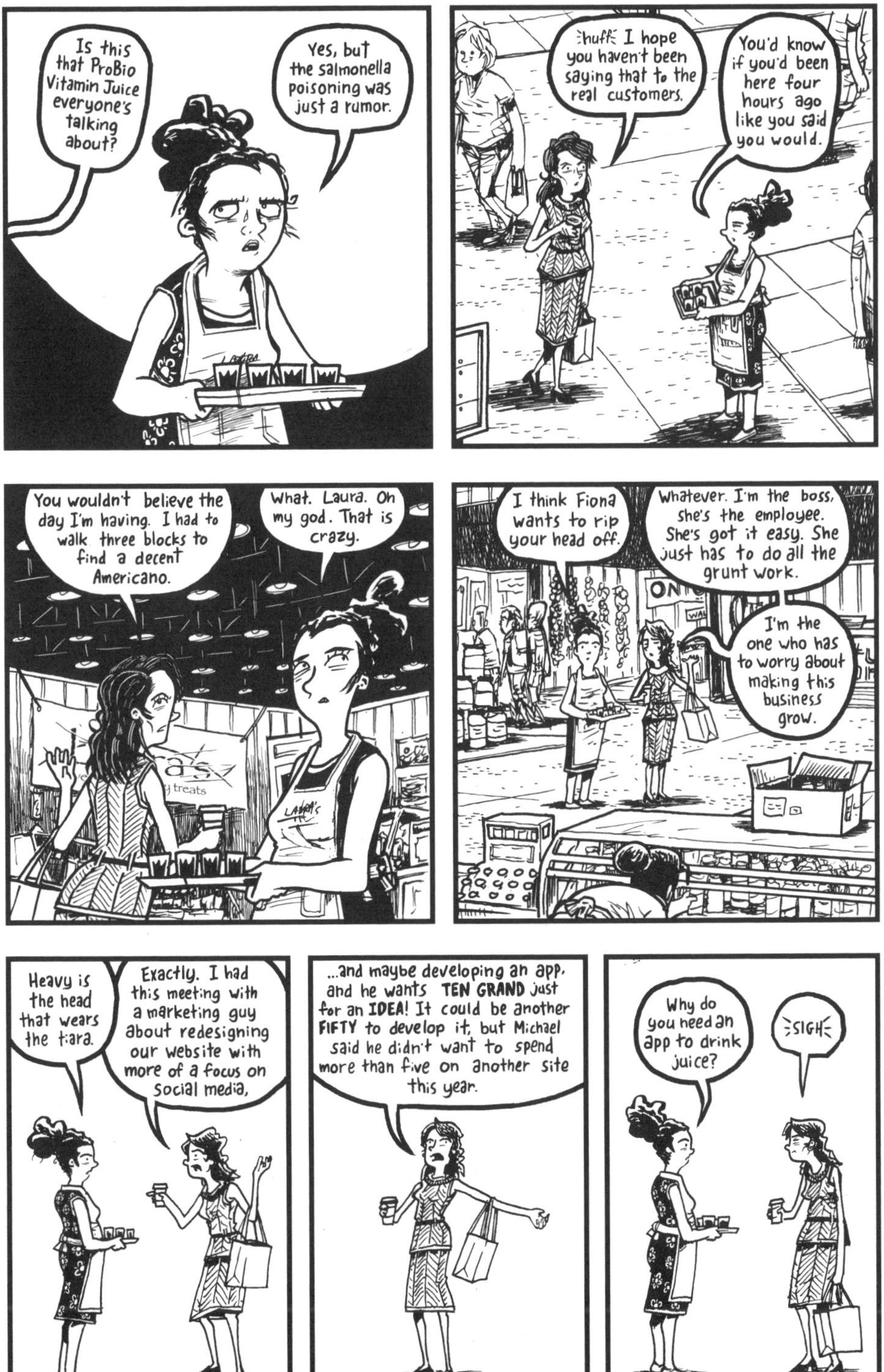
Is this that ProBio Vitamin Juice everyone's talking about?
Yes, but the salmonella poisoning was just a rumor.
huff I hope you haven't been saying that to the real customers.
You'd know if you'd been here four hours ago like you said you would.
You wouldn't believe the day I'm having. I had to walk three blocks to find a decent Americano.
What. Laura. Oh my god. That is crazy.
I think Fiona wants to rip your head off.
Whatever. I'm the boss, she's the employee. She's got it easy. She just has to do all the grunt work.
I'm the one who has to worry about making this business grow.
Heavy is the head that wears the tiara.
Exactly. I had this meeting with a marketing guy about redesigning our website with more of a focus on social media,
...and maybe developing an app, and he wants TEN GRAND just for an IDEA! It could be another FIFTY to develop it, but Michael said he didn't want to spend more than five on another site this year.
Why do you need an app to drink juice?
SIGH

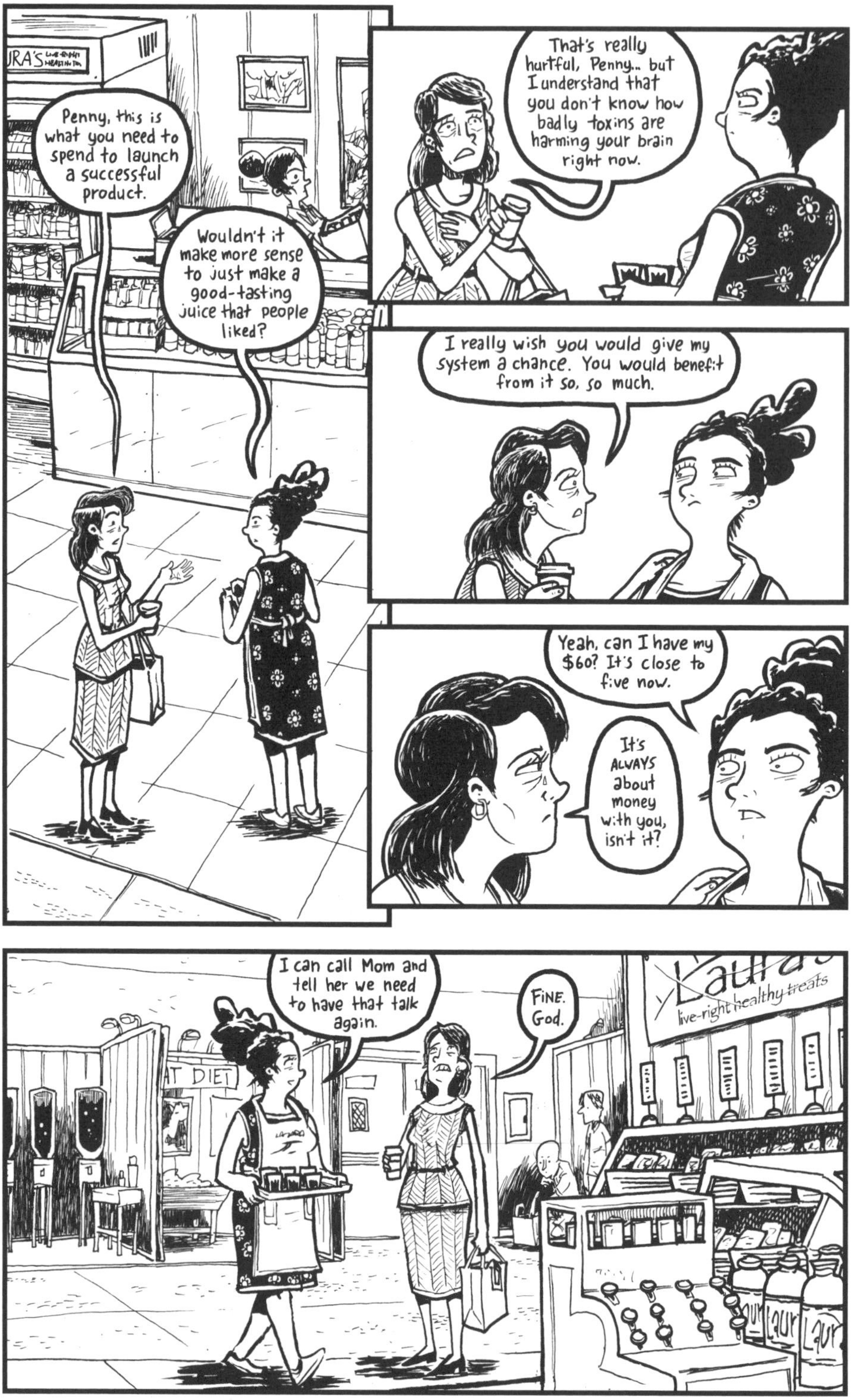

Penny, this is what you need to spend to launch a successful product.
Wouldn't it make more sense to just make a good-tasting juice that people liked?
That's really hurtful, Penny... but I understand that you don't know how badly toxins are harming your brain right now.
I really wish you would give my system a chance. You would benefit from it so, so much.
Yeah, can I have my $60? It's close to five now.
It's ALWAYS about money with you, isn't it?
I can call Mom and tell her we need to have that talk again.
FINE. God.
live-right healthy treats

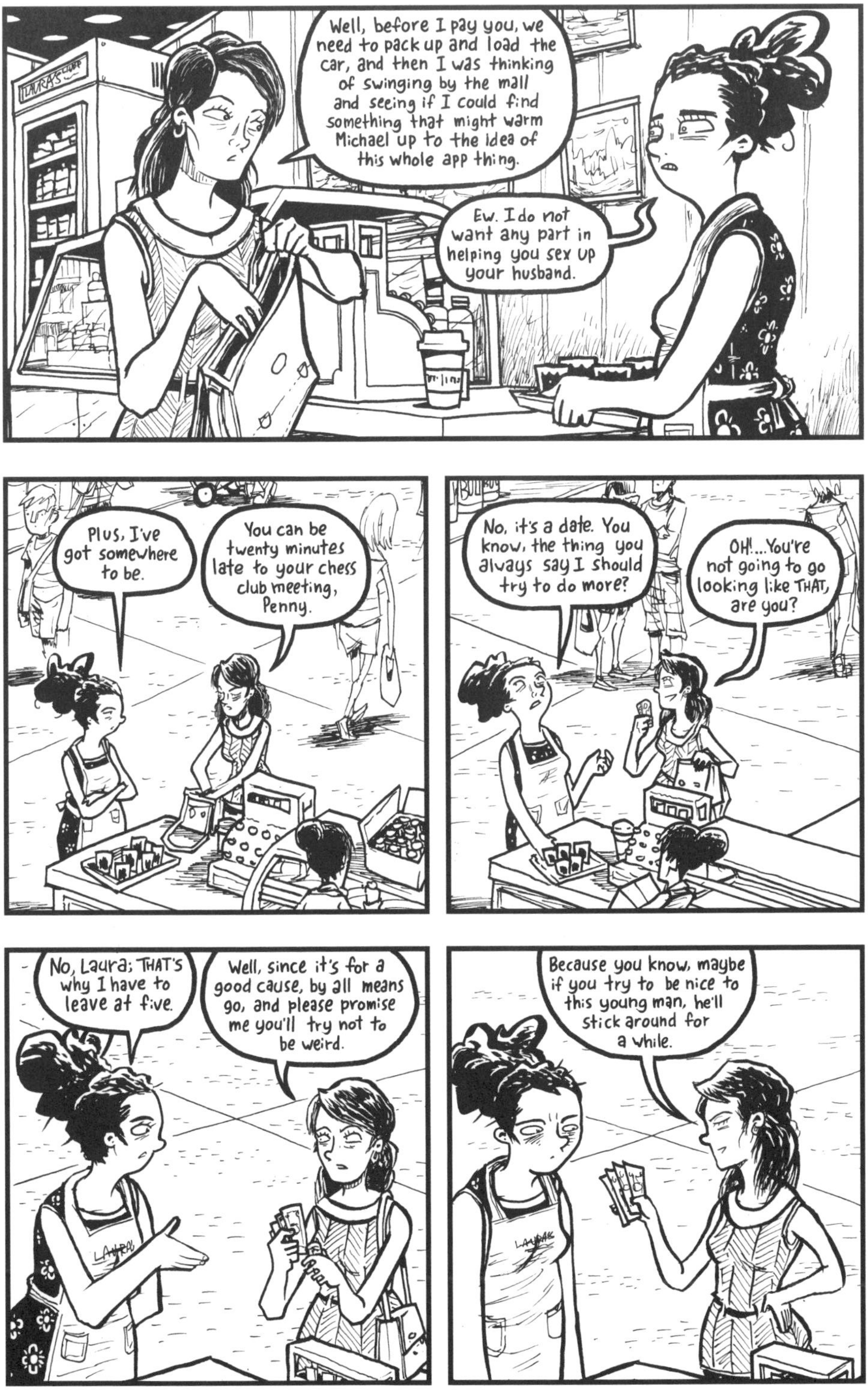
Well, before I pay you, we need to pack up and load the car, and then I was thinking of swinging by the mall and seeing if I could find something that might warm Michael up to the idea of this whole app thing.
Ew. I do not want any part in helping you sex up your husband.
Plus, I've got somewhere to be.
You can be twenty minutes late to your chess club meeting, Penny.
No, it's a date. You know, the thing you always say I should try to do more?
OH!...You're not going to go looking like THAT, are you?
No, Laura; THAT'S why I have to leave at five.
Well, since it's for a good cause, by all means go, and please promise me you'll try not to be weird.
Because you know, maybe if you try to be nice to this young man, he'll stick around for a while.

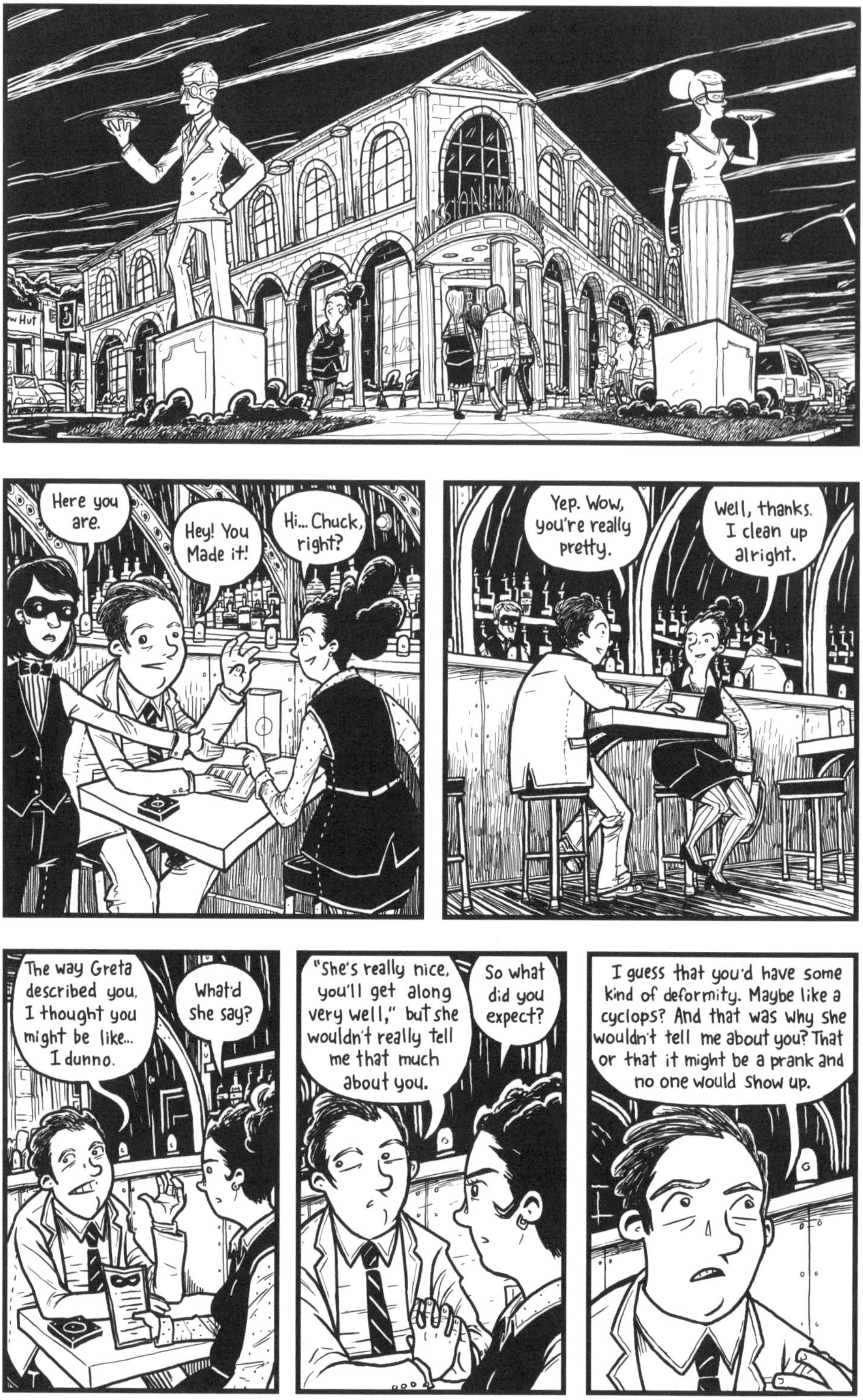
MISSION:IMPASTABLE
Here you are.
Hey! You Made it!
Hi... Chuck, right?
Yep. Wow, you're really pretty.
Well, thanks. I clean up alright.
The way Greta described you, I thought you might be like... I dunno.
What'd she say?
"She's really nice, you'll get along very well," but she wouldn't really tell me that much about you.
So what did you expect?
I guess that you'd have some kind of deformity. Maybe like a cyclops? And that was why she wouldn't tell me about you? That or that it might be a prank and no one would show up.

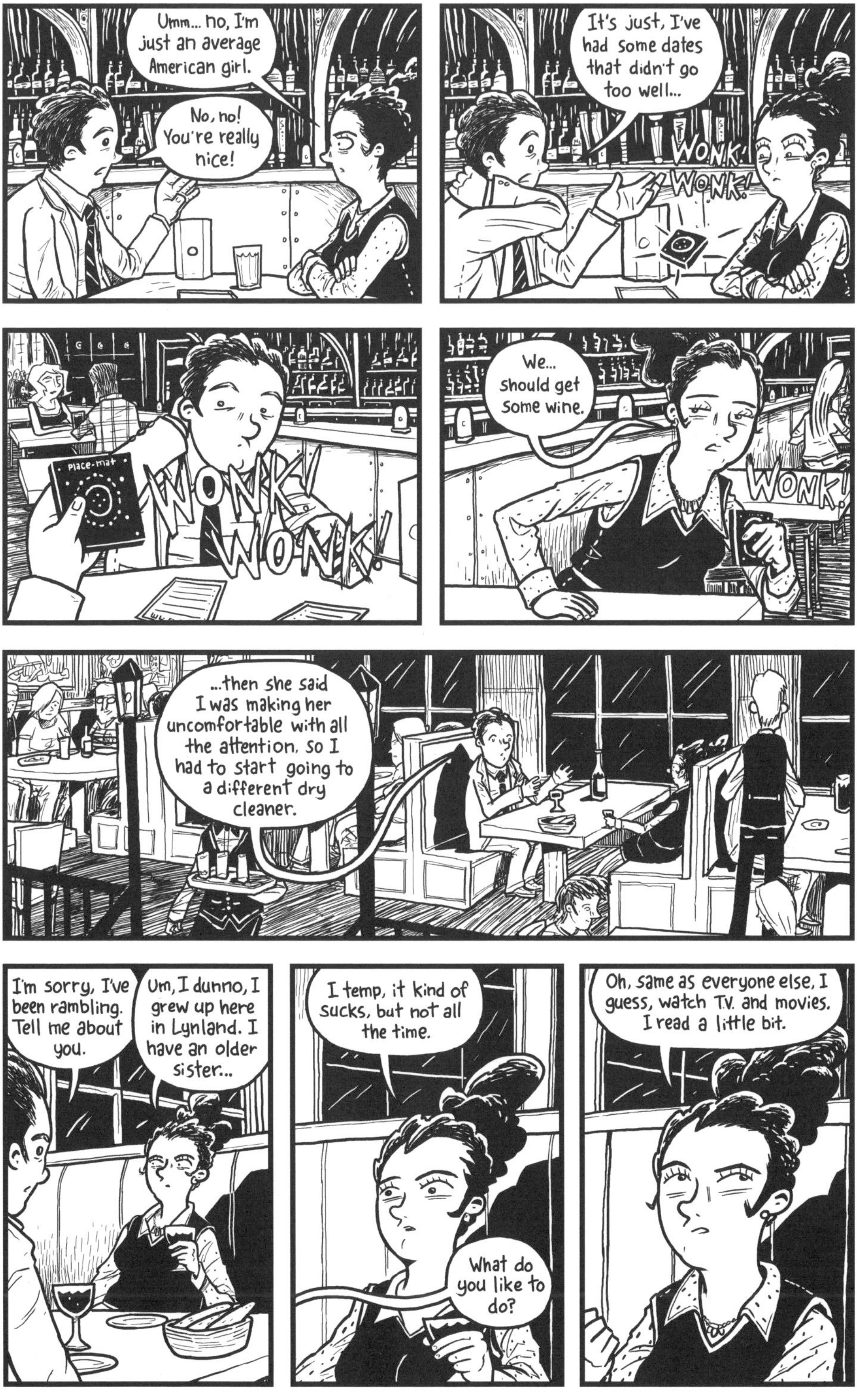
Umm... no, I'm just an average American girl.
No, no! You're really nice!
It's just, I've had some dates that didn't go too well...
WONK!
WONK!
Place-mat
WONK!
WONK!
We... should get some wine.
WONK!
...then she said I was making her uncomfortable with all the attention, so I had to start going to a different dry cleaner.
I'm sorry, I've been rambling. Tell me about you.
Um, I dunno, I grew up here in Lynland. I have an older sister...
I temp, it kind of sucks, but not all the time.
What do you like to do?
Oh, same as everyone else, I guess, watch T.V. and movies. I read a little bit.

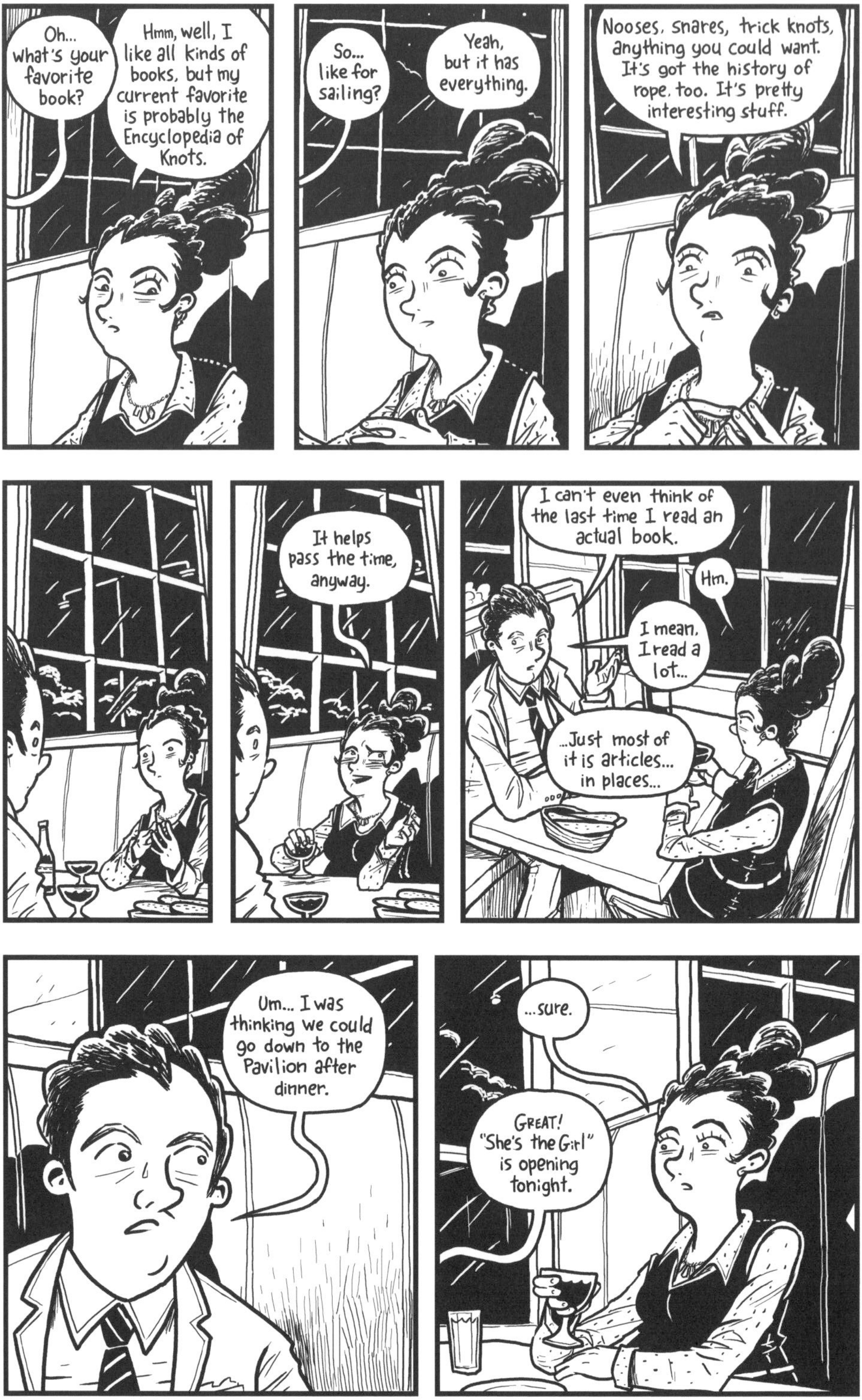
Oh... what's your favorite book?
Hmm, well, I like all kinds of books, but my current favorite is probably the Encyclopedia of Knots.
So... like for sailing?
Yeah, but it has everything.
Nooses, snares, trick knots, anything you could want. It's got the history of rope, too. It's pretty interesting stuff.
It helps pass the time, anyway.
I can't even think of the last time I read an actual book.
Hm.
I mean, I read a lot...
...Just most of it is articles... in places...
Um... I was thinking we could go down to the Pavilion after dinner.
...sure.
GREAT! "She's the Girl" is opening tonight.

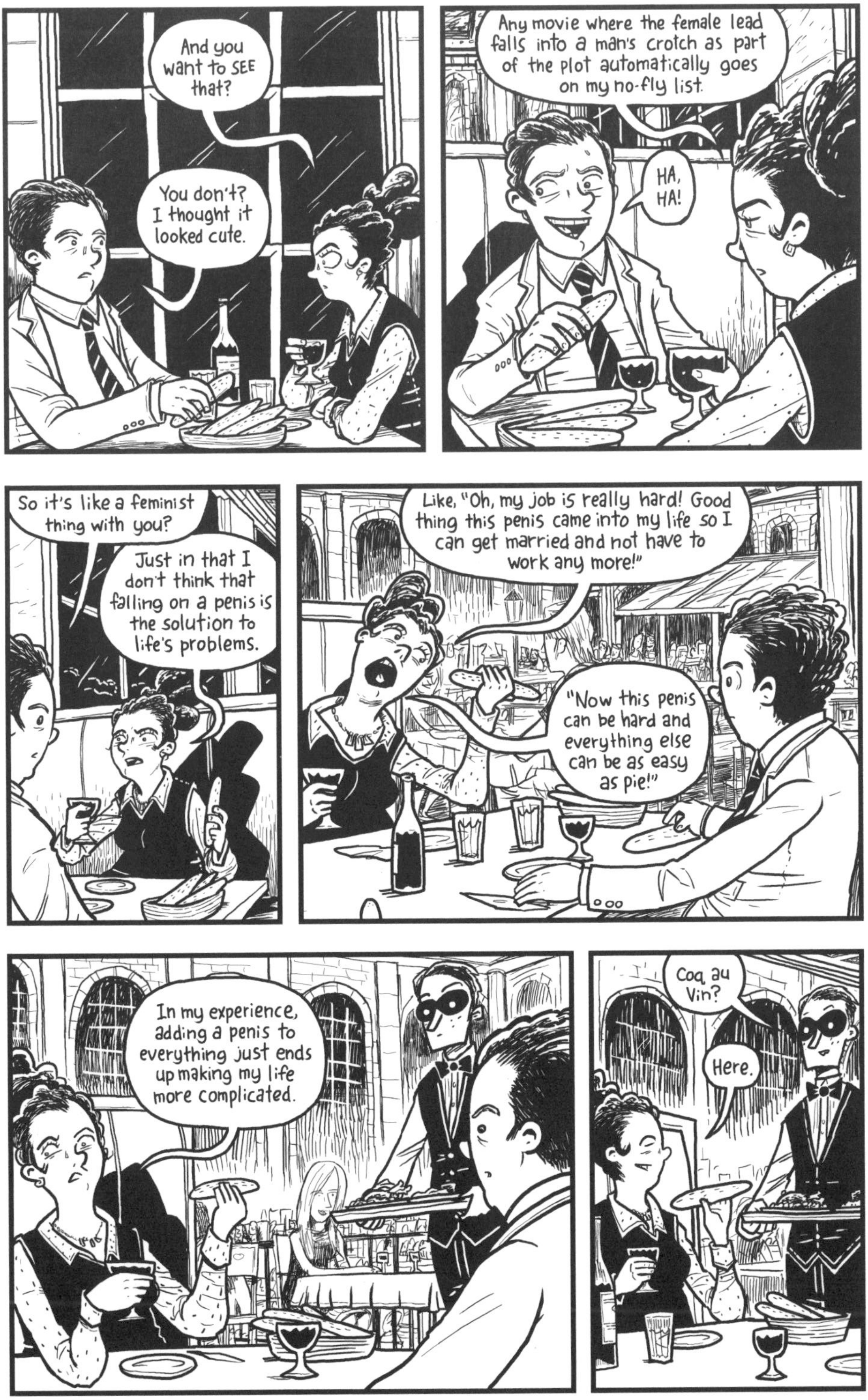
And you want to SEE that?
You don't? I thought it looked cute.
Any movie where the female lead falls into a man's crotch as part of the plot automatically goes on my no-fly list.
HA, HA!
So it's like a feminist thing with you?
Just in that I don't think that falling on a penis is the solution to life's problems.
Like, "Oh, my job is really hard! Good thing this penis came into my life so I can get married and not have to work any more!"
"Now this penis can be hard and everything else can be as easy as pie!"
In my experience, adding a penis to everything just ends up making my life more complicated.
Coq au Vin?
Here.

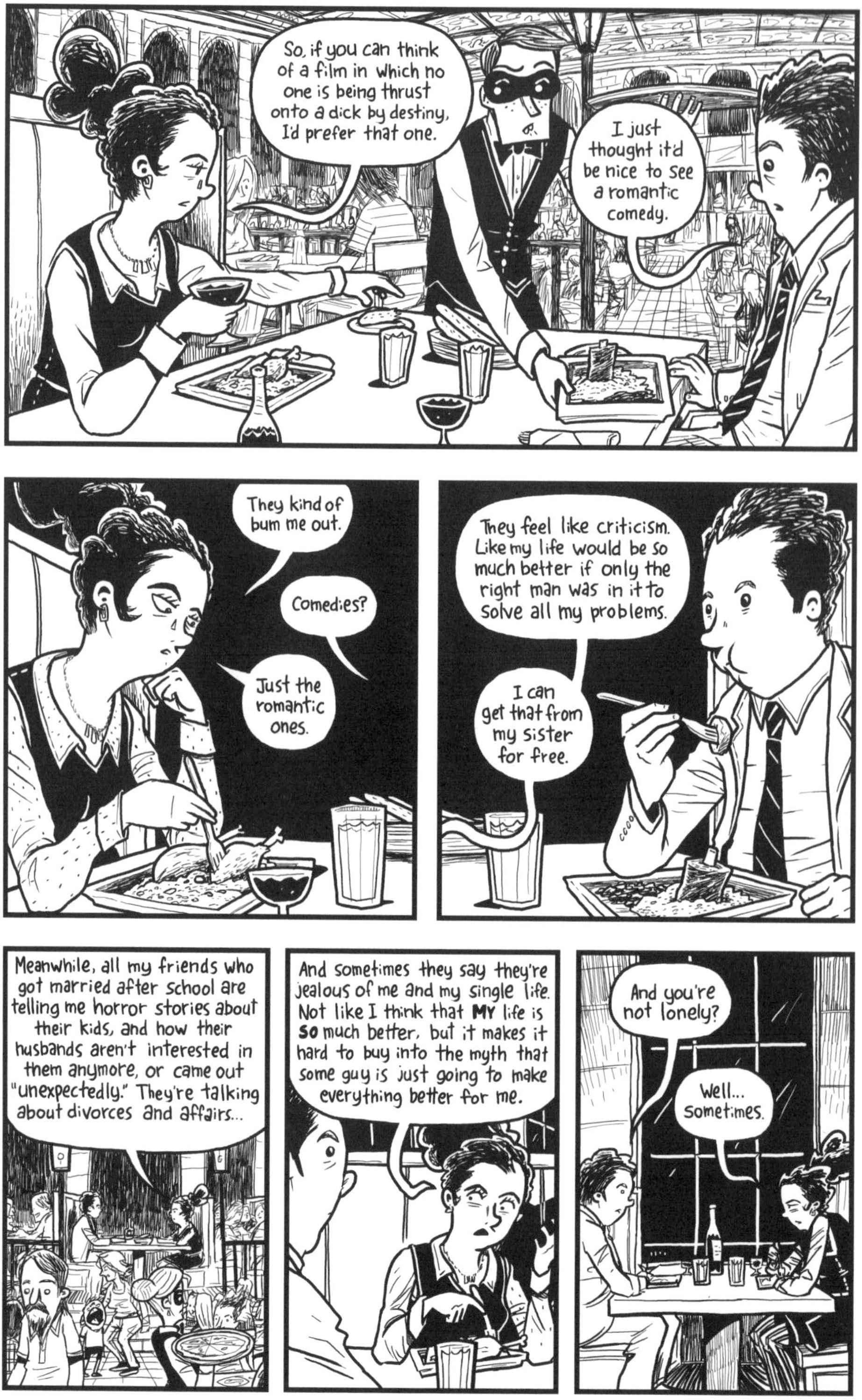
So, if you can think of a film in which no one is being thrust onto a dick by destiny, I'd prefer that one.
I just thought it'd be nice to see a romantic comedy.
They kind of bum me out.
Comedies?
Just the romantic ones.
They feel like criticism. Like my life would be so much better if only the right man was in it to solve all my problems.
I can get that from my sister for free.
Meanwhile, all my friends who got married after school are telling me horror stories about their kids, and how their husbands aren't interested in them anymore, or came out "unexpectedly." They're talking about divorces and affairs...
And sometimes they say they're jealous of me and my single life. Not like I think that MY life is SO much better, but it makes it hard to buy into the myth that some guy is just going to make everything better for me.
And you're not lonely?
Well... sometimes.

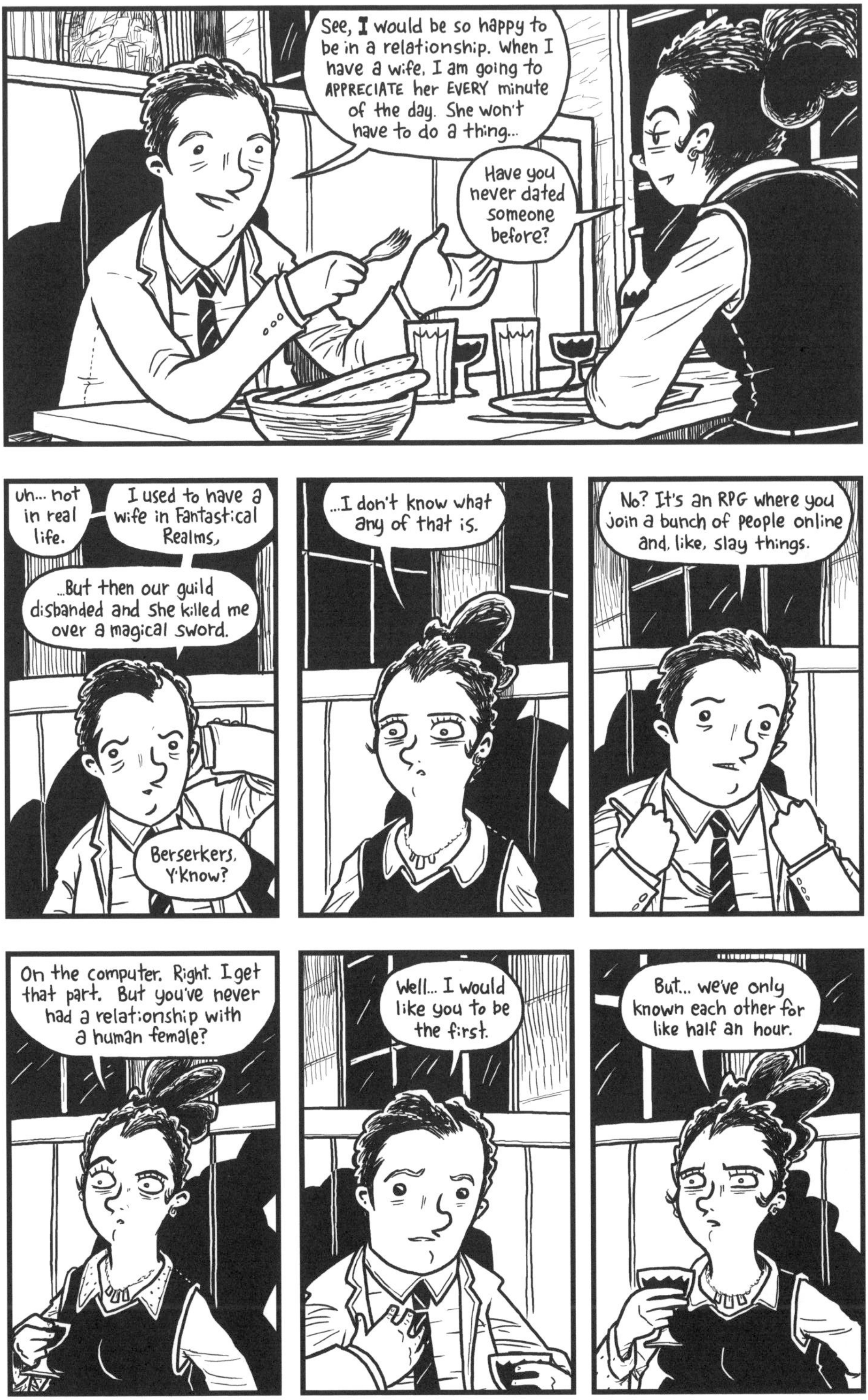
See, I would be so happy to be in a relationship. When I have a wife, I am going to APPRECIATE her EVERY minute of the day. She won't have to do a thing...
Have you never dated someone before?
uh... not in real life.
I used to have a wife in Fantastical Realms,
...But then our guild disbanded and she killed me over a magical sword.
Berserkers, Y'know?
...I don't know what any of that is.
No? It's an RPG where you join a bunch of people online and, like, slay things.
On the computer. Right. I get that part. But you've never had a relationship with a human female?
Well... I would like you to be the first.
But... we've only known each other for like half an hour.

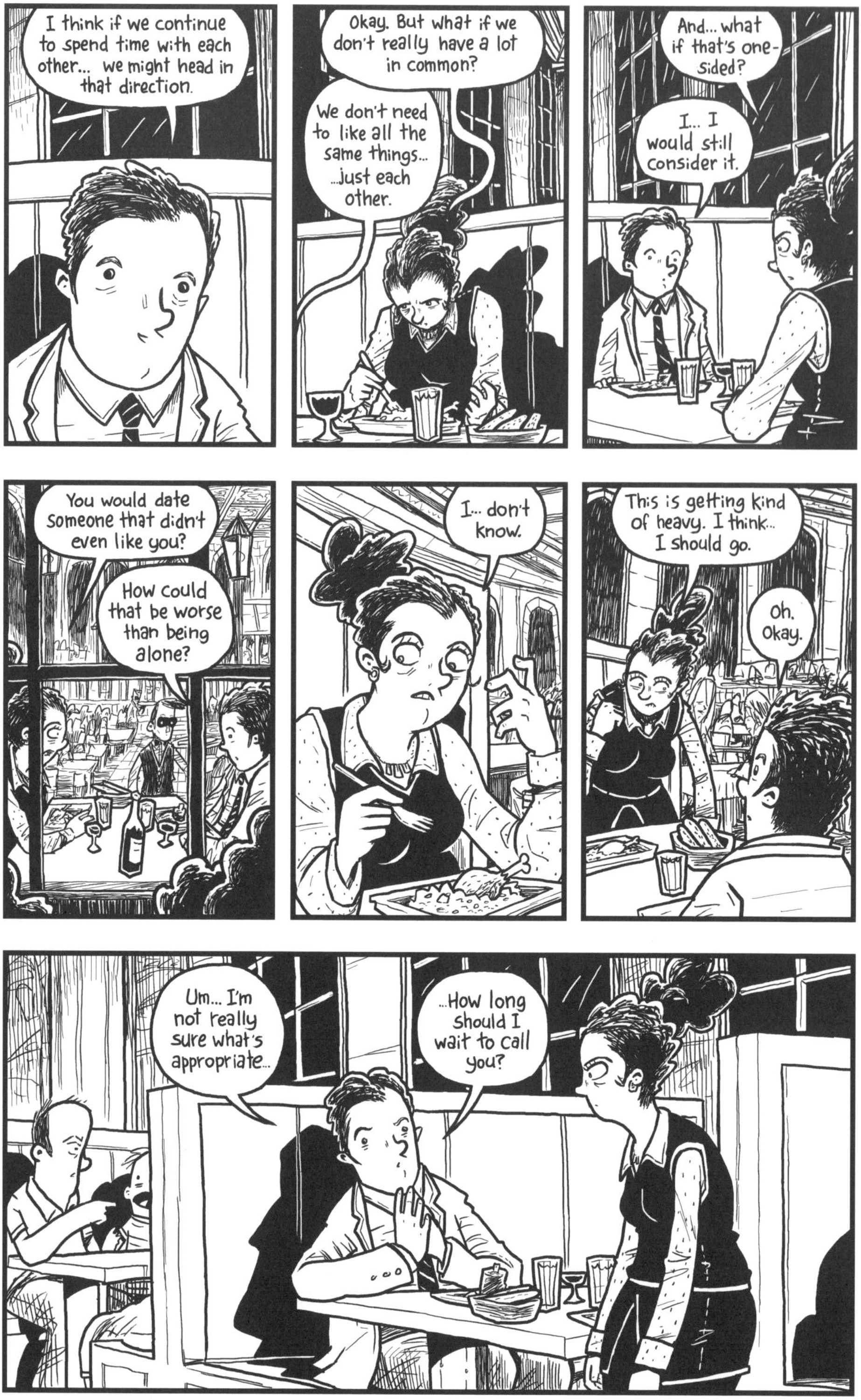
I think if we continue to spend time with each other... we might head in that direction.
Okay. But what if we don't really have a lot in common?
We don't need to like all the same things... ...just each other.
And... what if that's one-sided?
I... I would still consider it.
You would date someone that didn't even like you?
How could that be worse than being alone?
I... don't know.
This is getting kind of heavy. I think... I should go.
Oh. Okay.
Um... I'm not really sure what's appropriate...
...How long should I wait to call you?

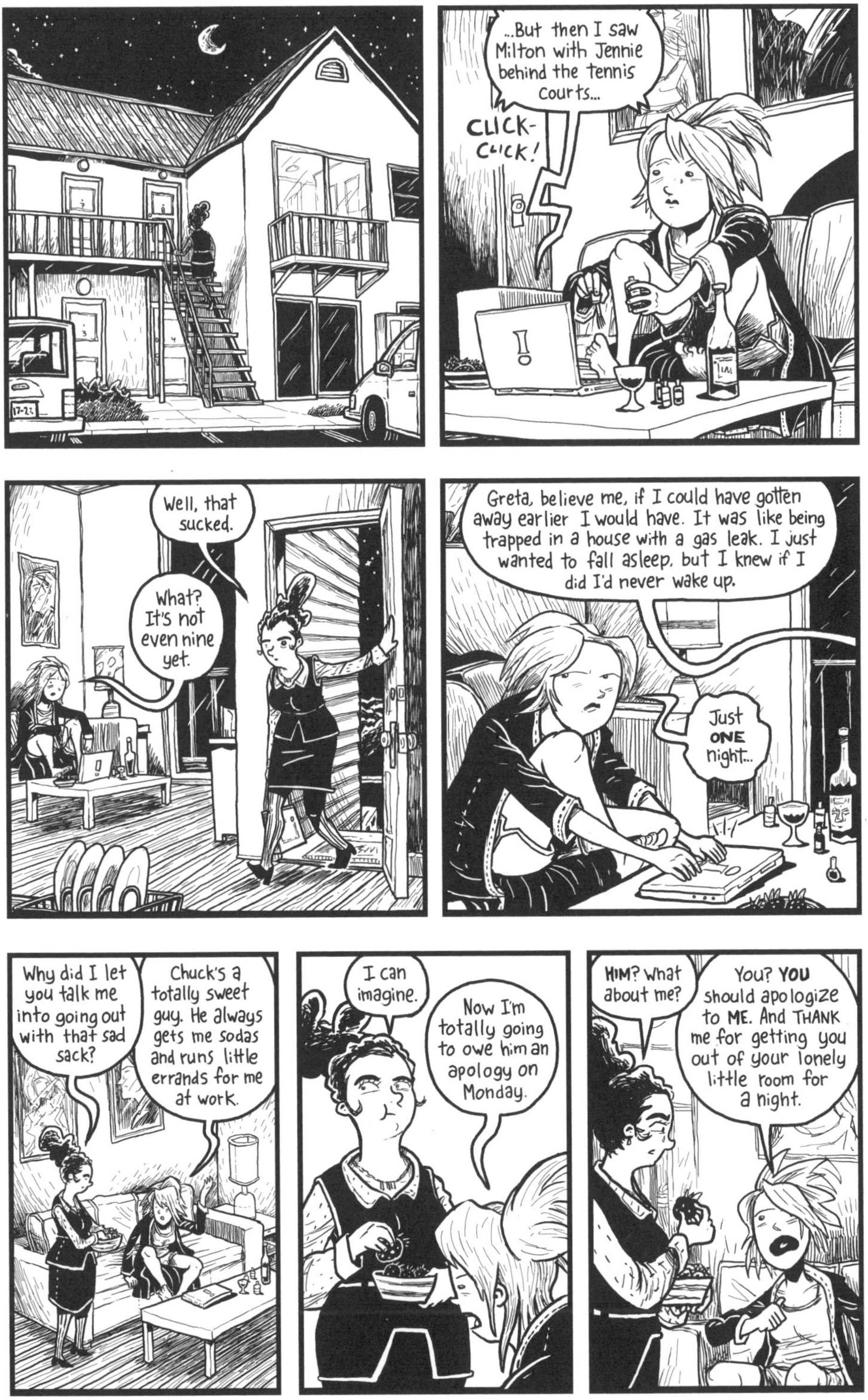

...But then I saw Milton with Jennie behind the tennis courts...
CLICK-CLICK!
Well, that sucked.
What? It's not even nine yet.
Greta, believe me, if I could have gotten away earlier I would have. It was like being trapped in a house with a gas leak. I just wanted to fall asleep, but I knew if I did I'd never wake up.
Just ONE night...
Why did I let you talk me into going out with that sad sack?
Chuck's a totally sweet guy. He always gets me sodas and runs little errands for me at work.
I can imagine.
Now I'm totally going to owe him an apology on Monday.
HIM? What about me?
You? YOU should apologize to ME. And THANK me for getting you out of your lonely little room for a night.

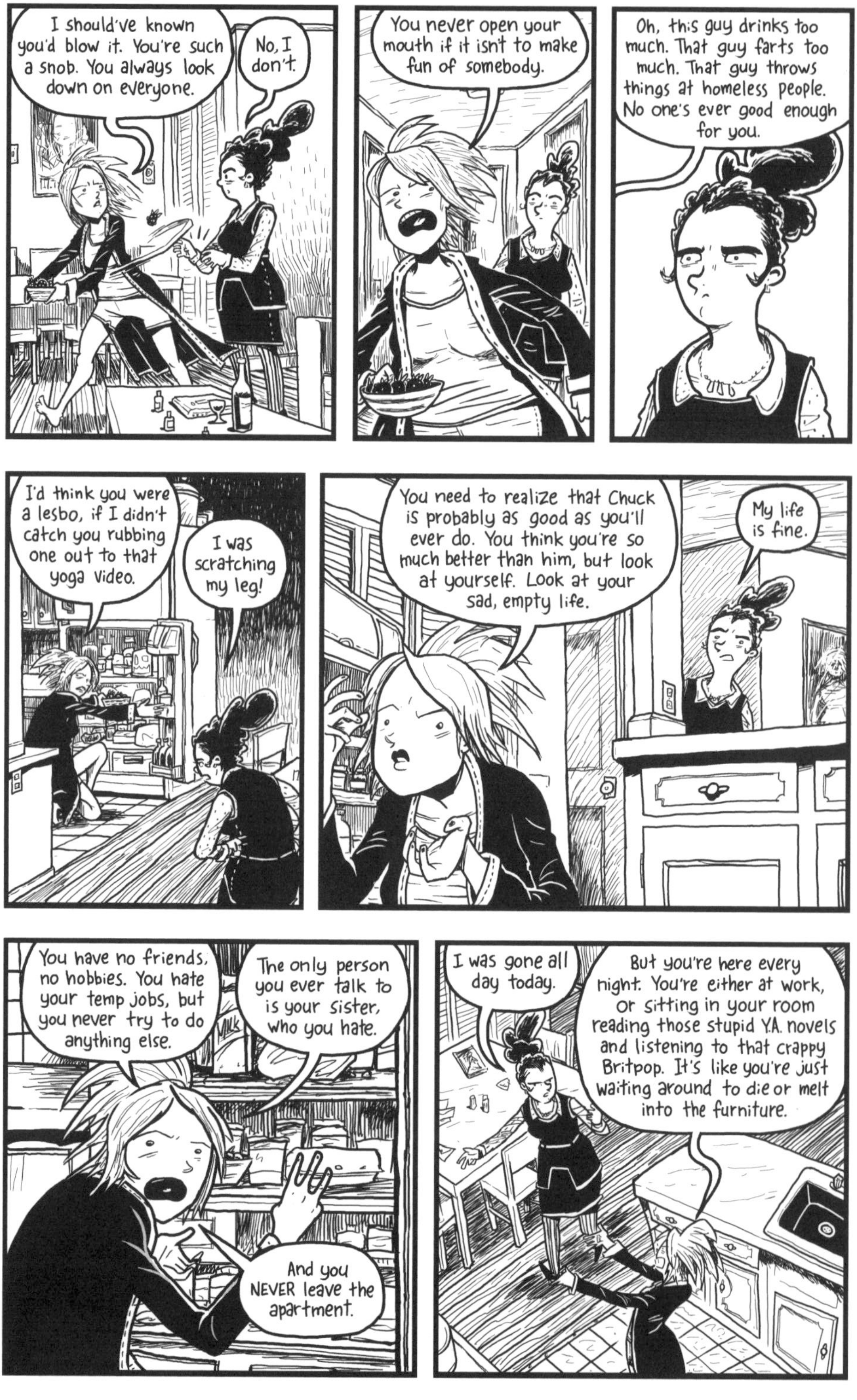
I should've known you'd blow it. You're such a snob. You always look down on everyone.
No, I don't.
You never open your mouth if it isn't to make fun of somebody.
Oh, this guy drinks too much. That guy farts too much. That guy throws things at homeless people. No one's ever good enough for you.
I'd think you were a lesbo, if I didn't catch you rubbing one out to that yoga video.
I was scratching my leg!
You need to realize that Chuck is probably as good as you'll ever do. You think you're so much better than him, but look at yourself. Look at your sad, empty life.
My life is fine.
You have no friends, no hobbies. You hate your temp jobs, but you never try to do anything else.
The only person you ever talk to is your sister, who you hate.
And you NEVER leave the apartment.
I was gone all day today.
But you're here every night. You're either at work, or sitting in your room reading those stupid Y.A. novels and listening to that crappy Britpop. It's like you're just waiting around to die or melt into the furniture.

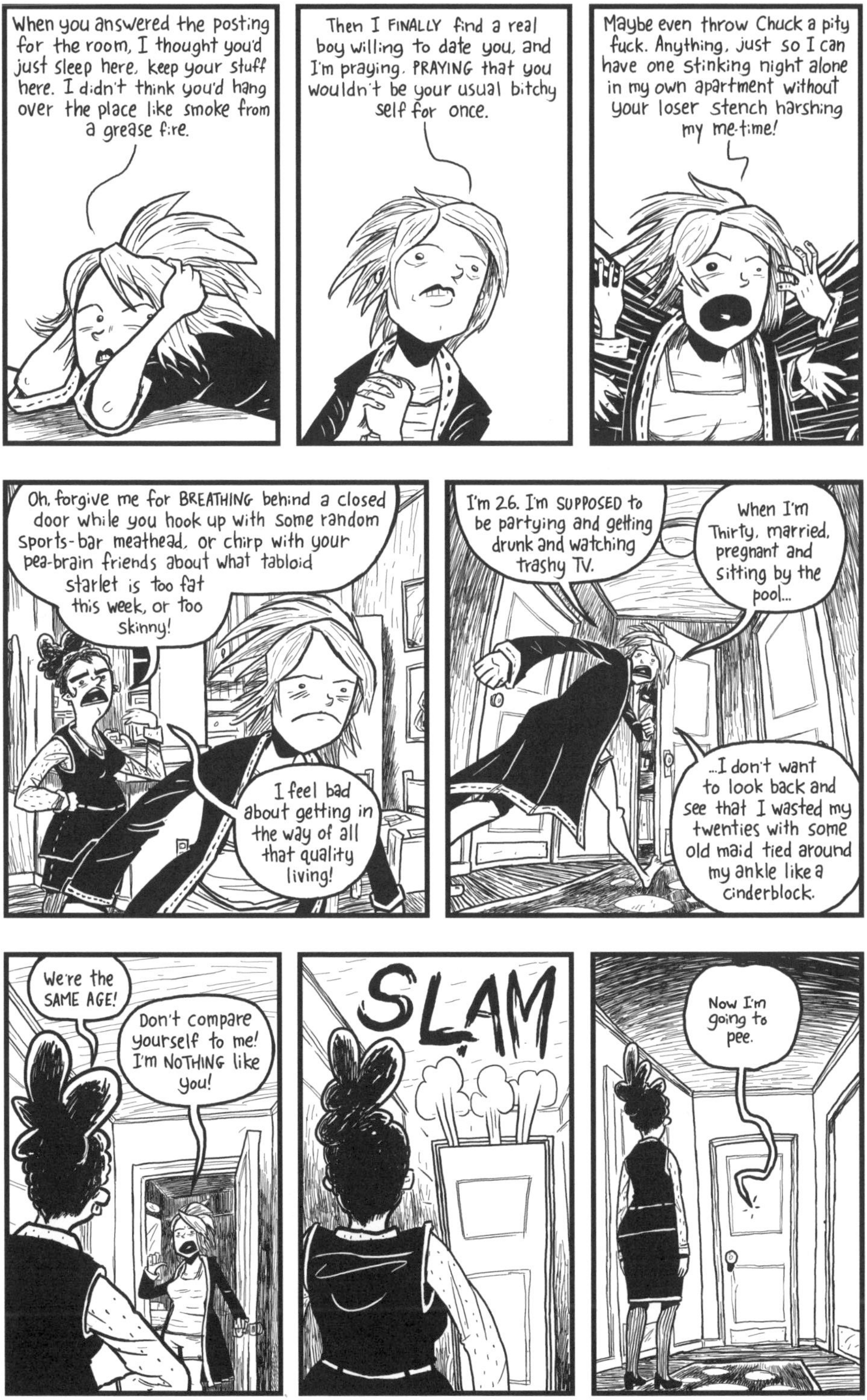
When you answered the posting for the room, I thought you'd just sleep here, keep your stuff here. I didn't think you'd hang over the place like smoke from a grease fire.
Then I FINALLY find a real boy willing to date you, and I'm praying, PRAYING that you wouldn't be your usual bitchy self for once.
Maybe even throw Chuck a pity fuck. Anything, just so I can have one stinking night alone in my own apartment without your loser stench harshing my me-time!
Oh, forgive me for BREATHING behind a closed door while you hook up with some random sports-bar meathead, or chirp with your pea-brain friends about what tabloid starlet is too fat this week, or too skinny!
I feel bad about getting in the way of all that quality living!
I'm 26. I'm SUPPOSED to be partying and getting drunk and watching trashy TV.
When I'm Thirty, married, pregnant and sitting by the pool...
...I don't want to look back and see that I wasted my twenties with some old maid tied around my ankle like a cinderblock.
We're the SAME AGE!
Don't compare yourself to me! I'm NOTHING like you!
SLAM
Now I'm going to pee.

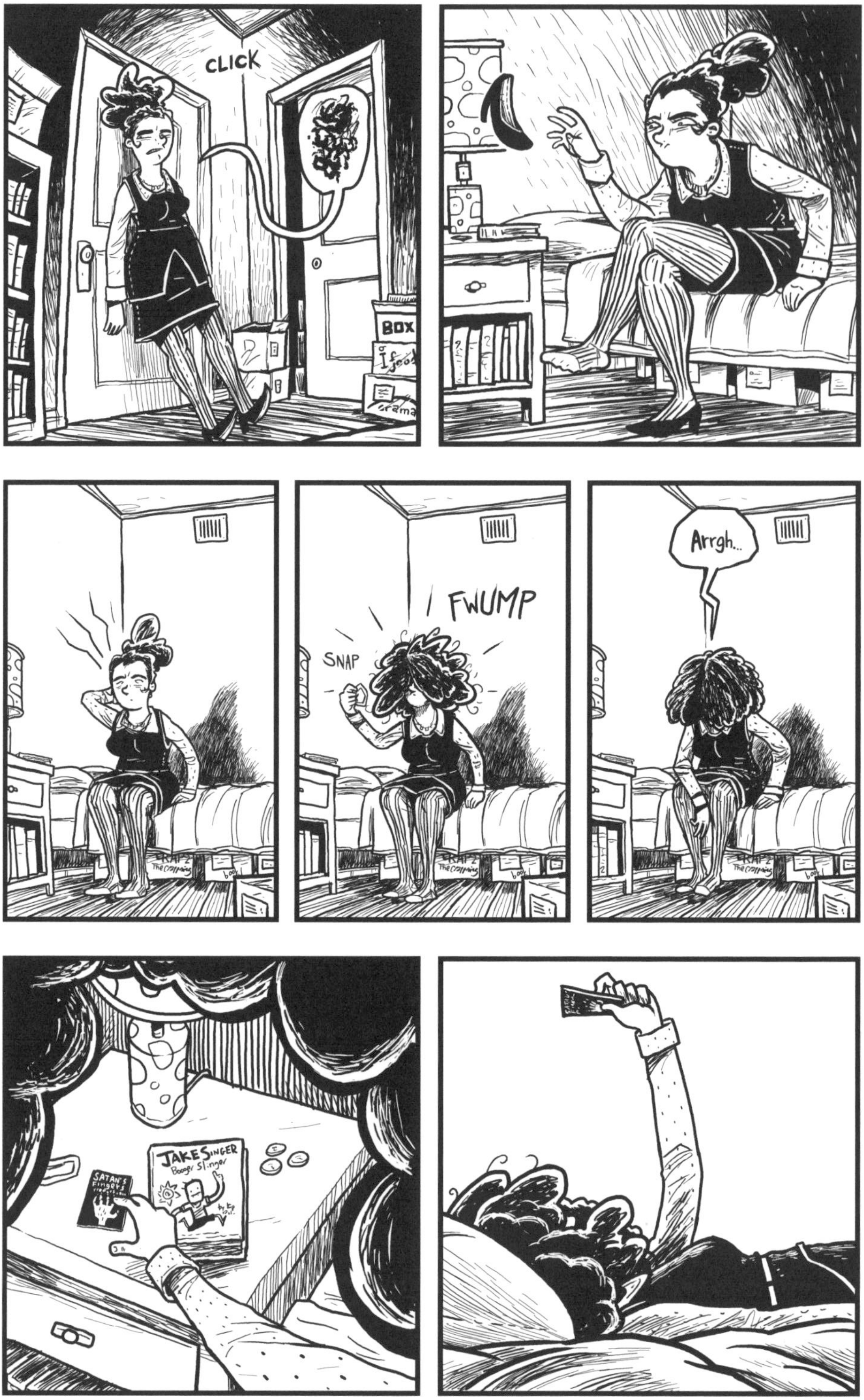
CLICK
BOX
SNAP
FWUMP
Arrgh...
JAKE SINGER

CHAPTER TWO

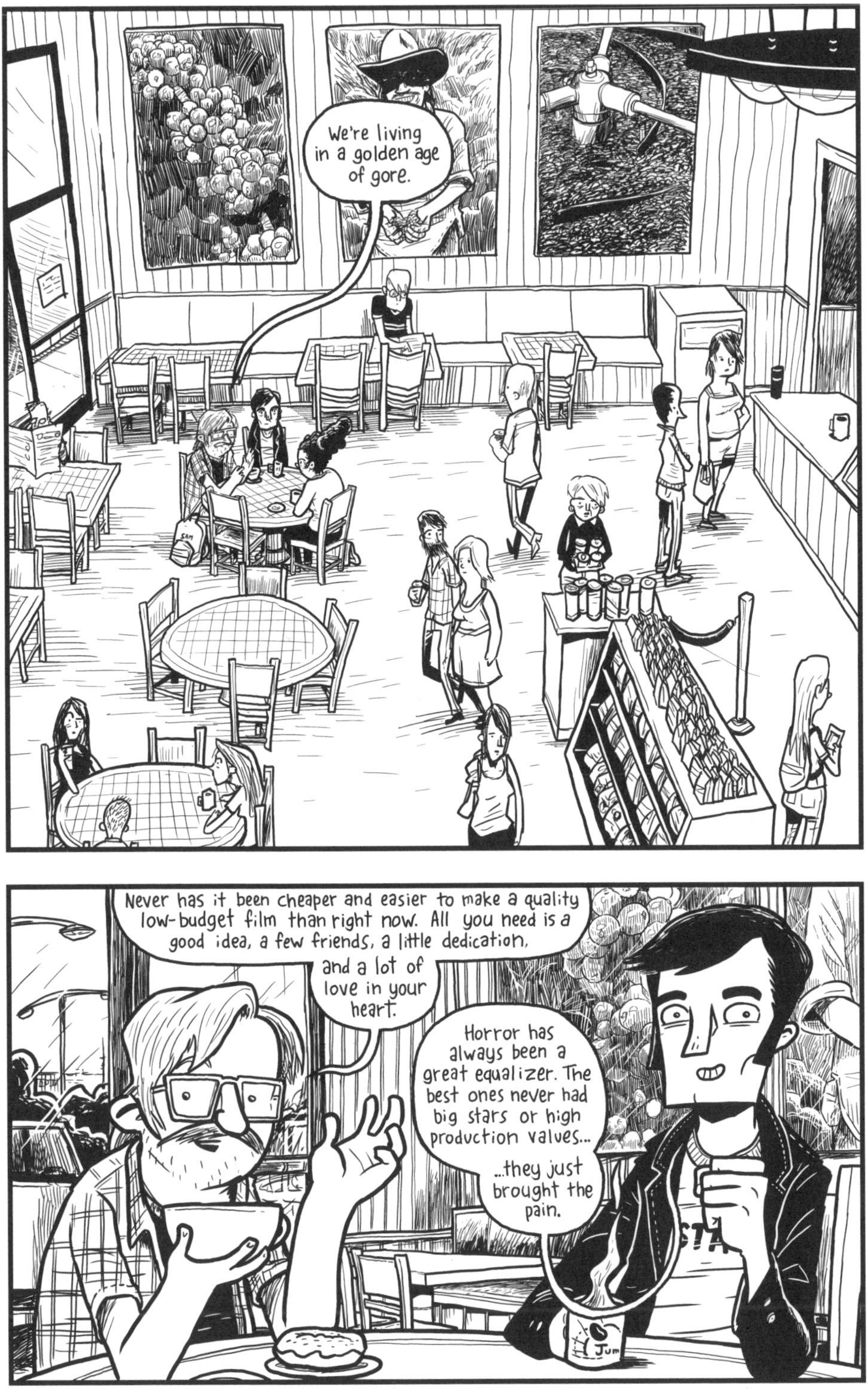
We're living in a golden age of gore.
Never has it been cheaper and easier to make a quality low-budget film than right now. All you need is a good idea, a few friends, a little dedication,
and a lot of love in your heart.
Horror has always been a great equalizer. The best ones never had big stars or high production values...
...they just brought the pain.

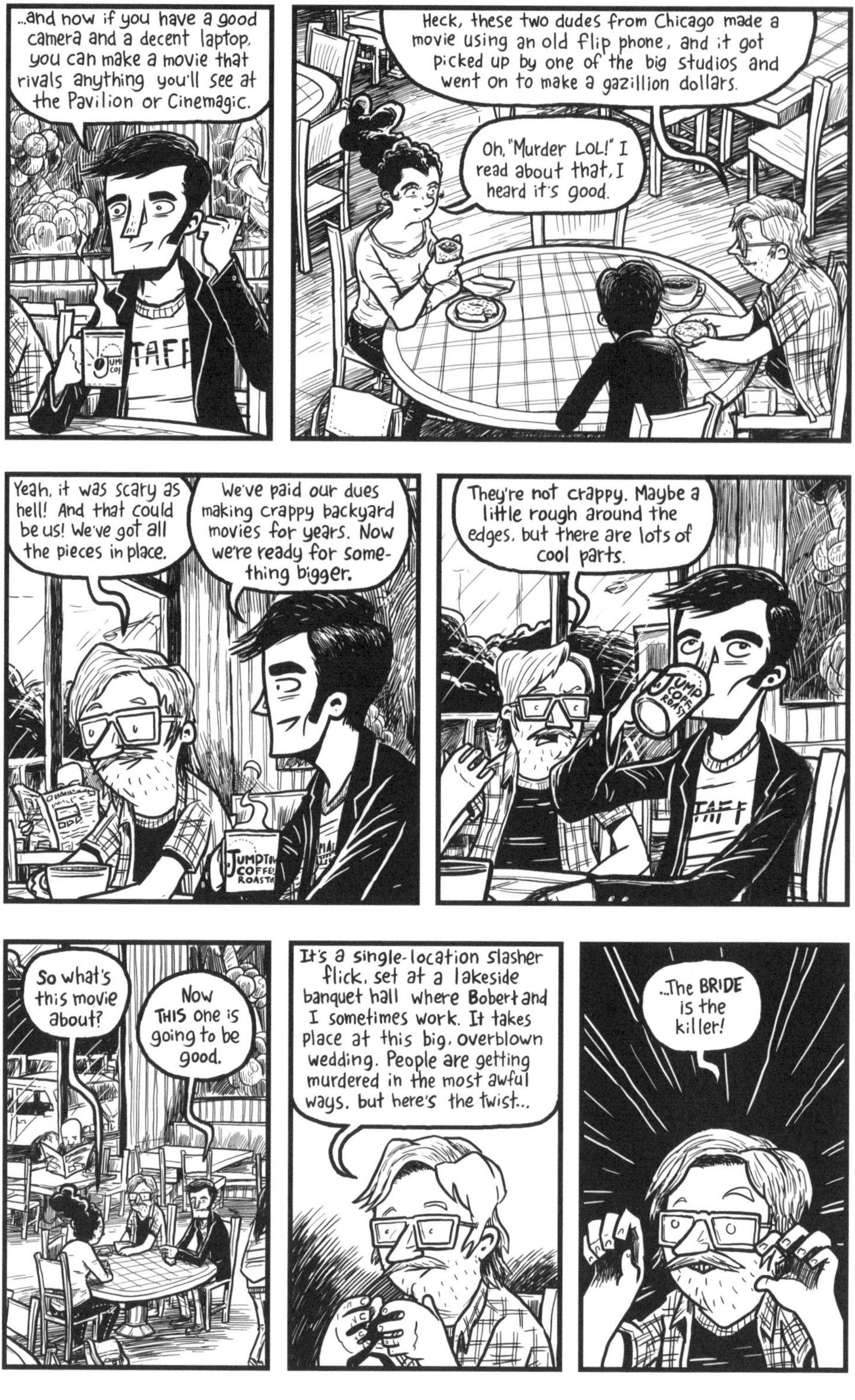
...and now if you have a good camera and a decent laptop, you can make a movie that rivals anything you'll see at the Pavilion or Cinemagic.
Heck, these two dudes from Chicago made a movie using an old flip phone, and it got picked up by one of the big studios and went on to make a gazillion dollars.
Oh, "Murder LOL!" I read about that, I heard it's good.
Yeah, it was scary as hell! And that could be us! We've got all the pieces in place.
We've paid our dues making crappy backyard movies for years. Now we're ready for something bigger.
They're not crappy. Maybe a little rough around the edges, but there are lots of cool parts.
So what's this movie about?
Now THIS one is going to be good.
It's a single-location slasher flick, set at a lakeside banquet hall where Bobert and I sometimes work. It takes place at this big, overblown wedding. People are getting murdered in the most awful ways, but here's the twist...
...The BRIDE is the killer!

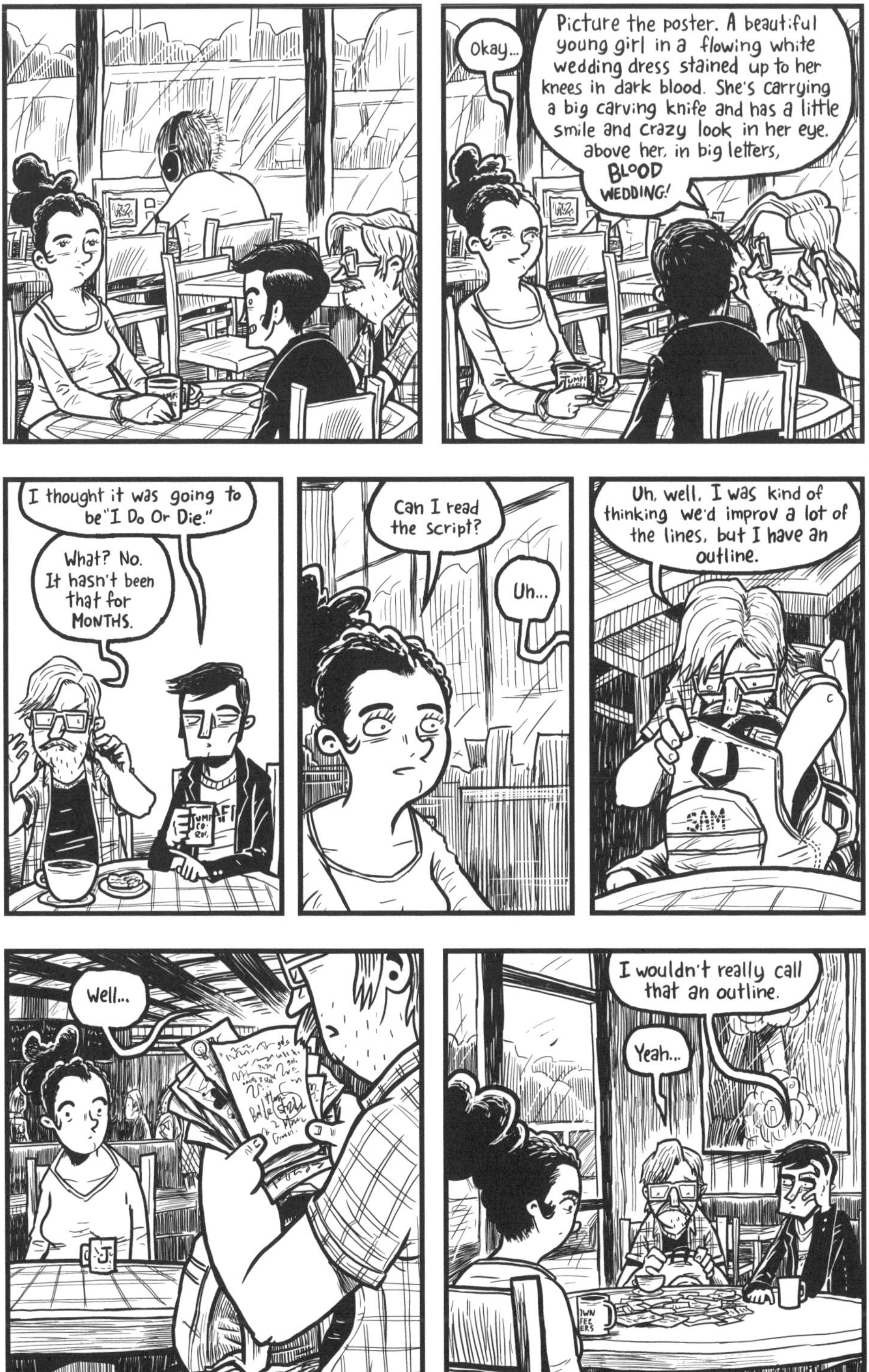

Okay...
Picture the poster. A beautiful young girl in a flowing white wedding dress stained up to her knees in dark blood. She's carrying a big carving knife and has a little smile and crazy look in her eye. above her, in big letters, BLOOD WEDDING!
I thought it was going to be "I Do Or Die."
What? No. It hasn't been that for MONTHS.
Can I read the script?
Uh...
Uh, well, I was kind of thinking we'd improv a lot of the lines, but I have an outline.
SAM
Well...
I wouldn't really call that an outline.
Yeah...

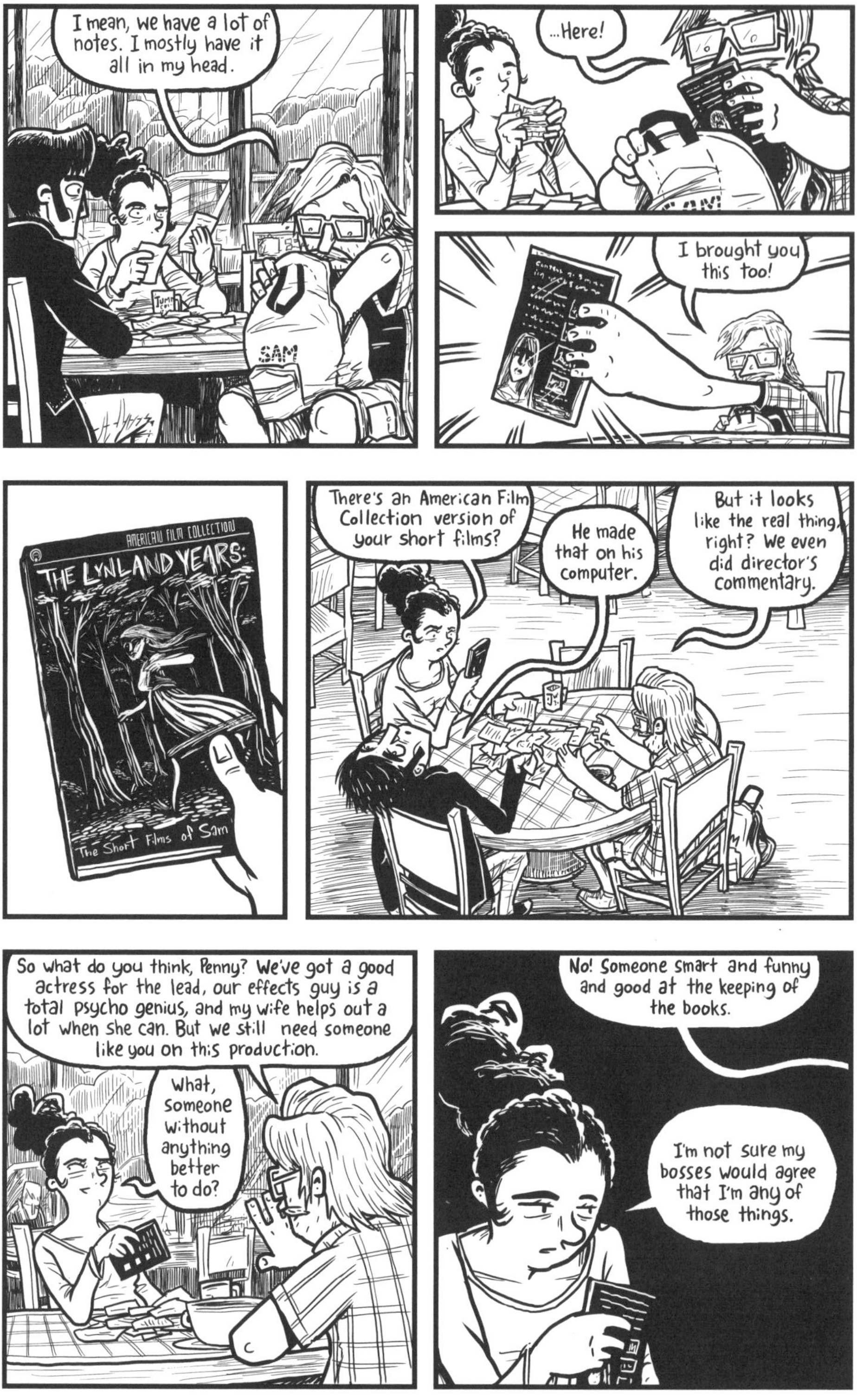

I mean, we have a lot of notes. I mostly have it all in my head.
SAM
...Here!
I brought you this too!
AMERICAN FILM COLLECTION
THE LYNLAND YEARS:
The Short Films of Sam
There's an American Film Collection version of your short films?
He made that on his computer.
But it looks like the real thing, right? We even did director's commentary.
So what do you think, Penny? We've got a good actress for the lead, our effects guy is a total psycho genius, and my wife helps out a lot when she can. But we still need someone like you on this production.
What, someone without anything better to do?
No! Someone smart and funny and good at the keeping of the books.
I'm not sure my bosses would agree that I'm any of those things.

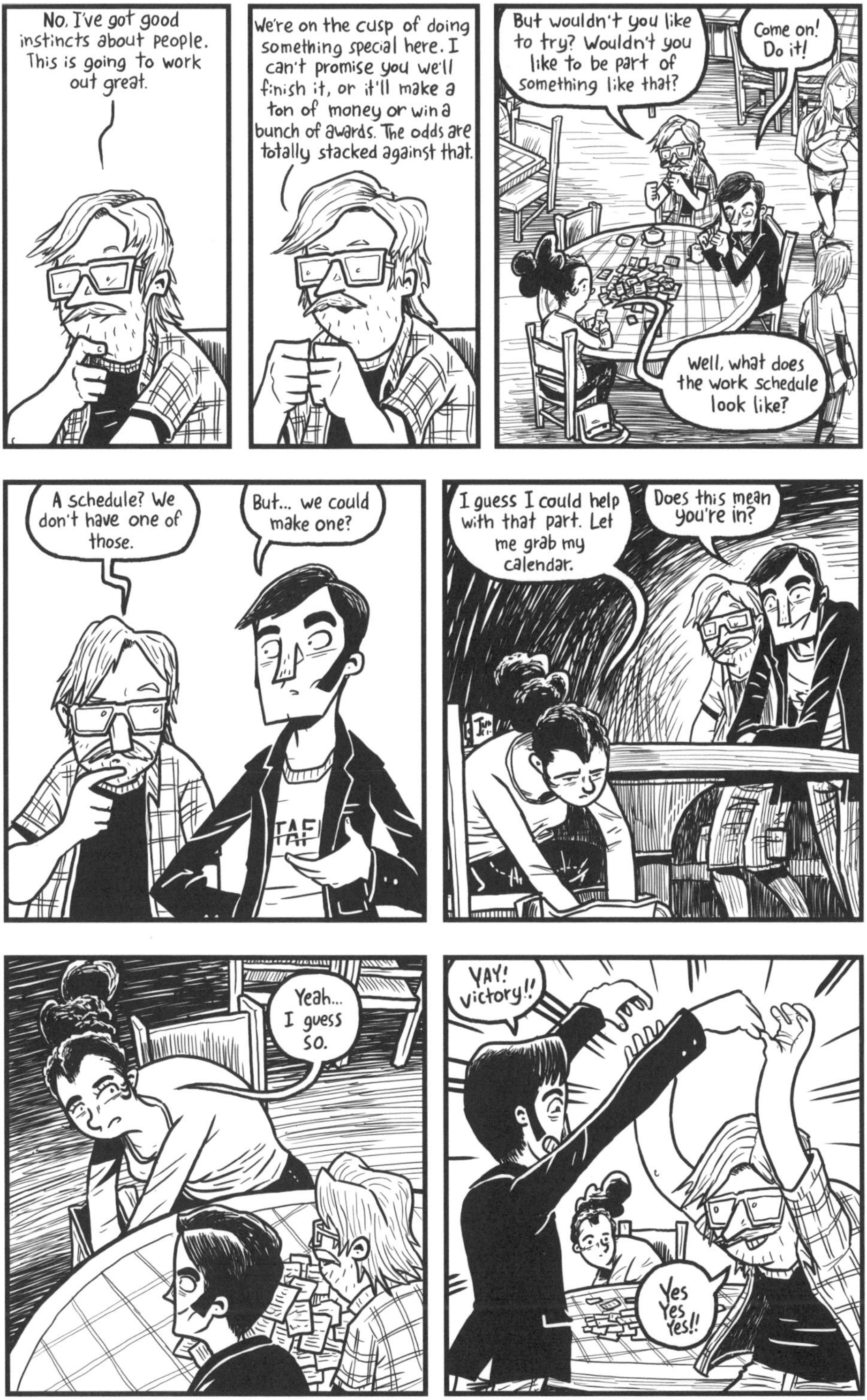

No. I've got good instincts about people. This is going to work out great.
We're on the cusp of doing something special here. I can't promise you we'll finish it, or it'll make a ton of money or win a bunch of awards. The odds are totally stacked against that.
But wouldn't you like to try? Wouldn't you like to be part of something like that?
Come on! Do it!
Well, what does the work schedule look like?
A schedule? We don't have one of those.
But... we could make one?
I guess I could help with that part. Let me grab my calendar.
Does this mean you're in?
Yeah... I guess so.
YAY! victory!!
Yes Yes Yes!!

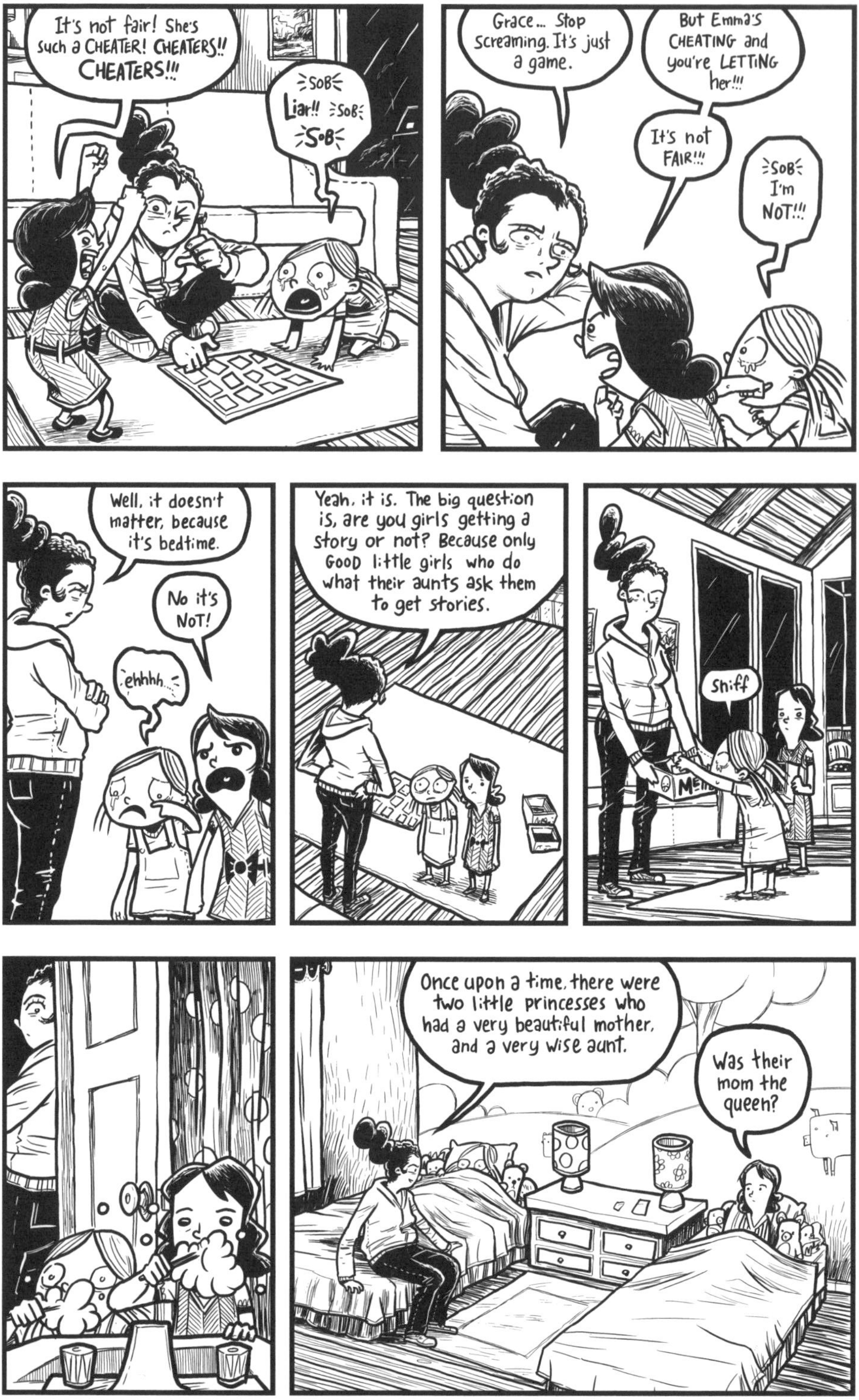
It's not fair! She's such a CHEATER! CHEATERS!! CHEATERS!!!
SOB
Liar!! SOB
SOB
Grace... Stop screaming. It's just a game.
But Emma's CHEATING and you're LETTING her!!!
It's not FAIR!!!
SOB
I'm NOT!!!
Well, it doesn't matter, because it's bedtime.
No it's NOT!
ehhhh...
Yeah, it is. The big question is, are you girls getting a story or not? Because only GOOD little girls who do what their aunts ask them to get stories.
Shiff
Once upon a time, there were two little princesses who had a very beautiful mother, and a very wise aunt.
Was their mom the queen?

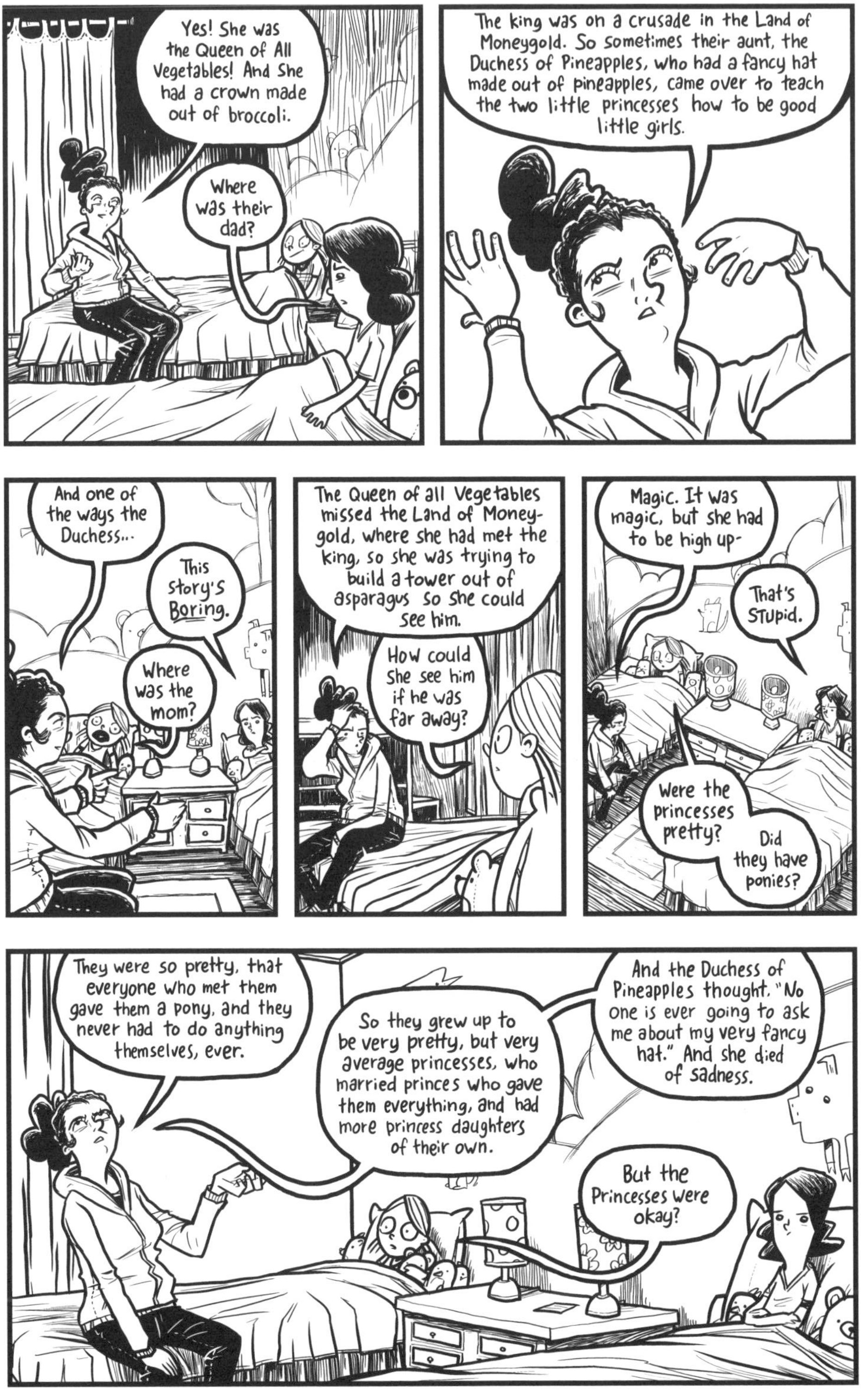
Yes! She was the Queen of All Vegetables! And She had a crown made out of broccoli.
Where was their dad?
The king was on a crusade in the Land of Moneygold. So sometimes their aunt, the Duchess of Pineapples, who had a fancy hat made out of pineapples, came over to teach the two little princesses how to be good little girls.
And one of the ways the Duchess...
This story's Boring.
Where was the mom?
The Queen of all Vegetables missed the Land of Moneygold, where she had met the king, so she was trying to build a tower out of asparagus so she could see him.
How could she see him if he was far away?
Magic. It was magic, but she had to be high up-
That's STUPID.
Were the princesses pretty?
Did they have ponies?
They were so pretty, that everyone who met them gave them a pony, and they never had to do anything themselves, ever.
So they grew up to be very pretty, but very average princesses, who married princes who gave them everything, and had more princess daughters of their own.
And the Duchess of Pineapples thought, "No one is ever going to ask me about my very fancy hat." And she died of sadness.
But the Princesses were okay?

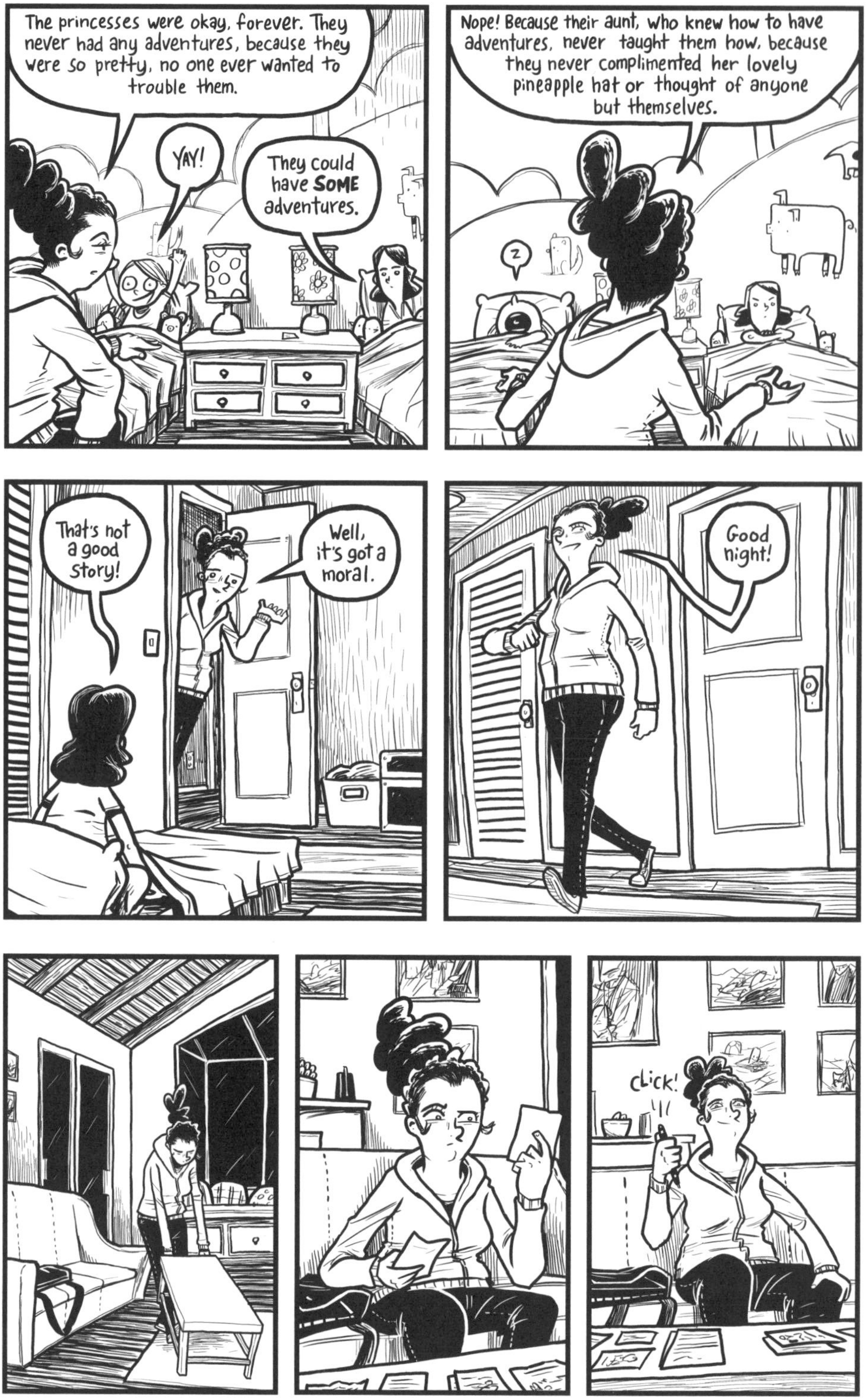
The princesses were okay, forever. They never had any adventures, because they were so pretty, no one ever wanted to trouble them.
YAY!
They could have **SOME** adventures.
Nope! Because their aunt, who knew how to have adventures, never taught them how, because they never complimented her lovely pineapple hat or thought of anyone but themselves.
That's not a good story!
Well, it's got a moral.
Good night!
CLICK!

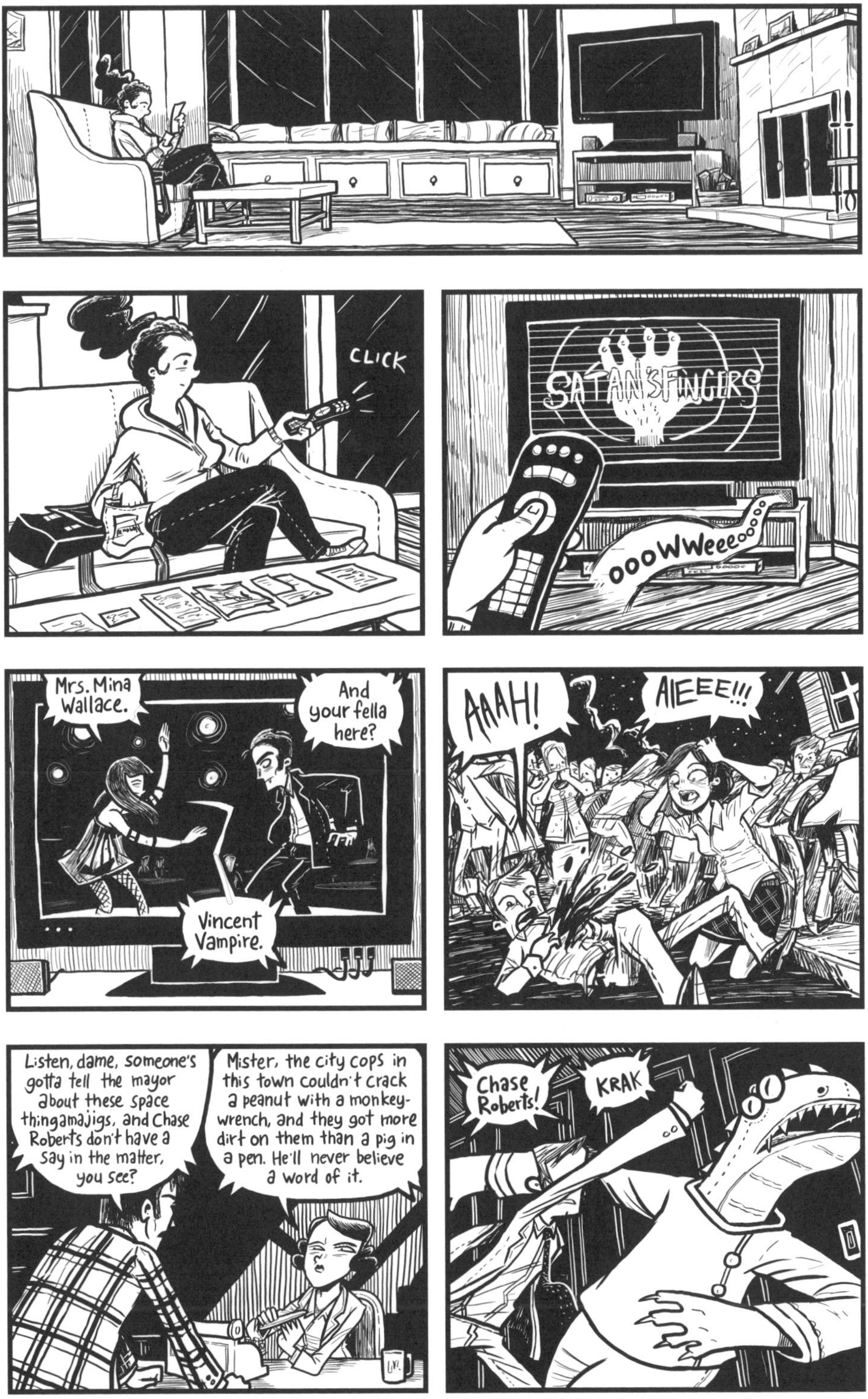
CLICK
SATAN'S FINGERS
OOOWWeeeooooo
Mrs. Mina Wallace.
And your fella here?
Vincent Vampire.
AAAH!
AIEEE!!!
Listen, dame, someone's gotta tell the mayor about these space thingamajigs, and Chase Roberts don't have a say in the matter, you see?
Mister, the city cops in this town couldn't crack a peanut with a monkey-wrench, and they got more dirt on them than a pig in a pen. He'll never believe a word of it.
Chase Roberts!
KRAK

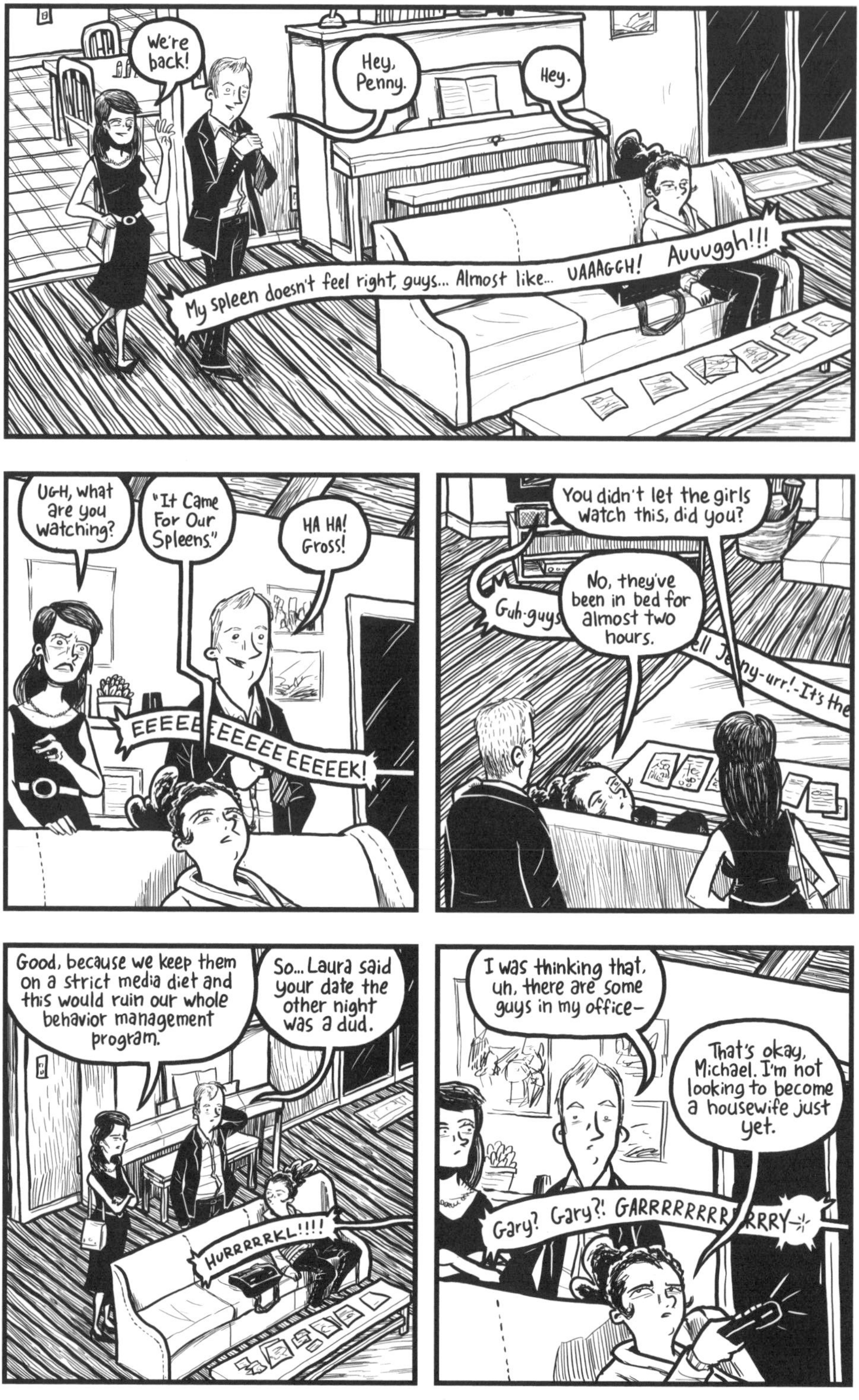
We're back!
Hey, Penny.
Hey.
My spleen doesn't feel right, guys... Almost like... UAAAGGH! Auuuggh!!!
UGH, what are you watching?
"It Came For Our Spleens."
HA HA! Gross!
EEEEEEEEEEEEEEEK!
You didn't let the girls watch this, did you?
Guh-guys
No, they've been in bed for almost two hours.
ny-urr!-It's the
Good, because we keep them on a strict media diet and this would ruin our whole behavior management program.
So... Laura said your date the other night was a dud.
HURRRRKL!!!!
I was thinking that, uh, there are some guys in my office-
That's okay, Michael. I'm not looking to become a housewife just yet.
Gary? Gary?! GARRRRRRRRRRRY

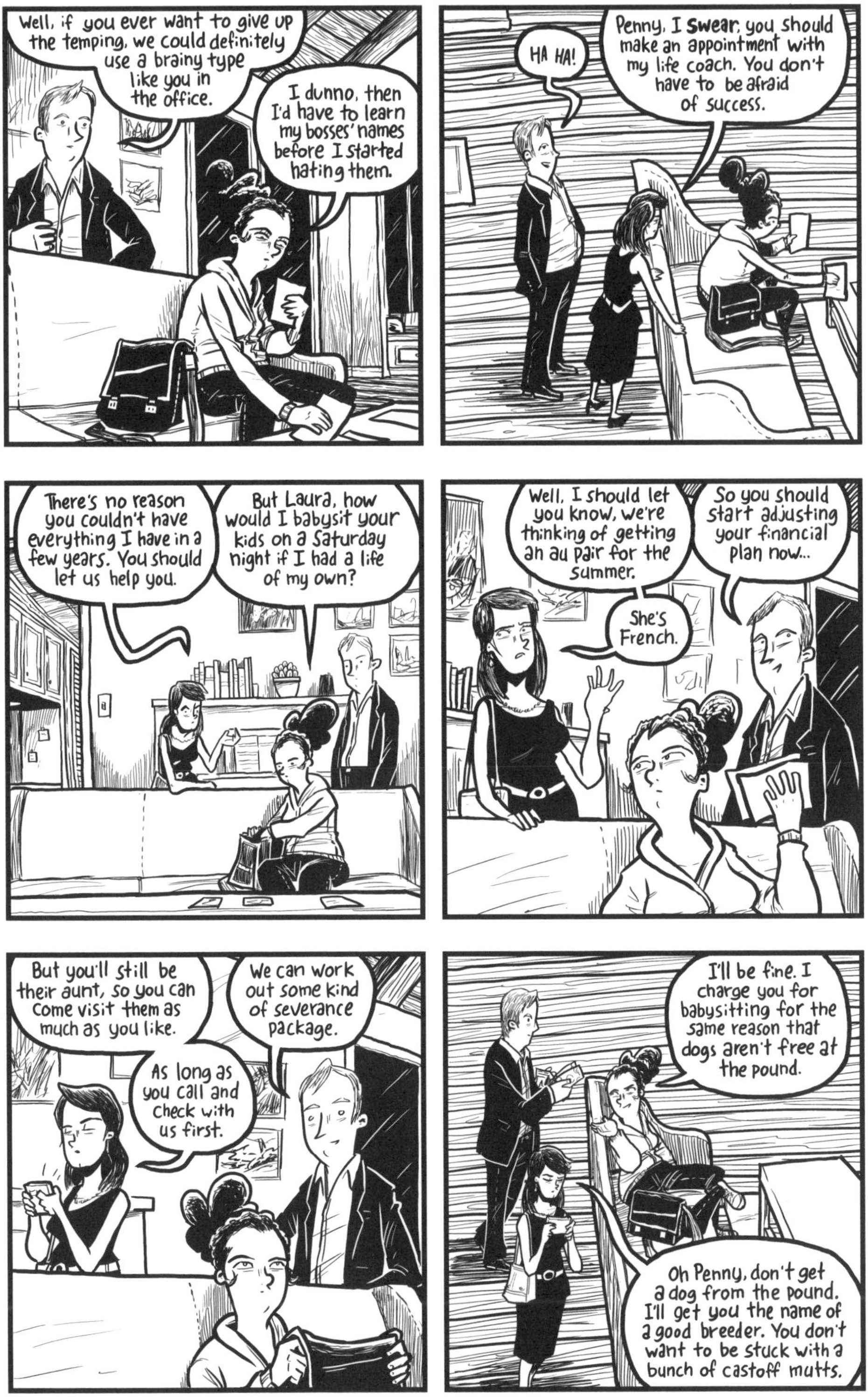
Well, if you ever want to give up the temping, we could definitely use a brainy type like you in the office.
I dunno, then I'd have to learn my bosses' names before I started hating them.
HA HA!
Penny, I **swear**, you should make an appointment with my life coach. You don't have to be afraid of success.
There's no reason you couldn't have everything I have in a few years. You should let us help you.
But Laura, how would I babysit your kids on a Saturday night if I had a life of my own?
Well, I should let you know, we're thinking of getting an au pair for the summer.
She's French.
So you should start adjusting your financial plan now...
But you'll still be their aunt, so you can come visit them as much as you like.
As long as you call and check with us first.
We can work out some kind of severance package.
I'll be fine. I charge you for babysitting for the same reason that dogs aren't free at the pound.
Oh Penny, don't get a dog from the pound. I'll get you the name of a good breeder. You don't want to be stuck with a bunch of castoff mutts.

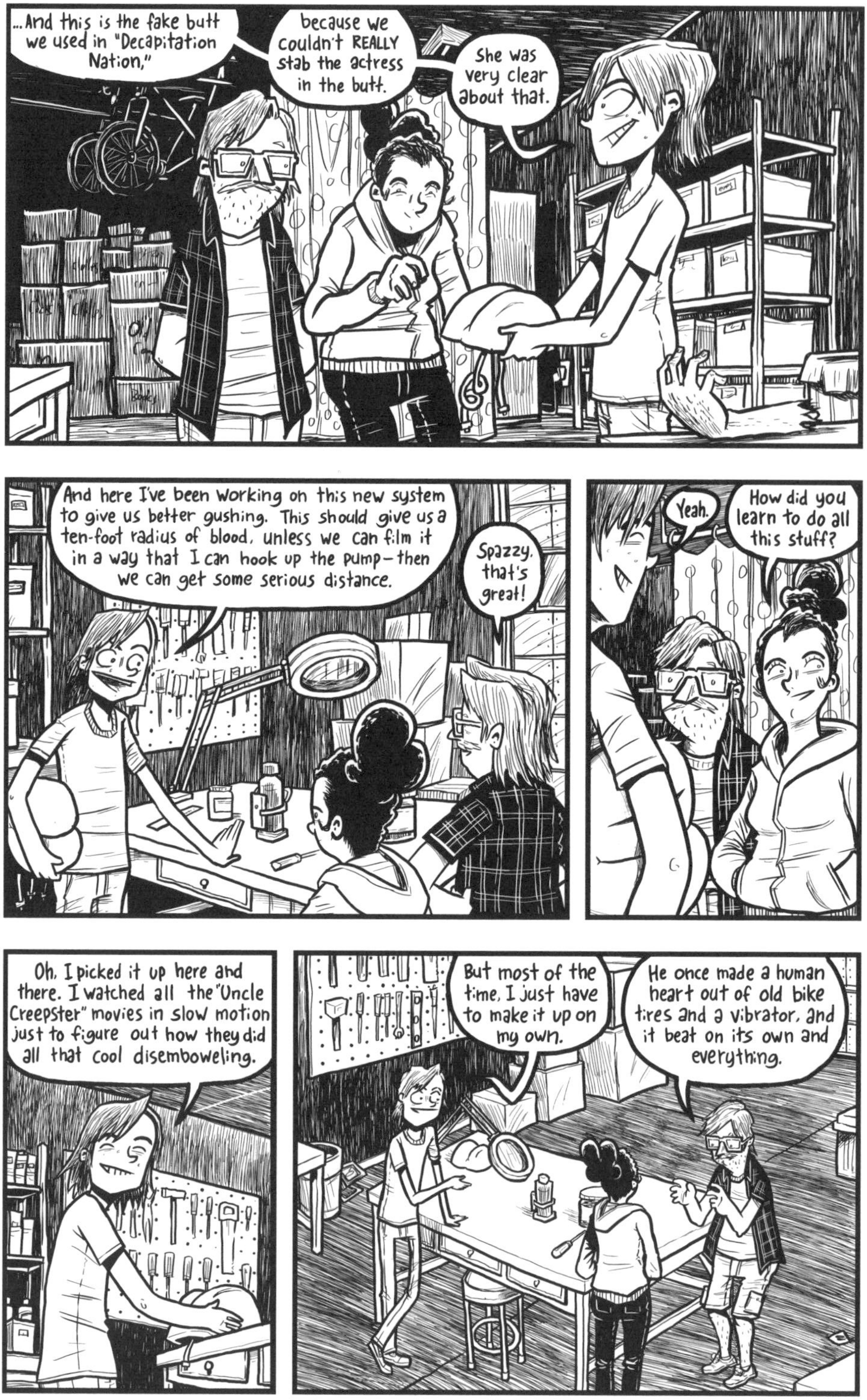
...And this is the fake butt we used in "Decapitation Nation,"
because we couldn't REALLY stab the actress in the butt.
She was very clear about that.
And here I've been working on this new system to give us better gushing. This should give us a ten-foot radius of blood, unless we can film it in a way that I can hook up the pump—then we can get some serious distance.
Spazzy, that's great!
Yeah.
How did you learn to do all this stuff?
Oh, I picked it up here and there. I watched all the "Uncle Creepster" movies in slow motion just to figure out how they did all that cool disemboweling.
But most of the time, I just have to make it up on my own.
He once made a human heart out of old bike tires and a vibrator, and it beat on its own and everything.

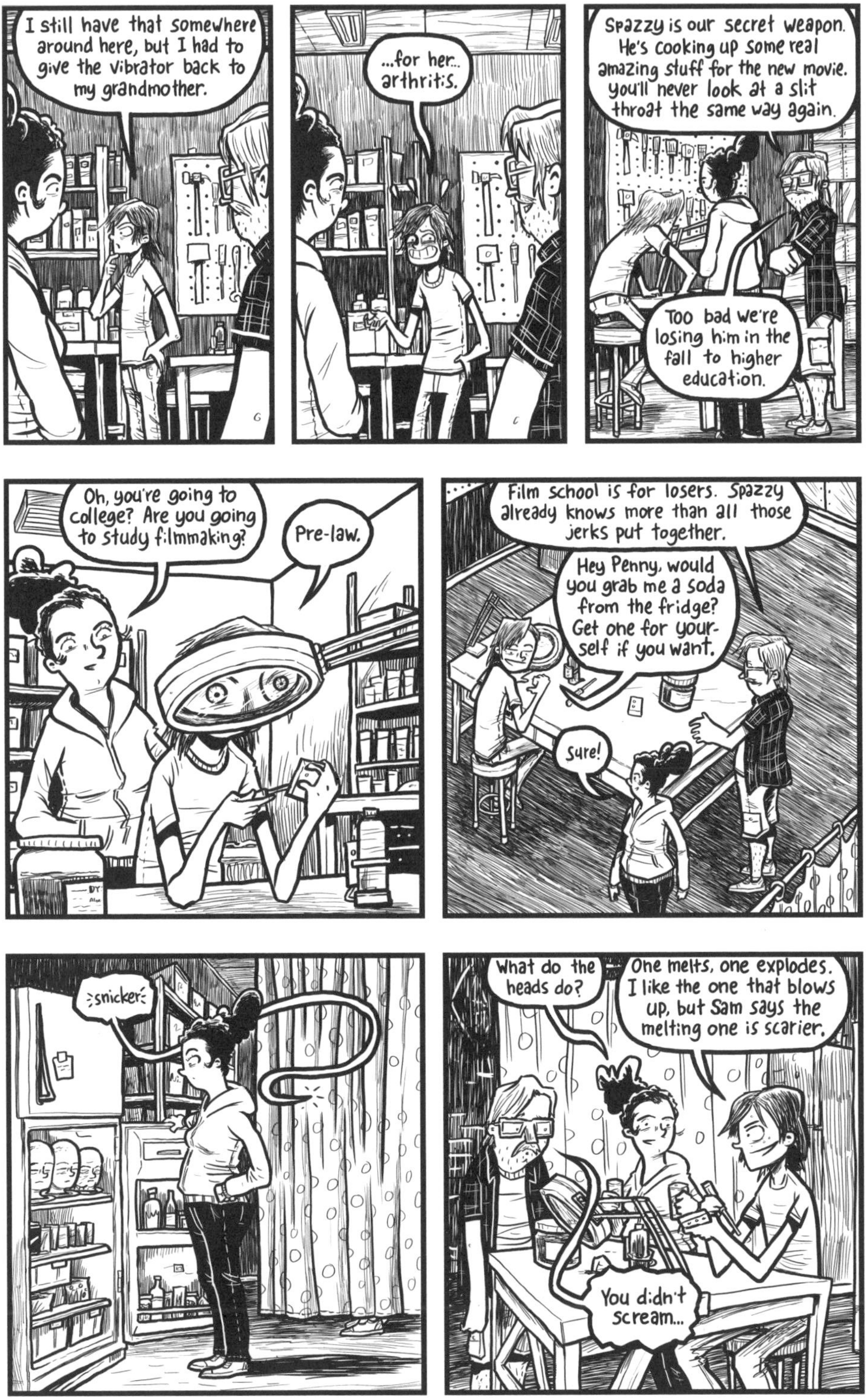
I still have that somewhere around here, but I had to give the vibrator back to my grandmother.
...for her... arthritis.
Spazzy is our secret weapon. He's cooking up some real amazing stuff for the new movie. You'll never look at a slit throat the same way again.
Too bad we're losing him in the fall to higher education.
Oh, you're going to college? Are you going to study filmmaking?
Pre-law.
Film school is for losers. Spazzy already knows more than all those jerks put together.
Hey Penny, would you grab me a soda from the fridge? Get one for yourself if you want.
Sure!
snicker
What do the heads do?
One melts, one explodes. I like the one that blows up, but Sam says the melting one is scarier.
You didn't scream...

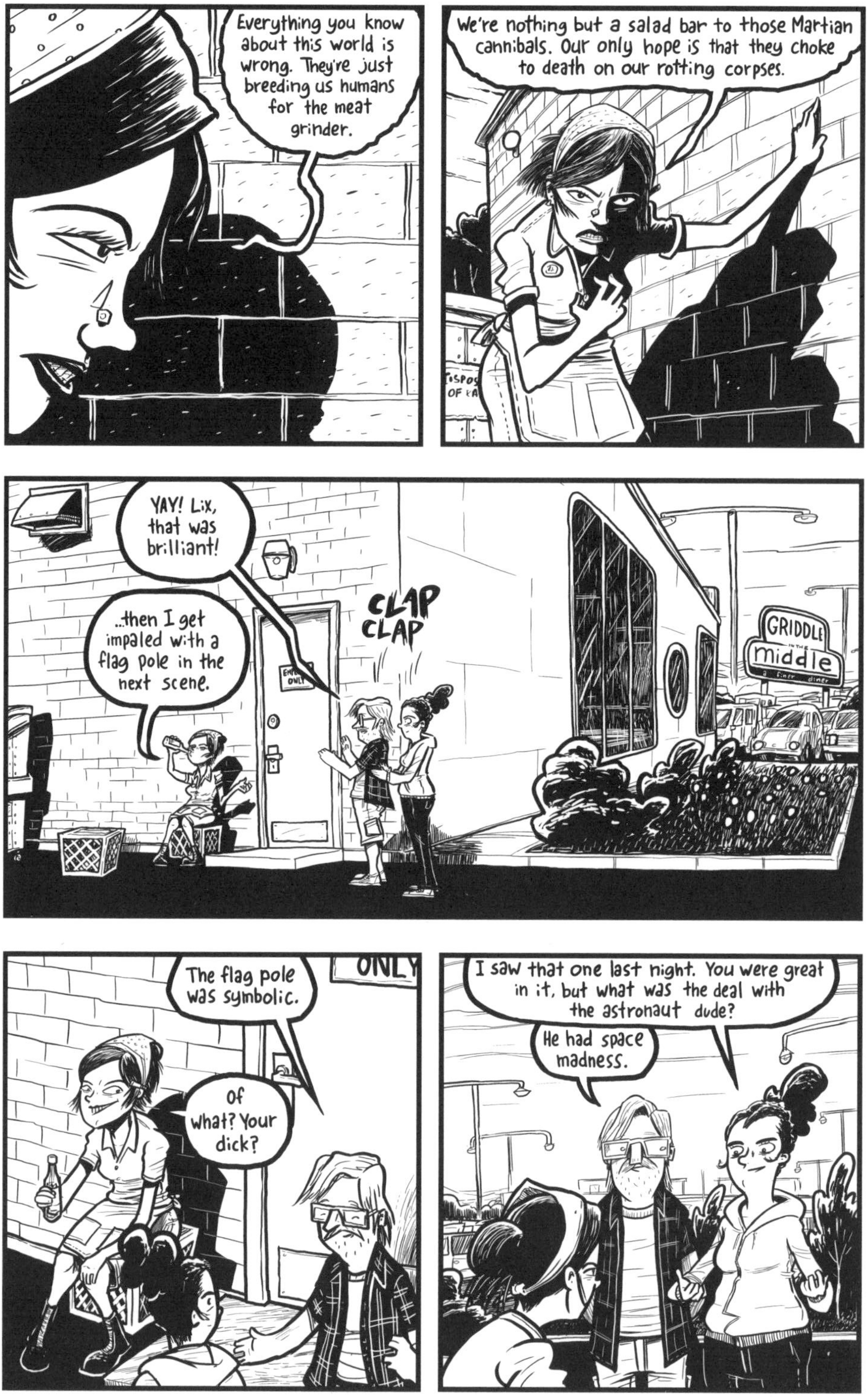
Everything you know about this world is wrong. They're just breeding us humans for the meat grinder.
We're nothing but a salad bar to those Martian cannibals. Our only hope is that they choke to death on our rotting corpses.
YAY! Lix, that was brilliant!
...then I get impaled with a flag pole in the next scene.
CLAP CLAP
GRIDDLE IN THE middle
The flag pole was symbolic.
ONLY
Of what? Your dick?
I saw that one last night. You were great in it, but what was the deal with the astronaut dude?
He had space madness.

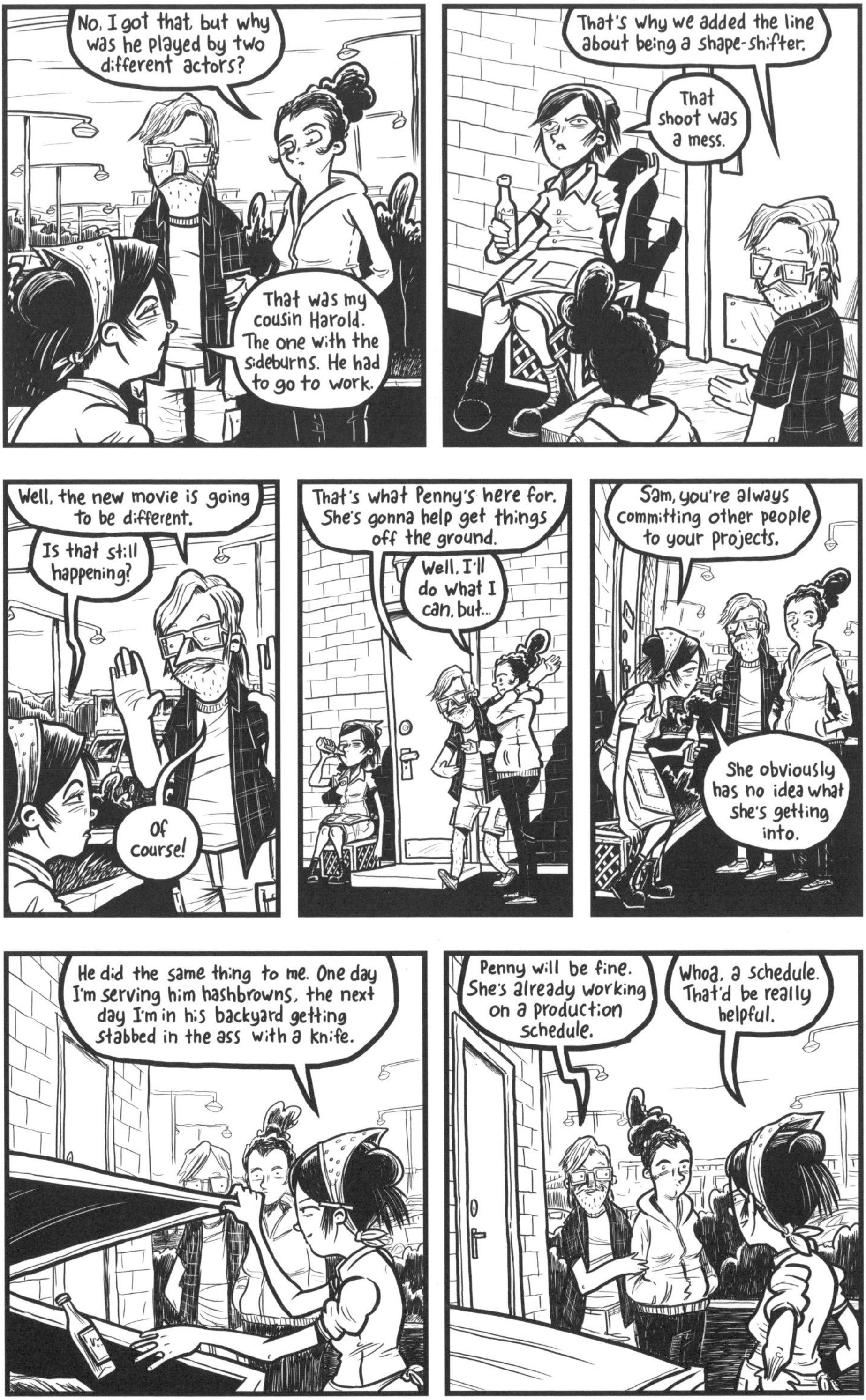
No, I got that, but why was he played by two different actors?
That was my cousin Harold. The one with the sideburns. He had to go to work.
That's why we added the line about being a shape-shifter.
That shoot was a mess.
Well, the new movie is going to be different.
Is that still happening?
Of course!
That's what Penny's here for. She's gonna help get things off the ground.
Well, I'll do what I can, but...
Sam, you're always committing other people to your projects.
She obviously has no idea what she's getting into.
He did the same thing to me. One day I'm serving him hashbrowns, the next day I'm in his backyard getting stabbed in the ass with a knife.
Penny will be fine. She's already working on a production schedule.
Whoa, a schedule. That'd be really helpful.

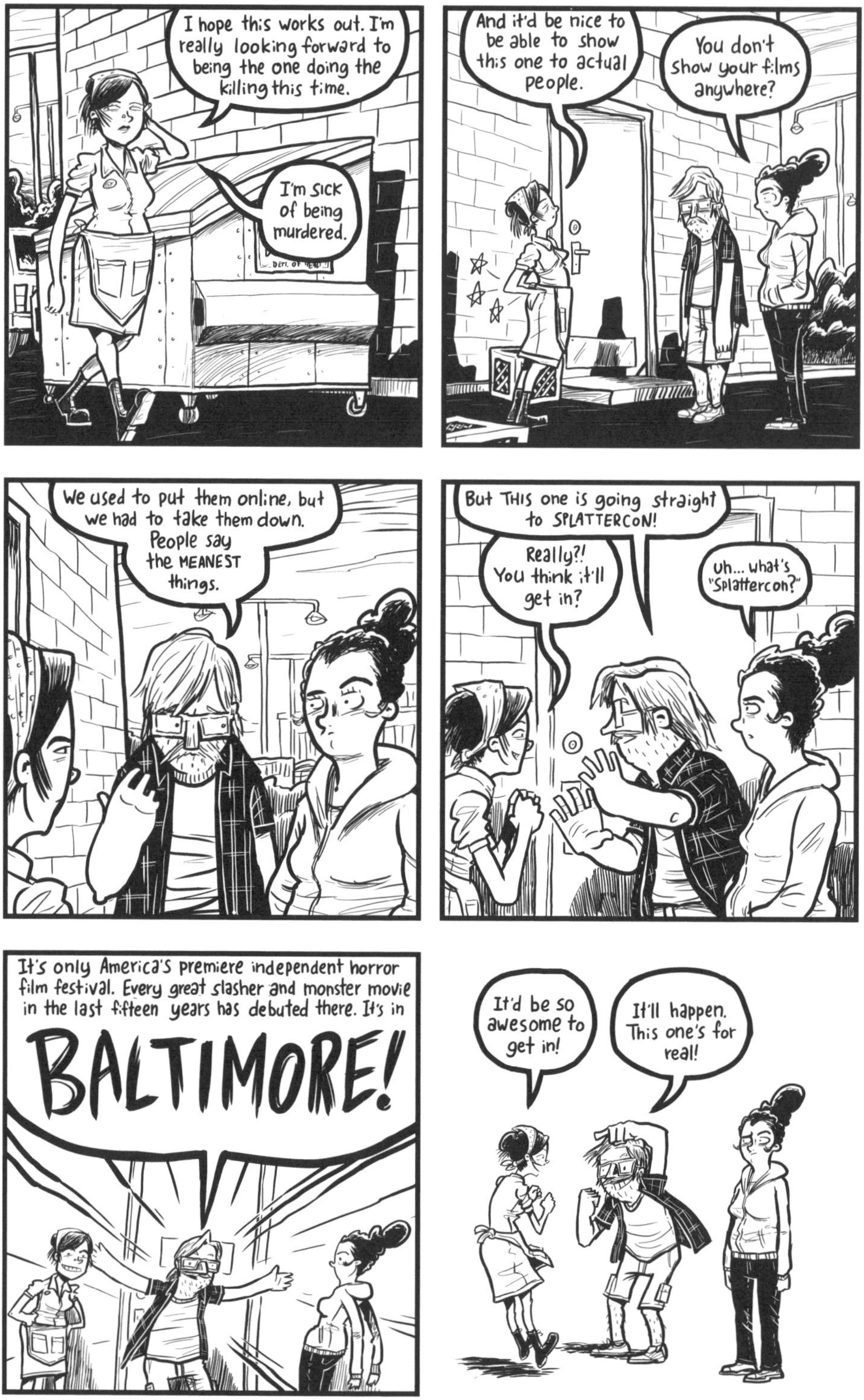
I hope this works out. I'm really looking forward to being the one doing the killing this time.
I'm SICK of being murdered.
And it'd be nice to be able to show this one to actual people.
You don't show your films anywhere?
We used to put them online, but we had to take them down. People say the MEANEST things.
But THIS one is going straight to SPLATTERCON!
Really?! You think it'll get in?
Uh... what's "Splattercon?"
It's only America's premiere independent horror film festival. Every great slasher and monster movie in the last fifteen years has debuted there. It's in
BALTIMORE!
It'd be so awesome to get in!
It'll happen. This one's for real!

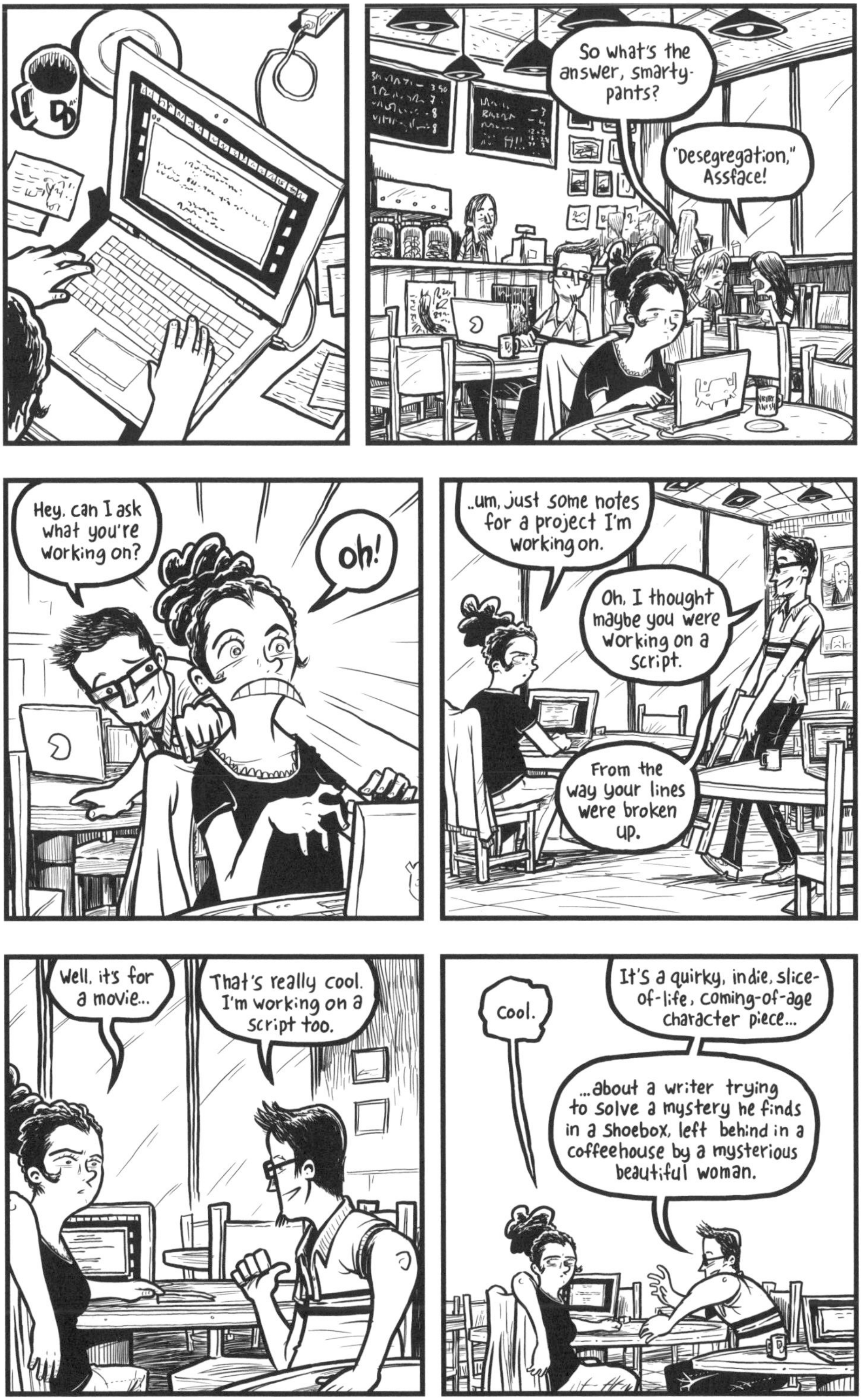
So what's the answer, smarty-pants?
"Desegregation," Assface!
Hey, can I ask what you're working on?
oh!
..um, just some notes for a project I'm working on.
Oh, I thought maybe you were working on a script.
From the way your lines were broken up.
Well, it's for a movie...
That's really cool. I'm working on a script too.
Cool.
It's a quirky, indie, slice-of-life, coming-of-age character piece...
...about a writer trying to solve a mystery he finds in a shoebox, left behind in a coffeehouse by a mysterious beautiful woman.

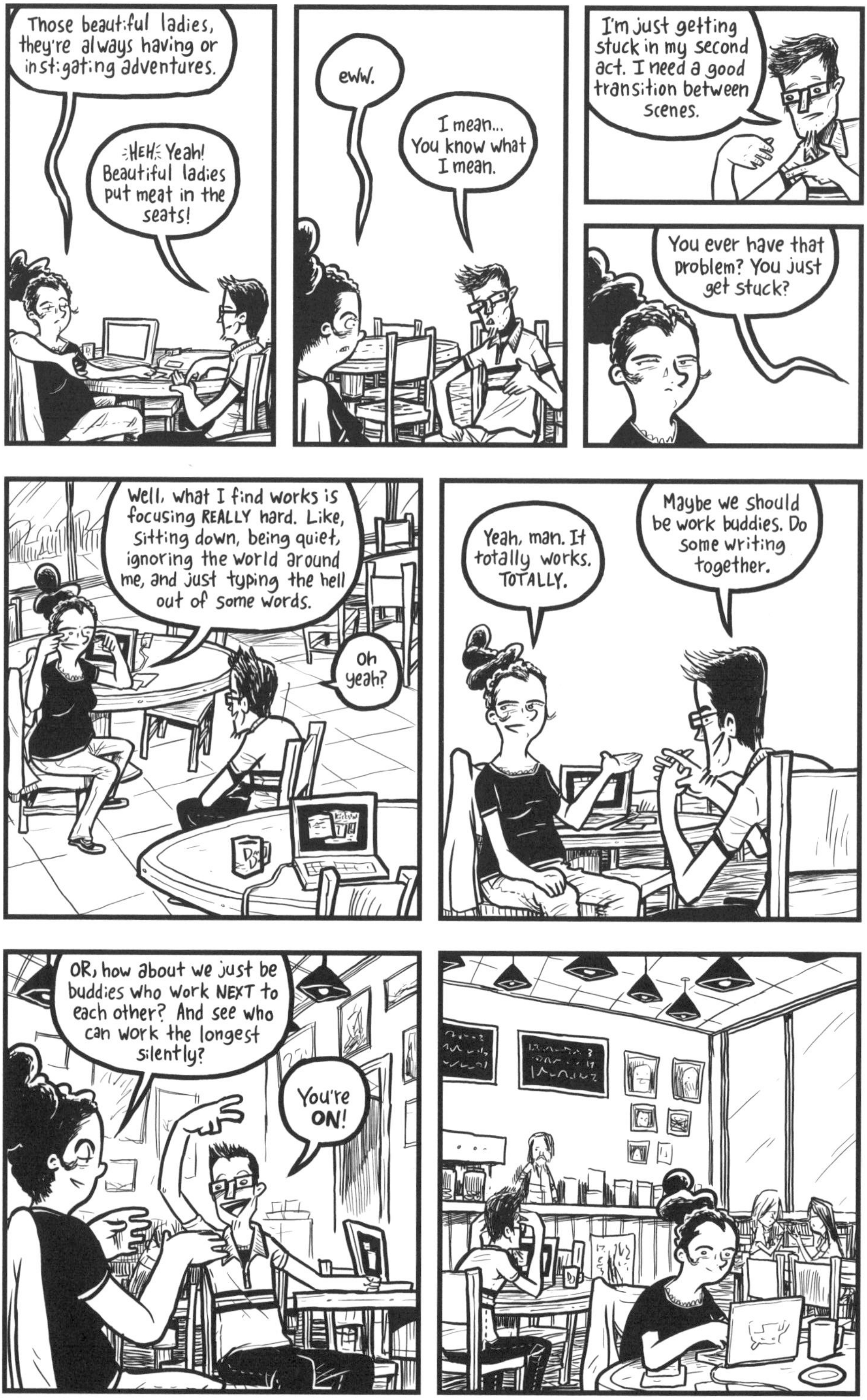
Those beautiful ladies, they're always having or instigating adventures.
HEH Yeah! Beautiful ladies put meat in the seats!
eww.
I mean... You know what I mean.
I'm just getting stuck in my second act. I need a good transition between scenes.
You ever have that problem? You just get stuck?
Well, what I find works is focusing REALLY hard. Like, sitting down, being quiet, ignoring the world around me, and just typing the hell out of some words.
Oh yeah?
Yeah, man. It totally works. TOTALLY.
Maybe we should be work buddies. Do some writing together.
OR, how about we just be buddies who work NEXT to each other? And see who can work the longest silently?
You're ON!

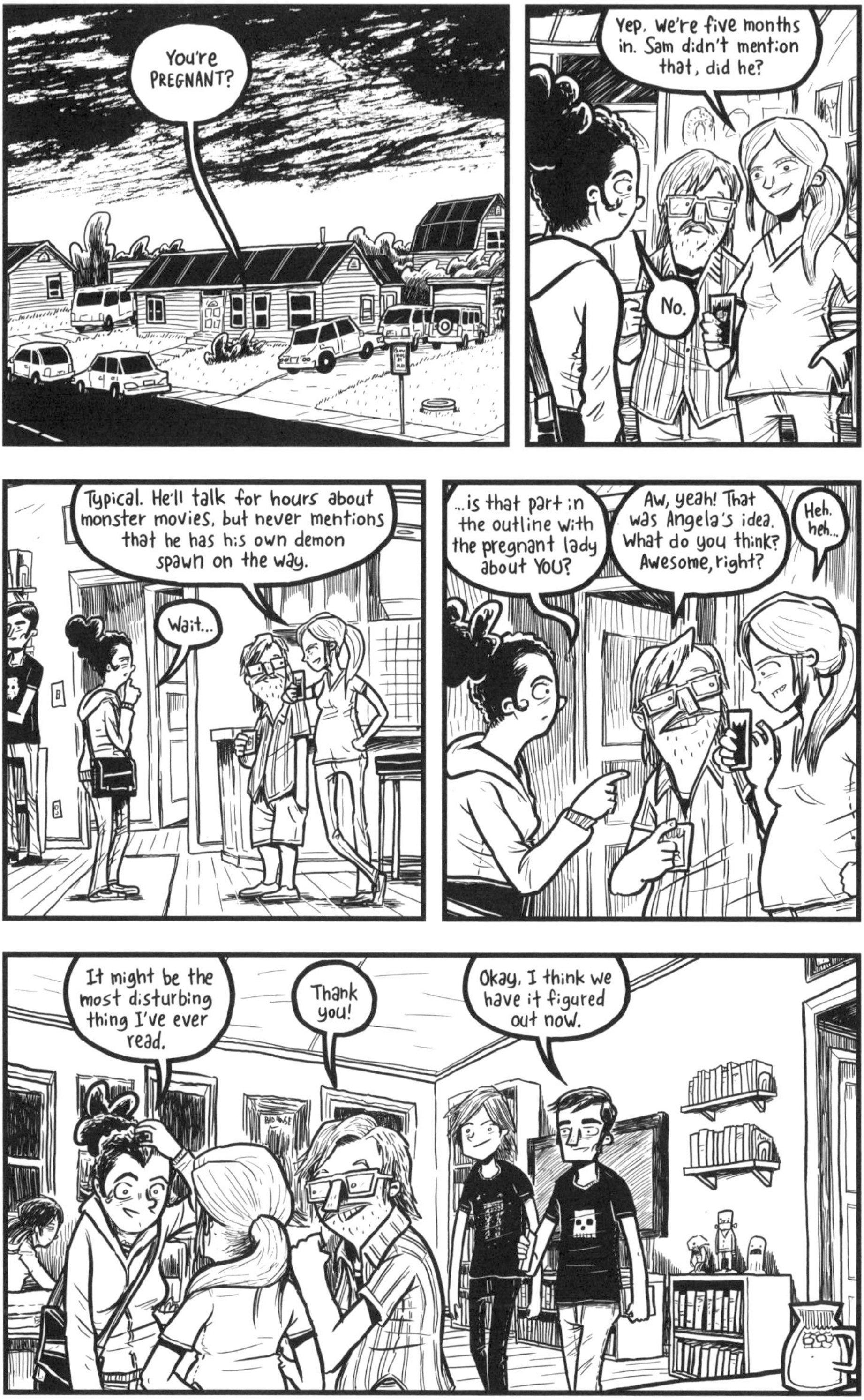
You're PREGNANT?
Yep, we're five months in. Sam didn't mention that, did he?
No.
Typical. He'll talk for hours about monster movies, but never mentions that he has his own demon spawn on the way.
Wait...
...is that part in the outline with the pregnant lady about YOU?
Aw, yeah! That was Angela's idea. What do you think? Awesome, right?
Heh. heh...
It might be the most disturbing thing I've ever read.
Thank you!
Okay, I think we have it figured out now.

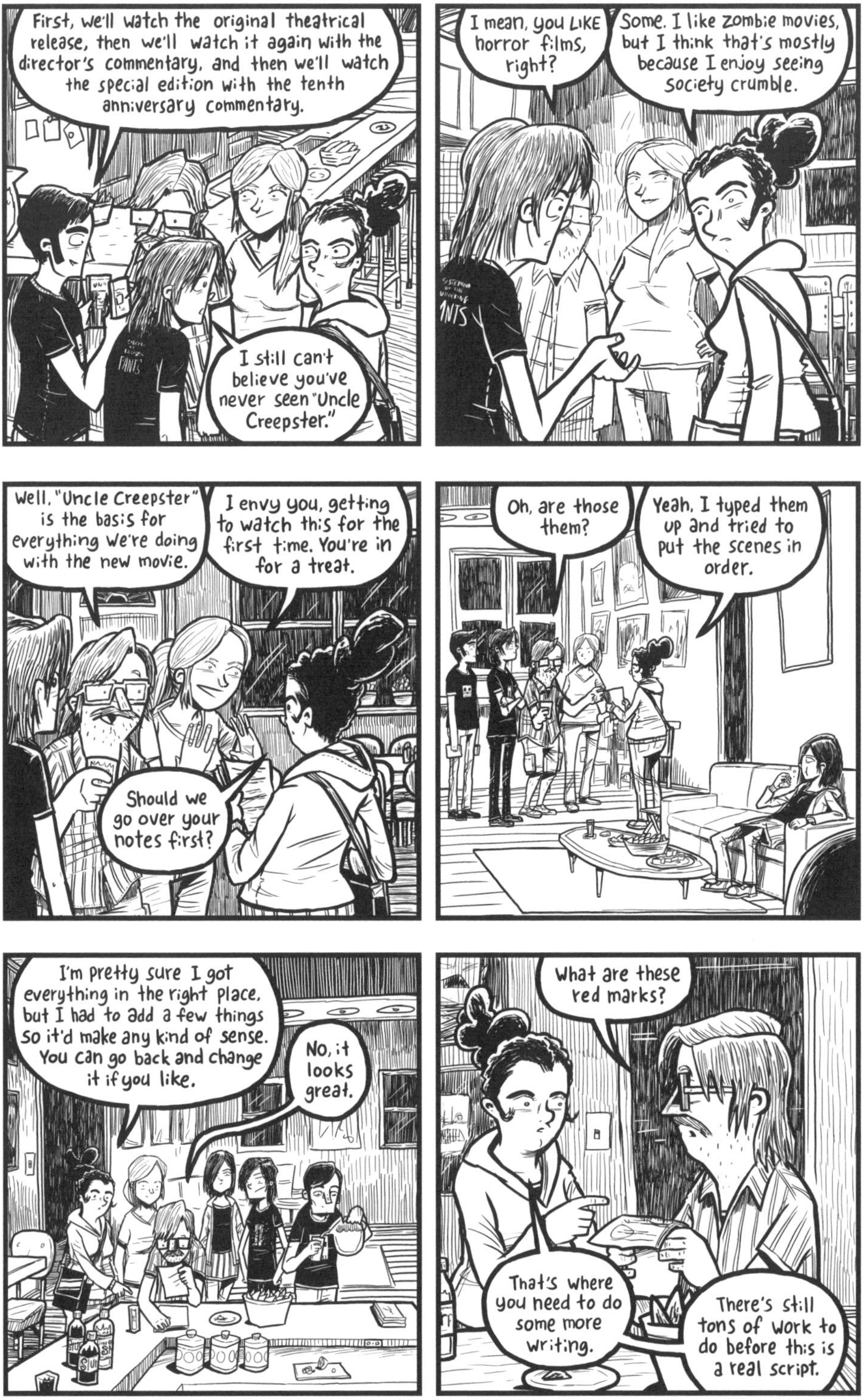
First, we'll watch the original theatrical release, then we'll watch it again with the director's commentary, and then we'll watch the special edition with the tenth anniversary commentary.
I still can't believe you've never seen "Uncle Creepster."
I mean, you LIKE horror films, right?
Some. I like zombie movies, but I think that's mostly because I enjoy seeing society crumble.
Well, "Uncle Creepster" is the basis for everything we're doing with the new movie.
I envy you, getting to watch this for the first time. You're in for a treat.
Should we go over your notes first?
Oh, are those them?
Yeah, I typed them up and tried to put the scenes in order.
I'm pretty sure I got everything in the right place, but I had to add a few things so it'd make any kind of sense. You can go back and change it if you like.
No, it looks great.
What are these red marks?
That's where you need to do some more writing.
There's still tons of work to do before this is a real script.

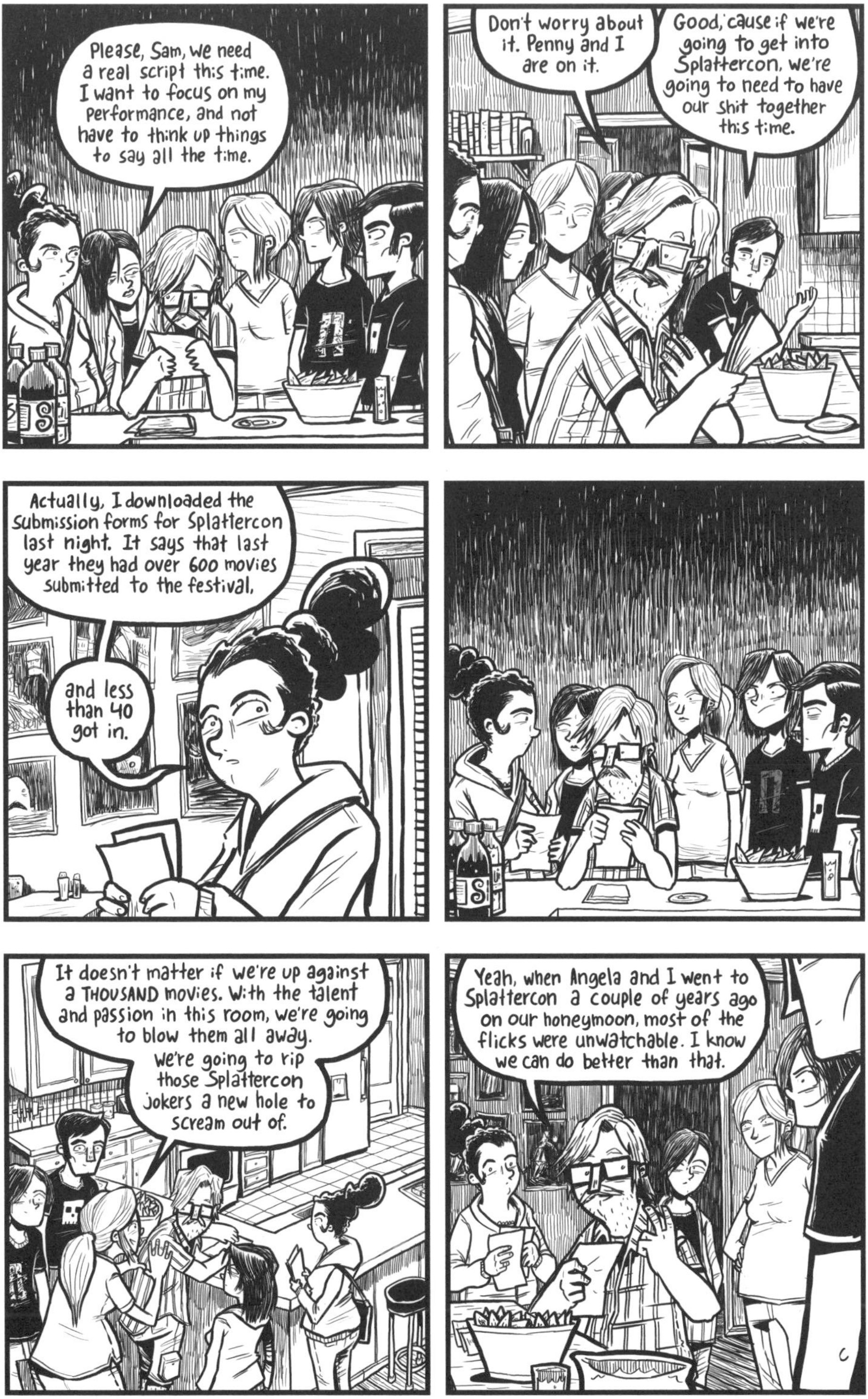
Please, Sam, we need a real script this time. I want to focus on my performance, and not have to think up things to say all the time.
Don't worry about it. Penny and I are on it.
Good, 'cause if we're going to get into Splattercon, we're going to need to have our shit together this time.
Actually, I downloaded the submission forms for Splattercon last night. It says that last year they had over 600 movies submitted to the festival,
and less than 40 got in.
It doesn't matter if we're up against a THOUSAND movies. With the talent and passion in this room, we're going to blow them all away.
We're going to rip those Splattercon jokers a new hole to scream out of.
Yeah, when Angela and I went to Splattercon a couple of years ago on our honeymoon, most of the flicks were unwatchable. I know we can do better than that.

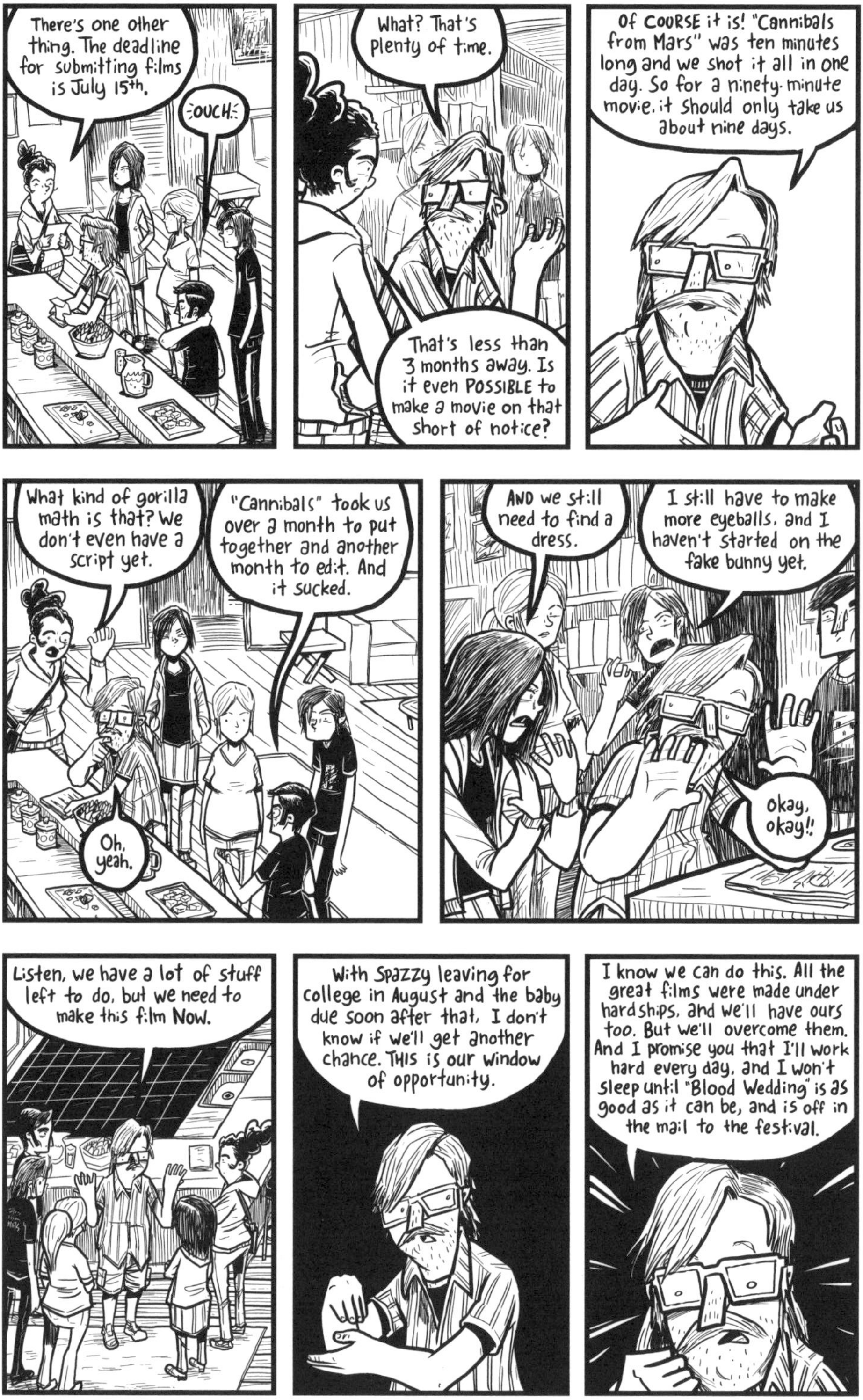

There's one other thing. The deadline for submitting films is July 15th.
OUCH.
What? That's plenty of time.
That's less than 3 months away. Is it even POSSIBLE to make a movie on that short of notice?
Of COURSE it is! "Cannibals from Mars" was ten minutes long and we shot it all in one day. So for a ninety-minute movie, it should only take us about nine days.
What kind of gorilla math is that? We don't even have a script yet.
"Cannibals" took us over a month to put together and another month to edit. And it sucked.
Oh, yeah.
AND we still need to find a dress.
I still have to make more eyeballs, and I haven't started on the fake bunny yet.
Okay, okay!!
Listen, we have a lot of stuff left to do, but we need to make this film NOW.
With Spazzy leaving for college in August and the baby due soon after that, I don't know if we'll get another chance. THIS is our window of opportunity.
I know we can do this. All the great films were made under hardships, and we'll have ours too. But we'll overcome them. And I promise you that I'll work hard every day, and I won't sleep until "Blood Wedding" is as good as it can be, and is off in the mail to the festival.

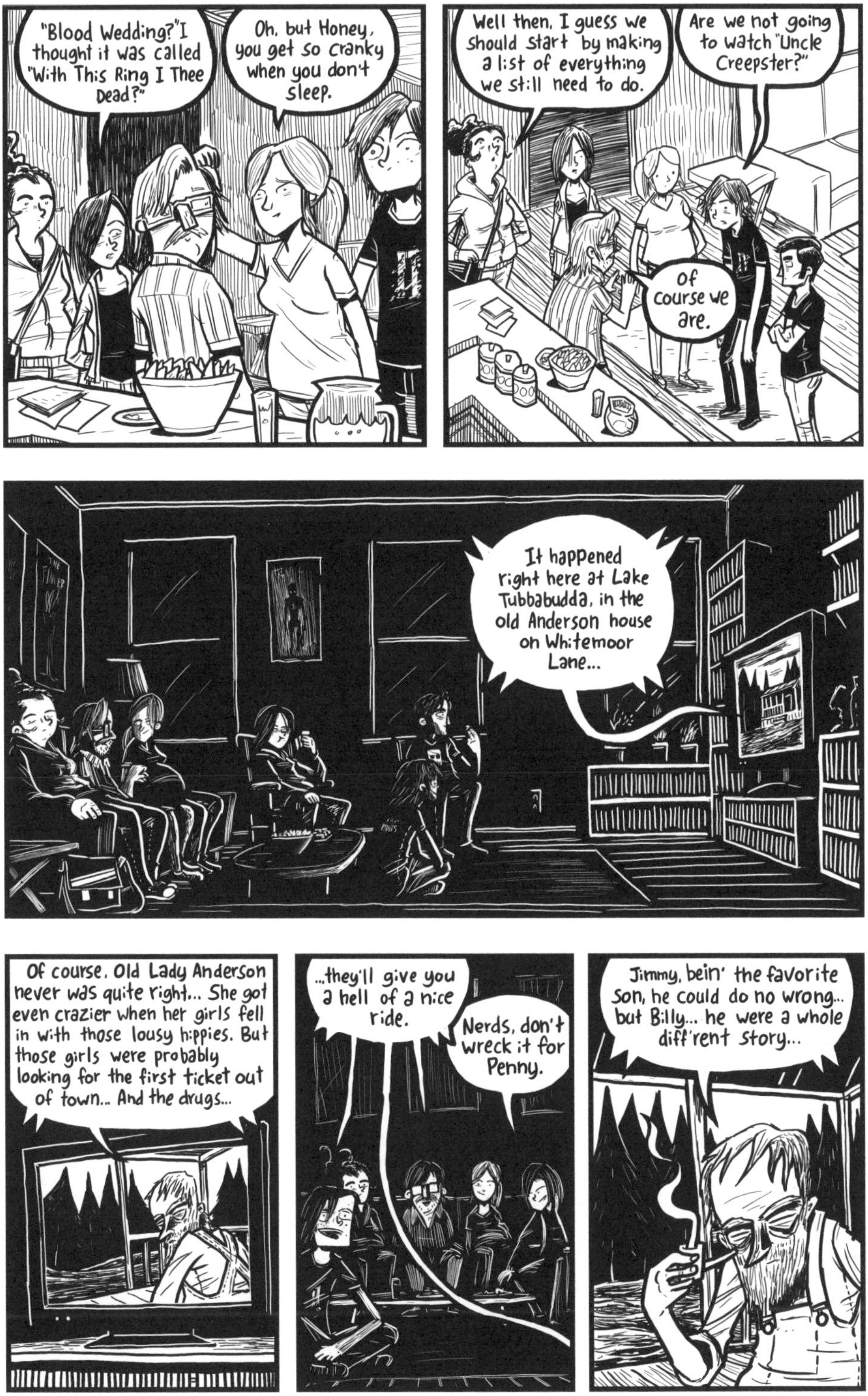
"Blood Wedding?" I thought it was called "With This Ring I Thee Dead?"
Oh, but Honey, you get so cranky when you don't sleep.
Well then, I guess we should start by making a list of everything we still need to do.
Are we not going to watch "Uncle Creepster?"
Of course we are.
It happened right here at Lake Tubbabudda, in the old Anderson house on Whitemoor Lane...
Of course, Old Lady Anderson never was quite right... She got even crazier when her girls fell in with those lousy hippies. But those girls were probably looking for the first ticket out of town... And the drugs...
...they'll give you a hell of a nice ride.
Nerds, don't wreck it for Penny.
Jimmy, bein' the favorite son, he could do no wrong... but Billy... he were a whole diff'rent story...

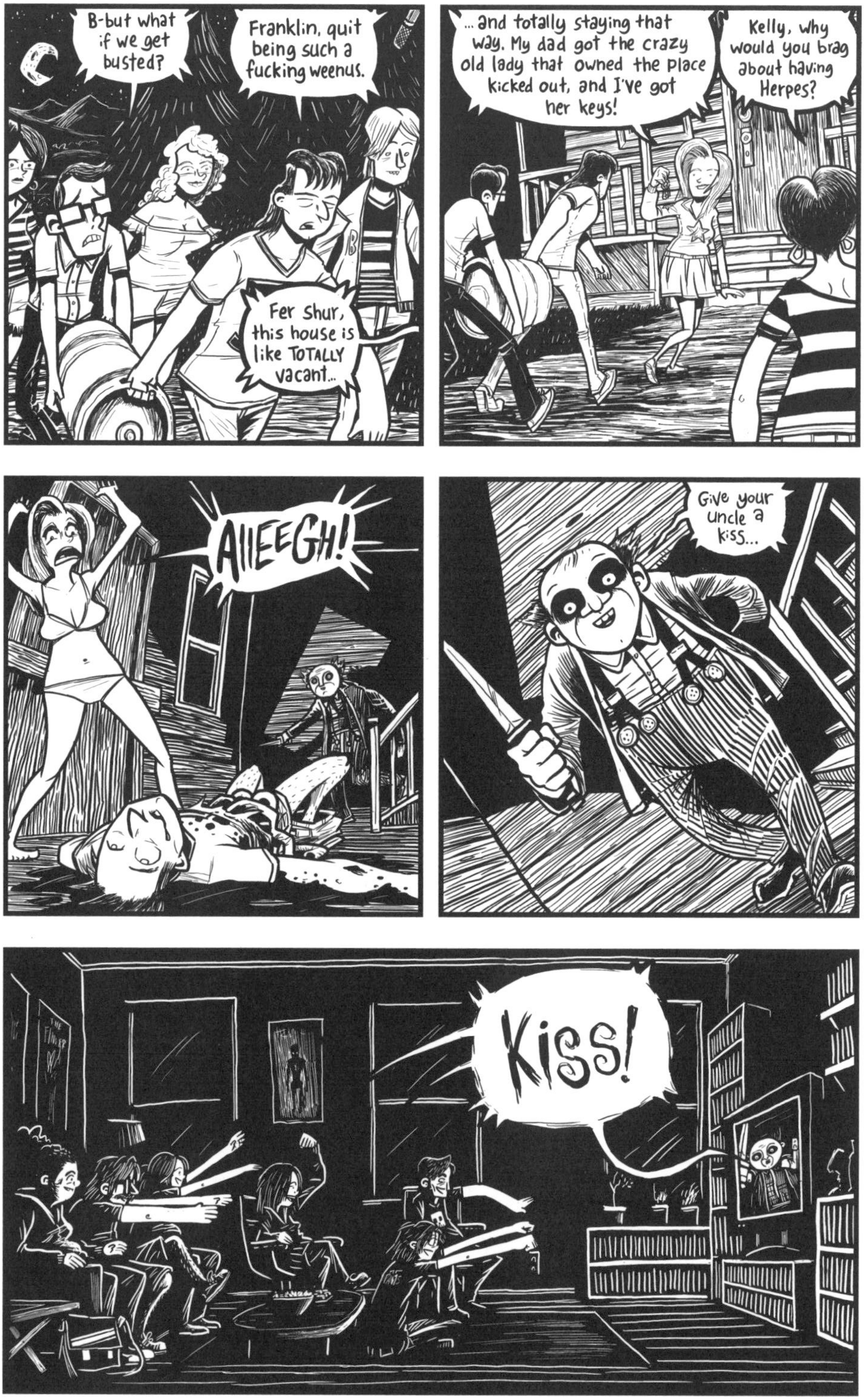
B-but what if we get busted?
Franklin, quit being such a fucking weenus.
Fer shur, this house is like TOTALLY vacant...
...and totally staying that way. My dad got the crazy old lady that owned the place kicked out, and I've got her keys!
Kelly, why would you brag about having Herpes?
AIIEEGH!
Give your uncle a kiss...
Kiss!

CHAPTER THREE

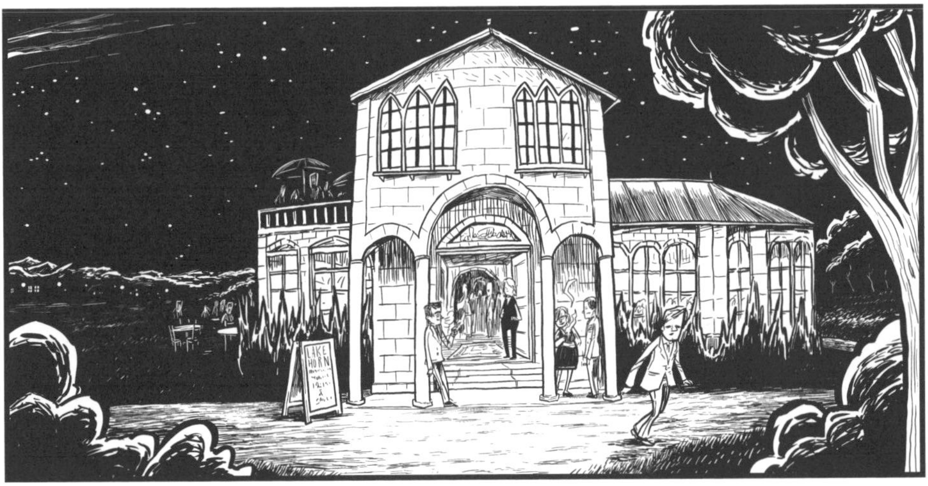
LAKE HORN

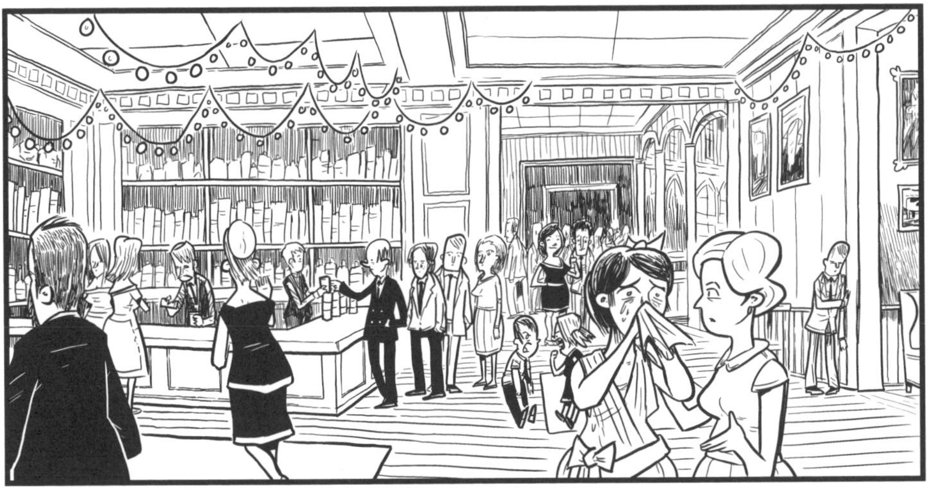

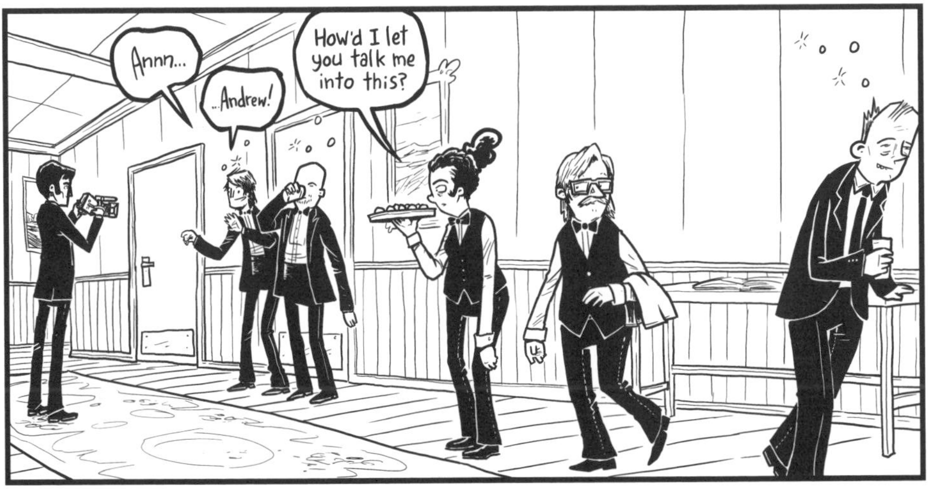
Annn...
..Andrew!
How'd I let you talk me into this?

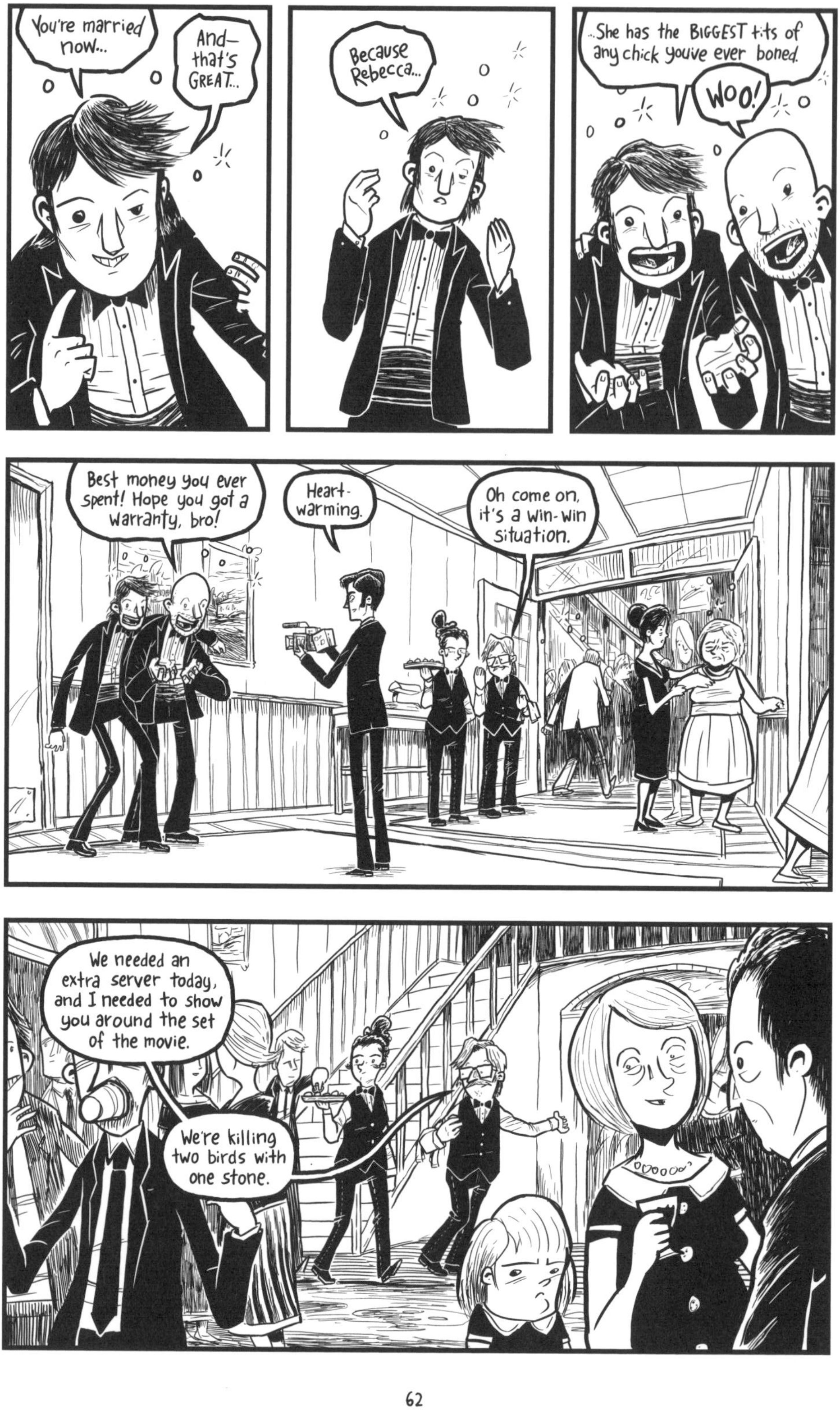
You're married now...
And— that's GREAT...
Because Rebecca...
...She has the BIGGEST tits of any chick you've ever boned.
WOO!
Best money you ever spent! Hope you got a warranty, bro!
Heart-warming.
Oh come on, it's a win-win situation.
We needed an extra server today, and I needed to show you around the set of the movie.
We're killing two birds with one stone.

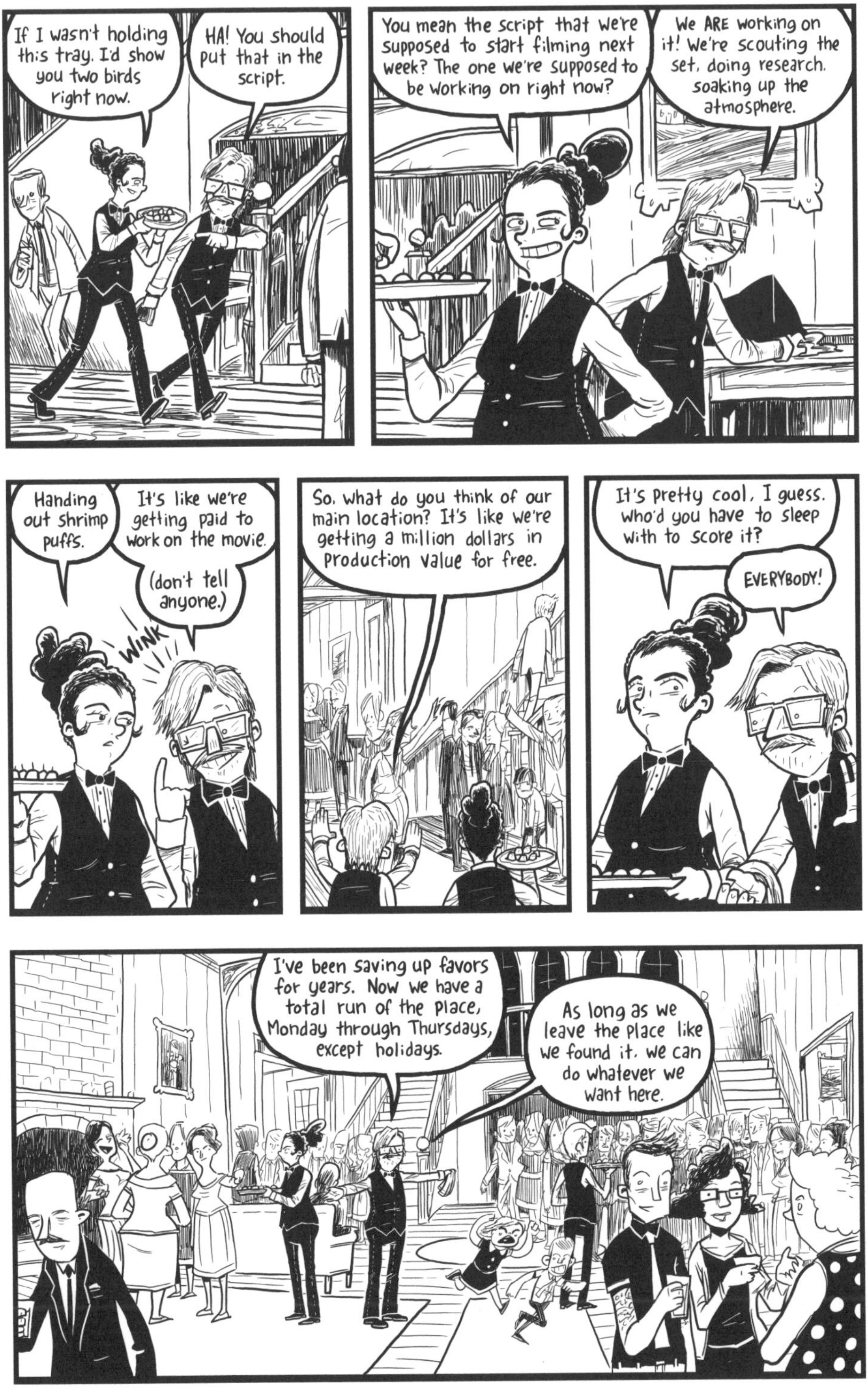
If I wasn't holding this tray, I'd show you two birds right now.
HA! You should put that in the script.
You mean the script that we're supposed to start filming next week? The one we're supposed to be working on right now?
We ARE working on it! We're scouting the set, doing research, soaking up the atmosphere.
Handing out shrimp puffs.
It's like we're getting paid to work on the movie.
(don't tell anyone.)
WINK
So, what do you think of our main location? It's like we're getting a million dollars in production value for free.
It's pretty cool, I guess. Who'd you have to sleep with to score it?
EVERYBODY!
I've been saving up favors for years. Now we have a total run of the place, Monday through Thursdays, except holidays.
As long as we leave the place like we found it, we can do whatever we want here.

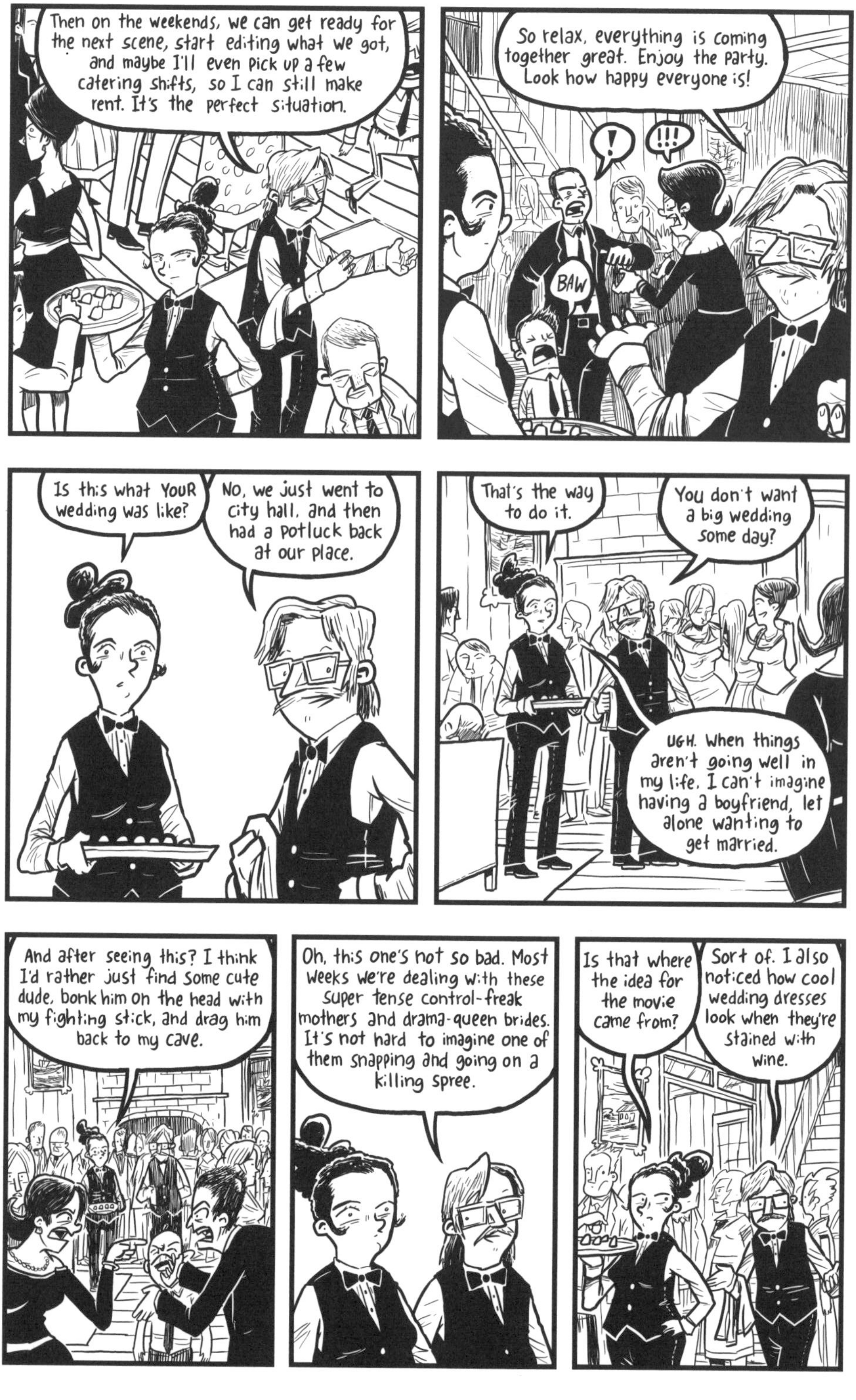
Then on the weekends, we can get ready for the next scene, start editing what we got, and maybe I'll even pick up a few catering shifts, so I can still make rent. It's the perfect situation.
So relax, everything is coming together great. Enjoy the party. Look how happy everyone is!
!
!!!
BAW
Is this what YOUR wedding was like?
No, we just went to city hall, and then had a potluck back at our place.
That's the way to do it.
You don't want a big wedding some day?
UGH. When things aren't going well in my life, I can't imagine having a boyfriend, let alone wanting to get married.
And after seeing this? I think I'd rather just find some cute dude, bonk him on the head with my fighting stick, and drag him back to my cave.
Oh, this one's not so bad. Most weeks we're dealing with these super tense control-freak mothers and drama-queen brides. It's not hard to imagine one of them snapping and going on a killing spree.
Is that where the idea for the movie came from?
Sort of. I also noticed how cool wedding dresses look when they're stained with wine.

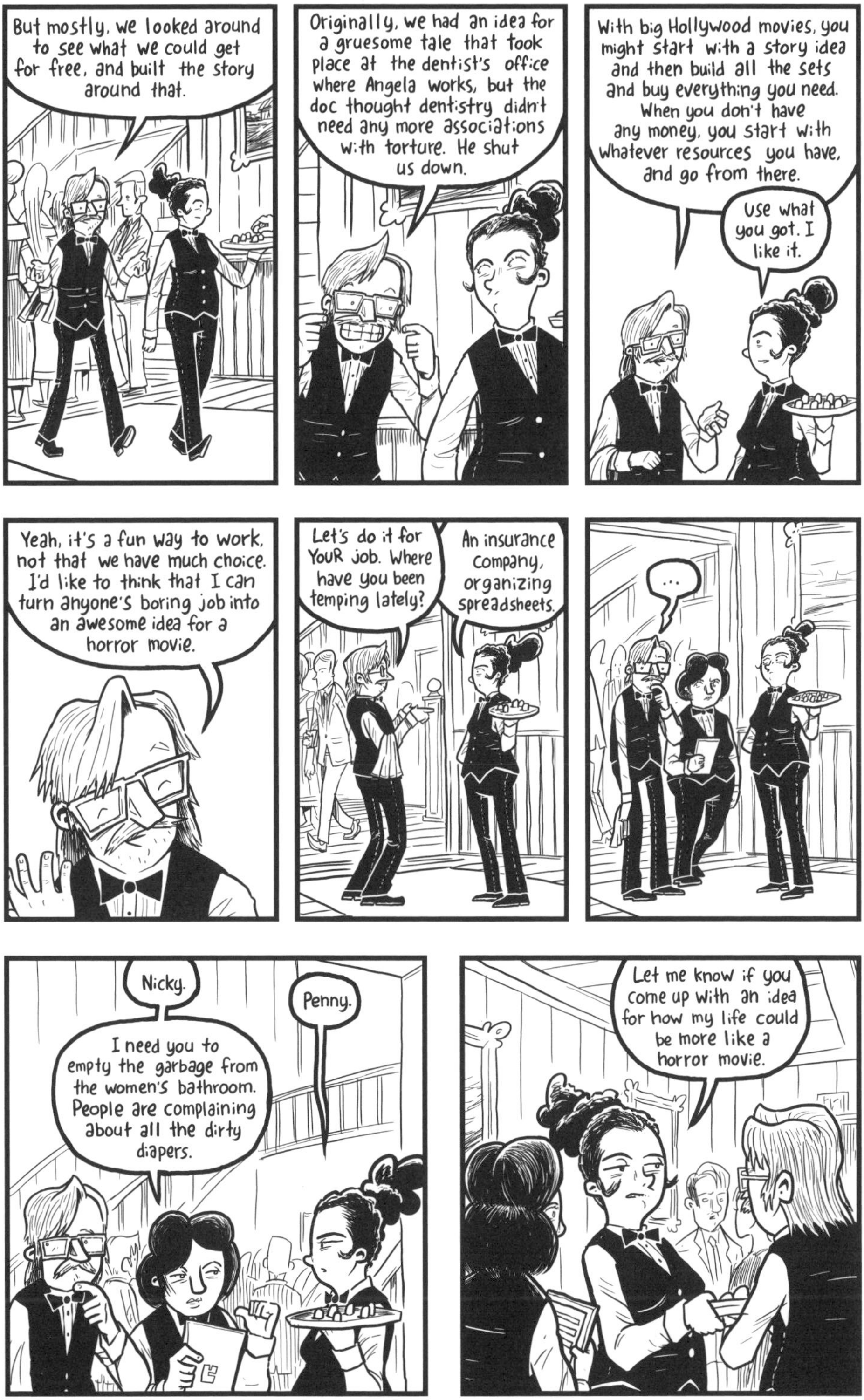
But mostly, we looked around to see what we could get for free, and built the story around that.
Originally, we had an idea for a gruesome tale that took place at the dentist's office where Angela works, but the doc thought dentistry didn't need any more associations with torture. He shut us down.
With big Hollywood movies, you might start with a story idea and then build all the sets and buy everything you need. When you don't have any money, you start with whatever resources you have, and go from there.
Use what you got. I like it.
Yeah, it's a fun way to work, not that we have much choice. I'd like to think that I can turn anyone's boring job into an awesome idea for a horror movie.
Let's do it for YOUR job. Where have you been temping lately?
An insurance company, organizing spreadsheets.
...
Nicky.
Penny.
I need you to empty the garbage from the women's bathroom. People are complaining about all the dirty diapers.
Let me know if you come up with an idea for how my life could be more like a horror movie.

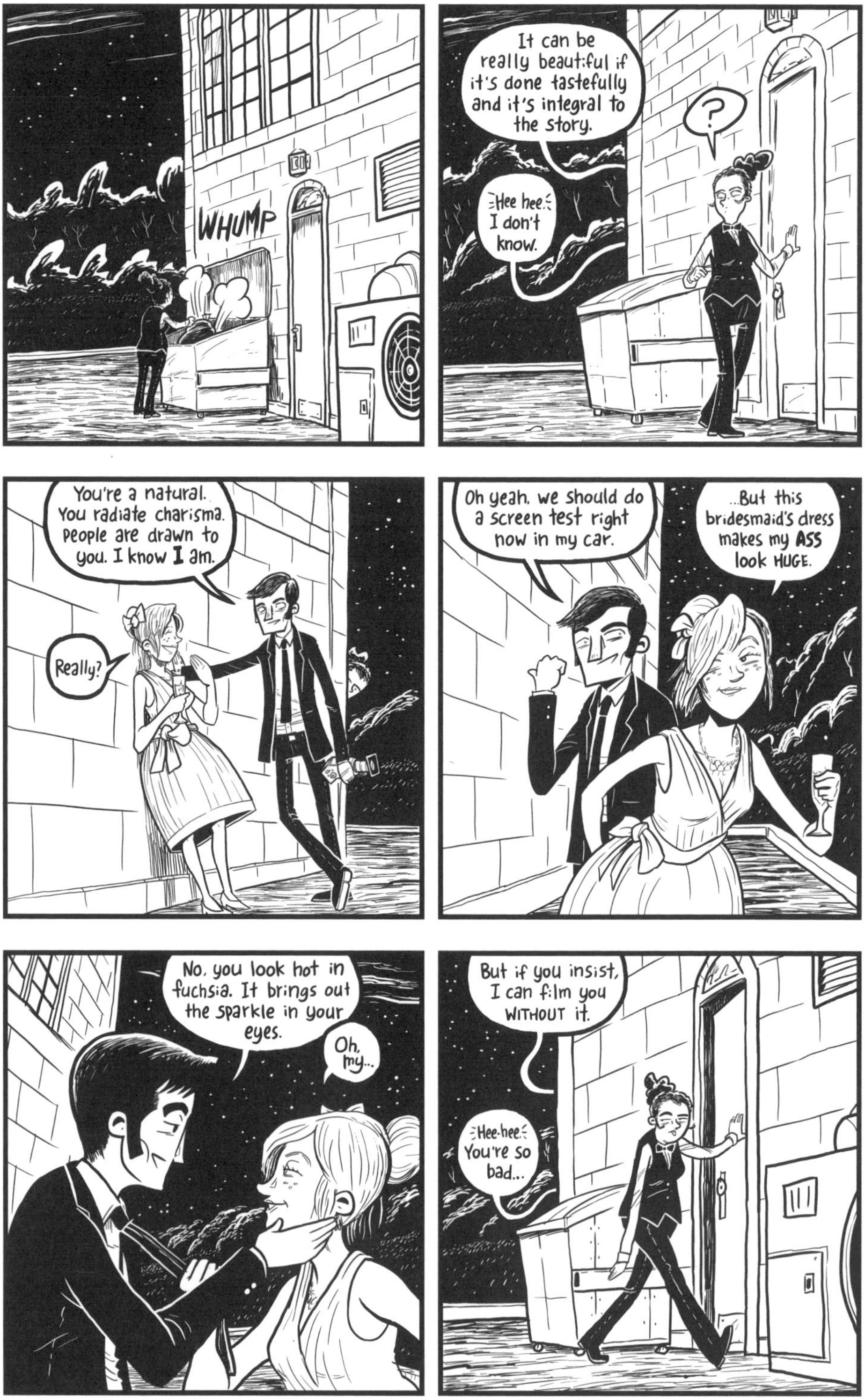
WHUMP
It can be really beautiful if it's done tastefully and it's integral to the story.
?
Hee hee. I don't know.
You're a natural. You radiate charisma. People are drawn to you. I know I am.
Really?
Oh yeah, we should do a screen test right now in my car.
...But this bridesmaid's dress makes my ASS look HUGE.
No, you look hot in fuchsia. It brings out the sparkle in your eyes.
Oh, my...
But if you insist, I can film you WITHOUT it.
Hee-hee. You're so bad...

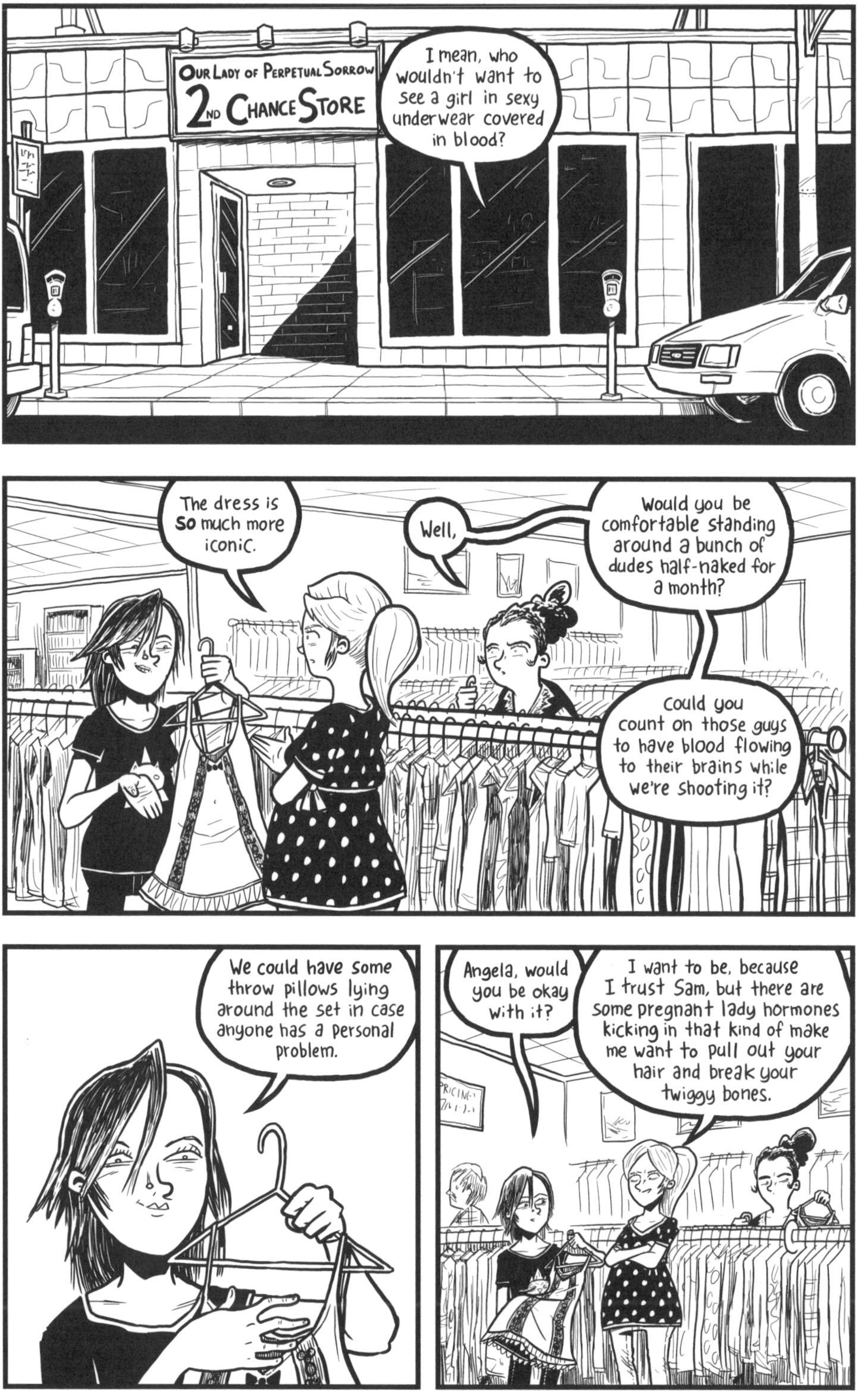
OUR LADY OF PERPETUAL SORROW
2ND CHANCE STORE
I mean, who wouldn't want to see a girl in sexy underwear covered in blood?
The dress is SO much more iconic.
Well,
Would you be comfortable standing around a bunch of dudes half-naked for a month?
Could you count on those guys to have blood flowing to their brains while we're shooting it?
We could have some throw pillows lying around the set in case anyone has a personal problem.
Angela, would you be okay with it?
I want to be, because I trust Sam, but there are some pregnant lady hormones kicking in that kind of make me want to pull out your hair and break your twiggy bones.

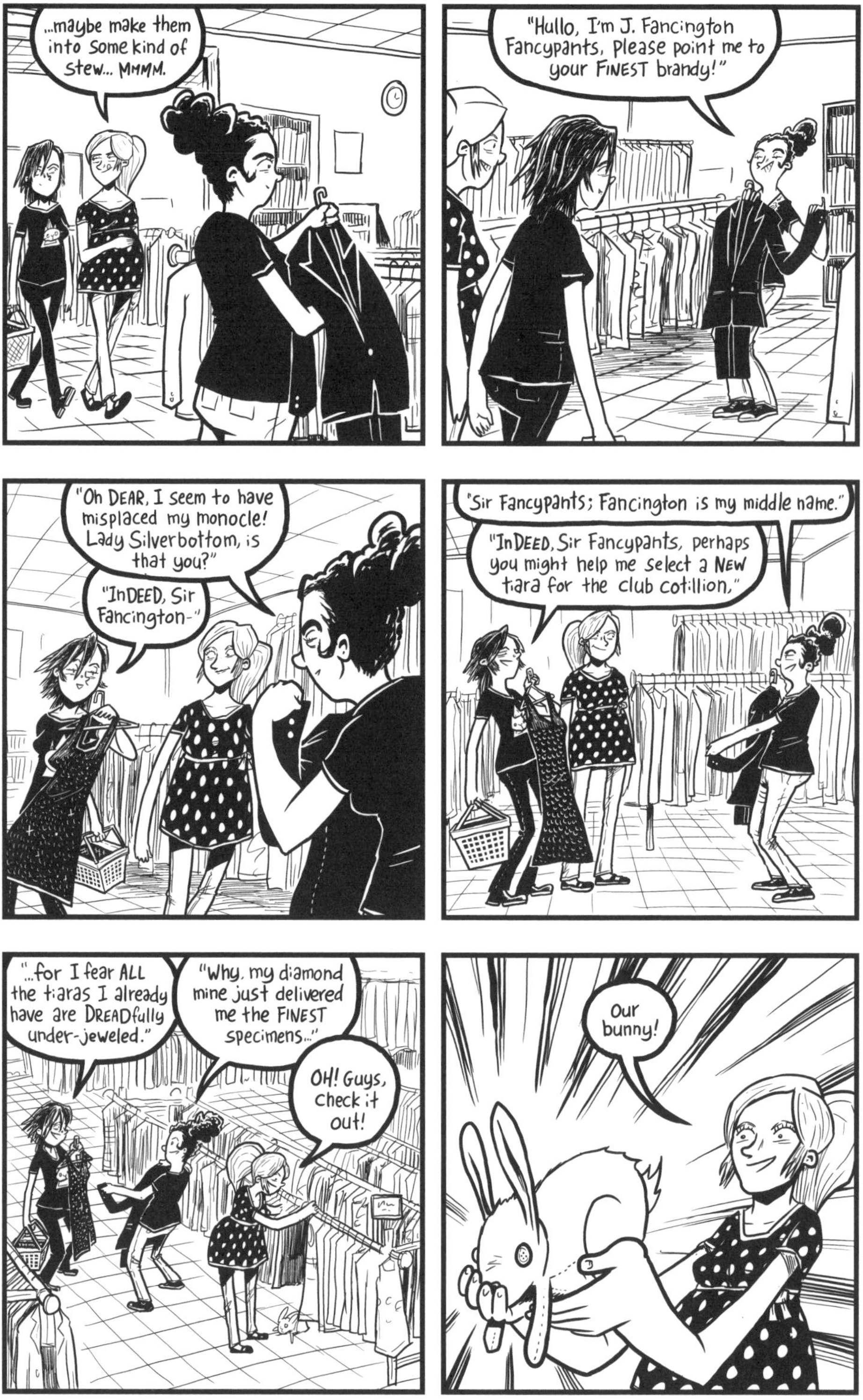
...maybe make them into Some kind of Stew... MMMM.
"Hullo, I'm J. Fancington Fancypants, please point me to your FINEST brandy!"
"Oh DEAR, I seem to have misplaced my monocle! Lady Silverbottom, is that you?"
"InDEED, Sir Fancington-"
"Sir Fancypants; Fancington is my middle name."
"InDEED, Sir Fancypants, perhaps you might help me select a NEW tiara for the club cotillion,"
"...for I fear ALL the tiaras I already have are DREADfully under-jeweled."
"Why, my diamond mine just delivered me the FINEST specimens..."
OH! Guys, check it out!
Our bunny!

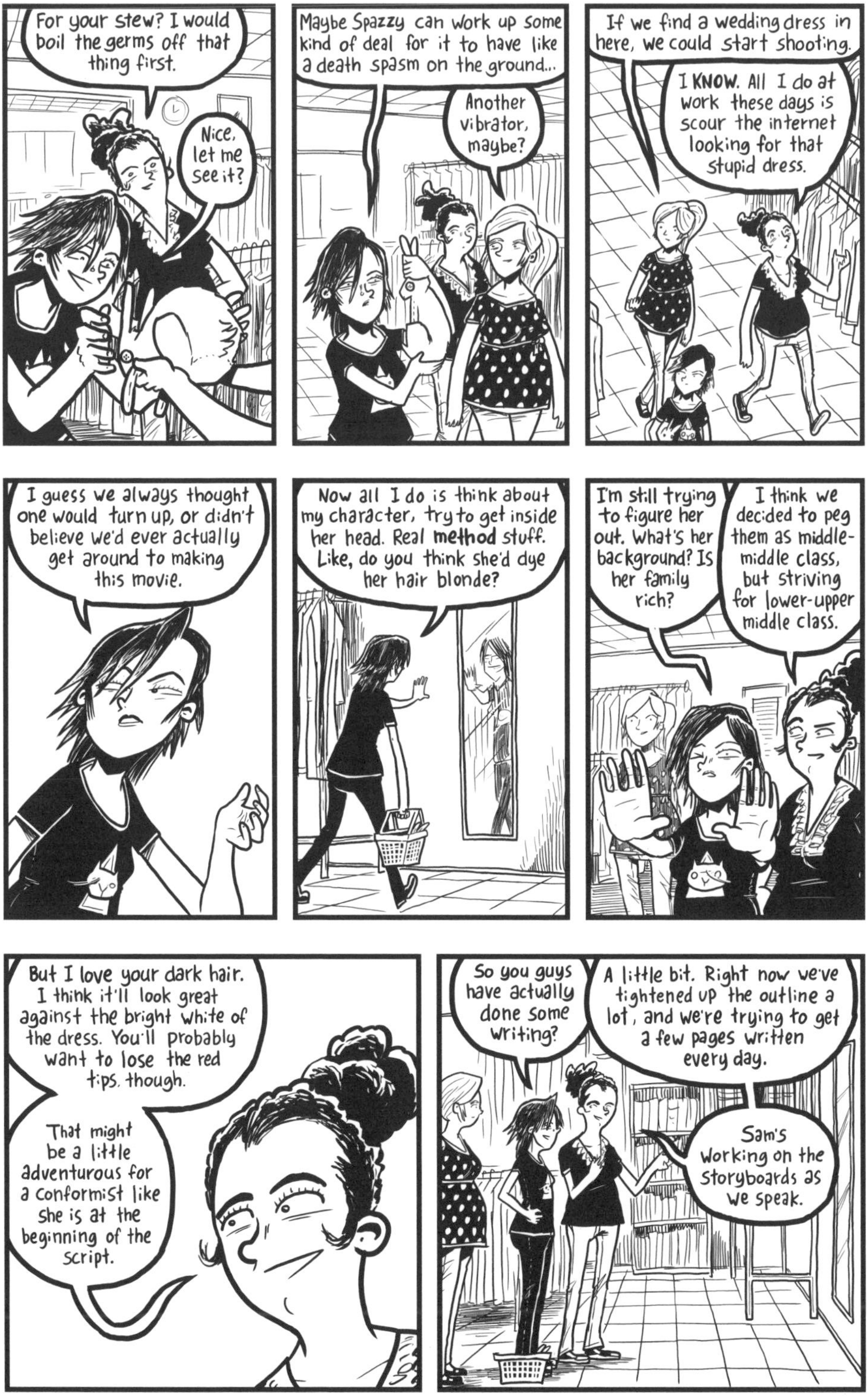
For your stew? I would boil the germs off that thing first.
Nice, let me see it?
Maybe Spazzy can work up some kind of deal for it to have like a death spasm on the ground...
Another vibrator, maybe?
If we find a wedding dress in here, we could start shooting.
I KNOW. All I do at work these days is scour the internet looking for that stupid dress.
I guess we always thought one would turn up, or didn't believe we'd ever actually get around to making this movie.
Now all I do is think about my character, try to get inside her head. Real method stuff. Like, do you think she'd dye her hair blonde?
I'm still trying to figure her out. What's her background? Is her family rich?
I think we decided to peg them as middle-middle class, but striving for lower-upper middle class.
But I love your dark hair. I think it'll look great against the bright white of the dress. You'll probably want to lose the red tips, though.
That might be a little adventurous for a conformist like she is at the beginning of the script.
So you guys have actually done some writing?
A little bit. Right now we've tightened up the outline a lot, and we're trying to get a few pages written every day.
Sam's working on the storyboards as we speak.

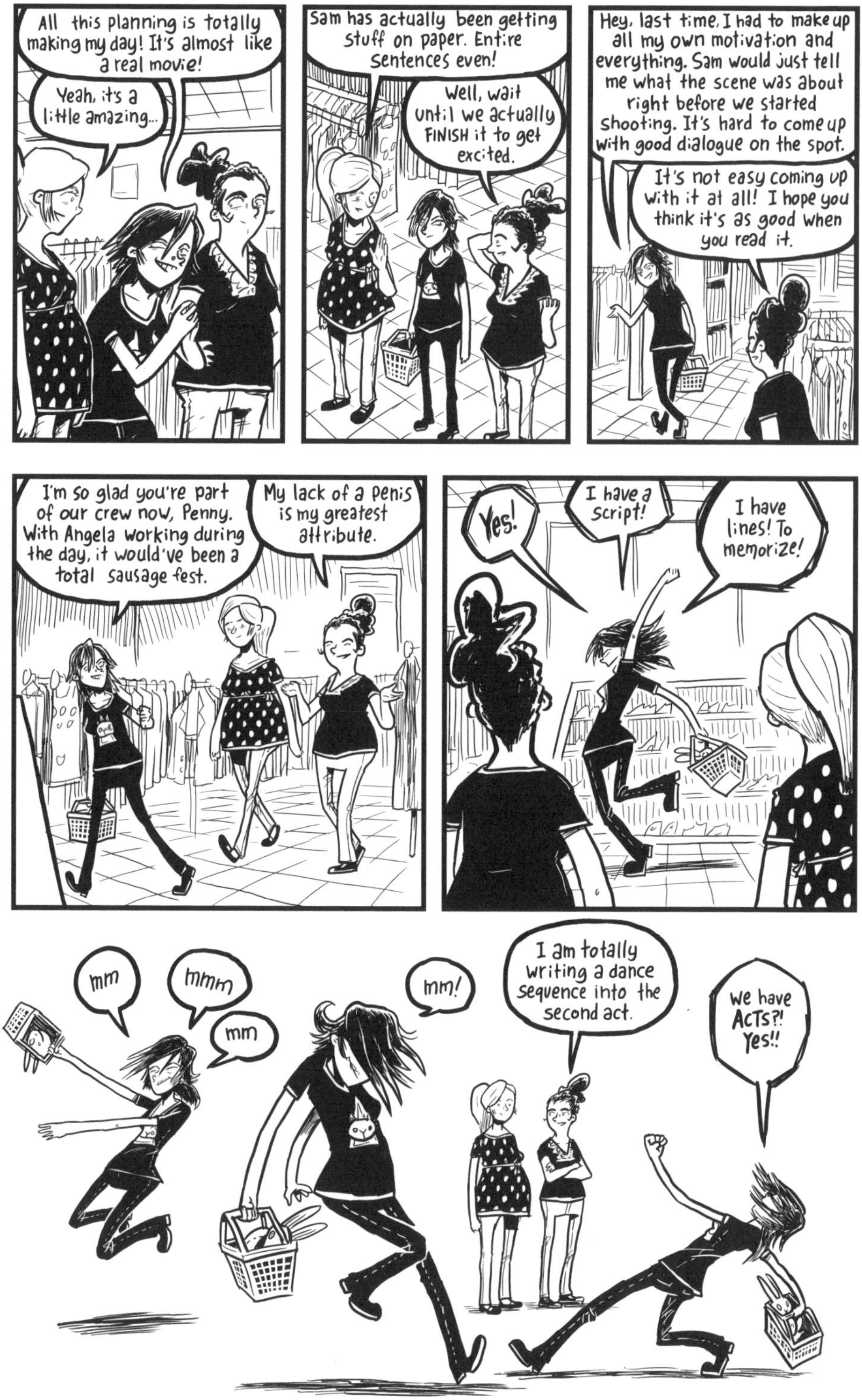
All this planning is totally making my day! It's almost like a real movie!
Yeah, it's a little amazing...
Sam has actually been getting stuff on paper. Entire sentences even!
Well, wait until we actually FINISH it to get excited.
Hey, last time, I had to make up all my own motivation and everything. Sam would just tell me what the scene was about right before we started shooting. It's hard to come up with good dialogue on the spot.
It's not easy coming up with it at all! I hope you think it's as good when you read it.
I'm so glad you're part of our crew now, Penny. With Angela working during the day, it would've been a total sausage fest.
My lack of a penis is my greatest attribute.
Yes!
I have a script!
I have lines! To memorize!
mm
mmm
mm
mm!
I am totally writing a dance sequence into the second act.
We have ACTS?! Yes!!

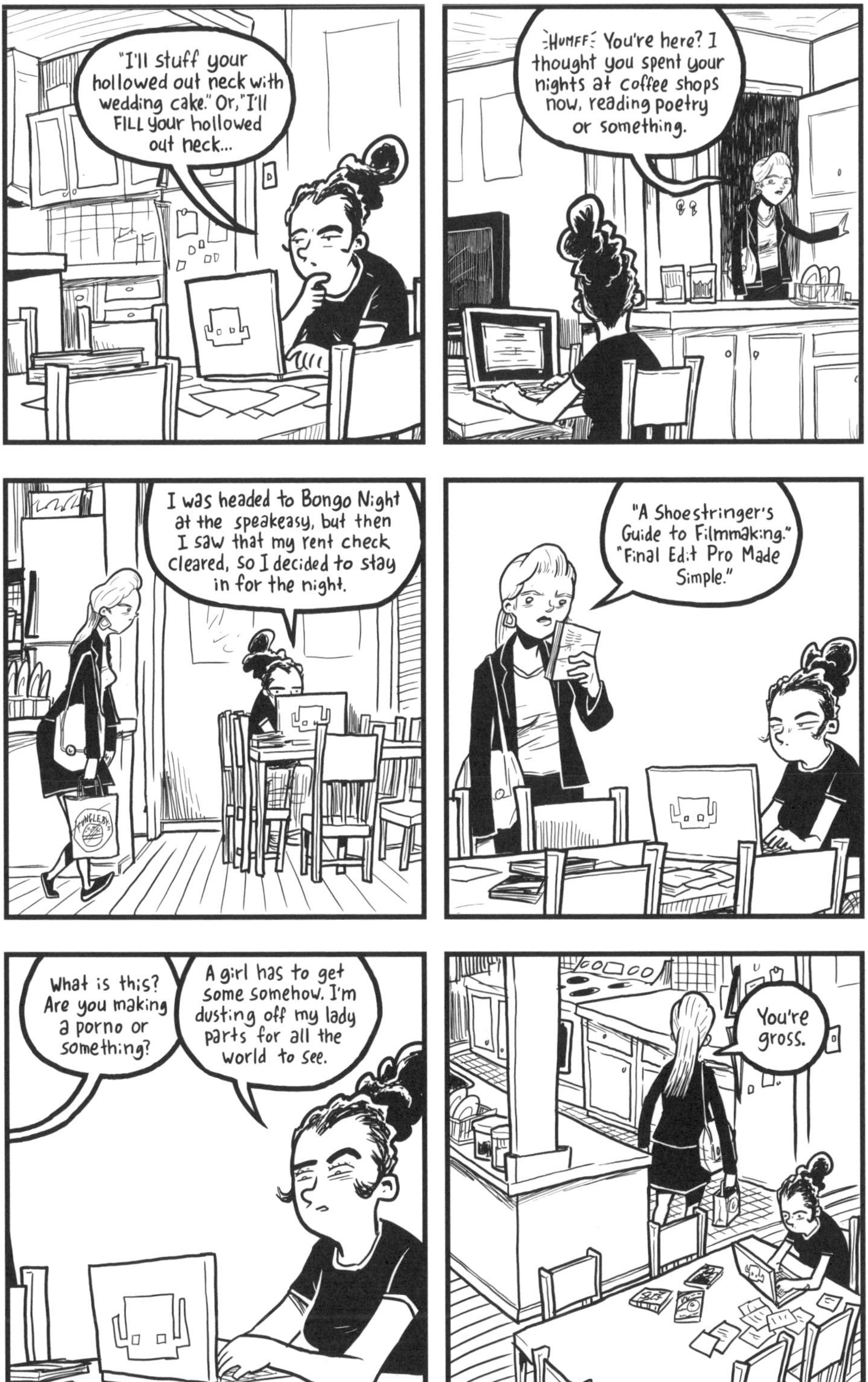
"I'll stuff your hollowed out neck with wedding cake." Or, "I'll FILL your hollowed out neck...
HUMFF You're here? I thought you spent your nights at coffee shops now, reading poetry or something.
I was headed to Bongo Night at the speakeasy, but then I saw that my rent check cleared, so I decided to stay in for the night.
"A Shoestringer's Guide to Filmmaking." "Final Edit Pro Made Simple."
What is this? Are you making a porno or something?
A girl has to get some somehow. I'm dusting off my lady parts for all the world to see.
You're gross.

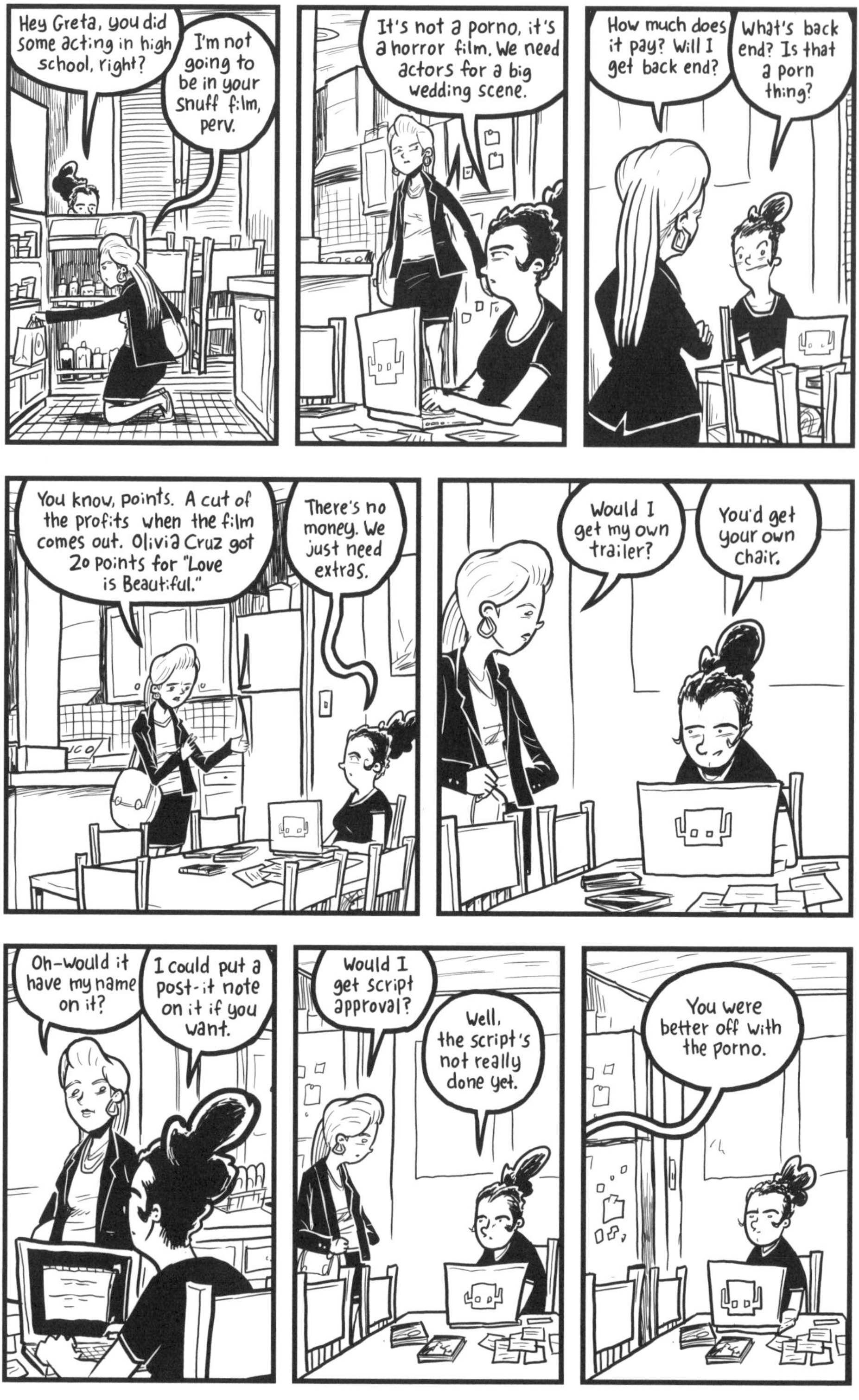
Hey Greta, you did some acting in high school, right?
I'm not going to be in your snuff film, perv.
It's not a porno, it's a horror film. We need actors for a big wedding scene.
How much does it pay? Will I get back end?
What's back end? Is that a porn thing?
You know, points. A cut of the profits when the film comes out. Olivia Cruz got 20 points for "Love is Beautiful."
There's no money. We just need extras.
Would I get my own trailer?
You'd get your own chair.
Oh-would it have my name on it?
I could put a post-it note on it if you want.
Would I get script approval?
Well, the script's not really done yet.
You were better off with the porno.

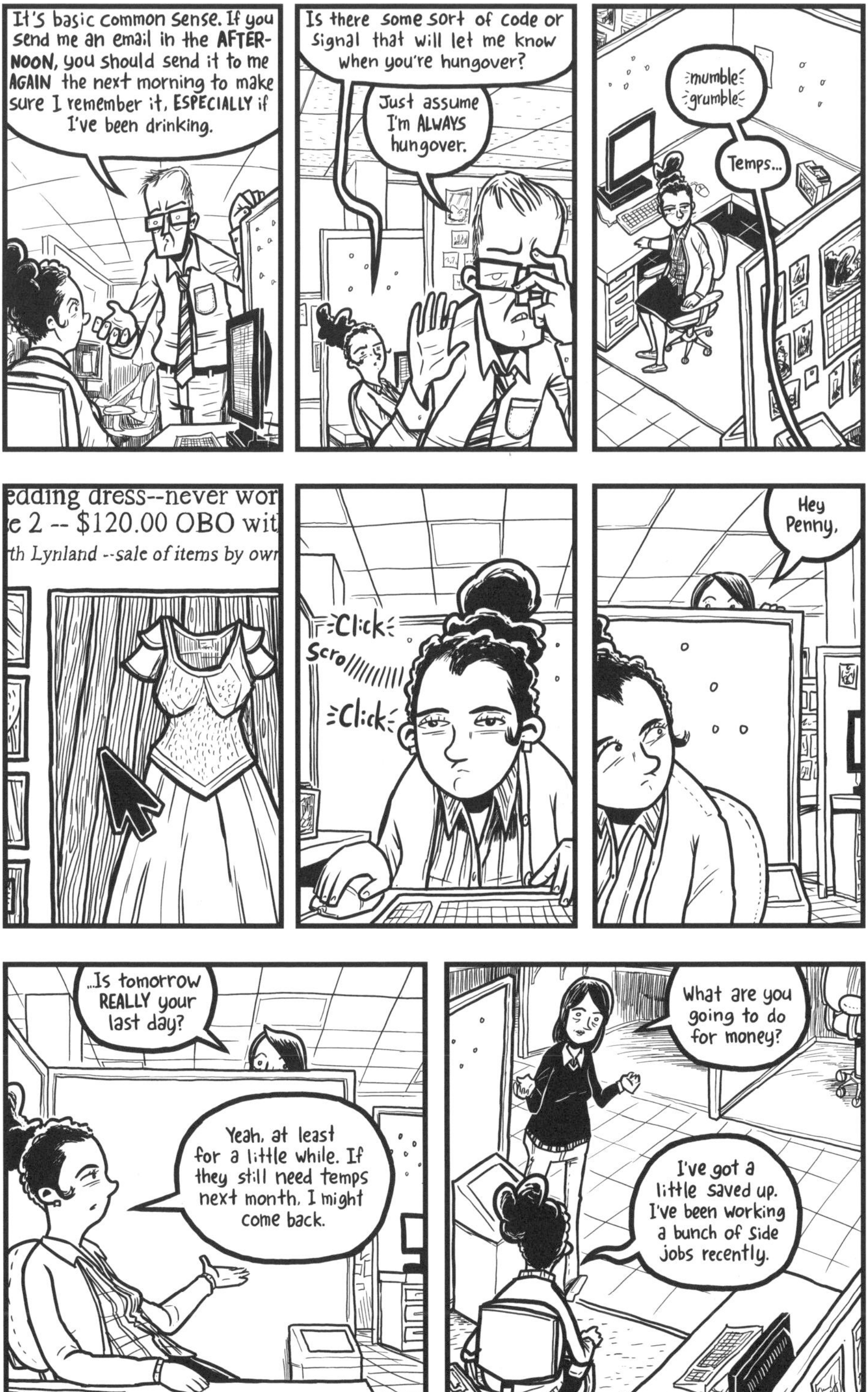
It's basic common sense. If you send me an email in the AFTERNOON, you should send it to me AGAIN the next morning to make sure I remember it, ESPECIALLY if I've been drinking.
Is there some sort of code or signal that will let me know when you're hungover?
Just assume I'm ALWAYS hungover.
mumble grumble
Temps...
edding dress--never wor
e 2 -- $120.00 OBO wit
th Lynland --sale of items by own
Click
Scroll
Click
Hey Penny,
...Is tomorrow REALLY your last day?
Yeah, at least for a little while. If they still need temps next month, I might come back.
What are you going to do for money?
I've got a little saved up. I've been working a bunch of side jobs recently.

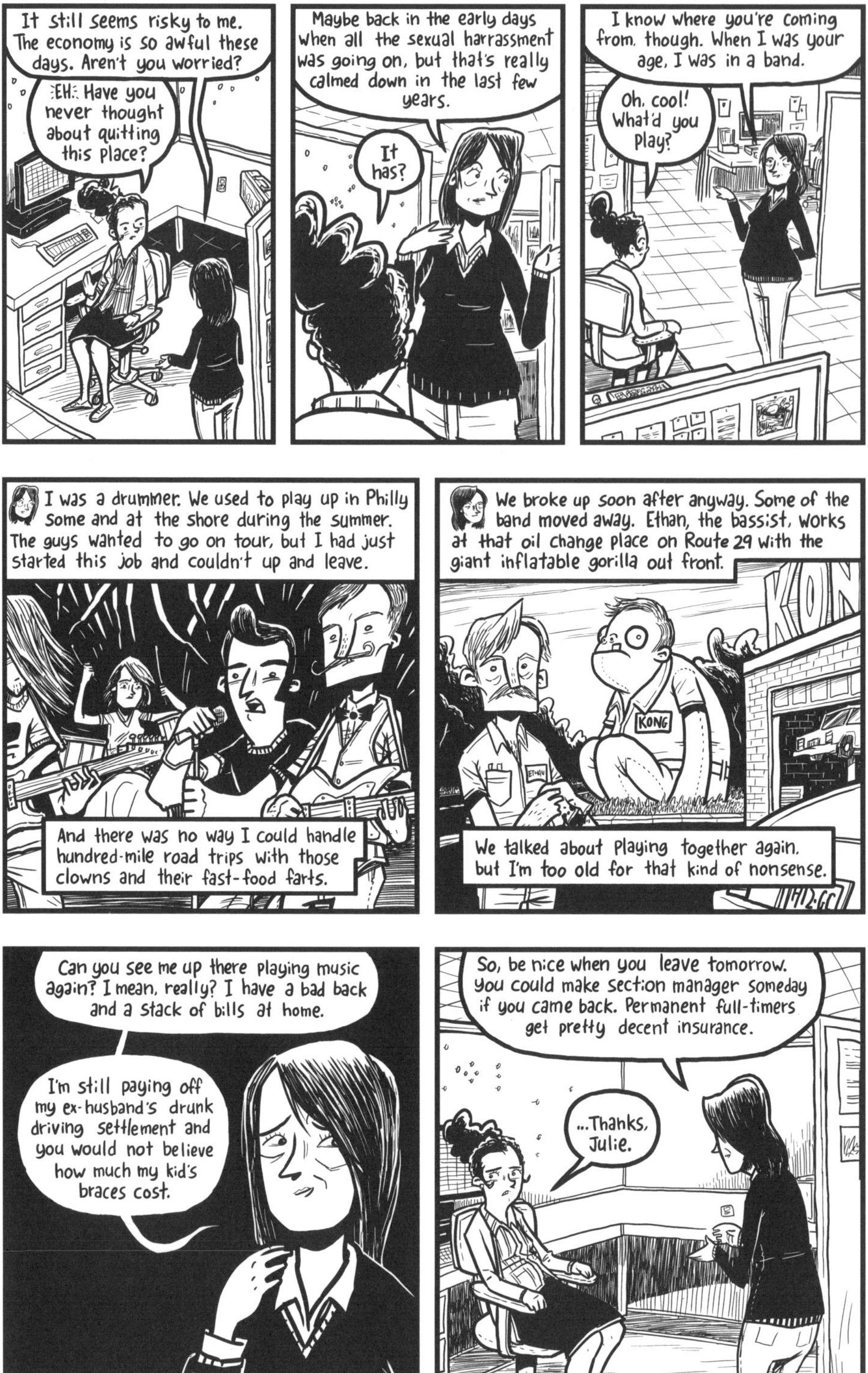

It still seems risky to me. The economy is so awful these days. Aren't you worried?
EH. Have you never thought about quitting this place?
Maybe back in the early days when all the sexual harrassment was going on, but that's really calmed down in the last few years.
It has?
I know where you're coming from, though. When I was your age, I was in a band.
Oh, cool! What'd you play?
I was a drummer. We used to play up in Philly some and at the shore during the summer. The guys wanted to go on tour, but I had just started this job and couldn't up and leave.
And there was no way I could handle hundred-mile road trips with those clowns and their fast-food farts.
We broke up soon after anyway. Some of the band moved away. Ethan, the bassist, works at that oil change place on Route 29 with the giant inflatable gorilla out front.
KONG
We talked about playing together again, but I'm too old for that kind of nonsense.
Can you see me up there playing music again? I mean, really? I have a bad back and a stack of bills at home.
I'm still paying off my ex-husband's drunk driving settlement and you would not believe how much my kid's braces cost.
So, be nice when you leave tomorrow. You could make section manager someday if you came back. Permanent full-timers get pretty decent insurance.
...Thanks, Julie.

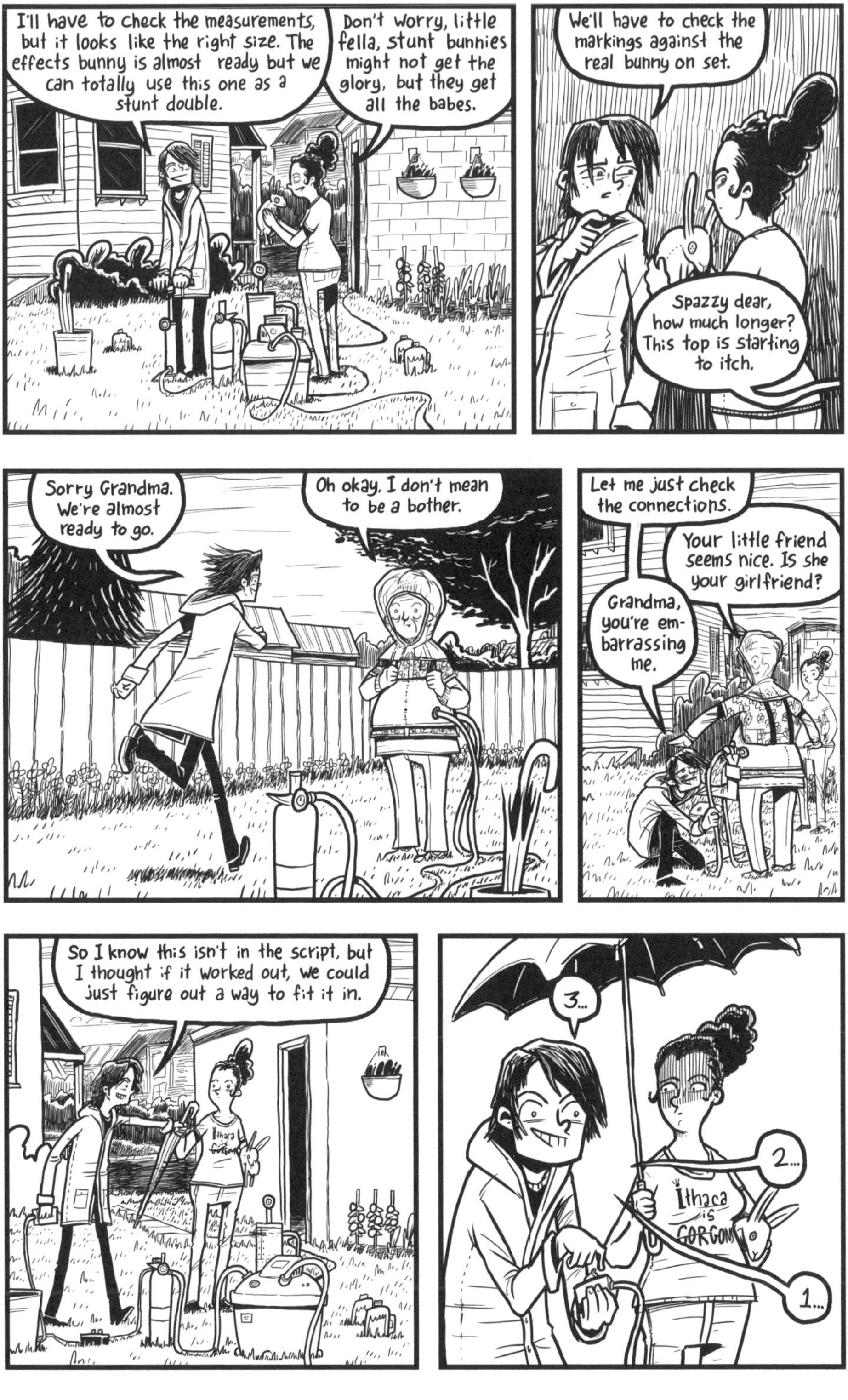

I'll have to check the measurements, but it looks like the right size. The effects bunny is almost ready but we can totally use this one as a stunt double.
Don't worry, little fella, stunt bunnies might not get the glory, but they get all the babes.
We'll have to check the markings against the real bunny on set.
Spazzy dear, how much longer? This top is starting to itch.
Sorry Grandma. We're almost ready to go.
Oh okay, I don't mean to be a bother.
Let me just check the connections.
Your little friend seems nice. Is she your girlfriend?
Grandma, you're em-barrassing me.
So I know this isn't in the script, but I thought if it worked out, we could just figure out a way to fit it in.
Ithaca is Gorgon
3...
2...
Ithaca is GORGON
1...

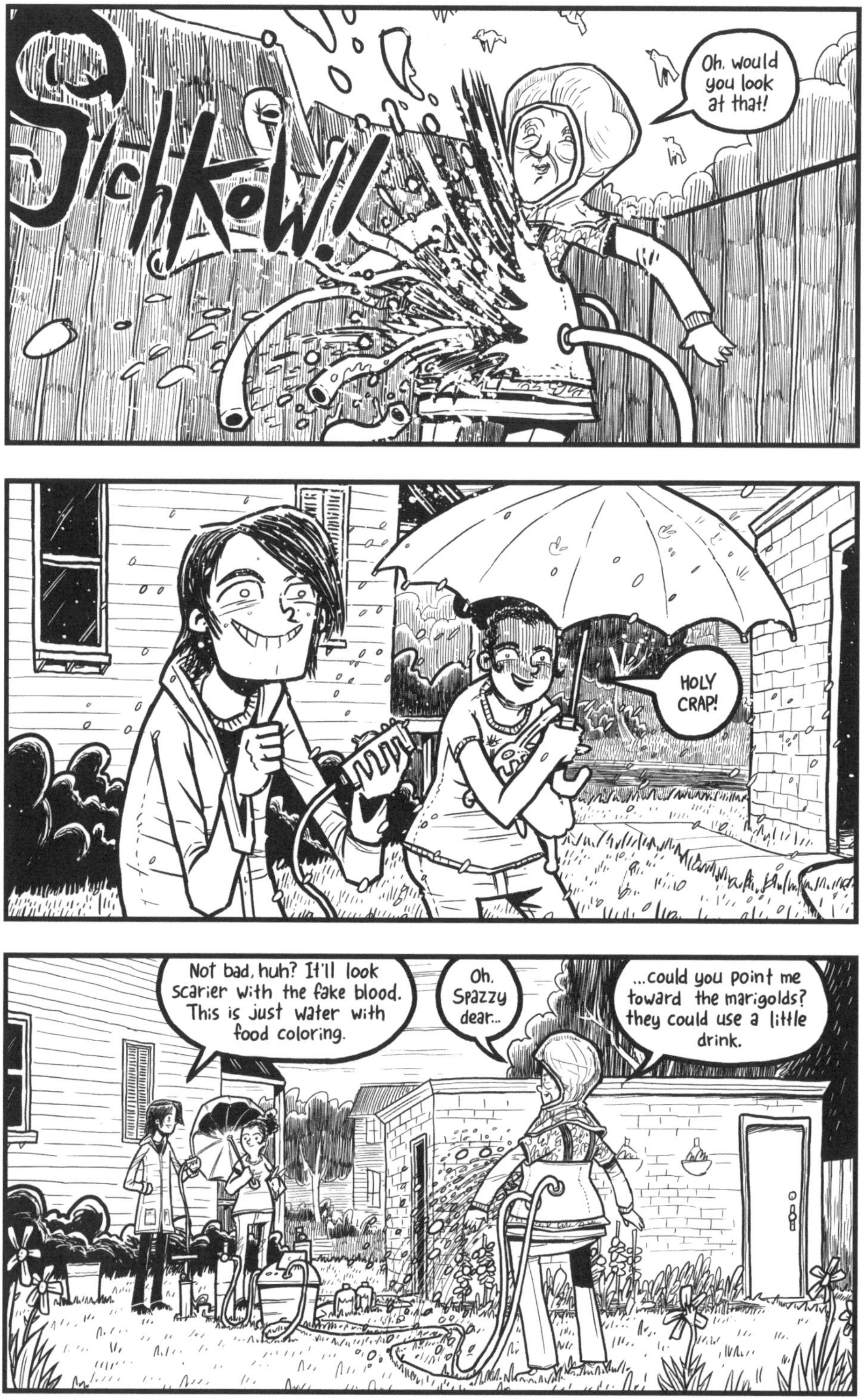
SPLOOSH!
Oh, would you look at that!
HOLY CRAP!
Not bad, huh? It'll look scarier with the fake blood. This is just water with food coloring.
Oh, Spazzy dear...
...could you point me toward the marigolds? they could use a little drink.

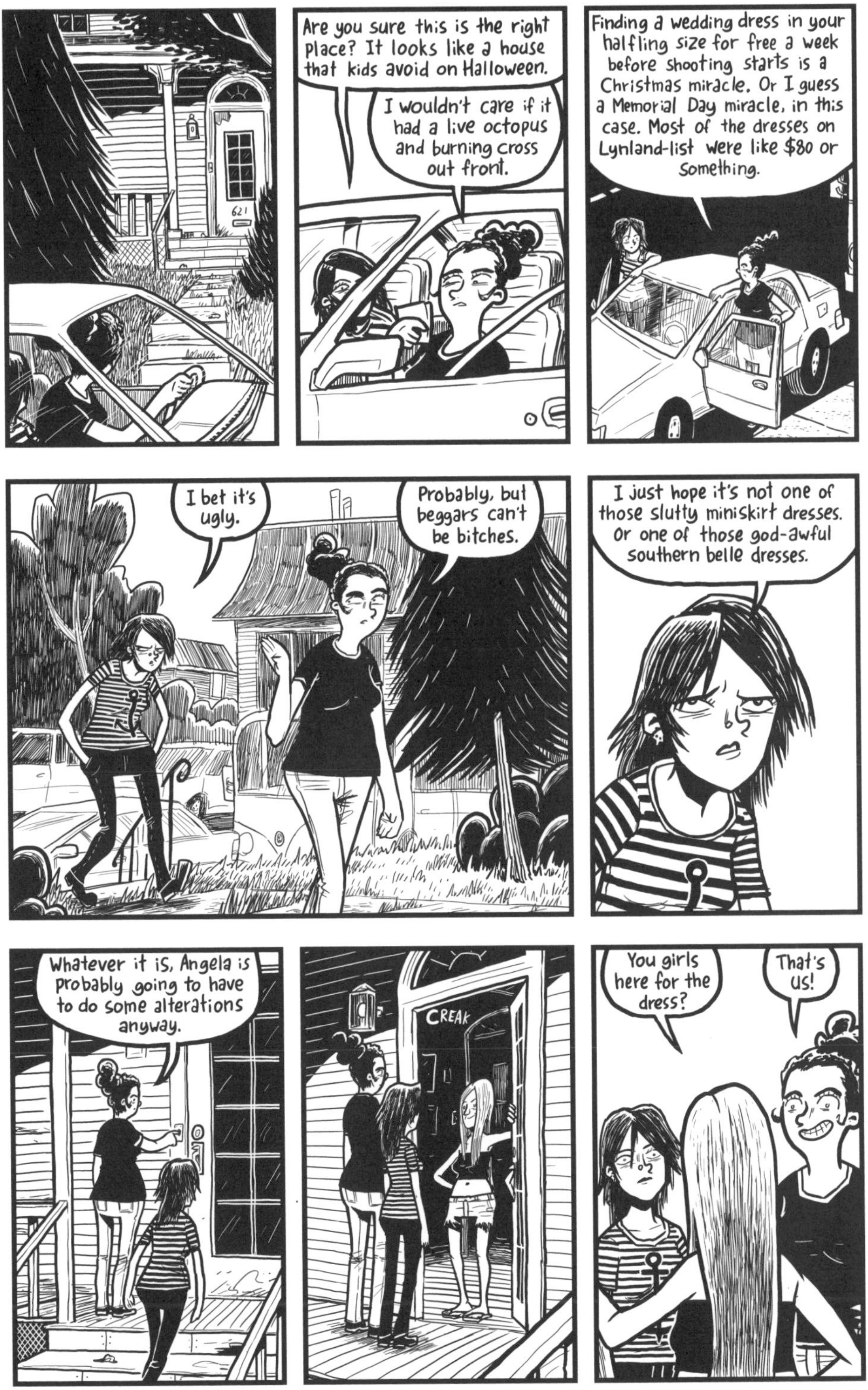

Are you sure this is the right place? It looks like a house that kids avoid on Halloween.
I wouldn't care if it had a live octopus and burning cross out front.
Finding a wedding dress in your halfling size for free a week before shooting starts is a Christmas miracle. Or I guess a Memorial Day miracle, in this case. Most of the dresses on Lynland-list were like $80 or something.
I bet it's ugly.
Probably, but beggars can't be bitches.
I just hope it's not one of those slutty miniskirt dresses. Or one of those god-awful southern belle dresses.
Whatever it is, Angela is probably going to have to do some alterations anyway.
CREAK
You girls here for the dress?
That's us!

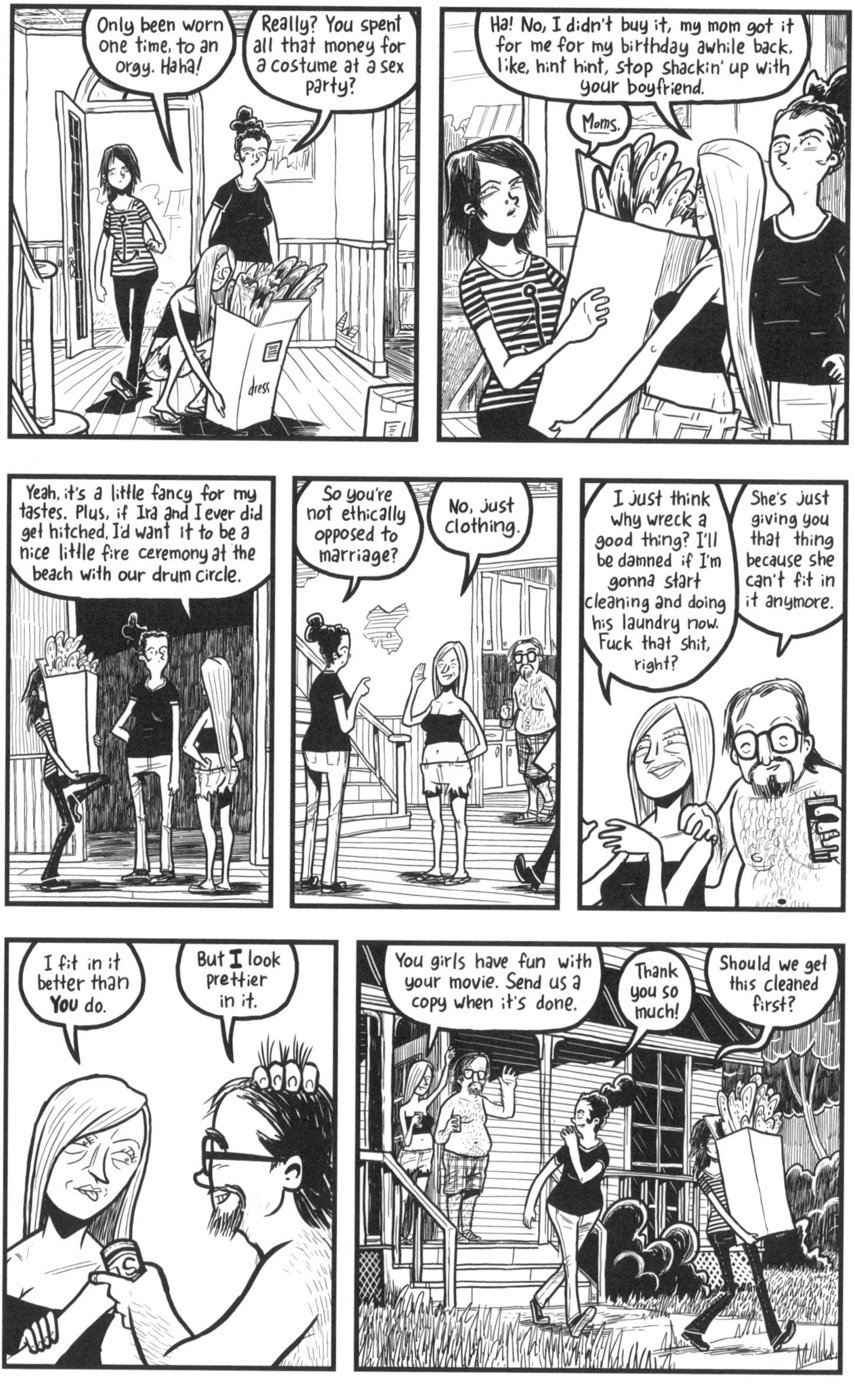
Only been worn one time, to an orgy. Haha!
Really? You spent all that money for a costume at a sex party?
dress
Ha! No, I didn't buy it, my mom got it for me for my birthday awhile back, like, hint hint, stop shackin' up with your boyfriend.
Moms.
Yeah, it's a little fancy for my tastes. Plus, if Ira and I ever did get hitched, I'd want it to be a nice little fire ceremony at the beach with our drum circle.
So you're not ethically opposed to marriage?
No, just clothing.
I just think why wreck a good thing? I'll be damned if I'm gonna start cleaning and doing his laundry now. Fuck that shit, right?
She's just giving you that thing because she can't fit in it anymore.
I fit in it better than YOU do.
But I look prettier in it.
You girls have fun with your movie. Send us a copy when it's done.
Thank you so much!
Should we get this cleaned first?

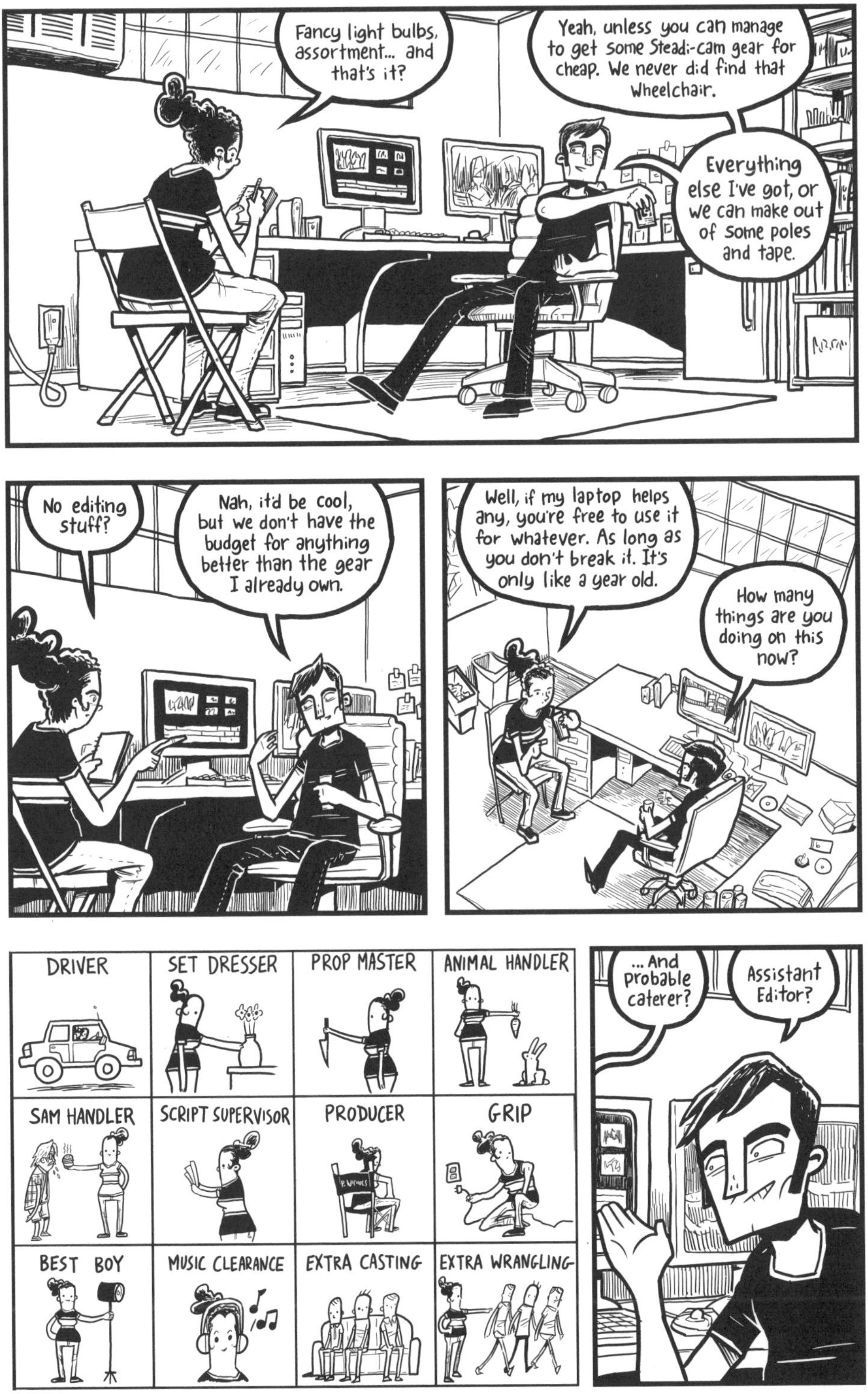
Fancy light bulbs, assortment... and that's it?
Yeah, unless you can manage to get some Steadi-cam gear for cheap. We never did find that Wheelchair.
Everything else I've got, or we can make out of some poles and tape.
No editing stuff?
Nah, it'd be cool, but we don't have the budget for anything better than the gear I already own.
Well, if my laptop helps any, you're free to use it for whatever. As long as you don't break it. It's only like a year old.
How many things are you doing on this now?
DRIVER
SET DRESSER
PROP MASTER
ANIMAL HANDLER
SAM HANDLER
SCRIPT SUPERVISOR
PRODUCER
GRIP
BEST BOY
MUSIC CLEARANCE
EXTRA CASTING
EXTRA WRANGLING
...And probable caterer?
Assistant Editor?

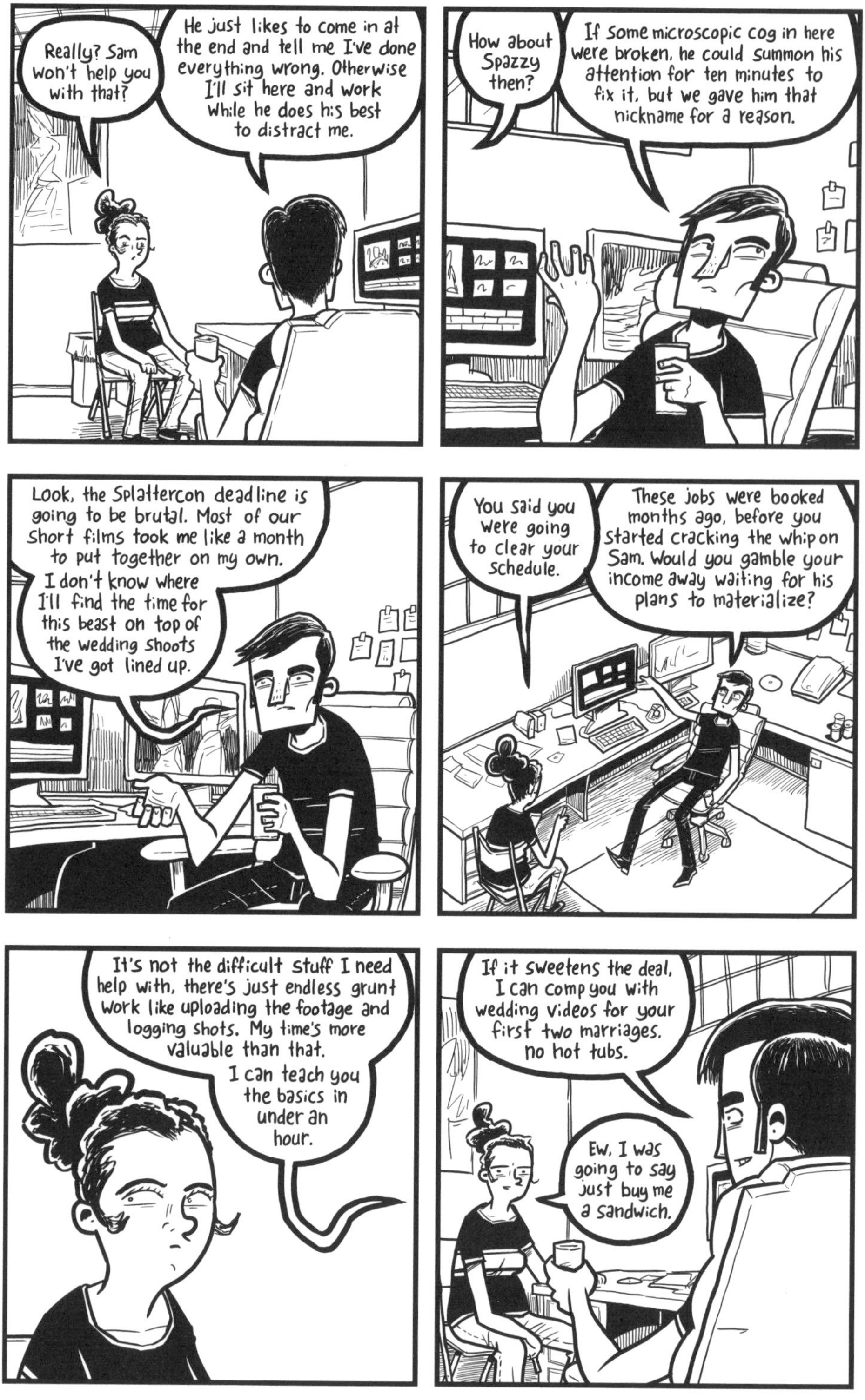
Really? Sam won't help you with that?
He just likes to come in at the end and tell me I've done everything wrong. Otherwise I'll sit here and work while he does his best to distract me.
How about Spazzy then?
If some microscopic cog in here were broken, he could summon his attention for ten minutes to fix it, but we gave him that nickname for a reason.
Look, the Splattercon deadline is going to be brutal. Most of our short films took me like a month to put together on my own.
I don't know where I'll find the time for this beast on top of the wedding shoots I've got lined up.
You said you were going to clear your schedule.
These jobs were booked months ago, before you started cracking the whip on Sam. Would you gamble your income away waiting for his plans to materialize?
It's not the difficult stuff I need help with, there's just endless grunt work like uploading the footage and logging shots. My time's more valuable than that.
I can teach you the basics in under an hour.
If it sweetens the deal, I can comp you with wedding videos for your first two marriages. no hot tubs.
Ew, I was going to say just buy me a sandwich.

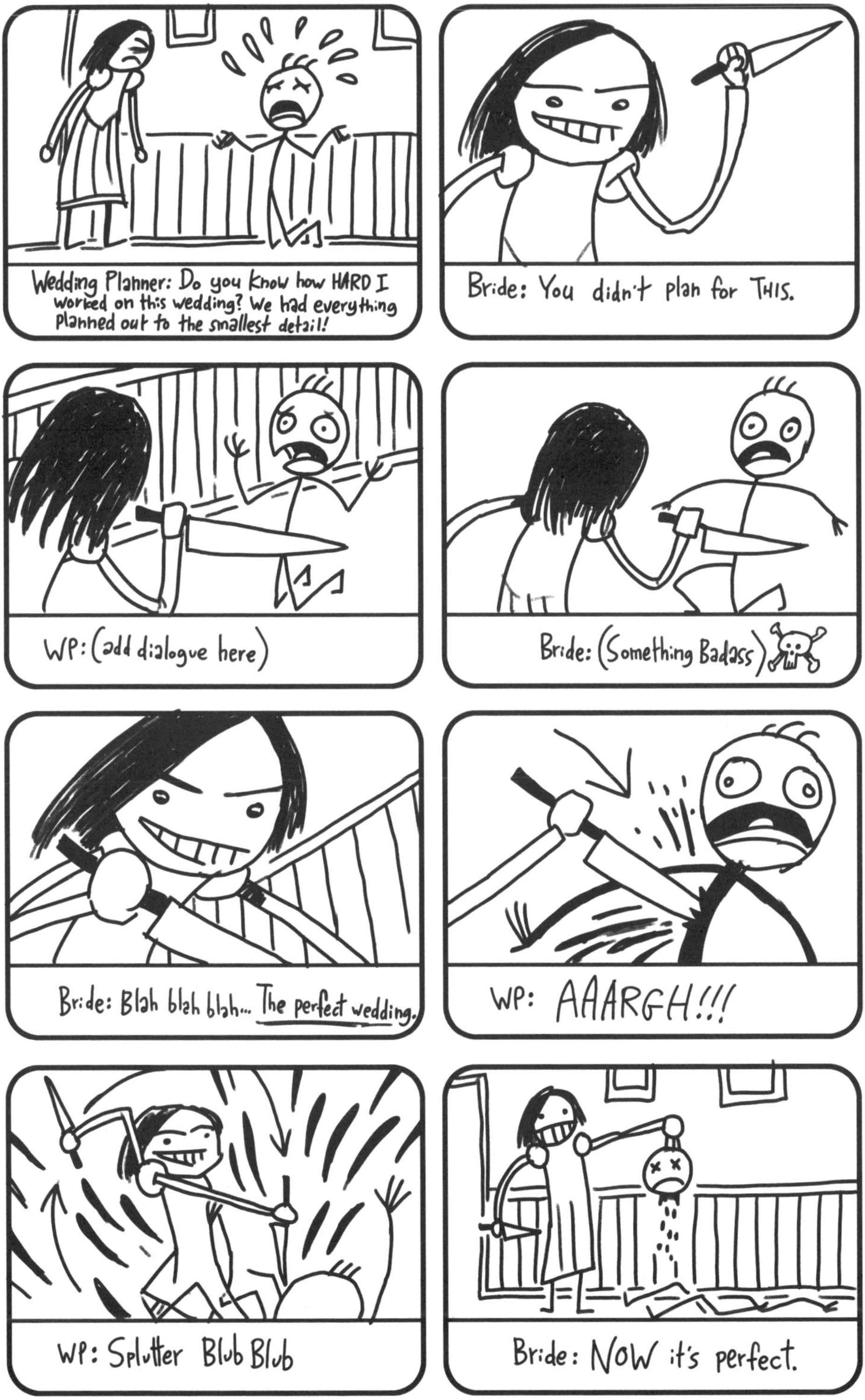
Wedding Planner: Do you know how HARD I worked on this wedding? We had everything planned out to the smallest detail!
Bride: You didn't plan for THIS.
WP: (add dialogue here)
Bride: (Something Badass)
Bride: Blah blah blah... The perfect wedding.
WP: AAARGH!!!
WP: Splutter Blub Blub
Bride: NOW it's perfect.

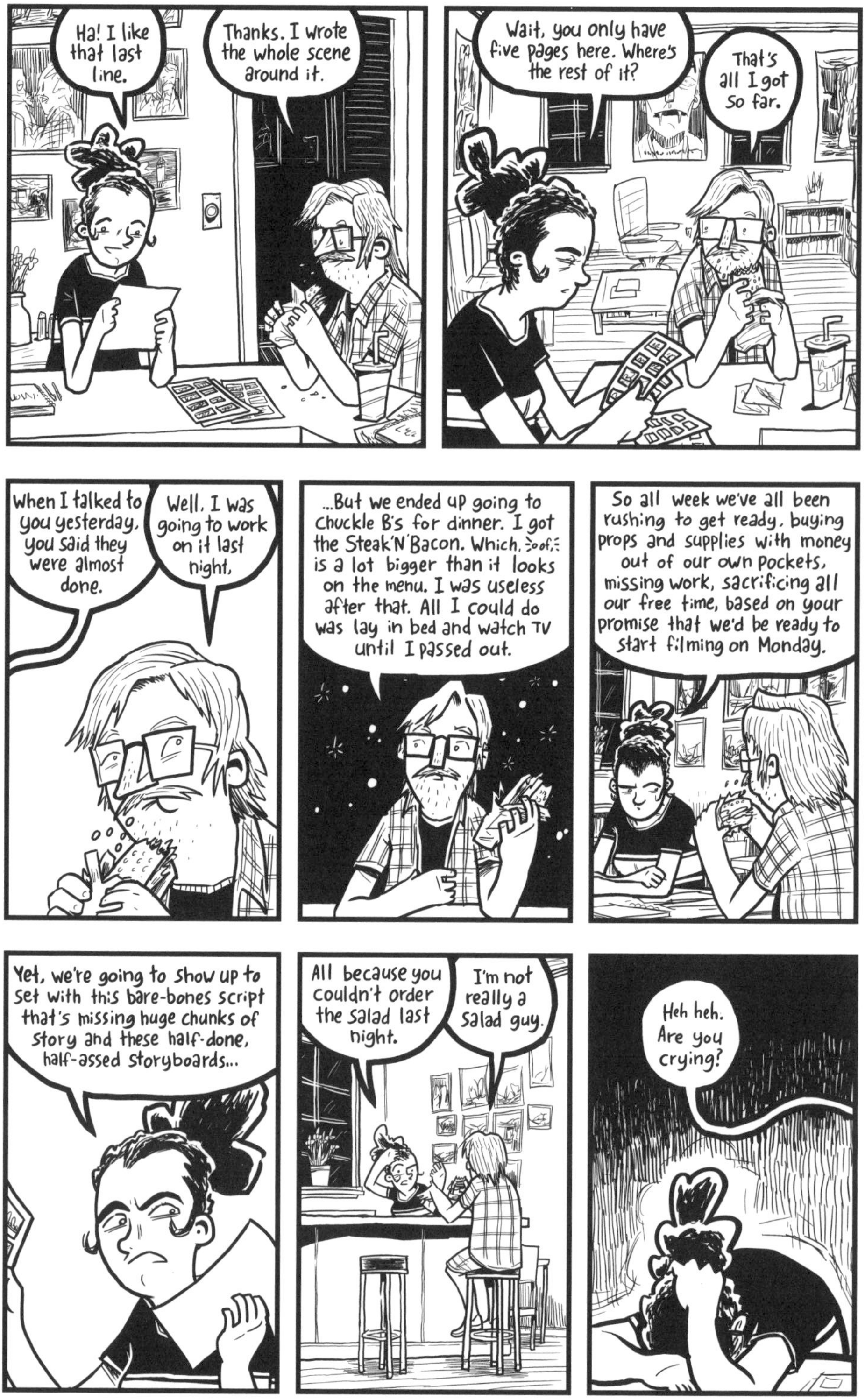
Ha! I like that last line.
Thanks. I wrote the whole scene around it.
Wait, you only have five pages here. Where's the rest of it?
That's all I got so far.
When I talked to you yesterday, you said they were almost done.
Well, I was going to work on it last night,
...But we ended up going to Chuckle B's for dinner. I got the Steak'N'Bacon. Which, oof, is a lot bigger than it looks on the menu. I was useless after that. All I could do was lay in bed and watch TV until I passed out.
So all week we've all been rushing to get ready, buying props and supplies with money out of our own pockets, missing work, sacrificing all our free time, based on your promise that we'd be ready to start filming on Monday.
Yet, we're going to show up to set with this bare-bones script that's missing huge chunks of story and these half-done, half-assed storyboards...
All because you couldn't order the salad last night.
I'm not really a salad guy.
Heh heh. Are you crying?

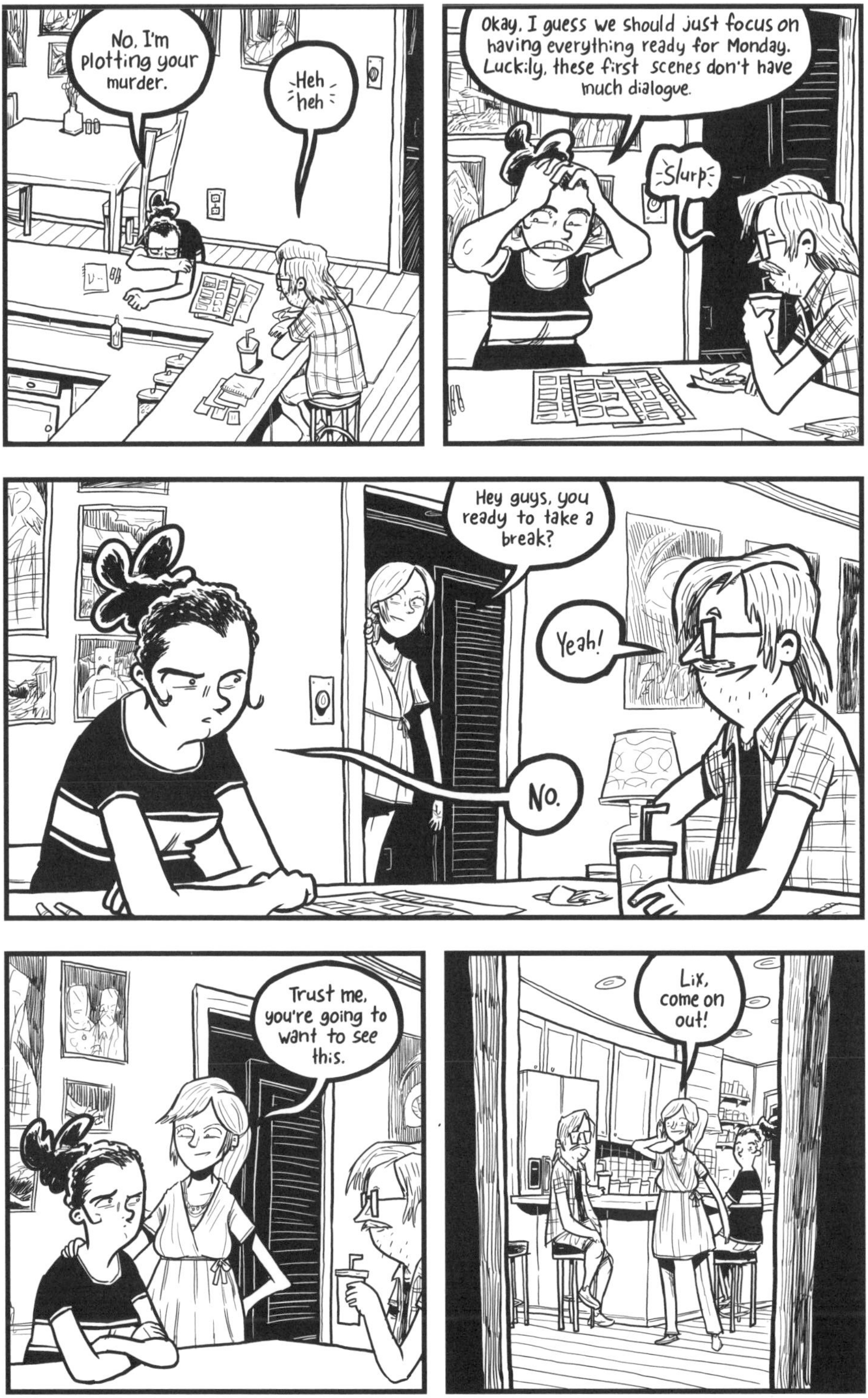
No, I'm plotting your murder.
Heh heh
Okay, I guess we should just focus on having everything ready for Monday. Luckily, these first scenes don't have much dialogue.
Slurp
Hey guys, you ready to take a break?
Yeah!
No.
Trust me, you're going to want to see this.
Lix, come on out!

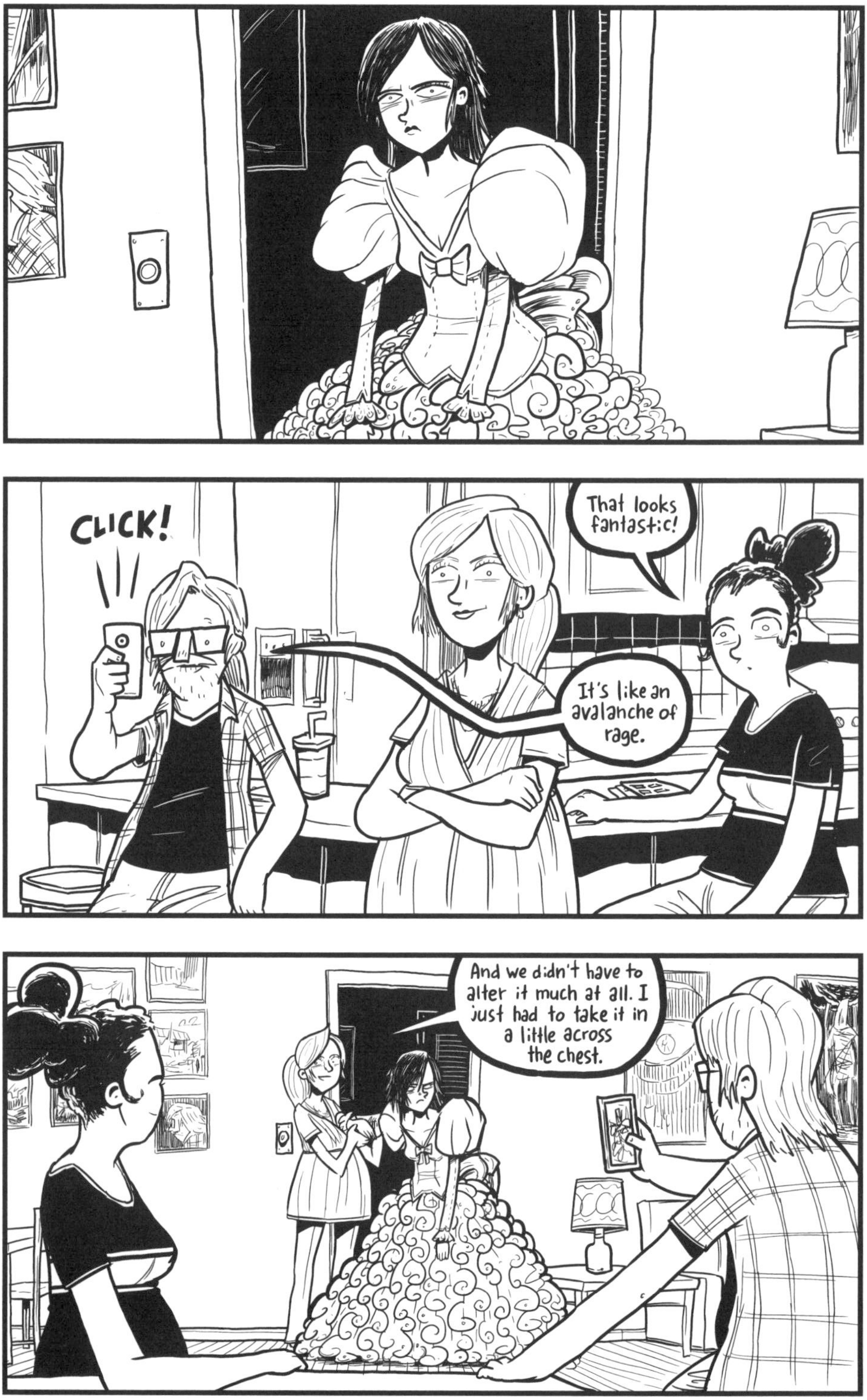
CLICK!
That looks fantastic!
It's like an avalanche of rage.
And we didn't have to alter it much at all. I just had to take it in a little across the chest.

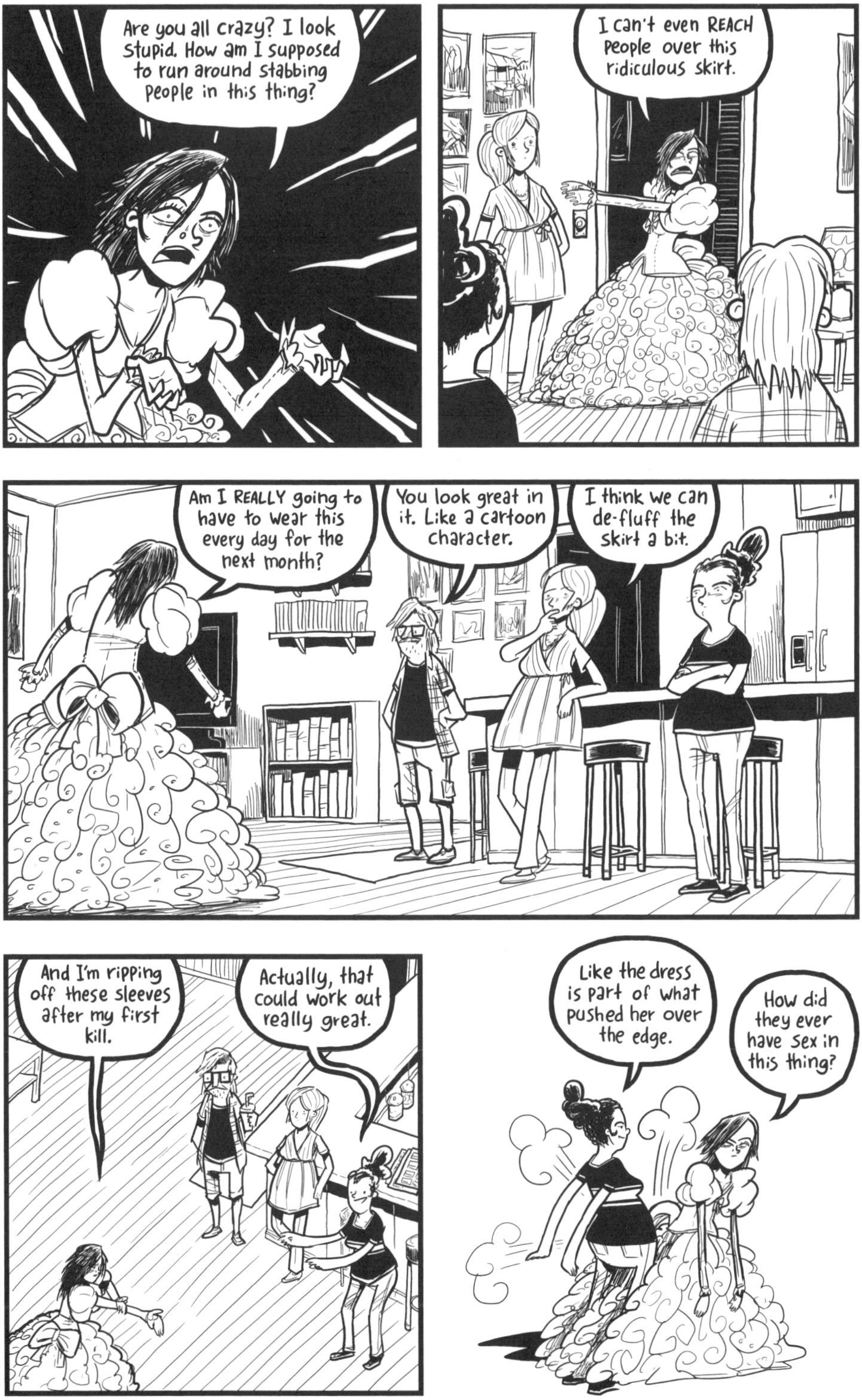
Are you all crazy? I look stupid. How am I supposed to run around stabbing people in this thing?
I can't even REACH people over this ridiculous skirt.
Am I REALLY going to have to wear this every day for the next month?
You look great in it. Like a cartoon character.
I think we can de-fluff the skirt a bit.
And I'm ripping off these sleeves after my first kill.
Actually, that could work out really great.
Like the dress is part of what pushed her over the edge.
How did they ever have sex in this thing?

CHAPTER FOUR

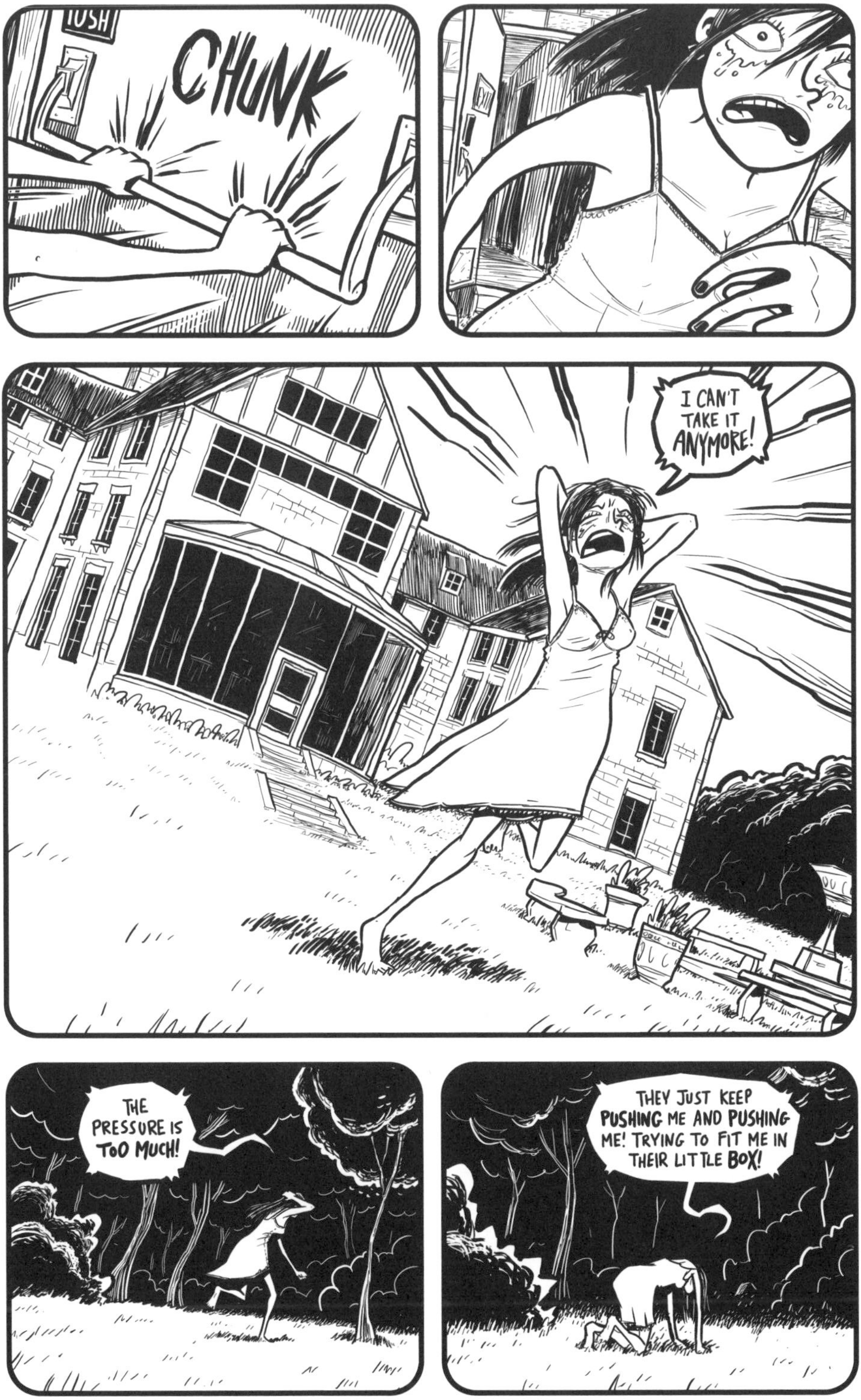

CHUNK
I CAN'T TAKE IT ANYMORE!
THE PRESSURE IS TOO MUCH!
THEY JUST KEEP PUSHING ME AND PUSHING ME! TRYING TO FIT ME IN THEIR LITTLE BOX!

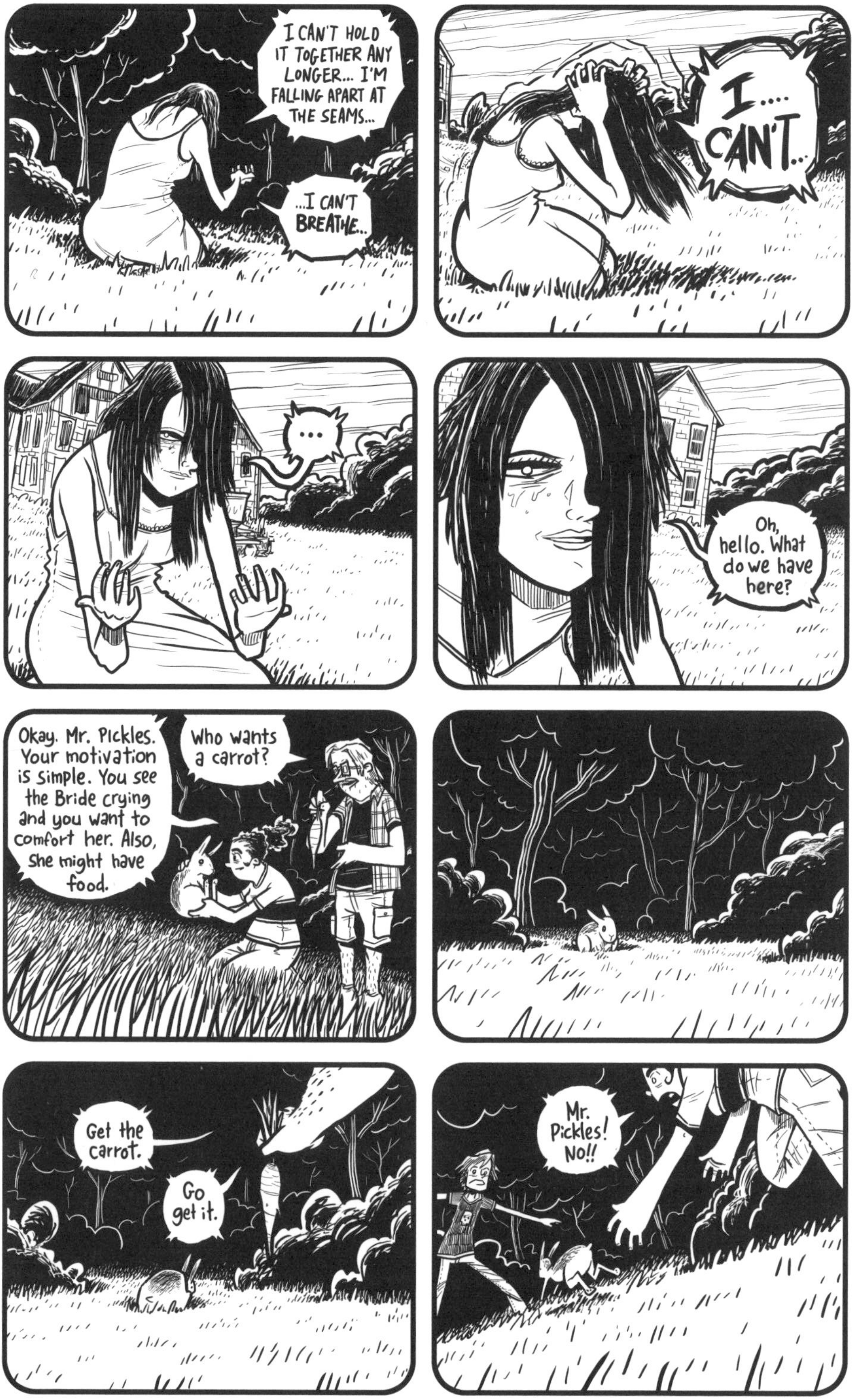
I CAN'T HOLD IT TOGETHER ANY LONGER... I'M FALLING APART AT THE SEAMS...
...I CAN'T BREATHE...
I.... CAN'T...
...
Oh, hello. What do we have here?
Okay. Mr. Pickles. Your motivation is simple. You see the Bride crying and you want to comfort her. Also, she might have food.
Who wants a carrot?
Get the carrot.
Go get it.
Mr. Pickles! No!!

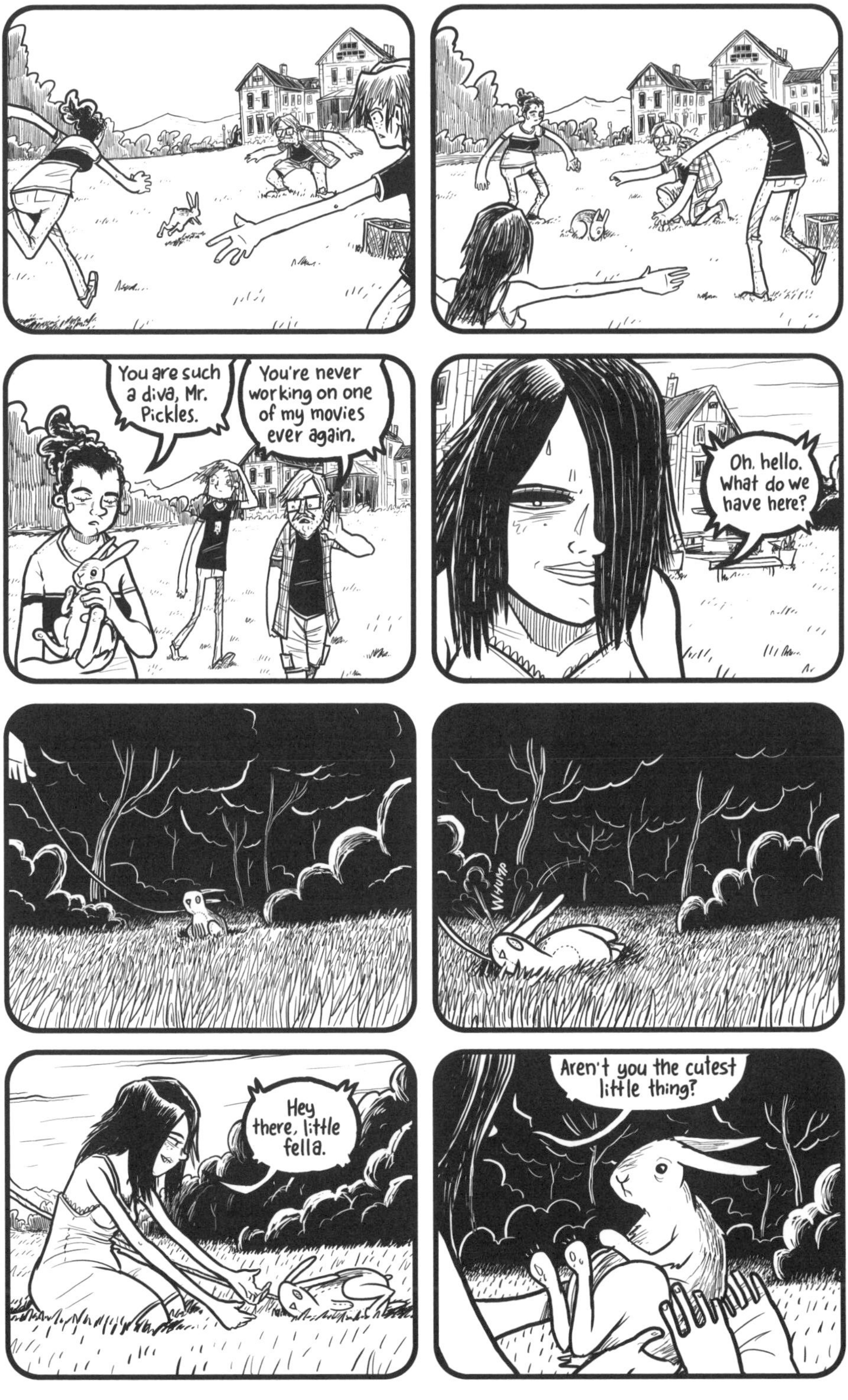
You are such a diva, Mr. Pickles.
You're never working on one of my movies ever again.
Oh. hello. What do we have here?
WHUMP
Hey there, little fella.
Aren't you the cutest little thing?

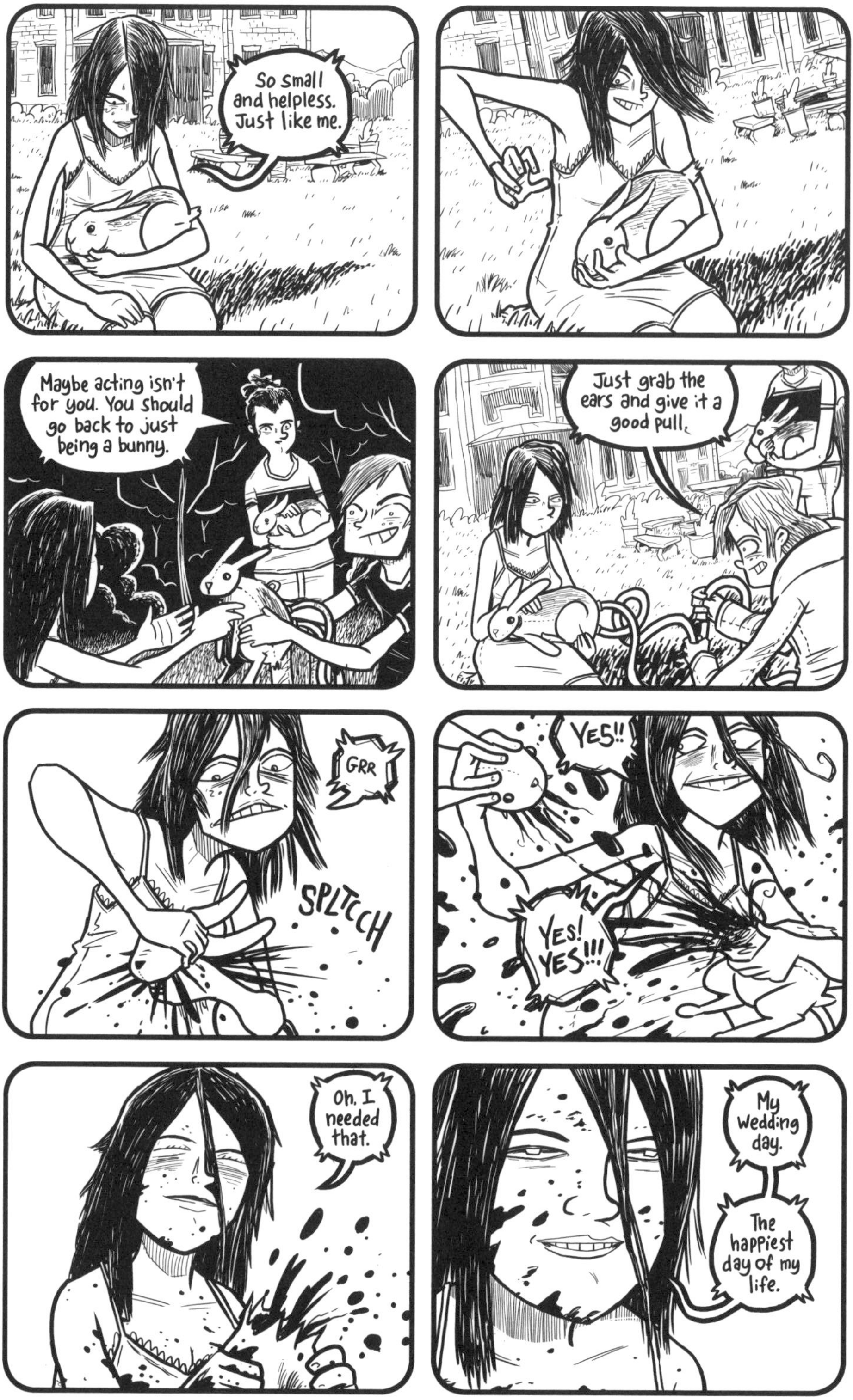
So small and helpless. Just like me.
Maybe acting isn't for you. You should go back to just being a bunny.
Just grab the ears and give it a good pull.
GRR
SPLTCCH
YES!!
YES! YES!!!
Oh, I needed that.
My wedding day.
The happiest day of my life.

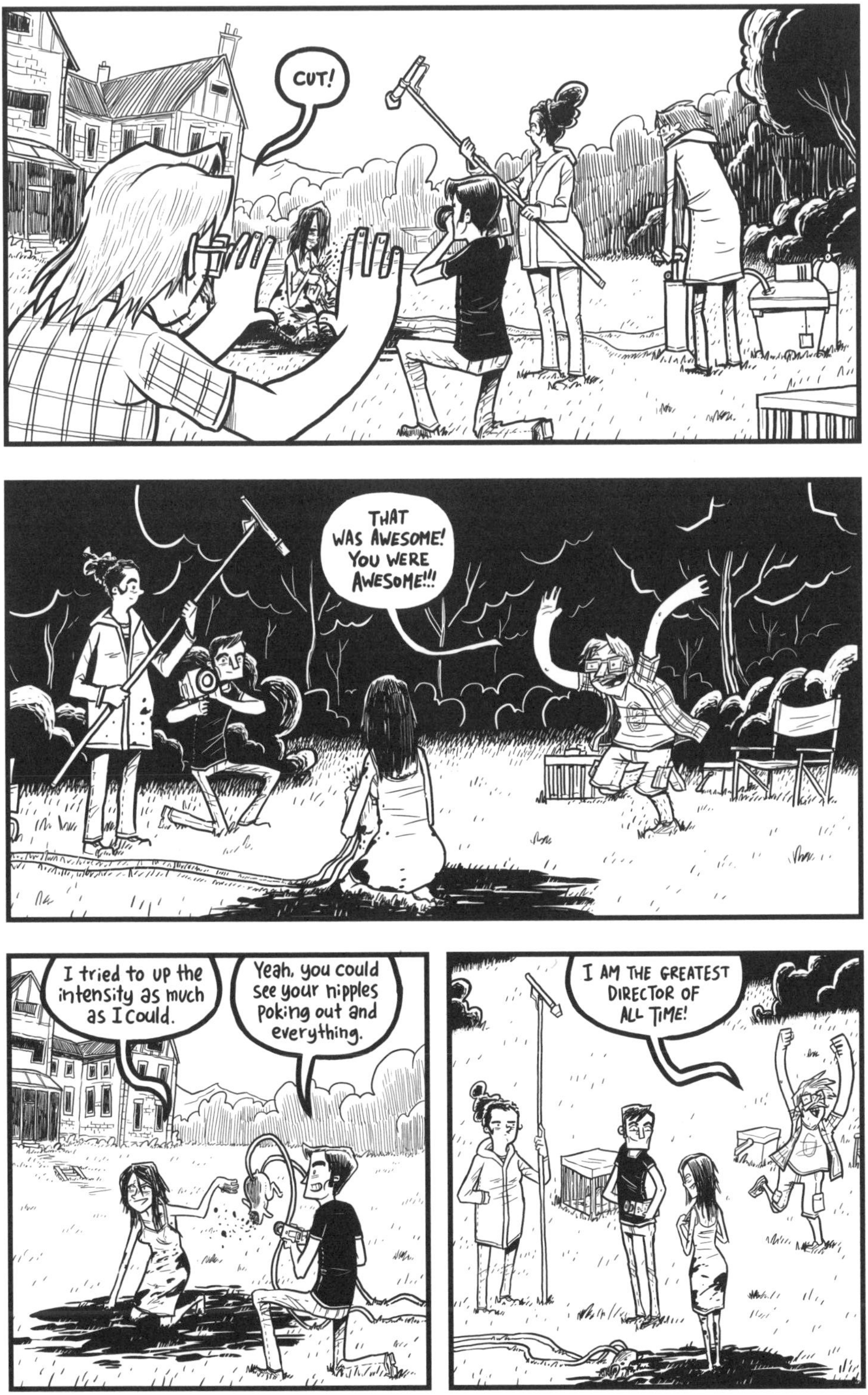
CUT!
THAT WAS AWESOME! YOU WERE AWESOME!!!
I tried to up the intensity as much as I could.
Yeah, you could see your nipples poking out and everything.
I AM THE GREATEST DIRECTOR OF ALL TIME!

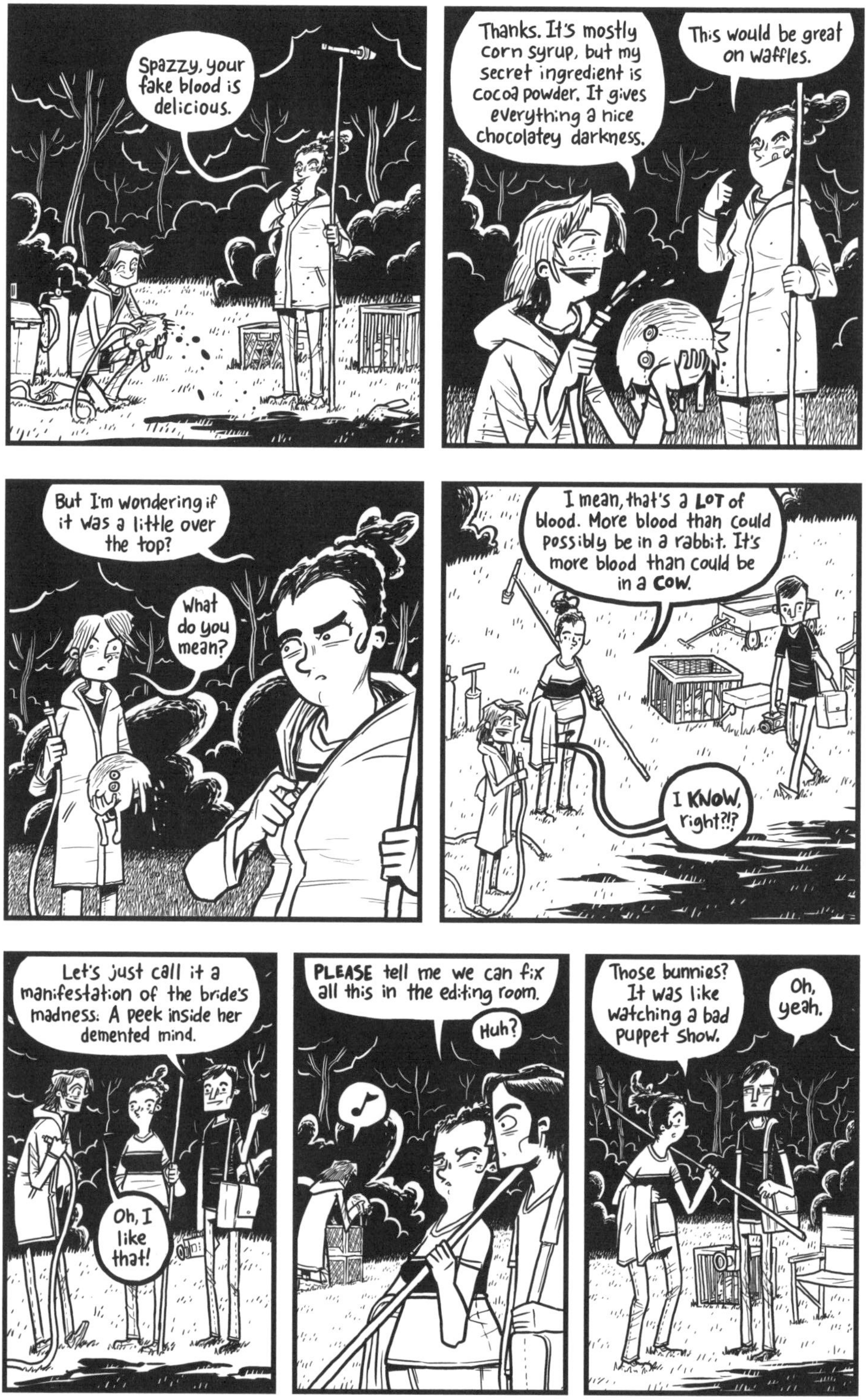
Spazzy, your fake blood is delicious.
Thanks. It's mostly corn syrup, but my secret ingredient is cocoa powder. It gives everything a nice chocolatey darkness.
This would be great on waffles.
But I'm wondering if it was a little over the top?
What do you mean?
I mean, that's a LOT of blood. More blood than could possibly be in a rabbit. It's more blood than could be in a COW.
I KNOW, right?!?
Let's just call it a manifestation of the bride's madness. A peek inside her demented mind.
Oh, I like that!
PLEASE tell me we can fix all this in the editing room.
Huh?
Those bunnies? It was like watching a bad puppet show.
Oh, yeah.

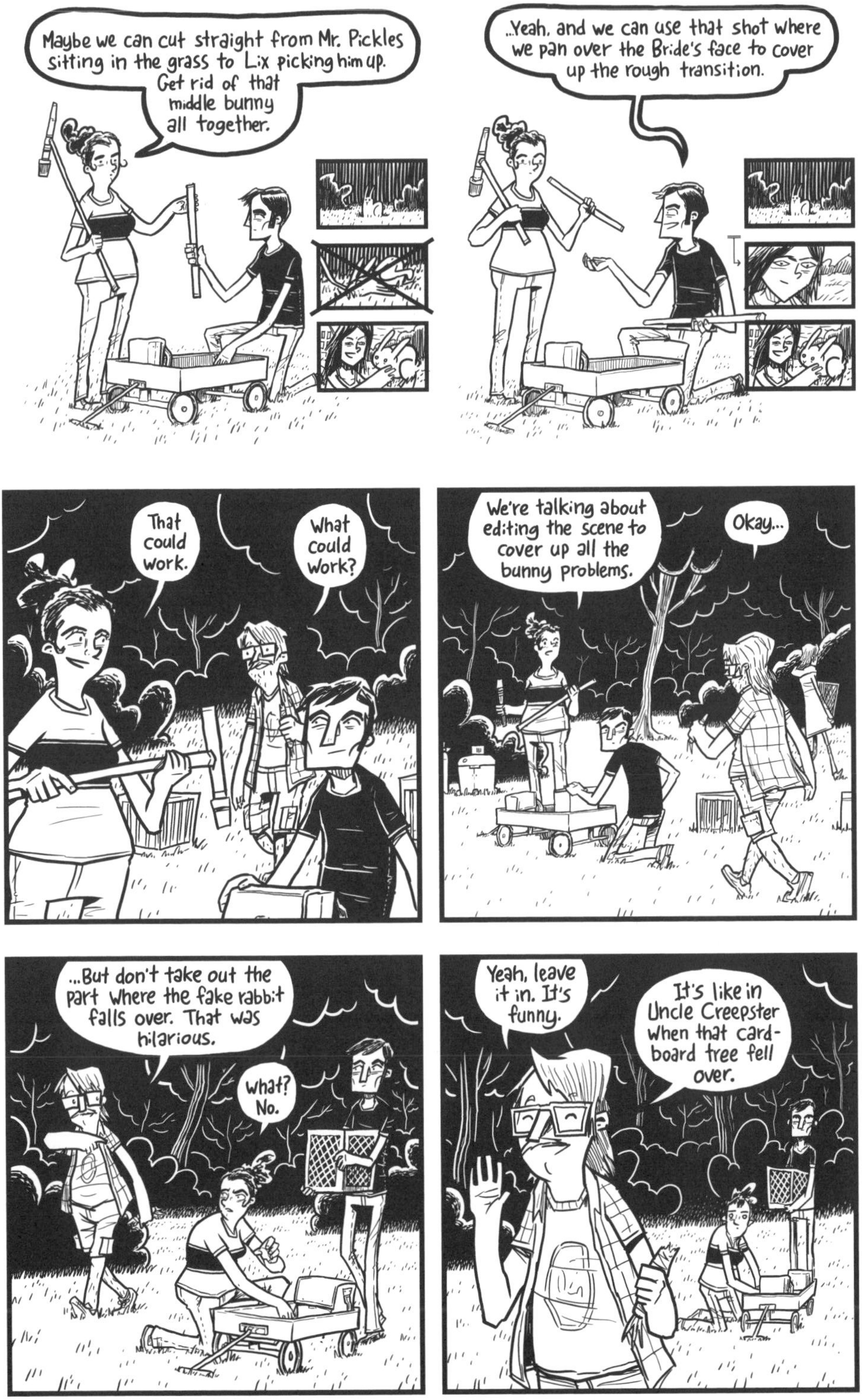
Maybe we can cut straight from Mr. Pickles sitting in the grass to Lix picking him up. Get rid of that middle bunny all together.
...Yeah, and we can use that shot where we pan over the Bride's face to cover up the rough transition.
That could work.
What could work?
We're talking about editing the scene to cover up all the bunny problems.
Okay...
...But don't take out the part where the fake rabbit falls over. That was hilarious.
What? No.
Yeah, leave it in. It's funny.
It's like in Uncle Creepster when that card-board tree fell over.

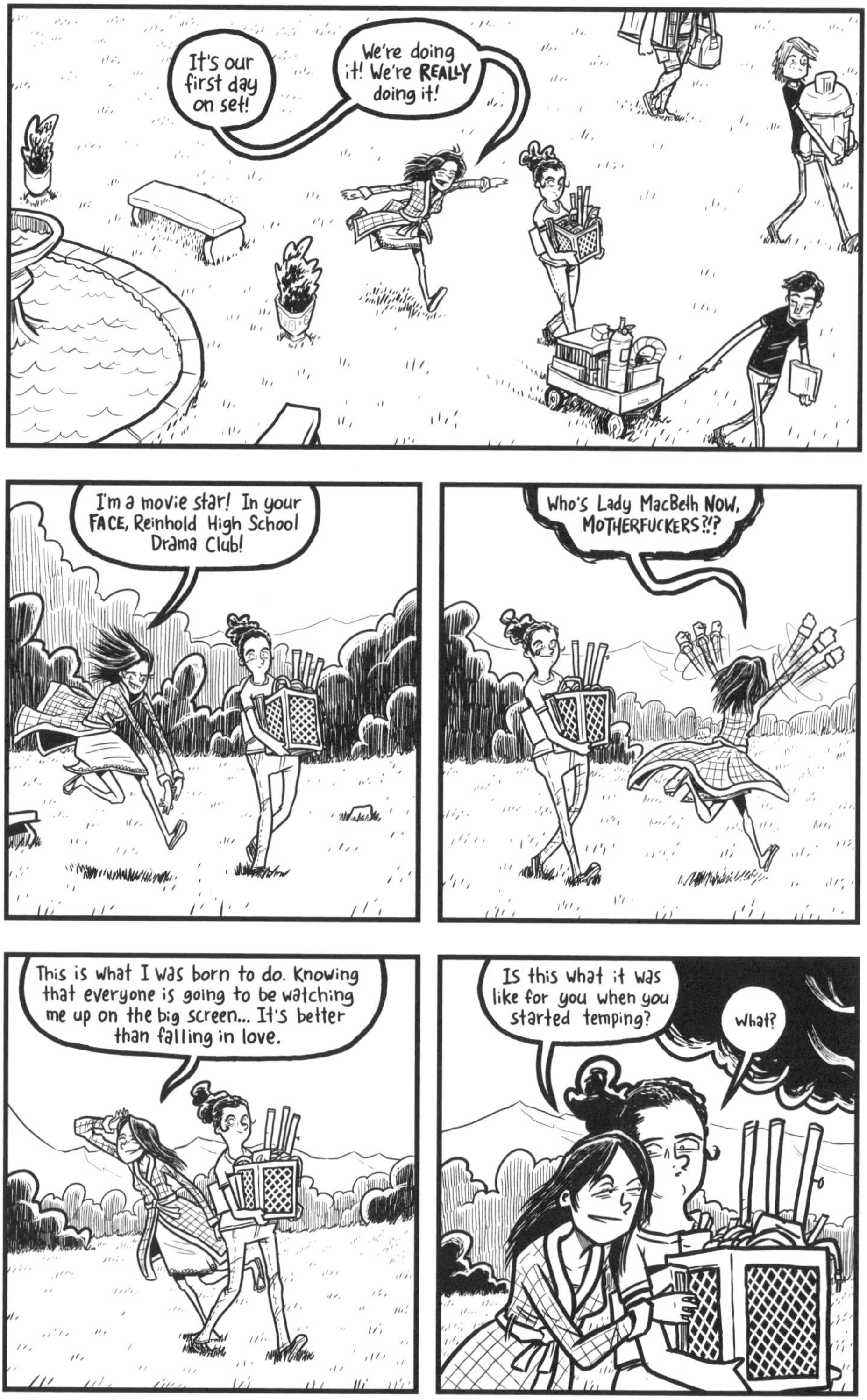
It's our first day on set!
We're doing it! We're REALLY doing it!
I'm a movie star! In your FACE, Reinhold High School Drama Club!
Who's Lady MacBeth NOW, MOTHERFUCKERS?!?
This is what I was born to do. Knowing that everyone is going to be watching me up on the big screen... It's better than falling in love.
Is this what it was like for you when you started temping?
What?

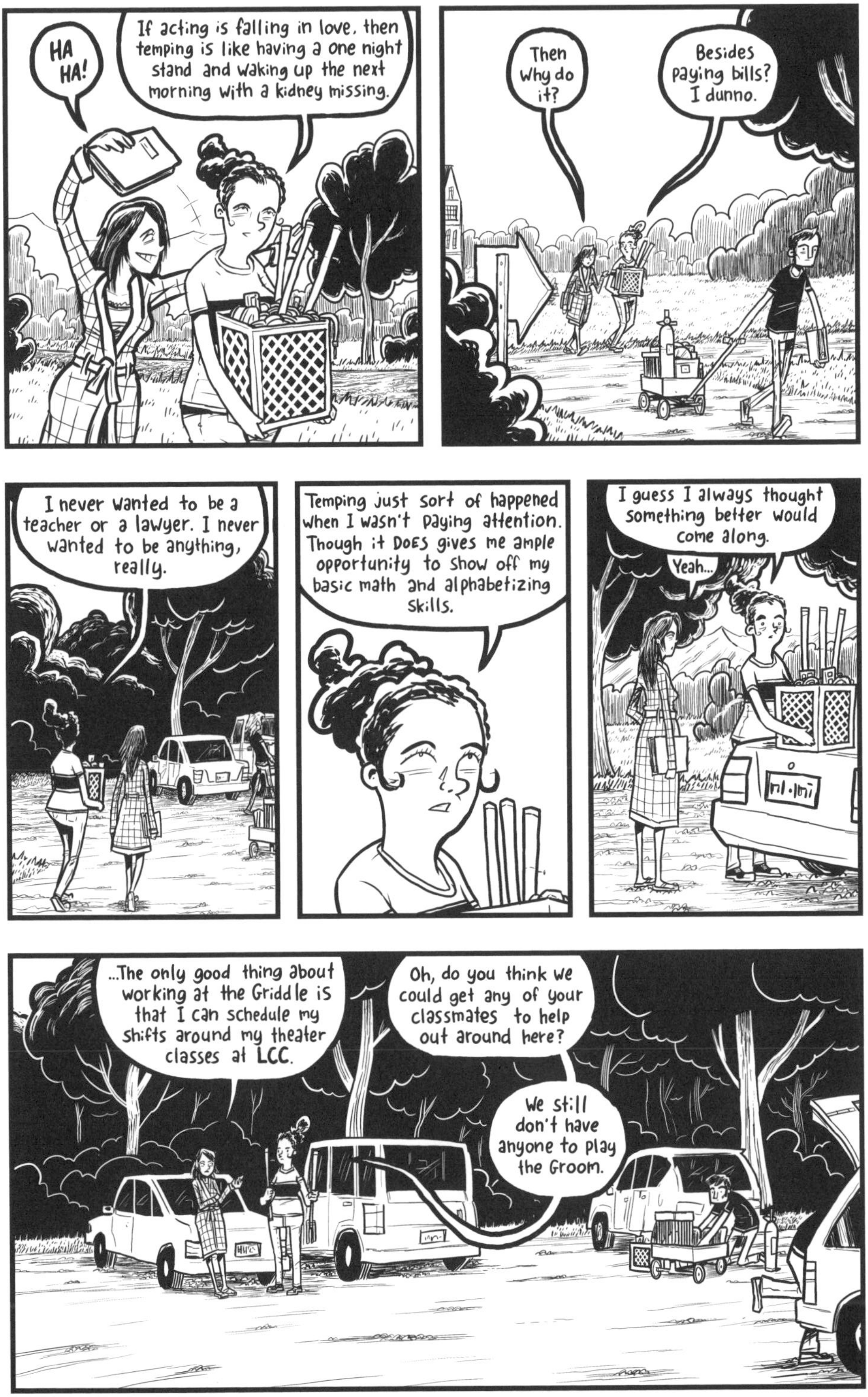
HA HA!
If acting is falling in love, then temping is like having a one night stand and waking up the next morning with a kidney missing.
Then why do it?
Besides paying bills? I dunno.
I never wanted to be a teacher or a lawyer. I never wanted to be anything, really.
Temping just sort of happened when I wasn't paying attention. Though it DOES gives me ample opportunity to show off my basic math and alphabetizing skills.
I guess I always thought something better would come along.
Yeah...
...The only good thing about working at the Griddle is that I can schedule my shifts around my theater classes at LCC.
Oh, do you think we could get any of your classmates to help out around here?
We still don't have anyone to play the Groom.

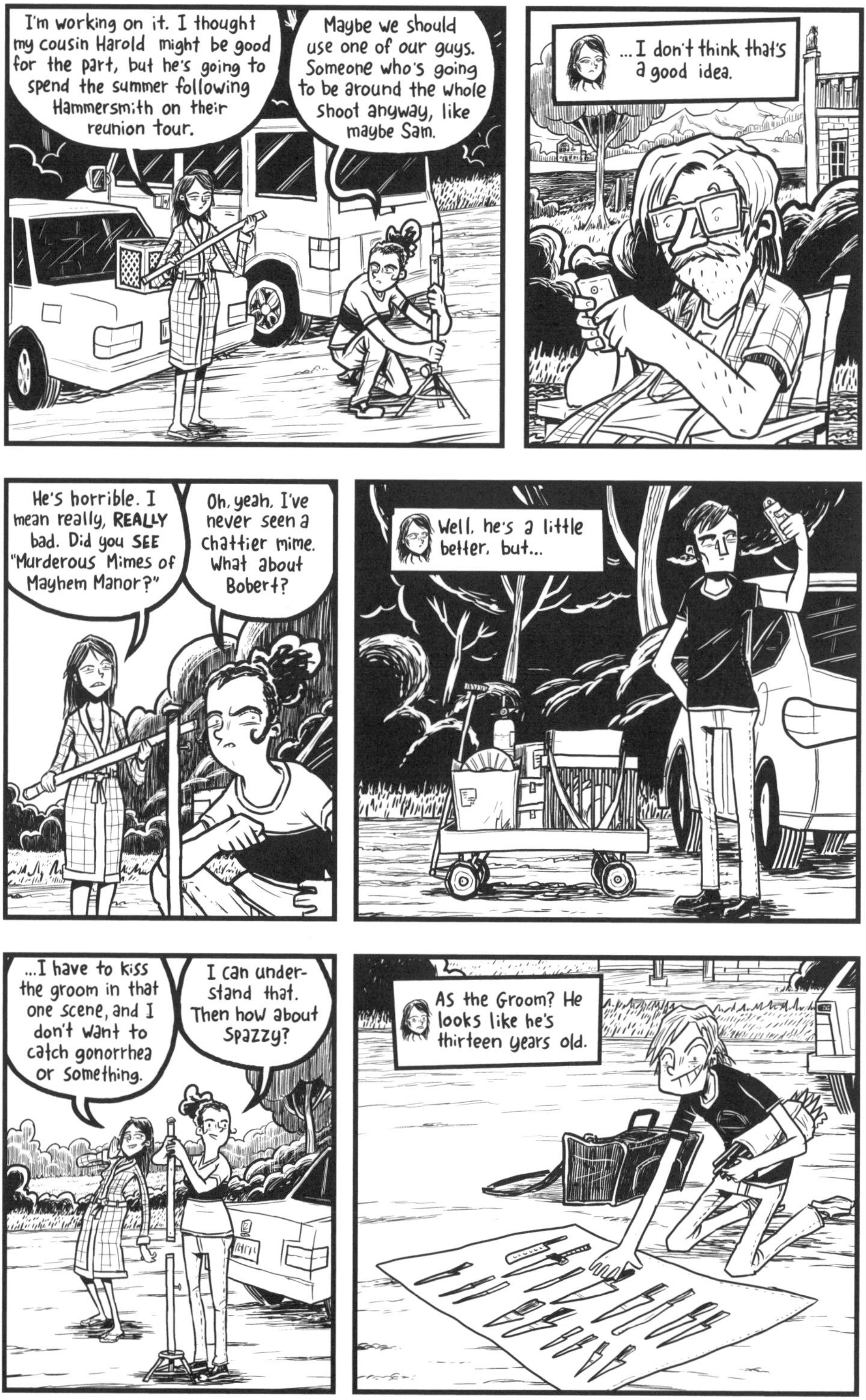
I'm working on it. I thought my cousin Harold might be good for the part, but he's going to spend the summer following Hammersmith on their reunion tour.
Maybe we should use one of our guys. Someone who's going to be around the whole shoot anyway, like maybe Sam.
...I don't think that's a good idea.
He's horrible. I mean really, REALLY bad. Did you SEE "Murderous Mimes of Mayhem Manor?"
Oh, yeah, I've never seen a chattier mime. What about Bobert?
Well, he's a little better, but...
...I have to kiss the groom in that one scene, and I don't want to catch gonorrhea or something.
I can understand that. Then how about Spazzy?
As the Groom? He looks like he's thirteen years old.

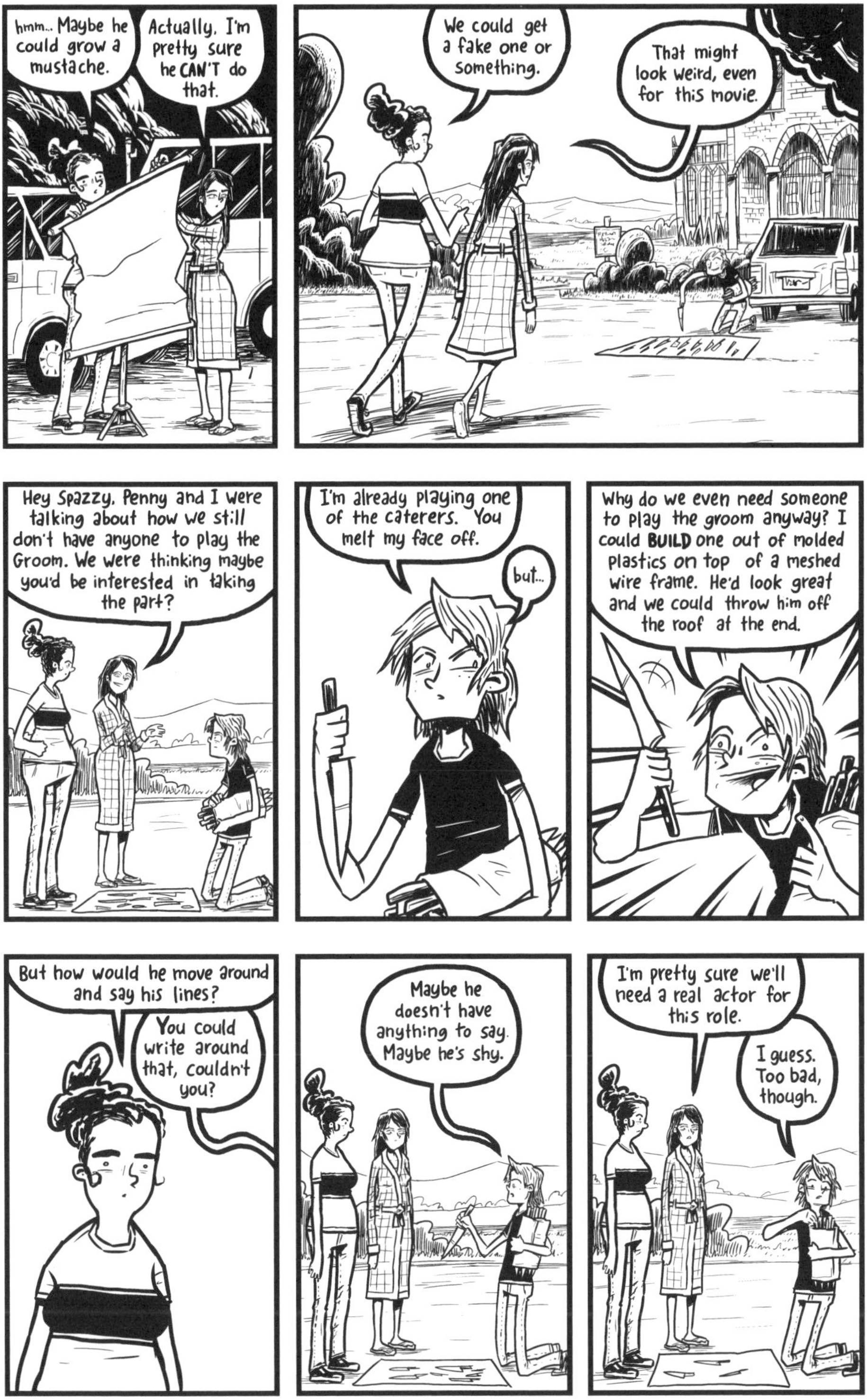
hmm.. Maybe he could grow a mustache.
Actually, I'm pretty sure he CAN'T do that.
We could get a fake one or something.
That might look weird, even for this movie.
Hey Spazzy, Penny and I were talking about how we still don't have anyone to play the Groom. We were thinking maybe you'd be interested in taking the part?
I'm already playing one of the caterers. You melt my face off.
but...
Why do we even need someone to play the groom anyway? I could BUILD one out of molded plastics on top of a meshed wire frame. He'd look great and we could throw him off the roof at the end.
But how would he move around and say his lines?
You could write around that, couldn't you?
Maybe he doesn't have anything to say. Maybe he's shy.
I'm pretty sure we'll need a real actor for this role.
I guess. Too bad, though.

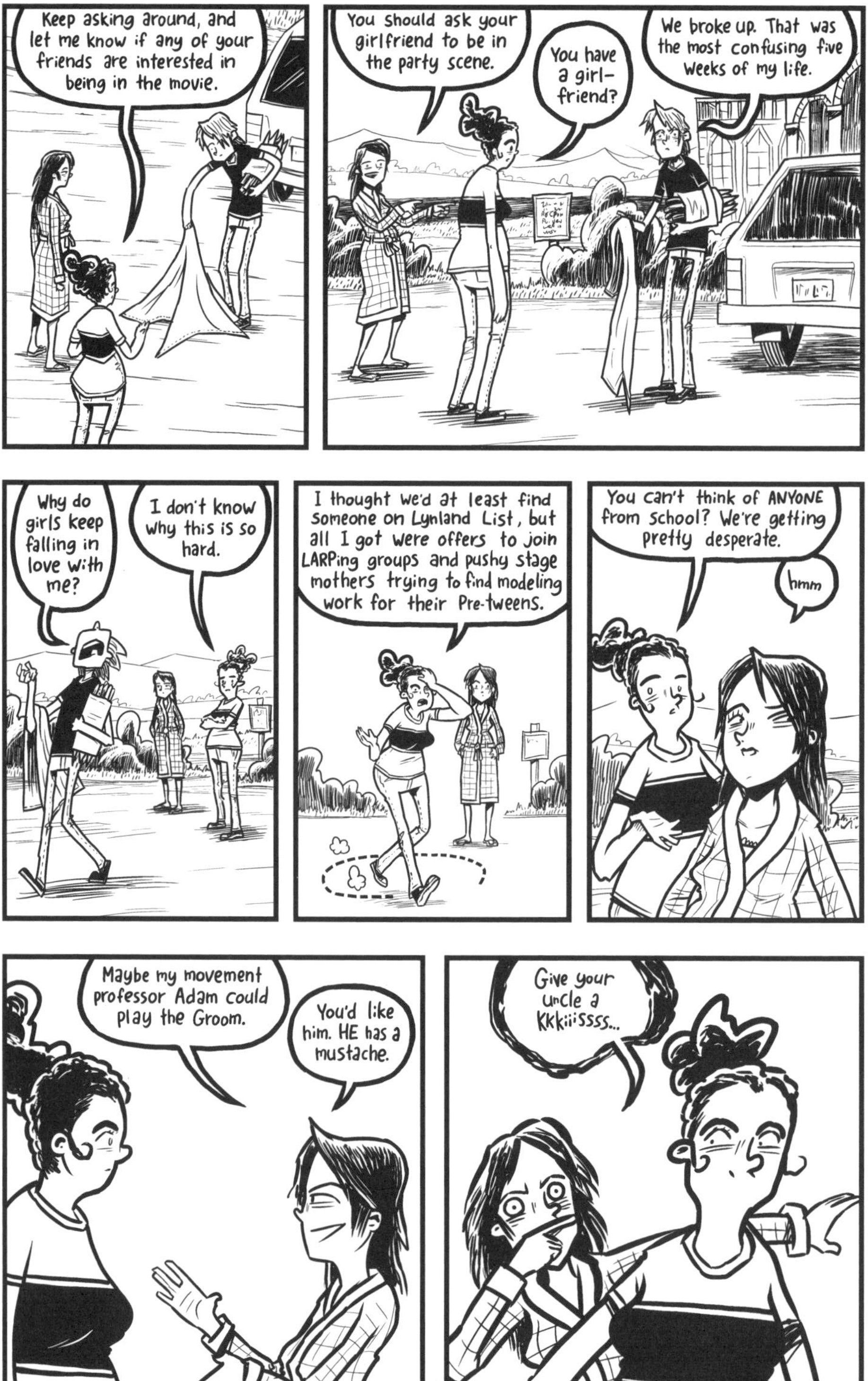
Keep asking around, and let me know if any of your friends are interested in being in the movie.
You should ask your girlfriend to be in the party scene.
You have a girl-friend?
We broke up. That was the most confusing five weeks of my life.
Why do girls keep falling in love with me?
I don't know why this is so hard.
I thought we'd at least find someone on Lynland List, but all I got were offers to join LARPing groups and pushy stage mothers trying to find modeling work for their Pre-tweens.
You can't think of ANYONE from school? We're getting pretty desperate.
hmm
Maybe my movement professor Adam could play the Groom.
You'd like him. HE has a mustache.
Give your uncle a Kkkiiissss...

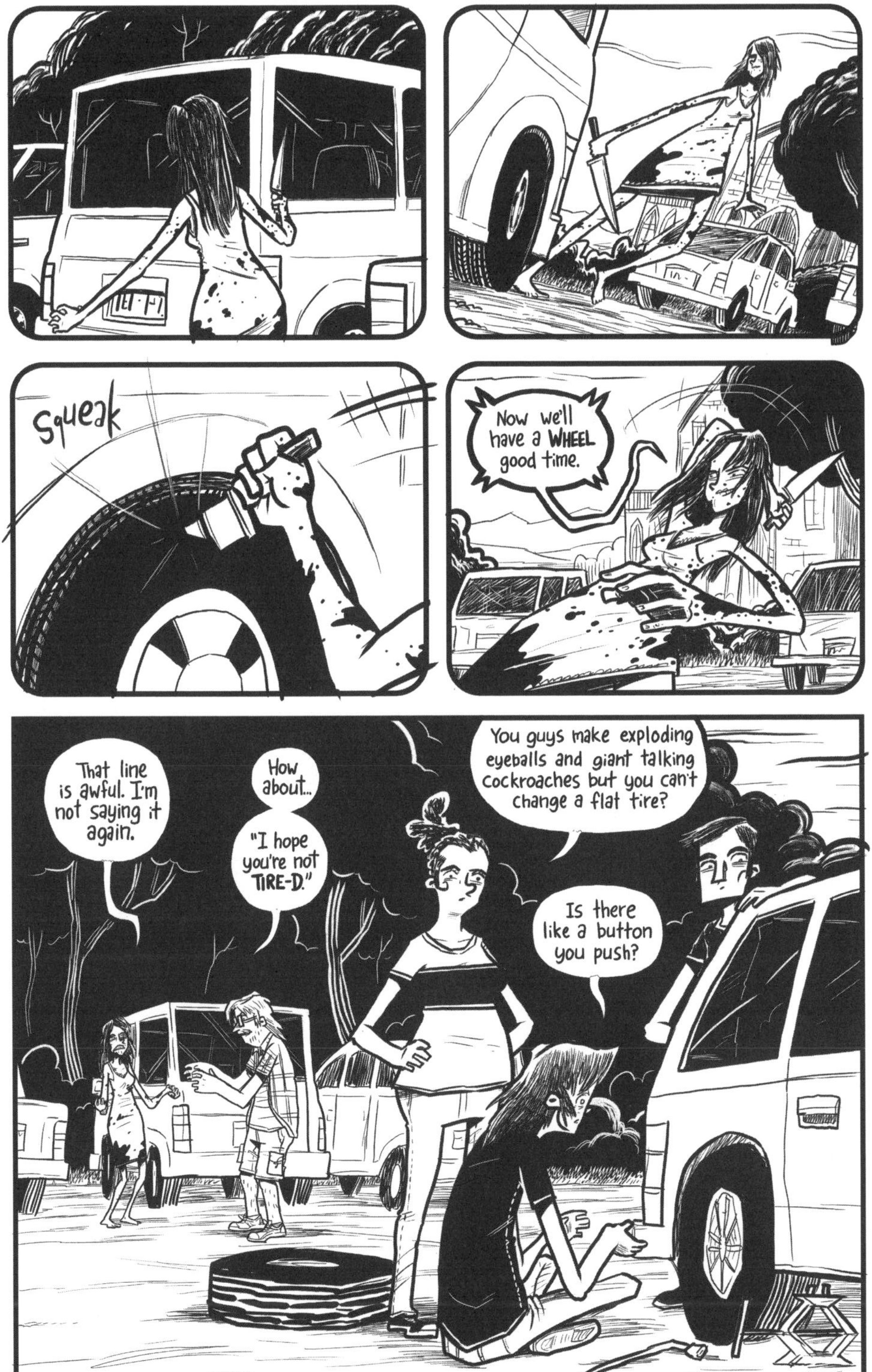
Squeak
Now we'll have a WHEEL good time.
That line is awful. I'm not saying it again.
How about...
"I hope you're not TIRE-D."
You guys make exploding eyeballs and giant talking cockroaches but you can't change a flat tire?
Is there like a button you push?

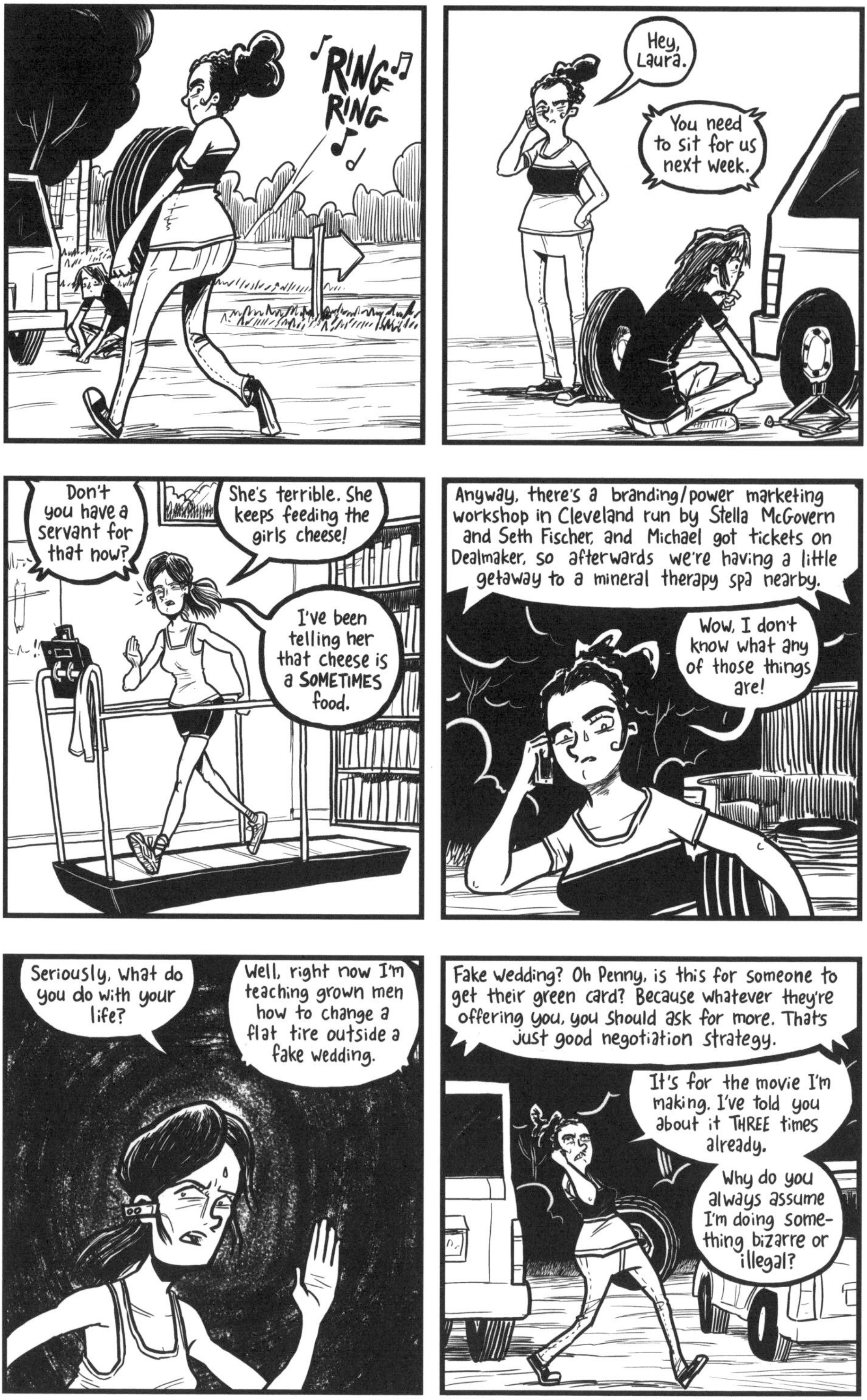
RING RING
Hey, Laura.
You need to sit for us next week.
Don't you have a servant for that now?
She's terrible. She keeps feeding the girls cheese!
I've been telling her that cheese is a SOMETIMES food.
Anyway, there's a branding/power marketing workshop in Cleveland run by Stella McGovern and Seth Fischer, and Michael got tickets on Dealmaker, so afterwards we're having a little getaway to a mineral therapy spa nearby.
Wow, I don't know what any of those things are!
Seriously, what do you do with your life?
Well, right now I'm teaching grown men how to change a flat tire outside a fake wedding.
Fake wedding? Oh Penny, is this for someone to get their green card? Because whatever they're offering you, you should ask for more. That's just good negotiation strategy.
It's for the movie I'm making. I've told you about it THREE times already.
Why do you always assume I'm doing something bizarre or illegal?

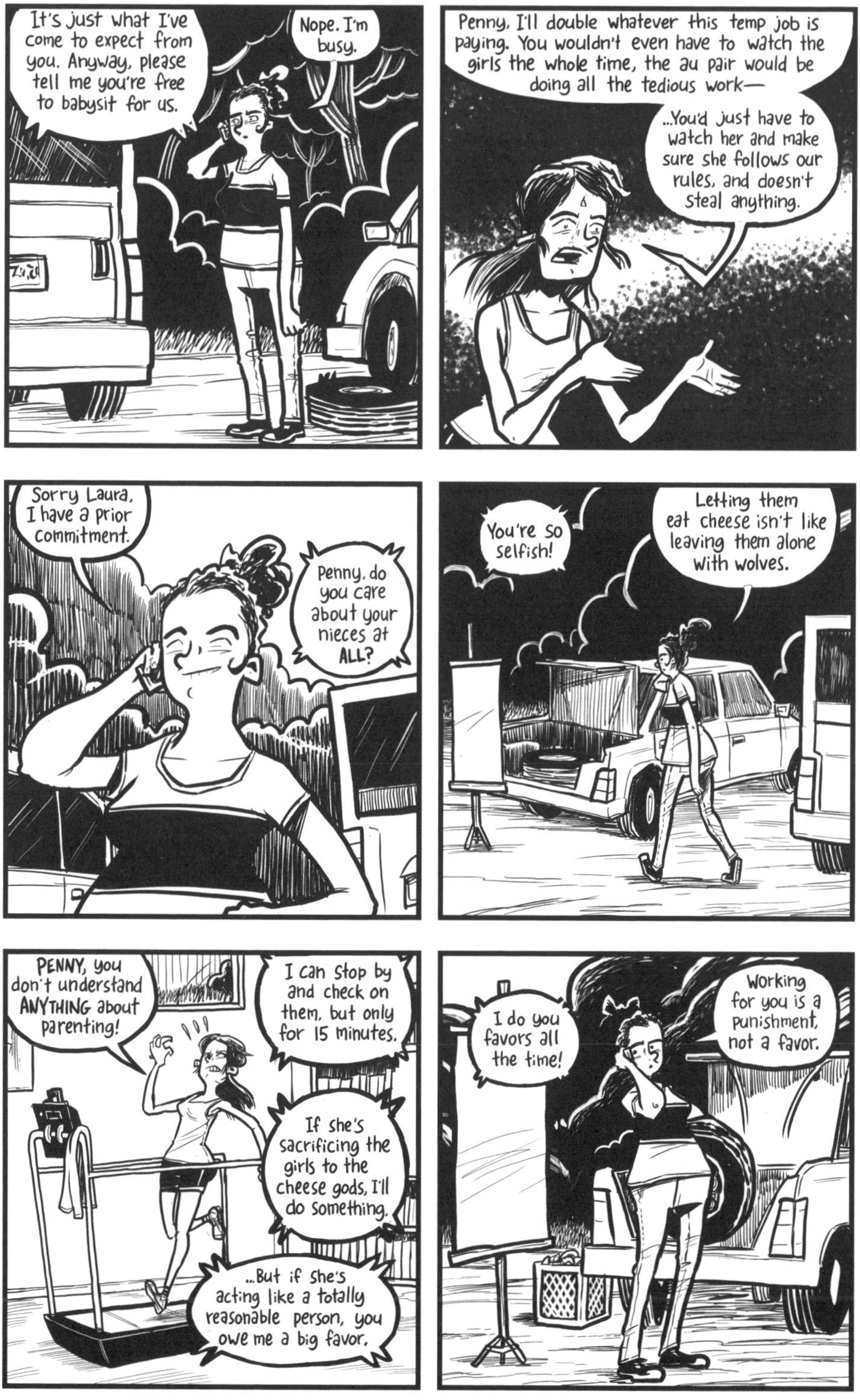
It's just what I've come to expect from you. Anyway, please tell me you're free to babysit for us.
Nope. I'm busy.
Penny, I'll double whatever this temp job is paying. You wouldn't even have to watch the girls the whole time, the au pair would be doing all the tedious work—
...You'd just have to watch her and make sure she follows our rules, and doesn't steal anything.
Sorry Laura, I have a prior commitment.
Penny, do you care about your nieces at ALL?
You're so selfish!
Letting them eat cheese isn't like leaving them alone with wolves.
PENNY, you don't understand ANYTHING about parenting!
I can stop by and check on them, but only for 15 minutes.
If she's sacrificing the girls to the cheese gods, I'll do something.
...But if she's acting like a totally reasonable person, you owe me a big favor.
I do you favors all the time!
Working for you is a punishment, not a favor.

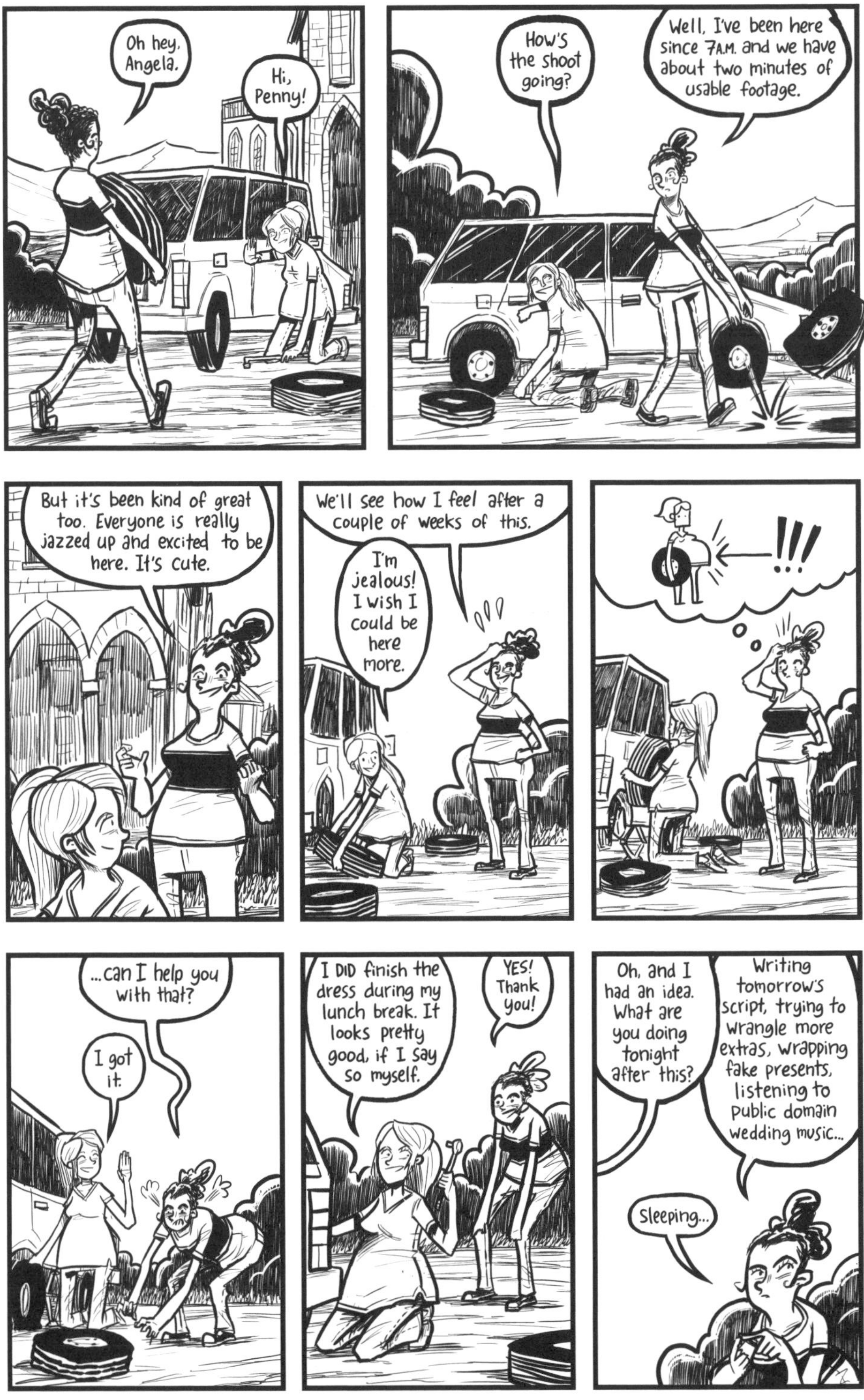

Oh hey, Angela.
Hi, Penny!
How's the shoot going?
Well, I've been here since 7A.M. and we have about two minutes of usable footage.
But it's been kind of great too. Everyone is really jazzed up and excited to be here. It's cute.
We'll see how I feel after a couple of weeks of this.
I'm jealous! I wish I could be here more.
!!!
...can I help you with that?
I got it.
I DID finish the dress during my lunch break. It looks pretty good, if I say so myself.
YES! Thank you!
Oh, and I had an idea. What are you doing tonight after this?
Writing tomorrow's script, trying to wrangle more extras, wrapping fake presents, listening to public domain wedding music...
Sleeping...

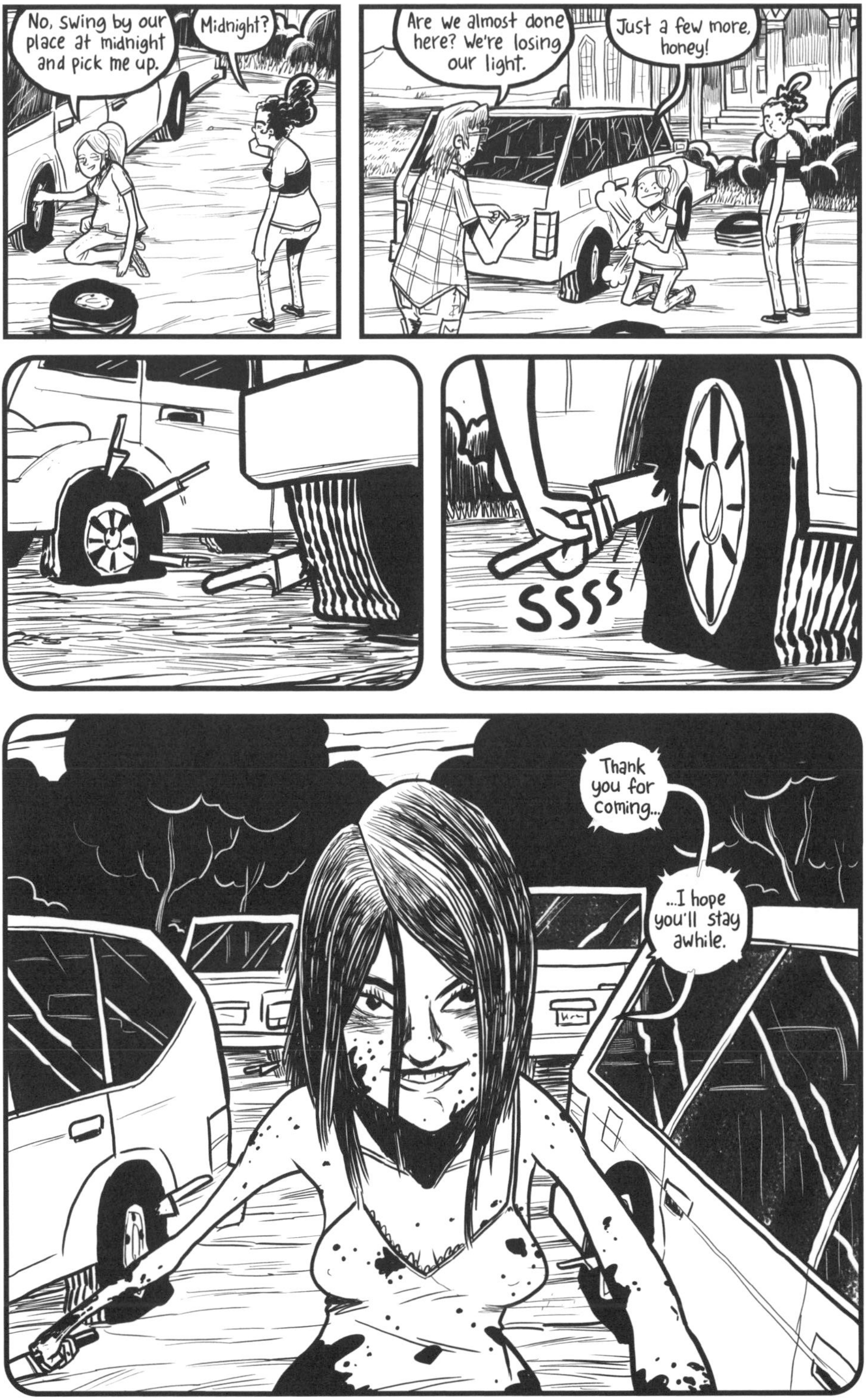
No, swing by our place at midnight and pick me up.
Midnight?
Are we almost done here? We're losing our light.
Just a few more, honey!
SSSS
Thank you for coming...
...I hope you'll stay awhile.

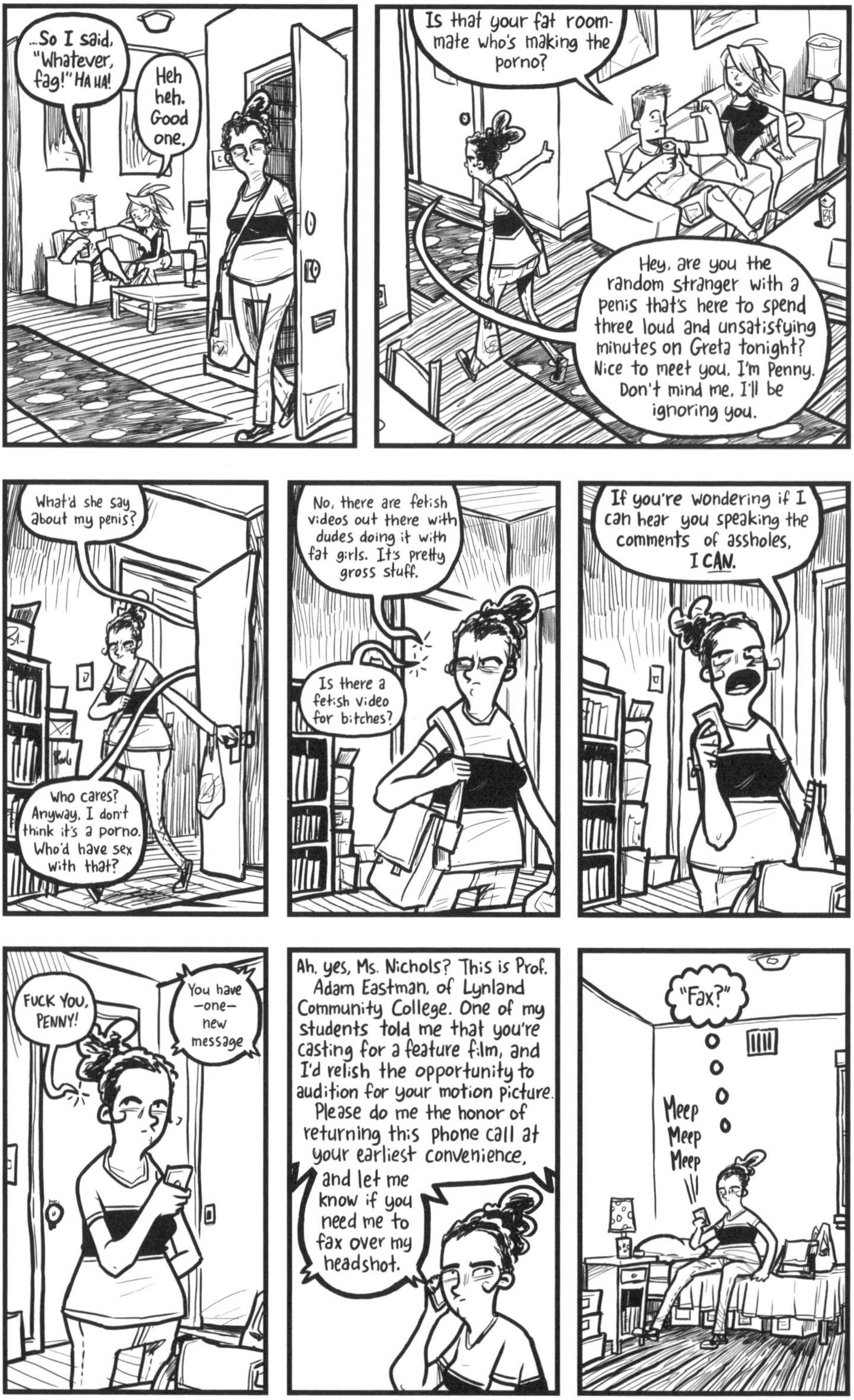
...So I said, "Whatever, fag!" HA HA!
Heh heh. Good one.
Is that your fat room-mate who's making the porno?
Hey, are you the random stranger with a penis that's here to spend three loud and unsatisfying minutes on Greta tonight? Nice to meet you, I'm Penny. Don't mind me, I'll be ignoring you.
What'd she say about my penis?
Who cares? Anyway, I don't think it's a porno. Who'd have sex with that?
No, there are fetish videos out there with dudes doing it with fat girls. It's pretty gross stuff.
Is there a fetish video for bitches?
If you're wondering if I can hear you speaking the comments of assholes, I CAN.
FUCK YOU, PENNY!
You have —one— new message
Ah, yes, Ms. Nichols? This is Prof. Adam Eastman, of Lynland Community College. One of my students told me that you're casting for a feature film, and I'd relish the opportunity to audition for your motion picture. Please do me the honor of returning this phone call at your earliest convenience,
and let me know if you need me to fax over my headshot.
"Fax?"
Meep Meep Meep

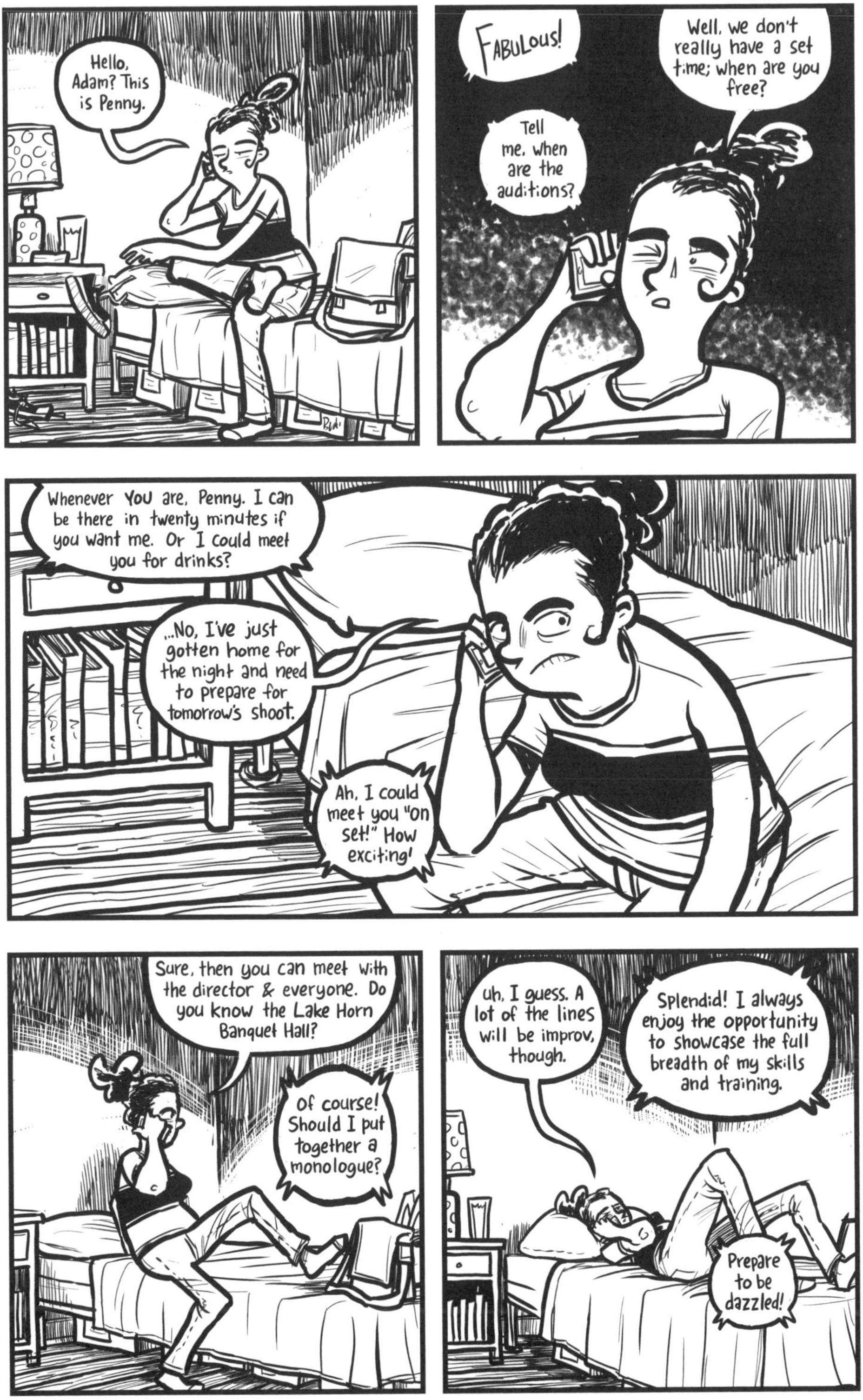
Hello, Adam? This is Penny.
FABULOUS!
Well, we don't really have a set time; when are you free?
Tell me, when are the auditions?
Whenever YOU are, Penny. I can be there in twenty minutes if you want me. Or I could meet you for drinks?
...No, I've just gotten home for the night and need to prepare for tomorrow's shoot.
Ah, I could meet you "on set!" How exciting!
Sure, then you can meet with the director & everyone. Do you know the Lake Horn Banquet Hall?
Of course! Should I put together a monologue?
Uh, I guess. A lot of the lines will be improv, though.
Splendid! I always enjoy the opportunity to showcase the full breadth of my skills and training.
Prepare to be dazzled!

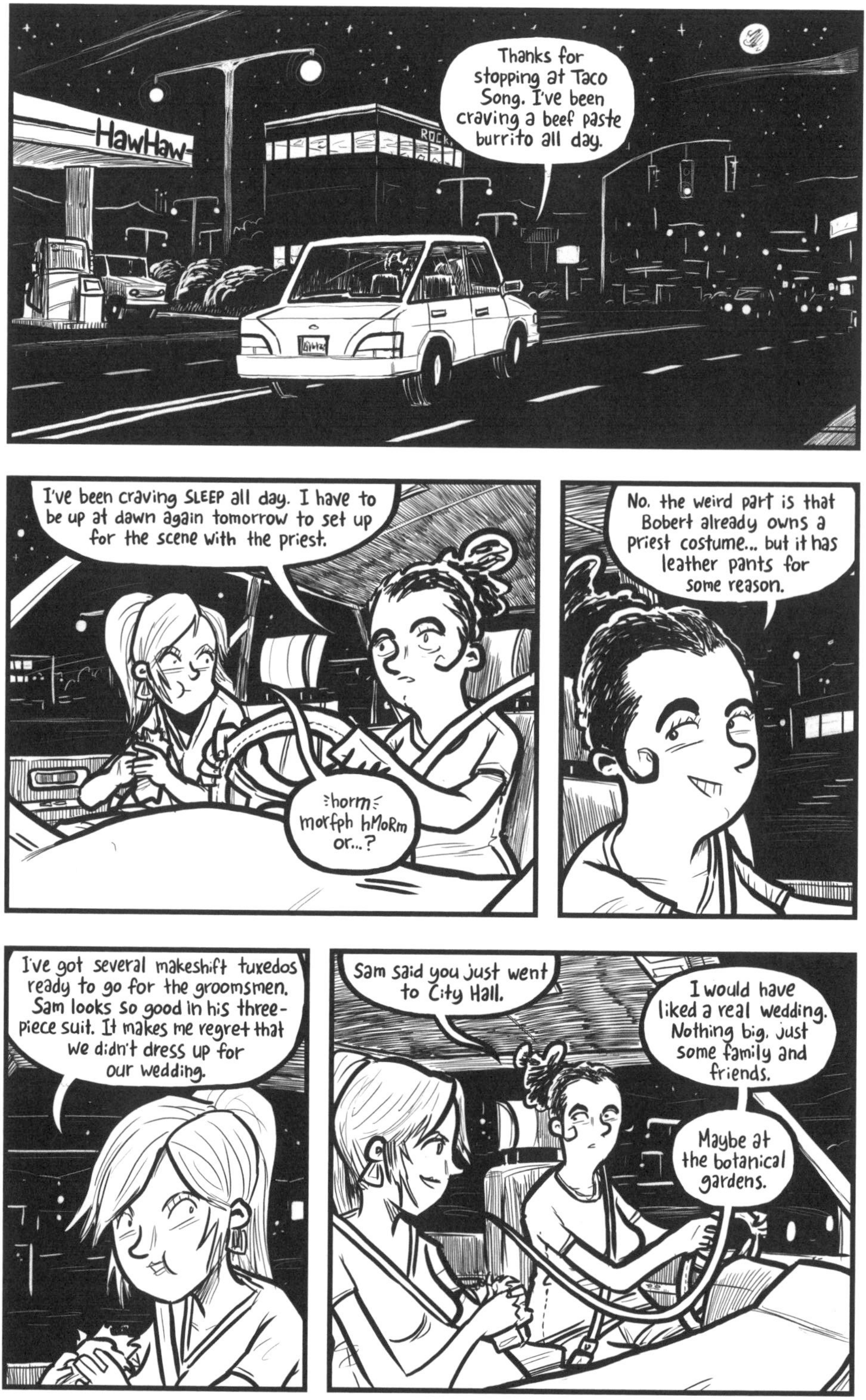

HawHaw
Thanks for stopping at Taco Song. I've been craving a beef paste burrito all day.
I've been craving SLEEP all day. I have to be up at dawn again tomorrow to set up for the scene with the priest.
horm morfph hMoRm or...?
No, the weird part is that Bobert already owns a priest costume... but it has leather pants for some reason.
I've got several makeshift tuxedos ready to go for the groomsmen. Sam looks so good in his three-piece suit. It makes me regret that we didn't dress up for our wedding.
Sam said you just went to City Hall.
I would have liked a real wedding. Nothing big, just some family and friends.
Maybe at the botanical gardens.

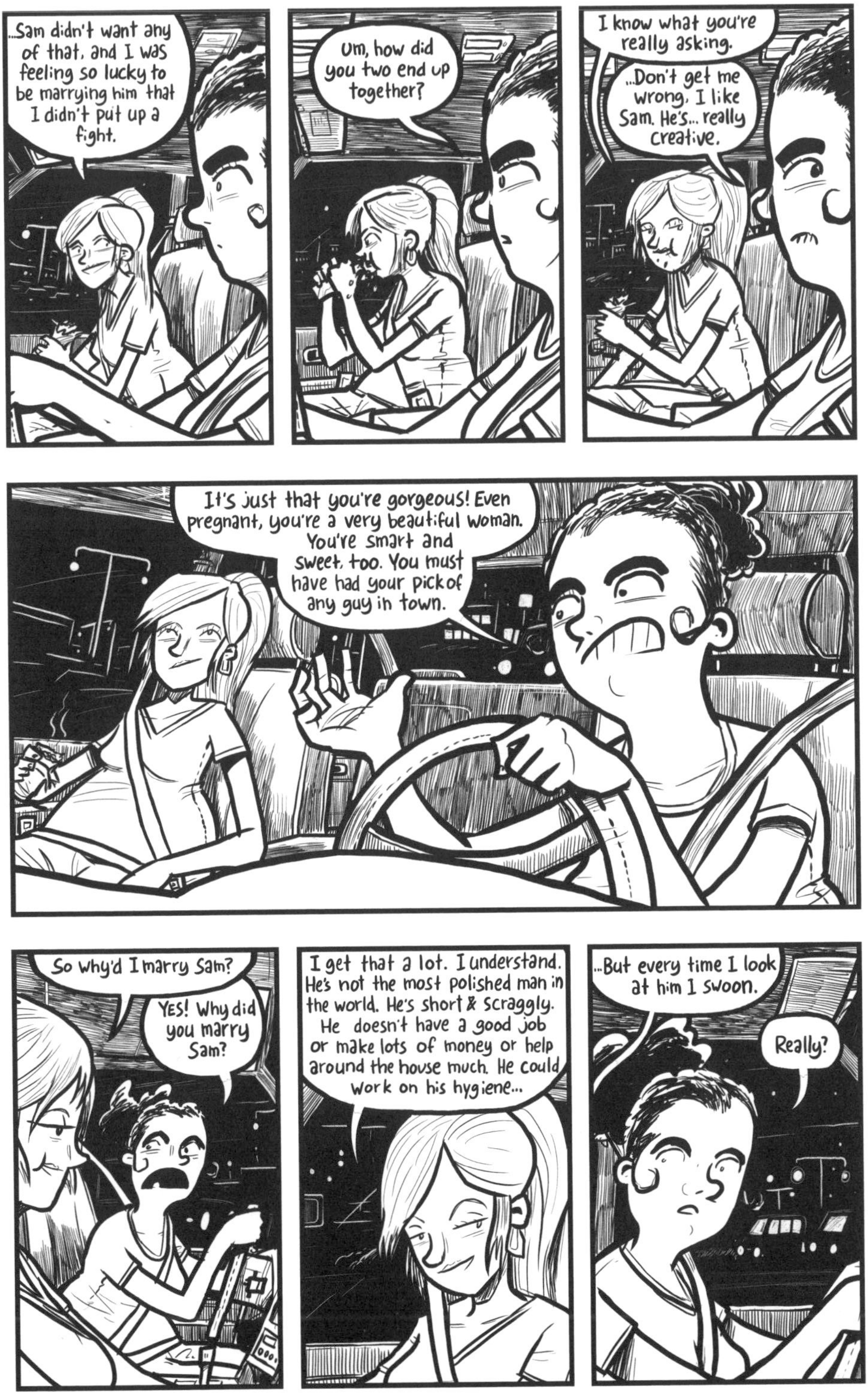
...Sam didn't want any of that, and I was feeling so lucky to be marrying him that I didn't put up a fight.
Um, how did you two end up together?
I know what you're really asking.
...Don't get me wrong, I like Sam. He's... really creative.
It's just that you're gorgeous! Even pregnant, you're a very beautiful woman. You're smart and sweet, too. You must have had your pick of any guy in town.
So why'd I marry Sam?
YES! Why did you marry Sam?
I get that a lot. I understand. He's not the most polished man in the world. He's short & scraggly. He doesn't have a good job or make lots of money or help around the house much. He could work on his hygiene...
...But every time I look at him I swoon.
Really?

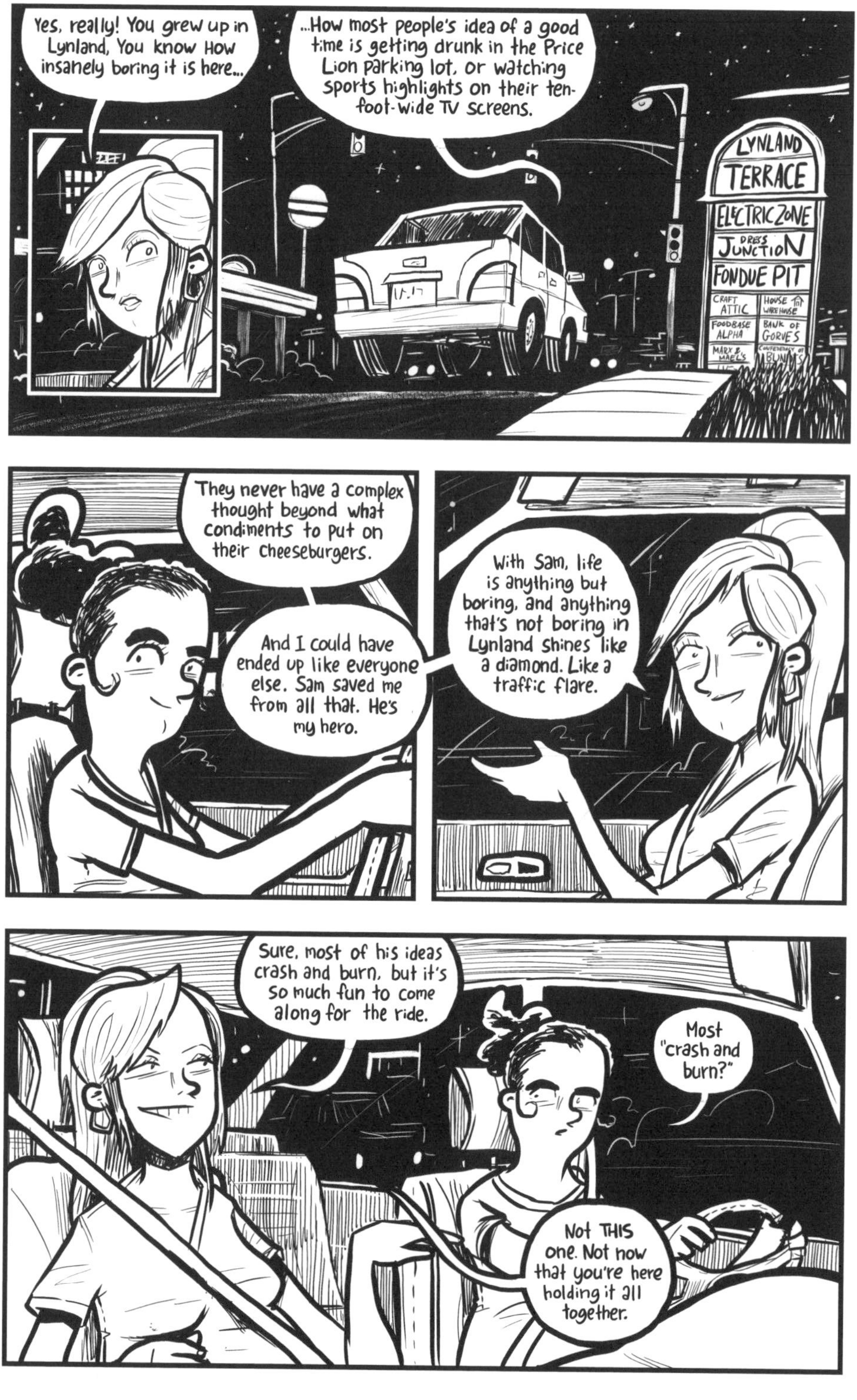
Yes, really! You grew up in Lynland, You know How insanely boring it is here...
...How most people's idea of a good time is getting drunk in the Price Lion parking lot, or watching sports highlights on their ten-foot-wide TV screens.
LYNLAND
TERRACE
ELECTRIC ZONE
DRESS JUNCTION
FONDUE PIT
CRAFT ATTIC
HOUSE WAREHOUSE
FOODBASE ALPHA
BANK OF GORVES
They never have a complex thought beyond what condiments to put on their cheeseburgers.
And I could have ended up like everyone else. Sam saved me from all that. He's my hero.
With Sam, life is anything but boring, and anything that's not boring in Lynland shines like a diamond. Like a traffic flare.
Sure, most of his ideas crash and burn, but it's so much fun to come along for the ride.
Most "crash and burn?"
Not THIS one. Not now that you're here holding it all together.

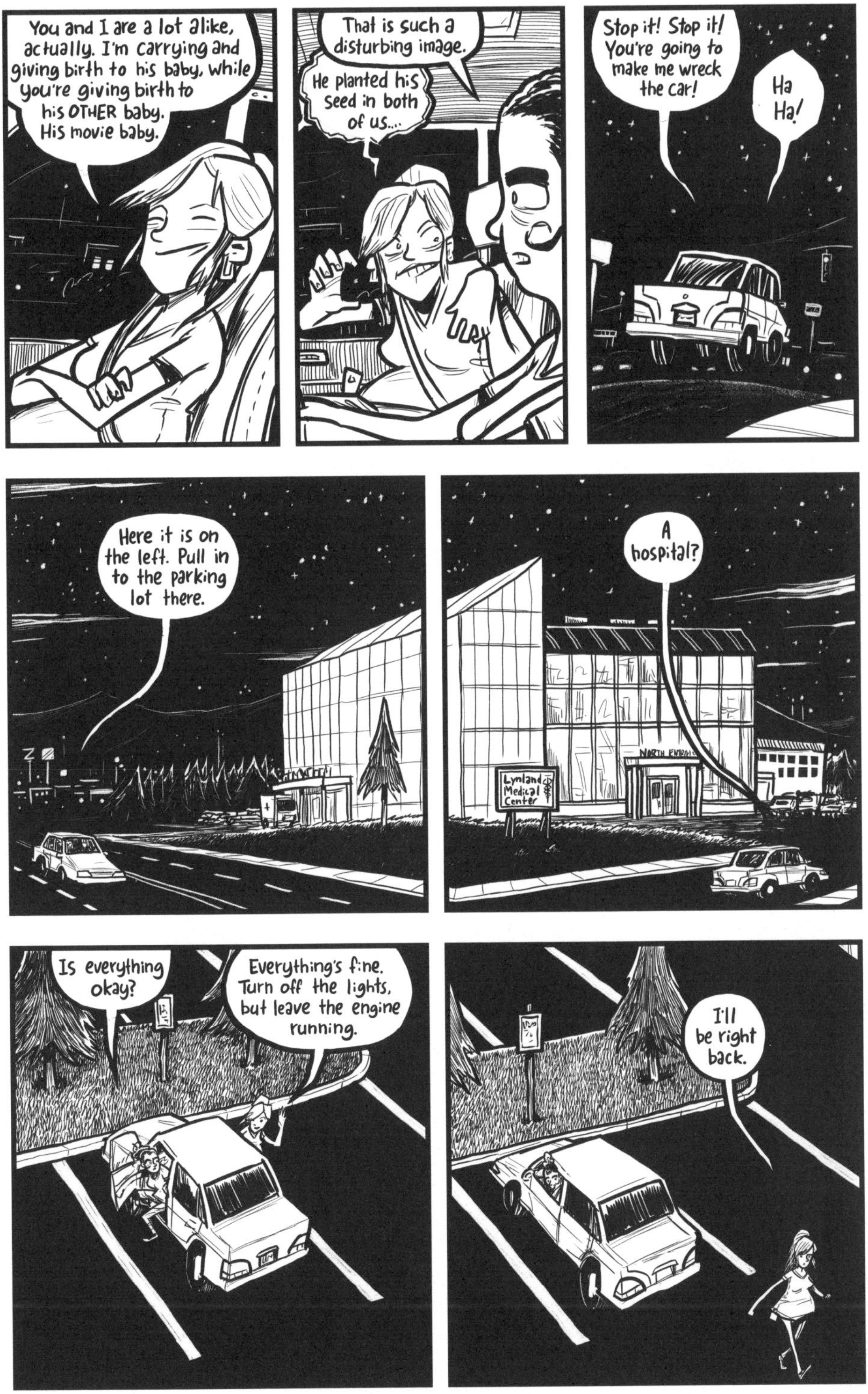
You and I are a lot alike, actually. I'm carrying and giving birth to his baby, while you're giving birth to his OTHER baby. His movie baby.
That is such a disturbing image.
He planted his seed in both of us...
Stop it! Stop it! You're going to make me wreck the car!
Ha Ha!
Here it is on the left. Pull in to the parking lot there.
A hospital?
Lynland Medical Center
Is everything okay?
Everything's fine. Turn off the lights, but leave the engine running.
I'll be right back.

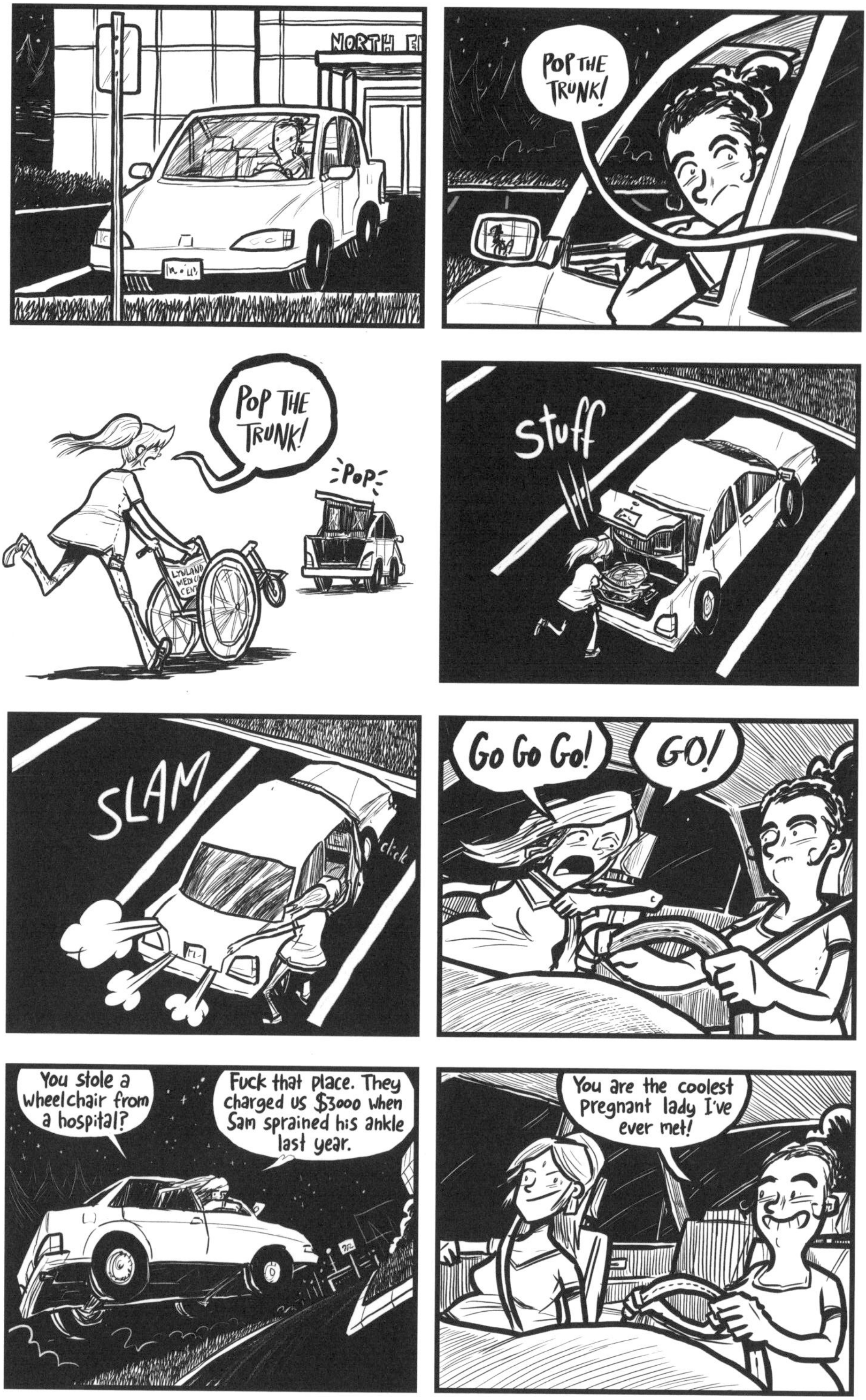
NORTH
POP THE TRUNK!
POP THE TRUNK!
POP
Stuff
SLAM
click
Go Go Go!
GO!
You stole a wheelchair from a hospital?
Fuck that place. They charged us $3000 when Sam sprained his ankle last year.
You are the coolest pregnant lady I've ever met!

CHAPTER FIVE

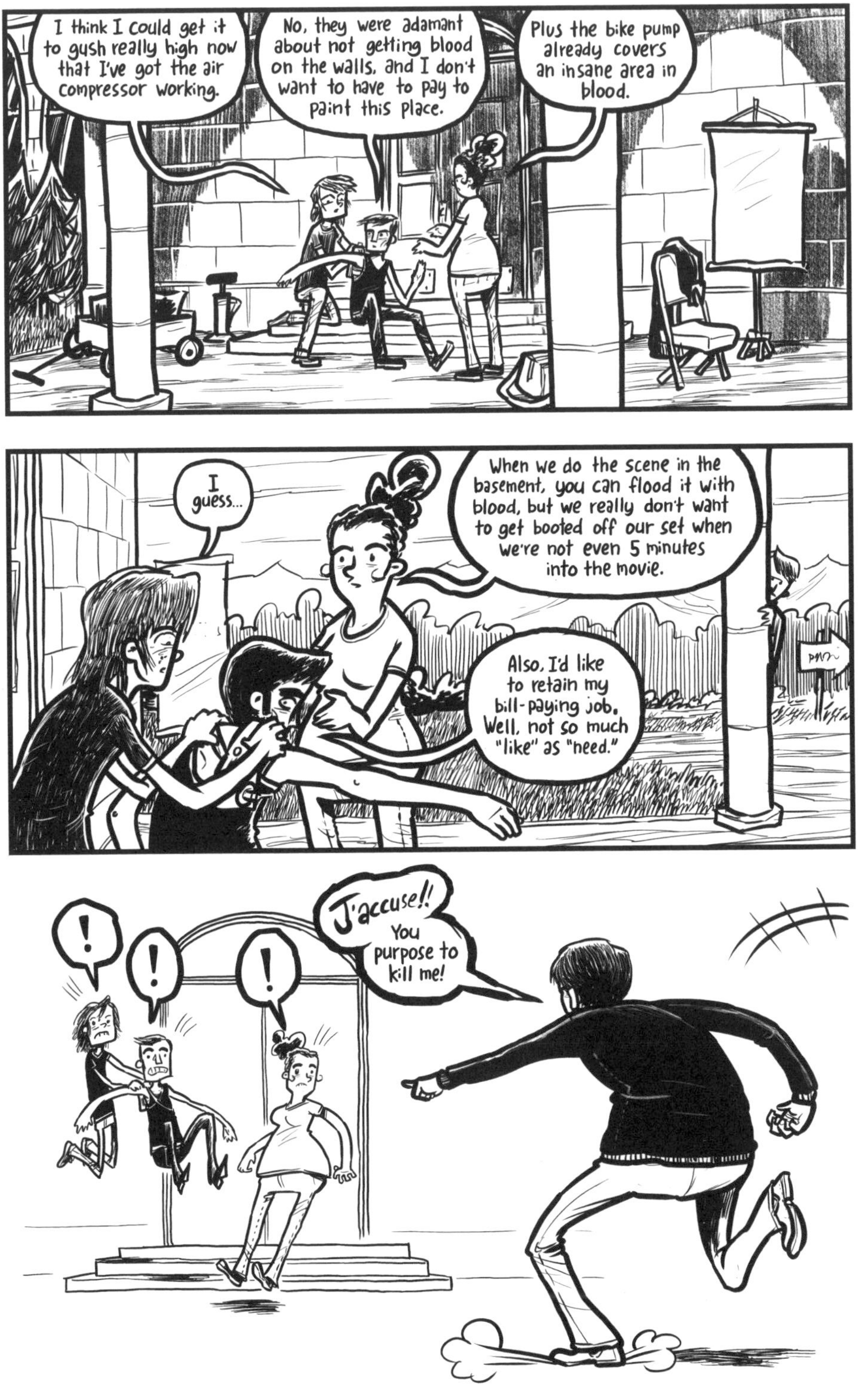
I think I could get it to gush really high now that I've got the air compressor working.
No, they were adamant about not getting blood on the walls, and I don't want to have to pay to paint this place.
Plus the bike pump already covers an insane area in blood.
I guess...
When we do the scene in the basement, you can flood it with blood, but we really don't want to get booted off our set when we're not even 5 minutes into the movie.
Also, I'd like to retain my bill-paying job. Well, not so much "like" as "need."
!
!
!
J'accuse!! You purpose to kill me!

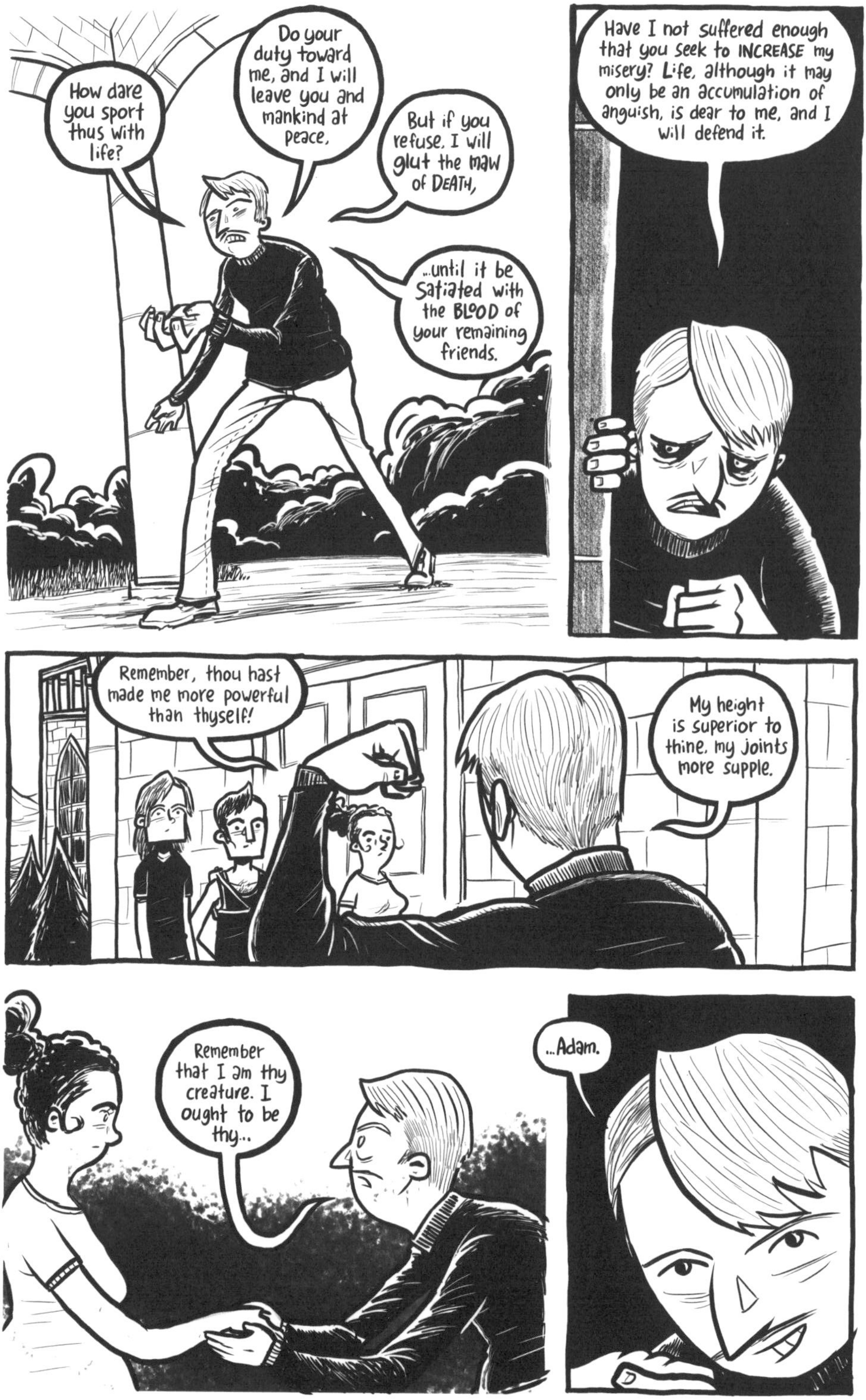
How dare you sport thus with life?
Do your duty toward me, and I will leave you and mankind at peace.
But if you refuse, I will glut the maw of DEATH,
...until it be satiated with the BLOOD of your remaining friends.
Have I not suffered enough that you seek to INCREASE my misery? Life, although it may only be an accumulation of anguish, is dear to me, and I will defend it.
Remember, thou hast made me more powerful than thyself!
My height is superior to thine, my joints more supple.
Remember that I am thy creature. I ought to be thy...
...Adam.

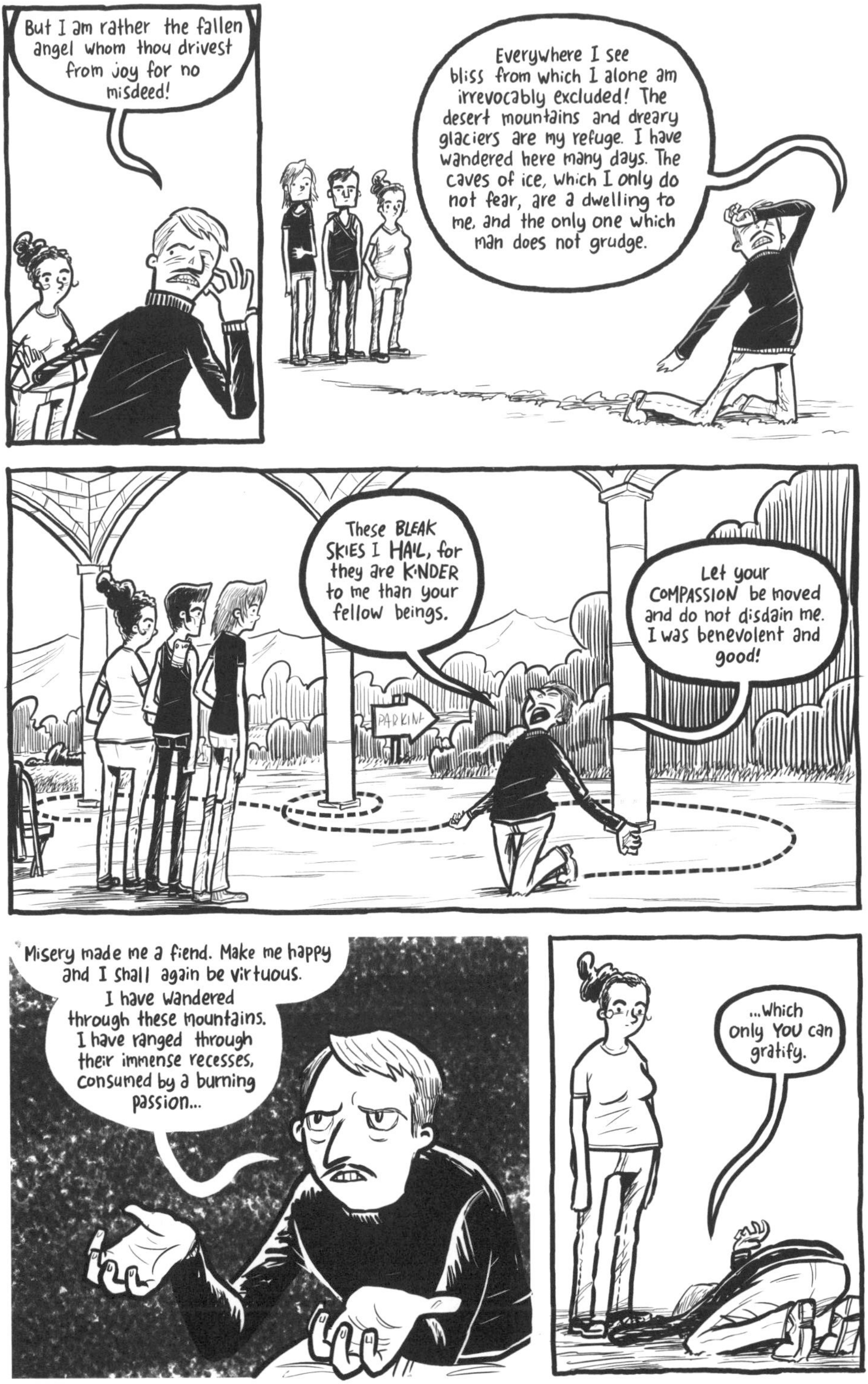
But I am rather the fallen angel whom thou drivest from joy for no misdeed!
Everywhere I see bliss from which I alone am irrevocably excluded! The desert mountains and dreary glaciers are my refuge. I have wandered here many days. The caves of ice, which I only do not fear, are a dwelling to me, and the only one which man does not grudge.
These BLEAK SKIES I HAIL, for they are KINDER to me than your fellow beings.
Let your COMPASSION be moved and do not disdain me. I was benevolent and good!
PARKING
Misery made me a fiend. Make me happy and I shall again be virtuous.
I have wandered through these mountains. I have ranged through their immense recesses, consumed by a burning passion...
...Which only YOU can gratify.

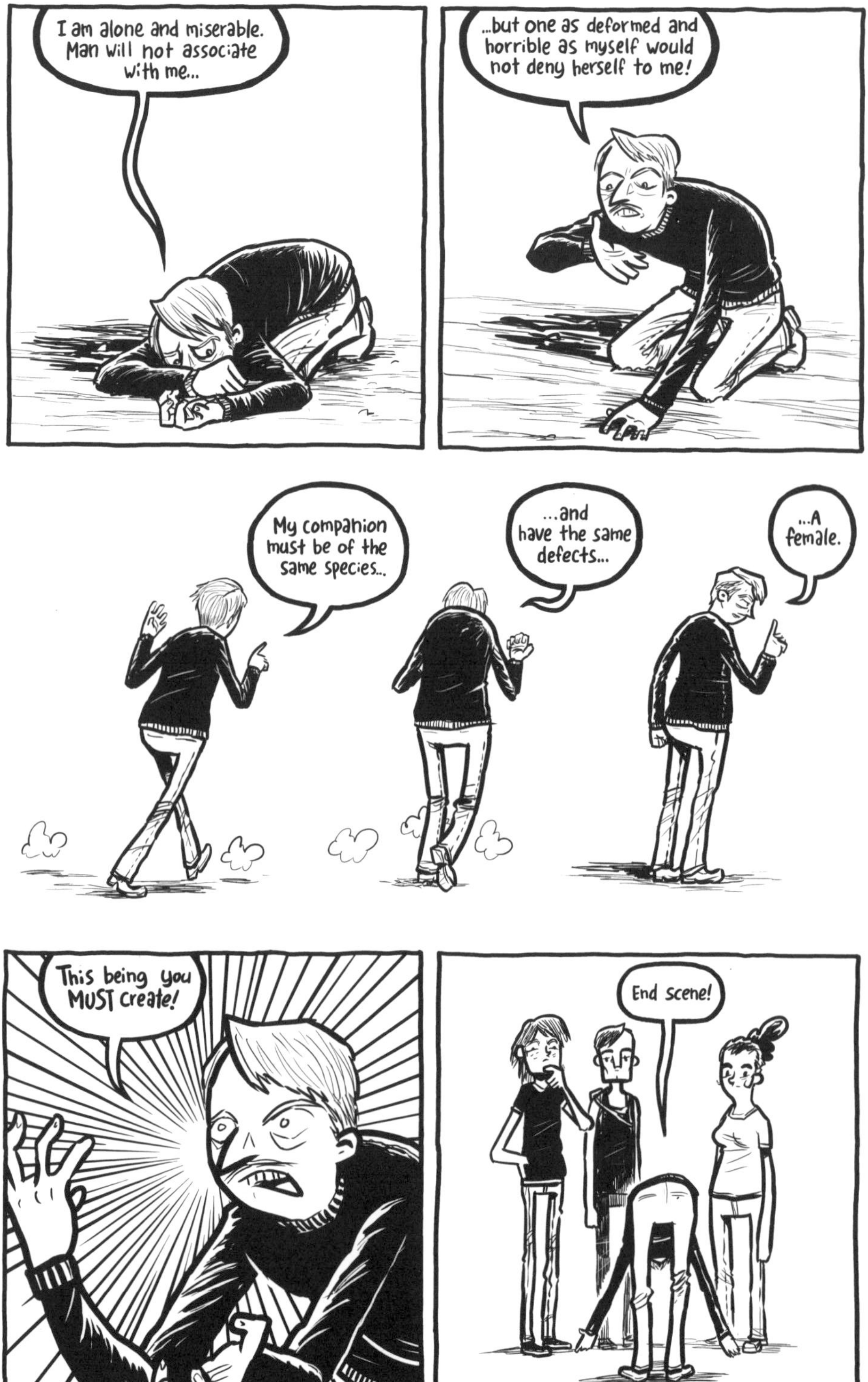
I am alone and miserable. Man will not associate with me...
...but one as deformed and horrible as myself would not deny herself to me!
My companion must be of the same species...
...and have the same defects...
...A female.
This being you MUST create!
End scene!

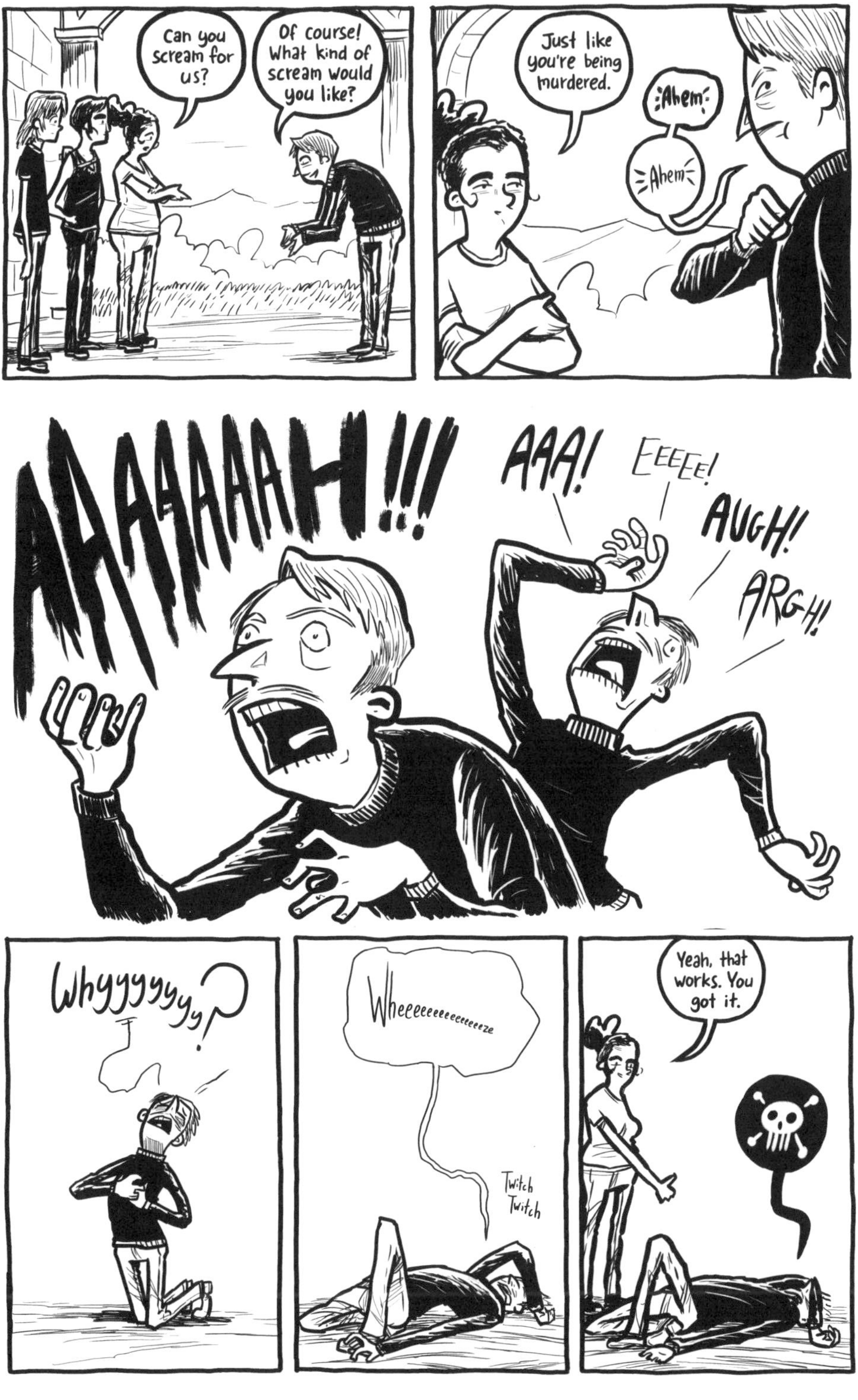
Can you scream for us?
Of course! What kind of scream would you like?
Just like you're being murdered.
Ahem
Ahem
AAAAAAH!!!
AAA!
EEEEE!
AUGH!
ARGH!
Whyyyyyy?
Wheeeeeeeeeeeeeeze
Twitch Twitch
Yeah, that works. You got it.

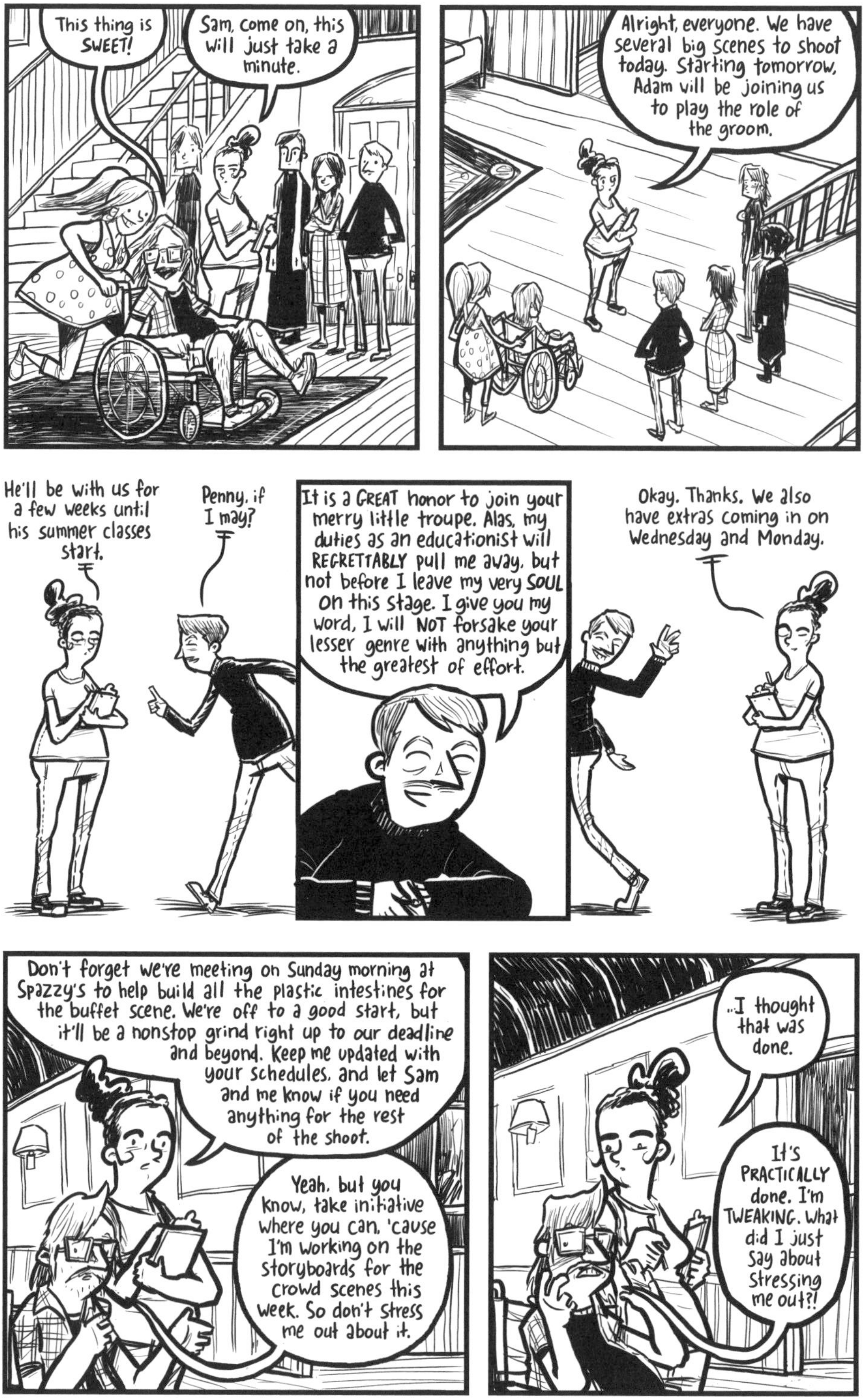
This thing is SWEET!
Sam, come on, this will just take a minute.
Alright, everyone. We have several big scenes to shoot today. Starting tomorrow, Adam will be joining us to play the role of the groom.
He'll be with us for a few weeks until his summer classes start.
Penny, if I may?
It is a GREAT honor to join your merry little troupe. Alas, my duties as an educationist will REGRETTABLY pull me away, but not before I leave my very SOUL on this stage. I give you my word, I will NOT forsake your lesser genre with anything but the greatest of effort.
Okay. Thanks. We also have extras coming in on Wednesday and Monday.
Don't forget we're meeting on Sunday morning at Spazzy's to help build all the plastic intestines for the buffet scene. We're off to a good start, but it'll be a nonstop grind right up to our deadline and beyond. Keep me updated with your schedules, and let Sam and me know if you need anything for the rest of the shoot.
Yeah, but you know, take initiative where you can, 'cause I'm working on the storyboards for the crowd scenes this week. So don't stress me out about it.
...I thought that was done.
It's PRACTICALLY done. I'm TWEAKING. What did I just say about stressing me out?!

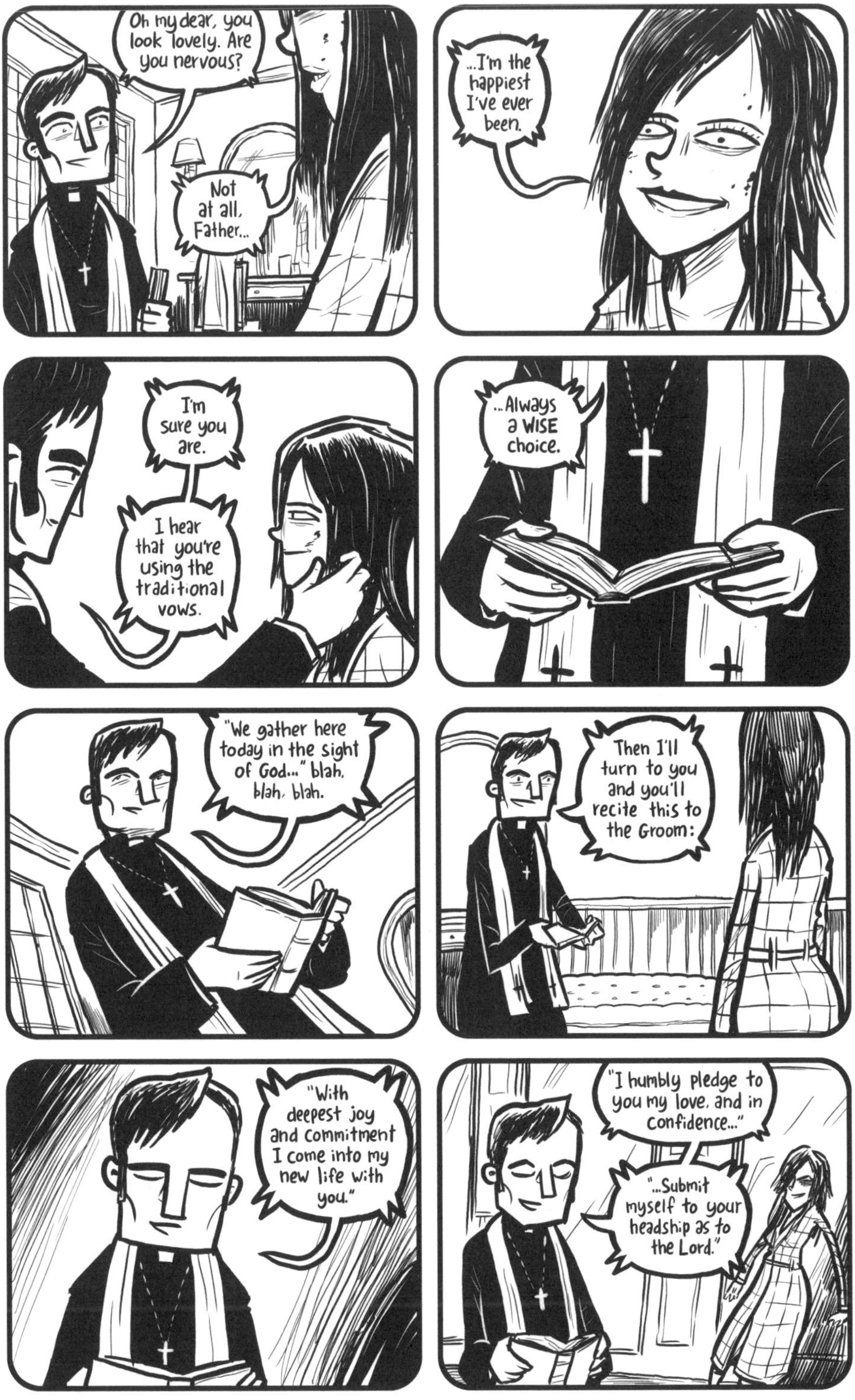
Oh my dear, you look lovely. Are you nervous?
Not at all, Father...
...I'm the happiest I've ever been.
I'm sure you are.
I hear that you're using the traditional vows.
...Always a WISE choice.
"We gather here today in the sight of God..." blah, blah, blah.
Then I'll turn to you and you'll recite this to the Groom:
"With deepest joy and commitment I come into my new life with you."
"I humbly pledge to you my love, and in confidence..."
"...Submit myself to your headship as to the Lord."

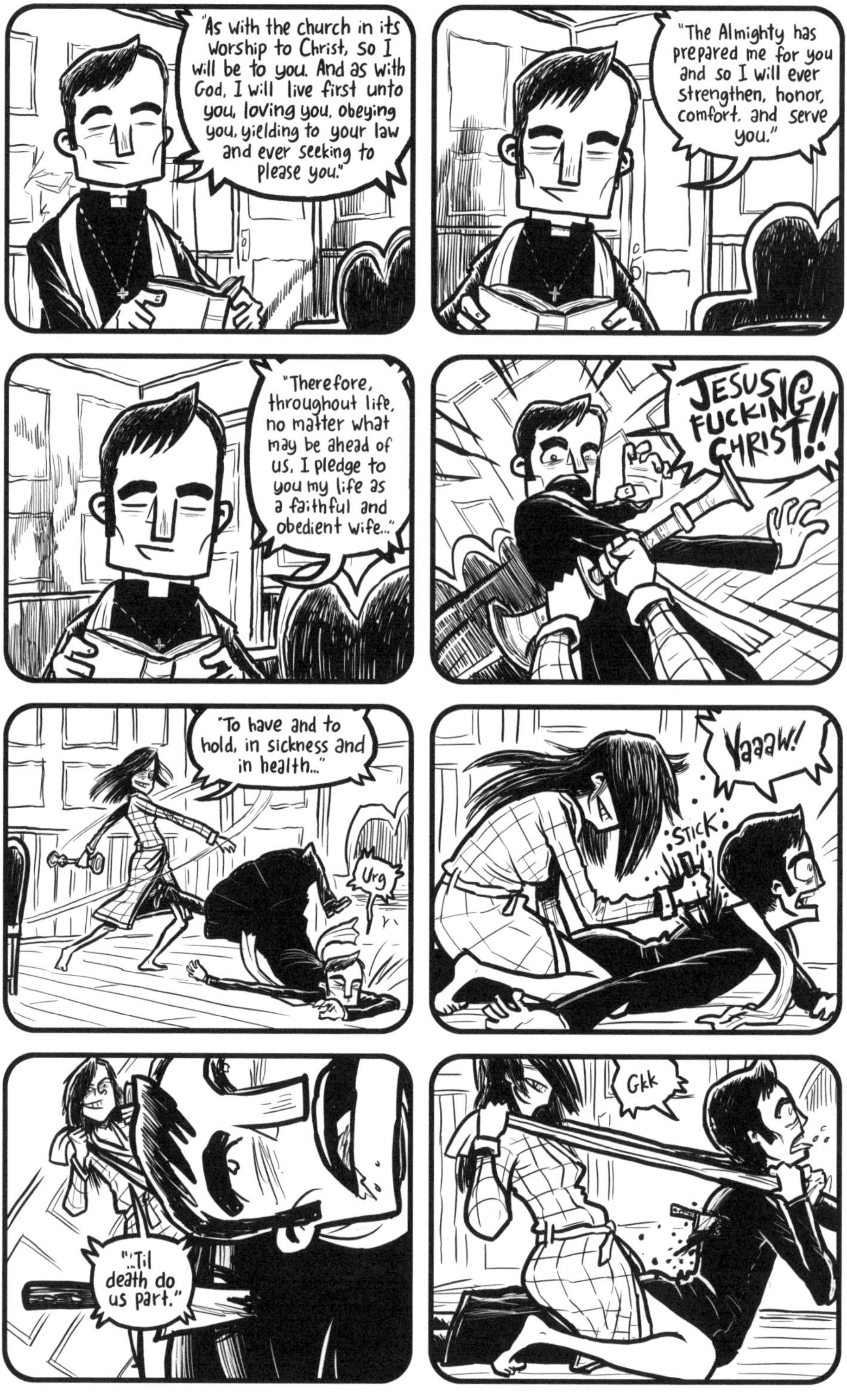
"As with the church in its worship to Christ, so I will be to you. And as with God, I will live first unto you, loving you, obeying you, yielding to your law and ever seeking to please you."
"The Almighty has prepared me for you and so I will ever strengthen, honor, comfort, and serve you."
"Therefore, throughout life, no matter what may be ahead of us, I pledge to you my life as a faithful and obedient wife..."
JESUS FUCKING CHRIST!!
"To have and to hold, in sickness and in health..."
Urg
Yaaaw!
STICK
"...Til death do us part."
Gkk

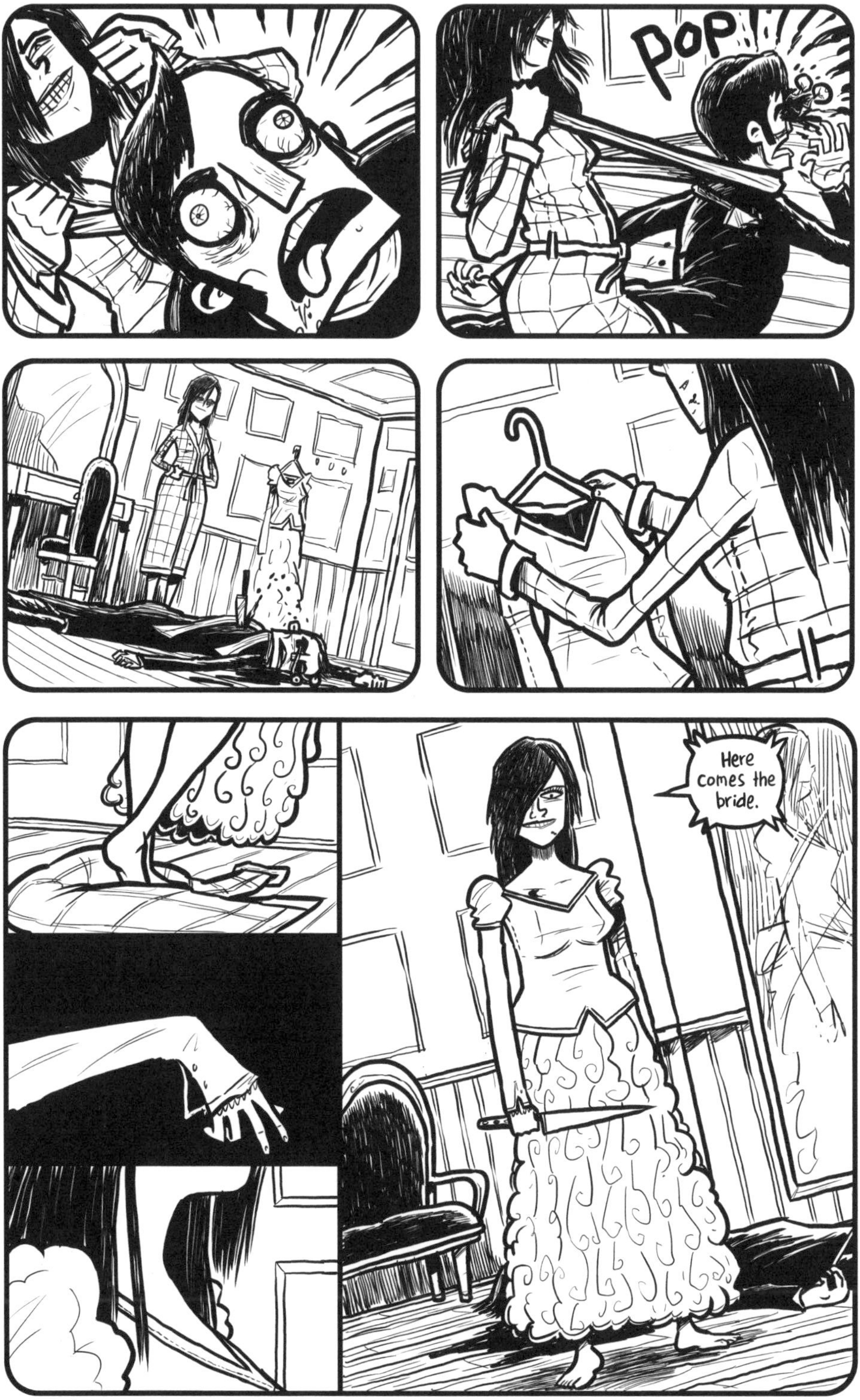
POP
Here comes the bride.

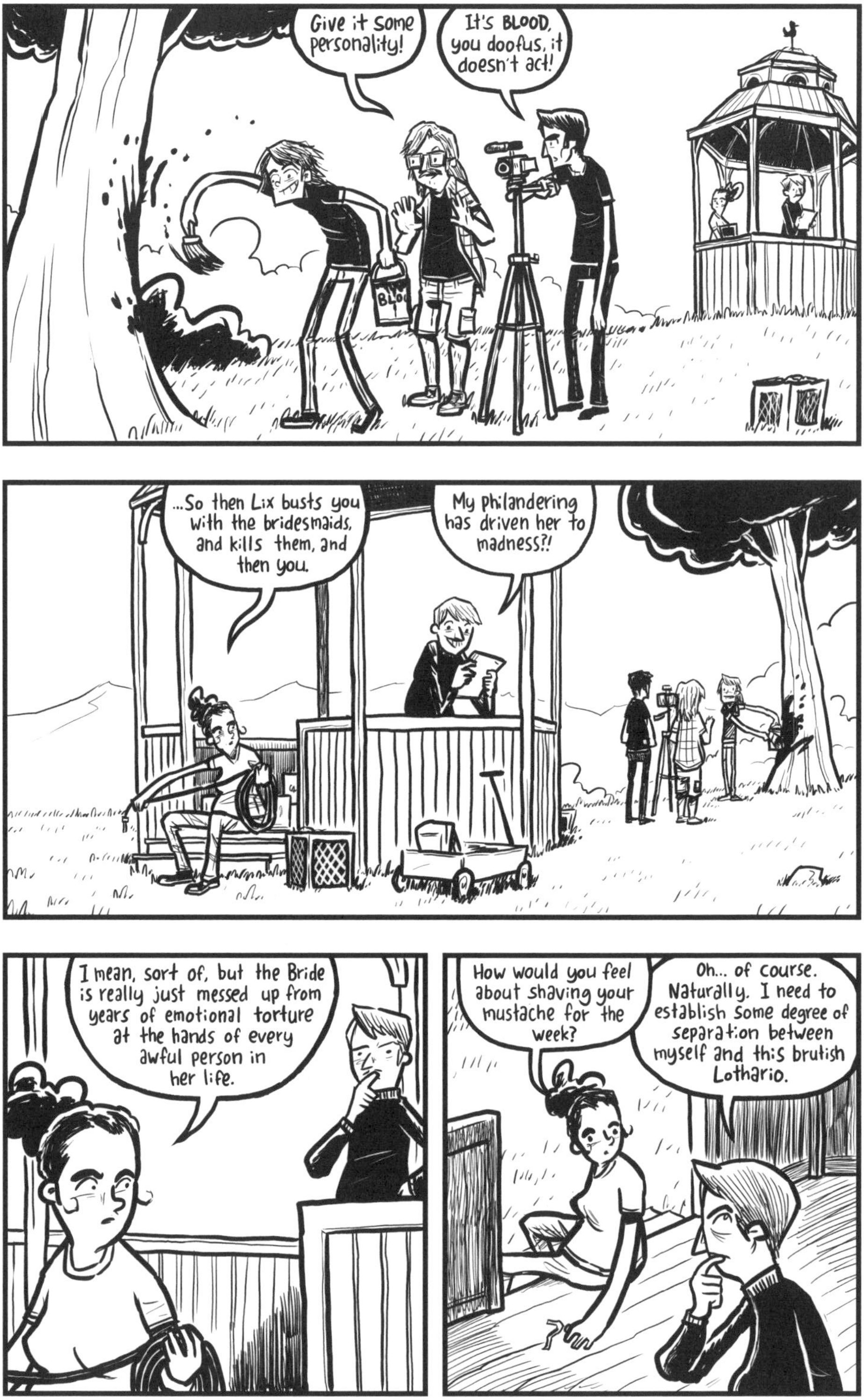
Give it some personality!
It's BLOOD, you doofus, it doesn't act!
BLOO
...So then Lix busts you with the bridesmaids, and kills them, and then you.
My philandering has driven her to madness?!
I mean, sort of, but the Bride is really just messed up from years of emotional torture at the hands of every awful person in her life.
How would you feel about shaving your mustache for the week?
Oh... of course. Naturally. I need to establish some degree of separation between myself and this brutish Lothario.

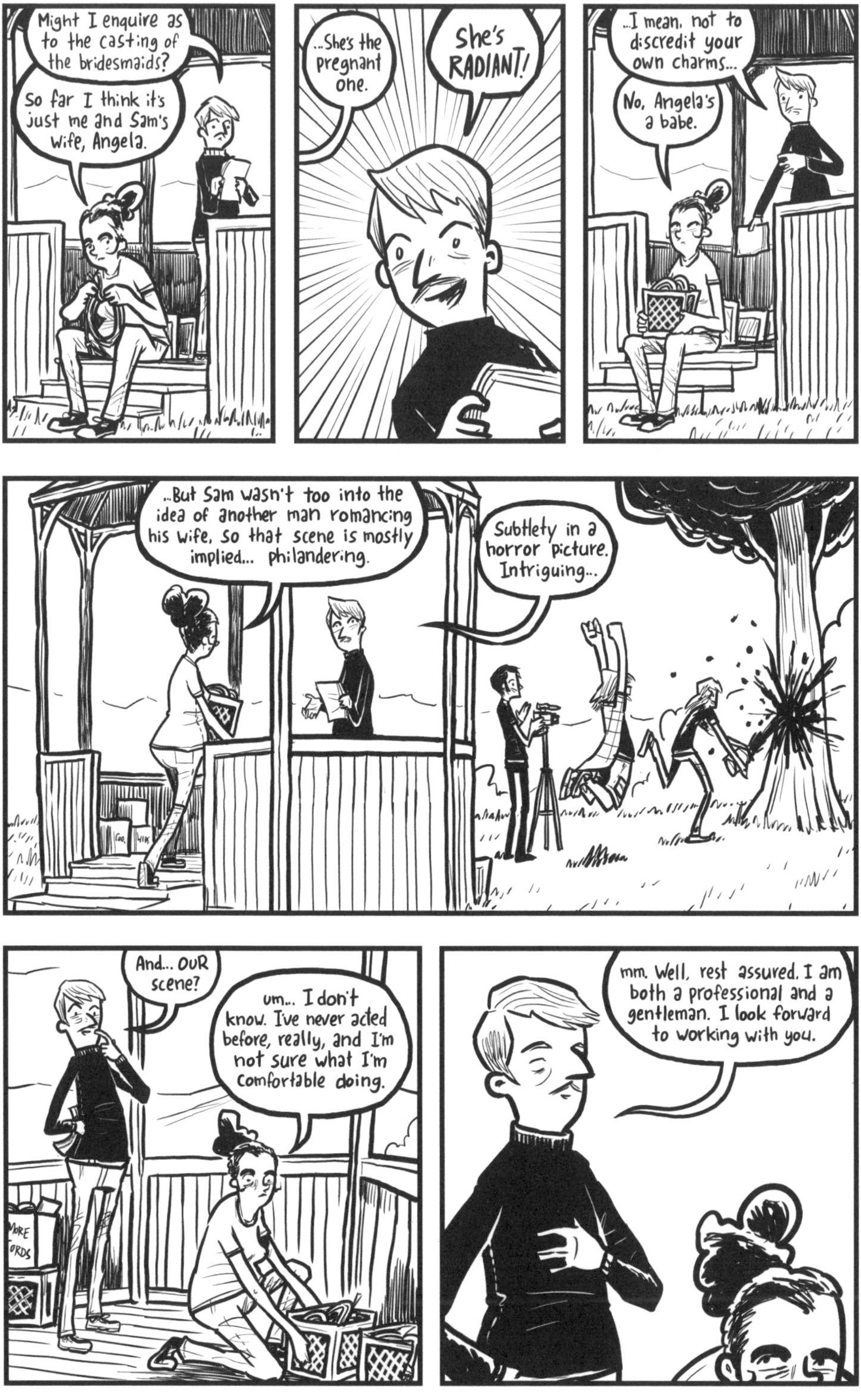
Might I enquire as to the casting of the bridesmaids?
So far I think it's just me and Sam's wife, Angela.
...She's the pregnant one.
She's RADIANT!
...I mean, not to discredit your own charms...
No, Angela's a babe.
..But Sam wasn't too into the idea of another man romancing his wife, so that scene is mostly implied... philandering.
Subtlety in a horror picture. Intriguing...
Angela
And... OUR scene?
um... I don't know. I've never acted before, really, and I'm not sure what I'm comfortable doing.
mm. Well, rest assured. I am both a professional and a gentleman. I look forward to working with you.

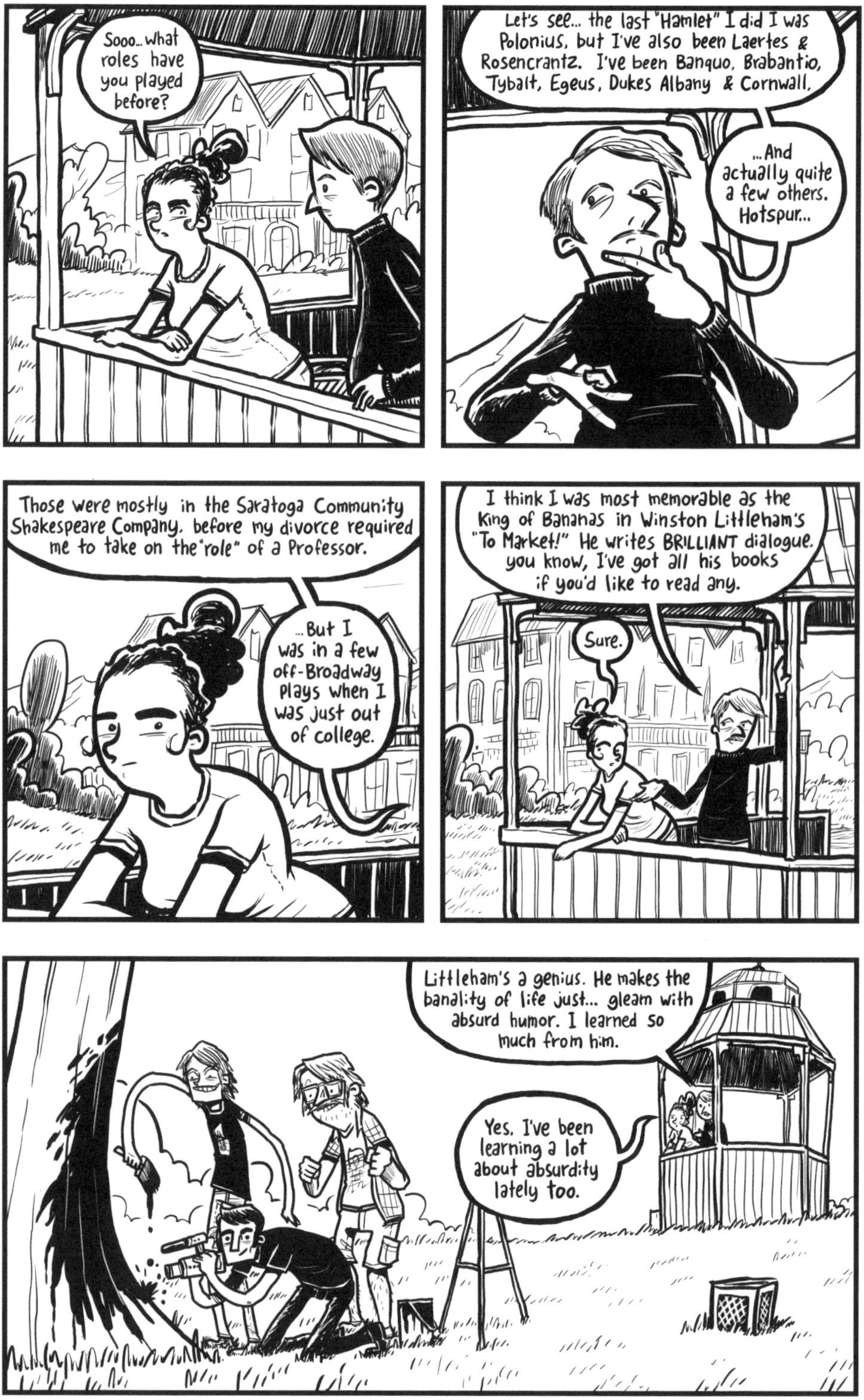
Sooo... what roles have you played before?
Let's see... the last "Hamlet" I did I was Polonius, but I've also been Laertes & Rosencrantz. I've been Banquo, Brabantio, Tybalt, Egeus, Dukes Albany & Cornwall,
...And actually quite a few others. Hotspur...
Those were mostly in the Saratoga Community Shakespeare Company, before my divorce required me to take on the "role" of a Professor.
...But I was in a few off-Broadway plays when I was just out of college.
I think I was most memorable as the King of Bananas in Winston Littleham's "To Market!" He writes BRILLIANT dialogue, you know, I've got all his books if you'd like to read any.
Sure.
Littleham's a genius. He makes the banality of life just... gleam with absurd humor. I learned so much from him.
Yes. I've been learning a lot about absurdity lately too.

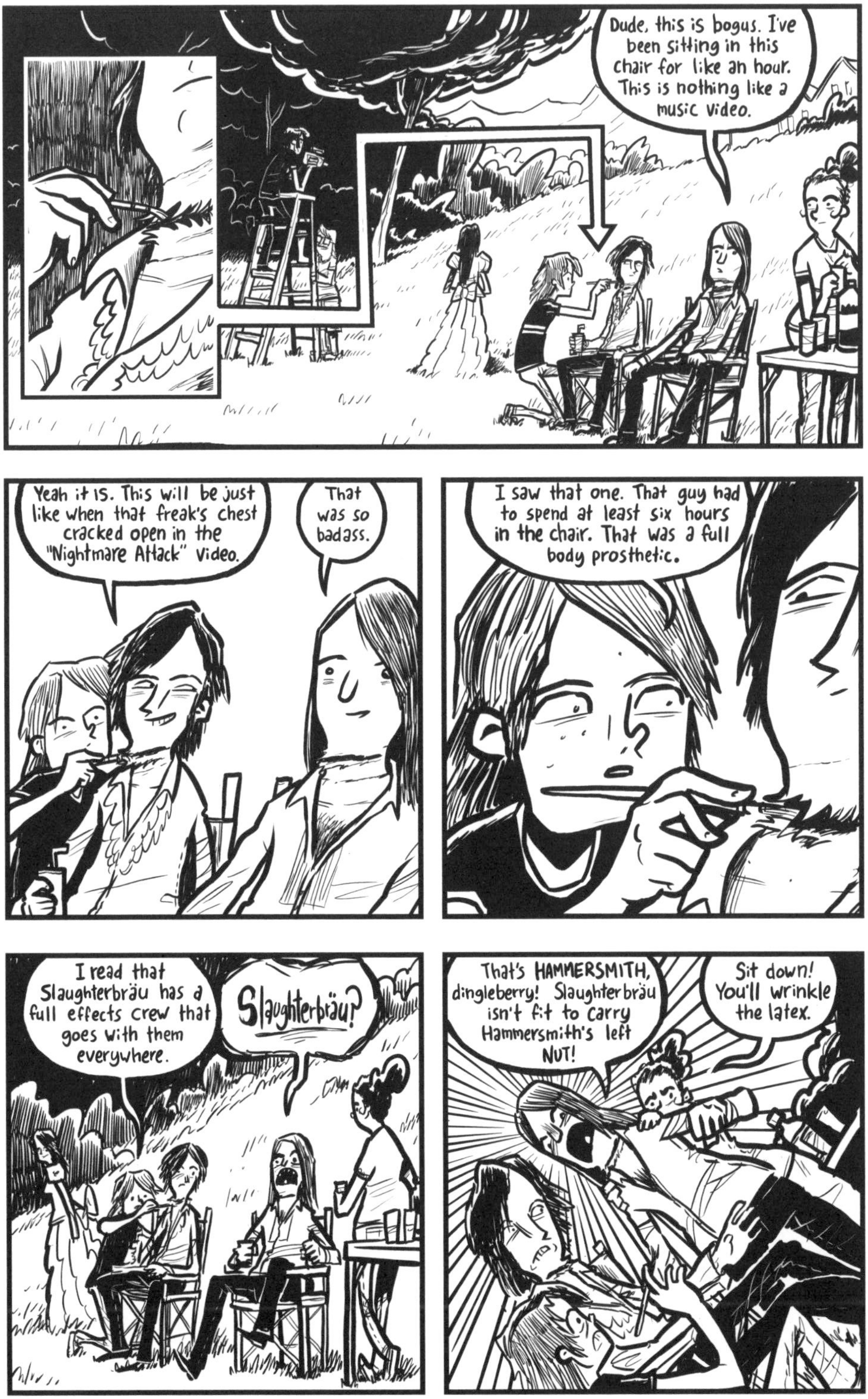
Dude, this is bogus. I've been sitting in this chair for like an hour. This is nothing like a music video.
Yeah it IS. This will be just like when that freak's chest cracked open in the "Nightmare Attack" video.
That was so badass.
I saw that one. That guy had to spend at least six hours in the chair. That was a full body prosthetic.
I read that Slaughterbräu has a full effects crew that goes with them everywhere.
Slaughterbräu?
That's HAMMERSMITH, dingleberry! Slaughterbräu isn't fit to carry Hammersmith's left NUT!
Sit down! You'll wrinkle the latex.

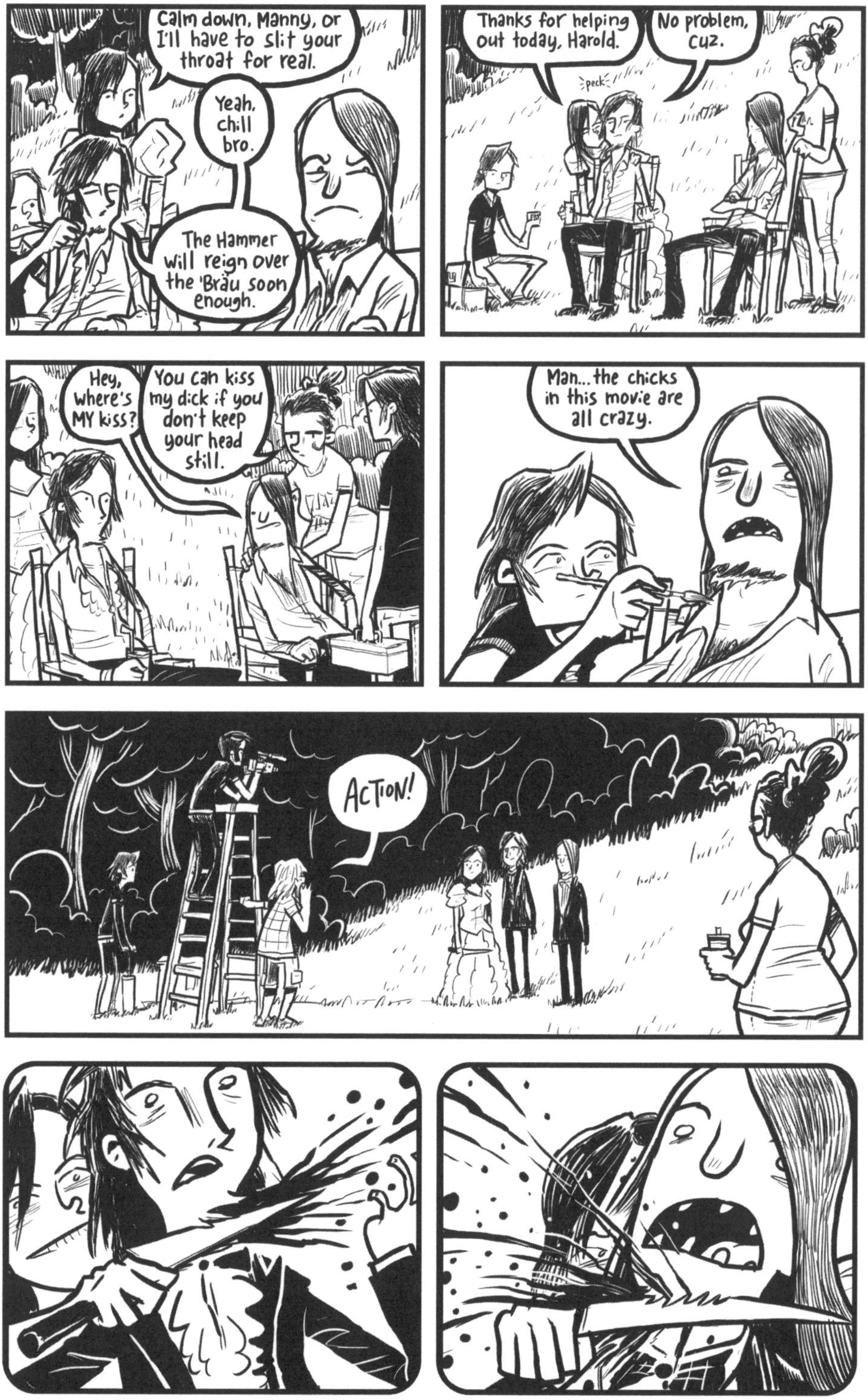
Calm down, Manny, or I'll have to slit your throat for real.
Yeah, chill bro.
The Hammer will reign over the 'Bräu soon enough.
Thanks for helping out today, Harold.
peck
No problem, cuz.
Hey, where's MY kiss?
You can kiss my dick if you don't keep your head still.
Man... the chicks in this movie are all crazy.
ACTION!

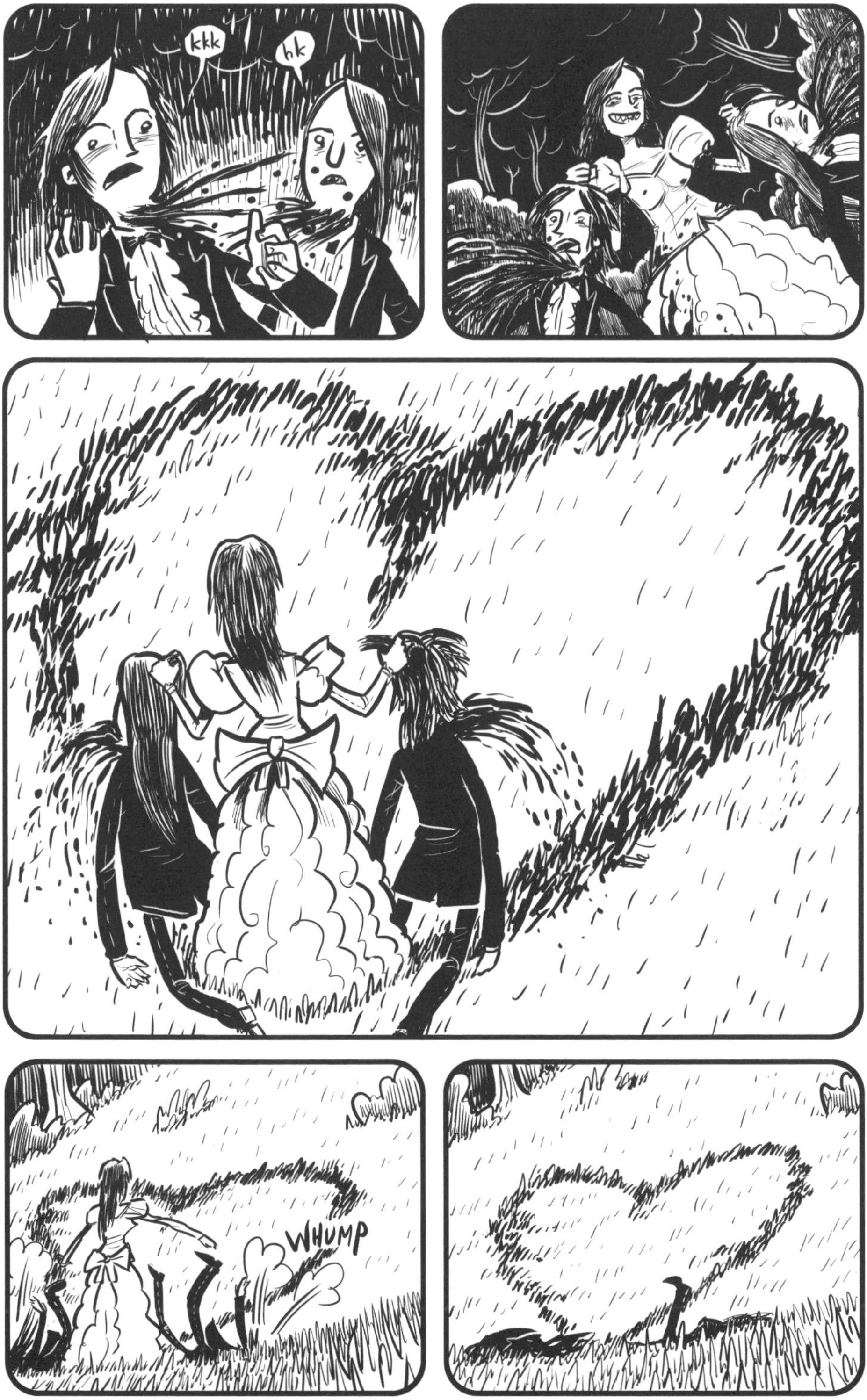
kkk
hk
WHUMP

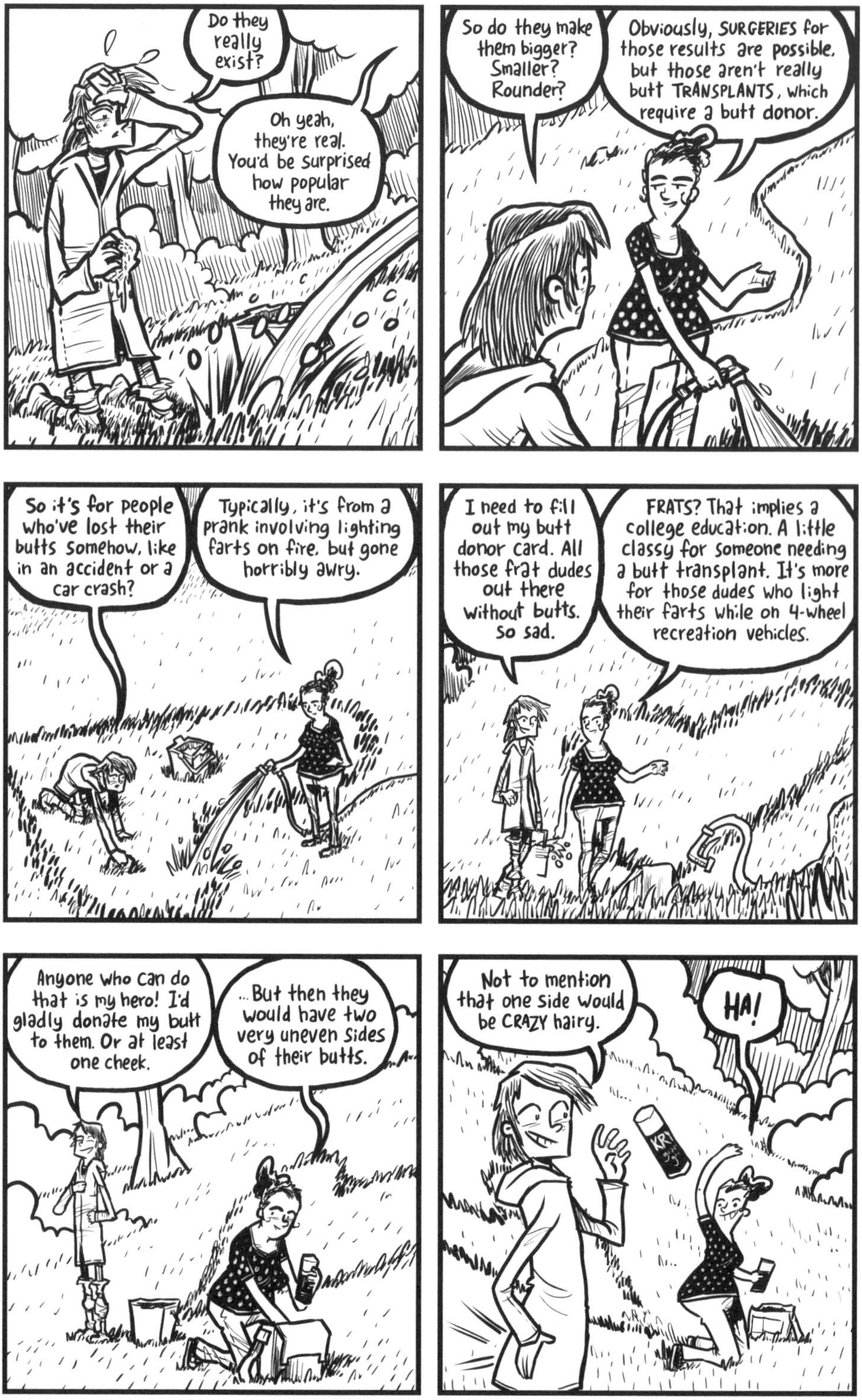
Do they really exist?
Oh yeah, they're real. You'd be surprised how popular they are.
So do they make them bigger? Smaller? Rounder?
Obviously, SURGERIES for those results are possible, but those aren't really butt TRANSPLANTS, which require a butt donor.
So it's for people who've lost their butts somehow, like in an accident or a car crash?
Typically, it's from a prank involving lighting farts on fire, but gone horribly awry.
I need to fill out my butt donor card. All those frat dudes out there without butts. So sad.
FRATS? That implies a college education. A little classy for someone needing a butt transplant. It's more for those dudes who light their farts while on 4-wheel recreation vehicles.
Anyone who can do that is my hero! I'd gladly donate my butt to them. Or at least one cheek.
...But then they would have two very uneven sides of their butts.
Not to mention that one side would be CRAZY hairy.
HA!

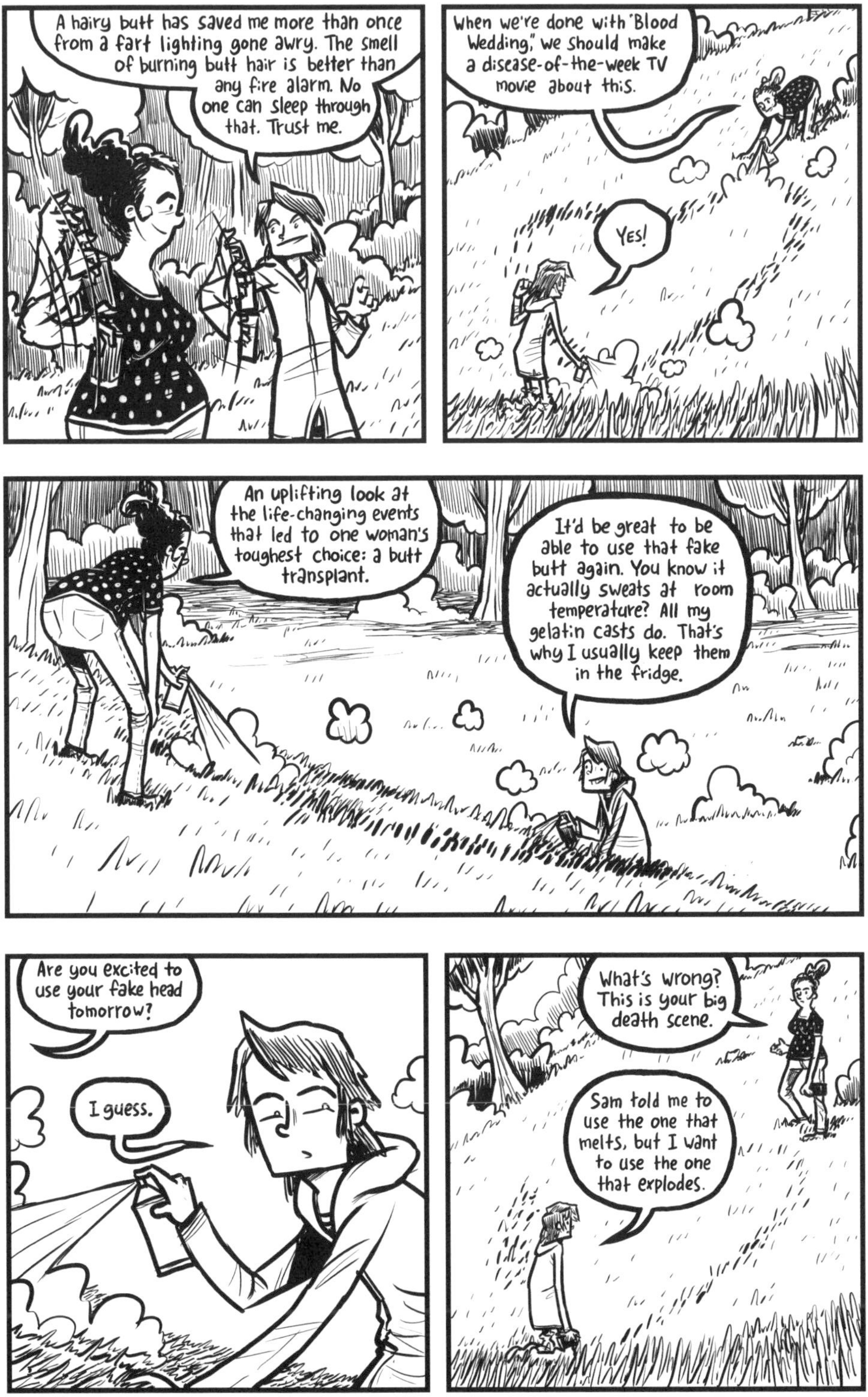
A hairy butt has saved me more than once from a fart lighting gone awry. The smell of burning butt hair is better than any fire alarm. No one can sleep through that. Trust me.
When we're done with "Blood Wedding," we should make a disease-of-the-week TV movie about this.
Yes!
An uplifting look at the life-changing events that led to one woman's toughest choice: a butt transplant.
It'd be great to be able to use that fake butt again. You know it actually sweats at room temperature? All my gelatin casts do. That's why I usually keep them in the fridge.
Are you excited to use your fake head tomorrow?
I guess.
What's wrong? This is your big death scene.
Sam told me to use the one that melts, but I want to use the one that explodes.

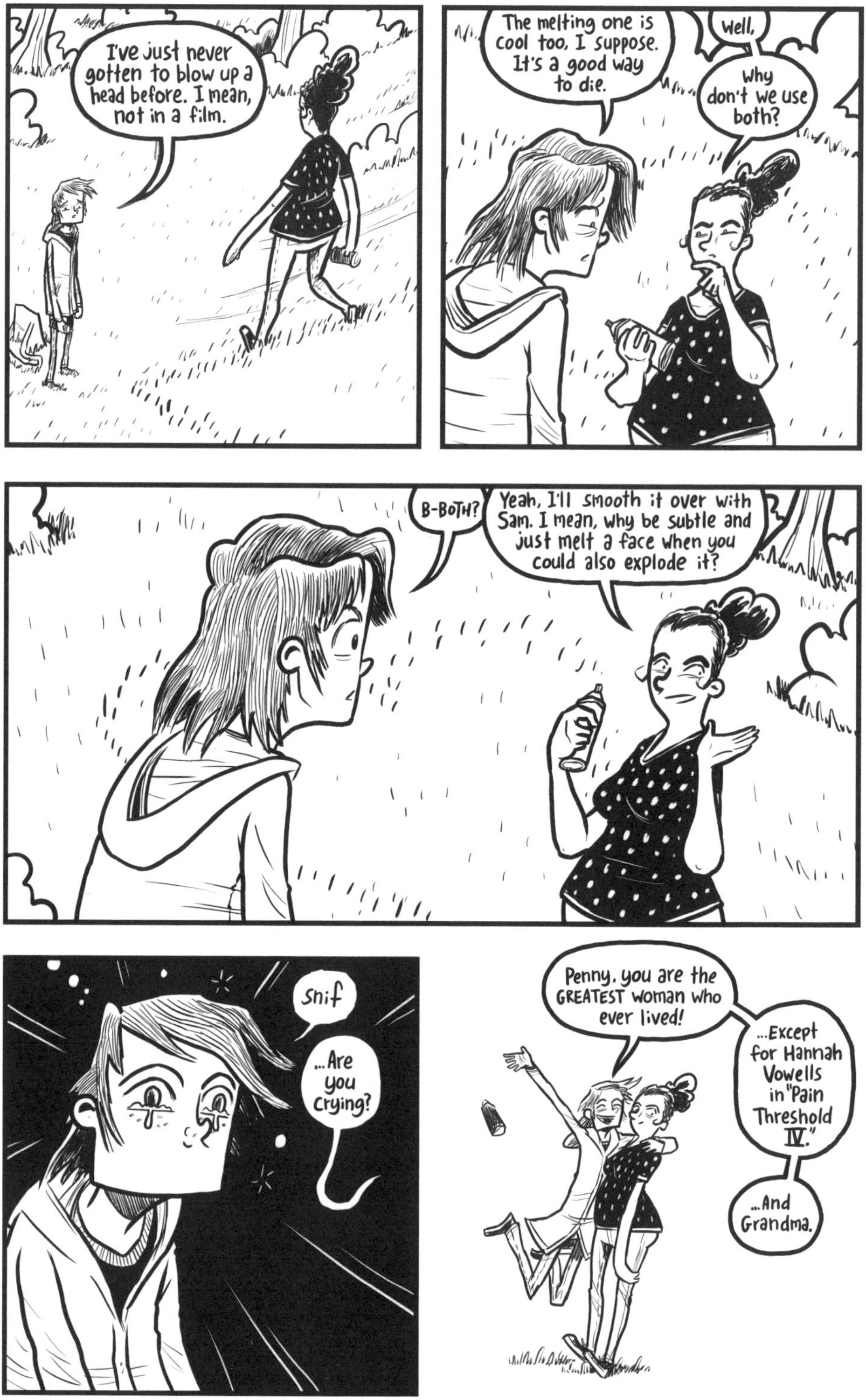
I've just never gotten to blow up a head before. I mean, not in a film.
The melting one is cool too, I suppose. It's a good way to die.
Well,
Why don't we use both?
B-BOTH?
Yeah, I'll smooth it over with Sam. I mean, why be subtle and just melt a face when you could also explode it?
snif
...Are you crying?
Penny, you are the GREATEST woman who ever lived!
...Except for Hannah Vowells in "Pain Threshold IV."
...And Grandma.

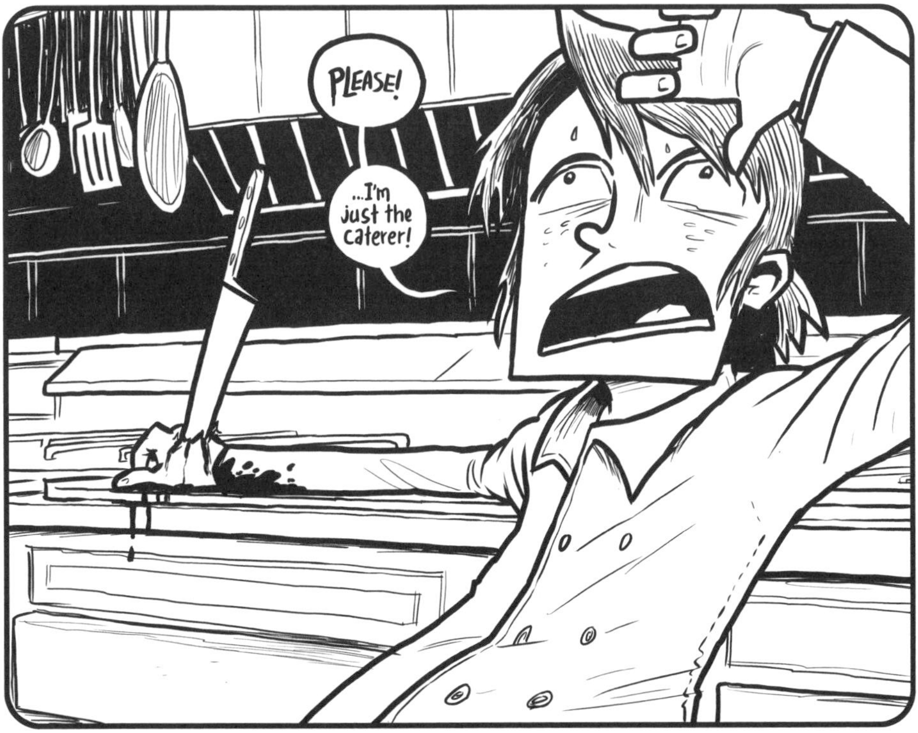
PLEASE!
...I'm just the caterer!

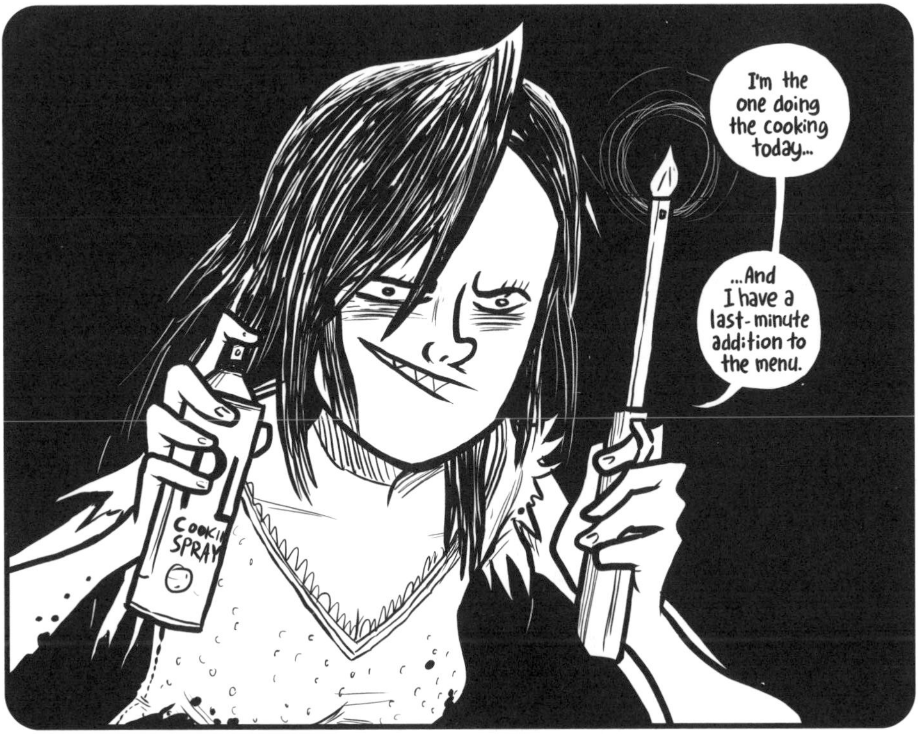
I'm the one doing the cooking today...
...And I have a last-minute addition to the menu.
COOKI
SPRAY

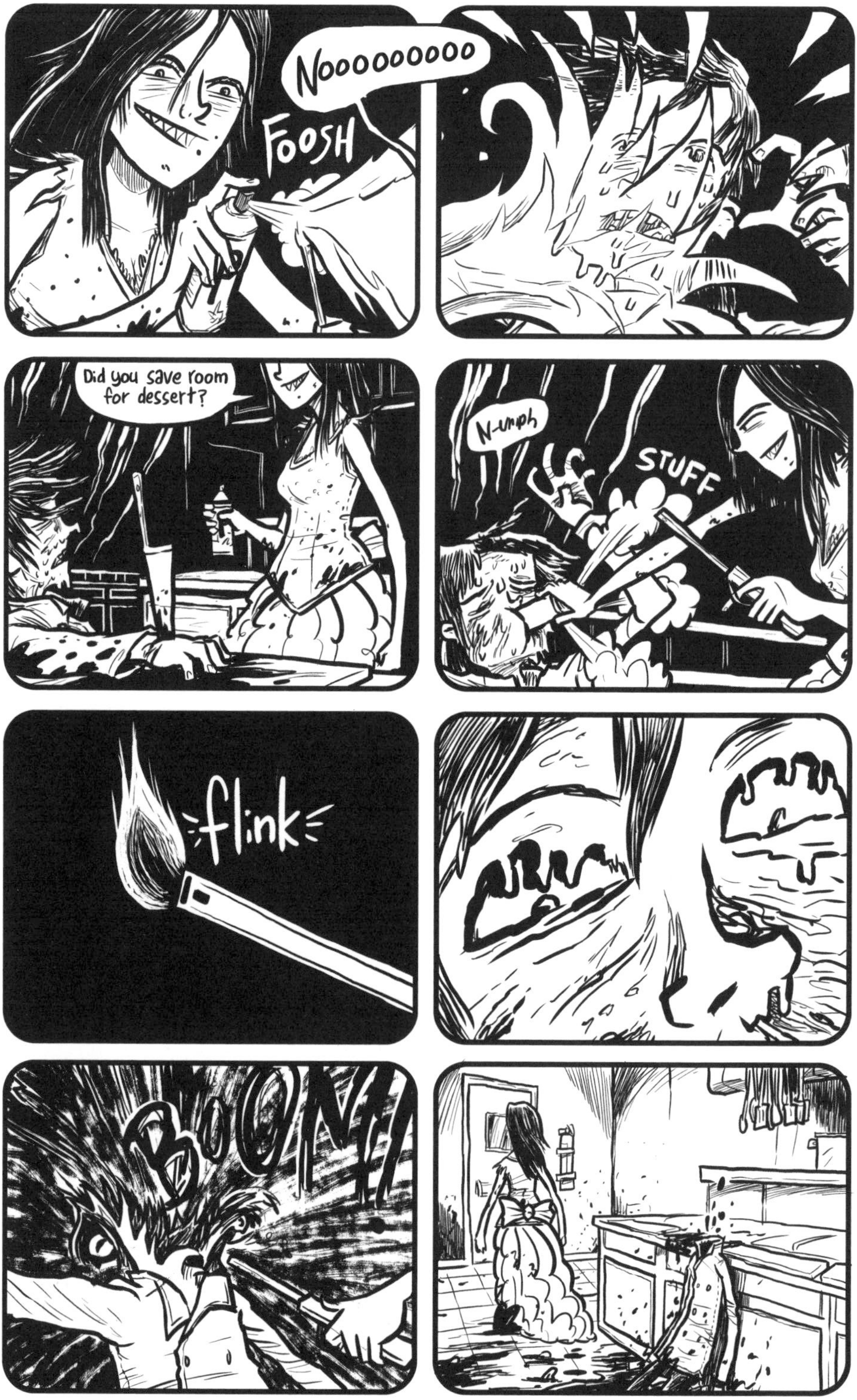
Nooooooooo
FOOSH
Did you save room for dessert?
N-umph
STUFF
flink
BOOM

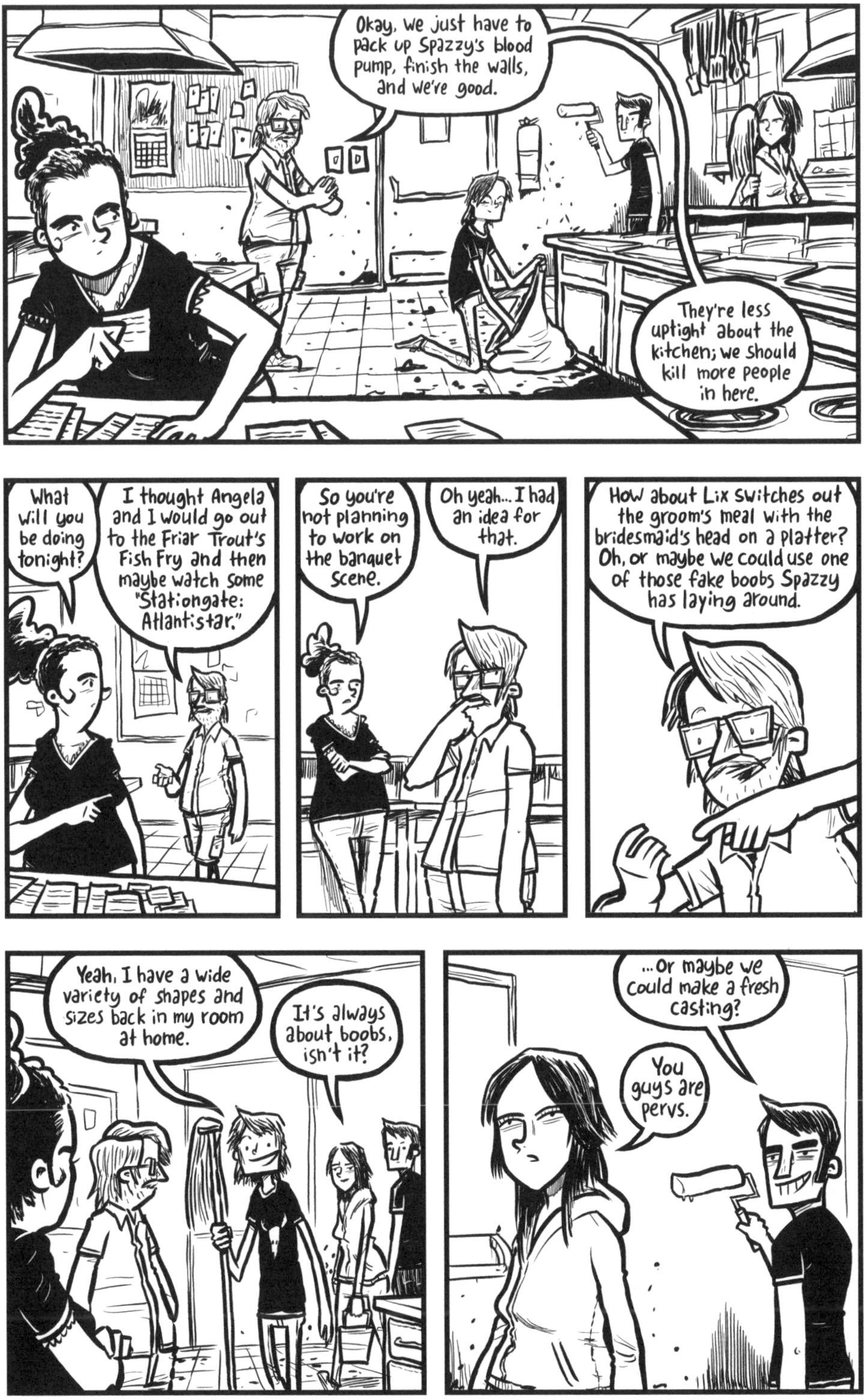
Okay, we just have to pack up Spazzy's blood pump, finish the walls, and we're good.
They're less uptight about the kitchen; we should kill more people in here.
What will you be doing tonight?
I thought Angela and I would go out to the Friar Trout's Fish Fry and then maybe watch some "Stationgate: Atlantistar."
So you're not planning to work on the banquet scene.
Oh yeah... I had an idea for that.
How about Lix switches out the groom's meal with the bridesmaid's head on a platter? Oh, or maybe we could use one of those fake boobs Spazzy has laying around.
Yeah, I have a wide variety of shapes and sizes back in my room at home.
It's always about boobs, isn't it?
...or maybe we could make a fresh casting?
You guys are pervs.

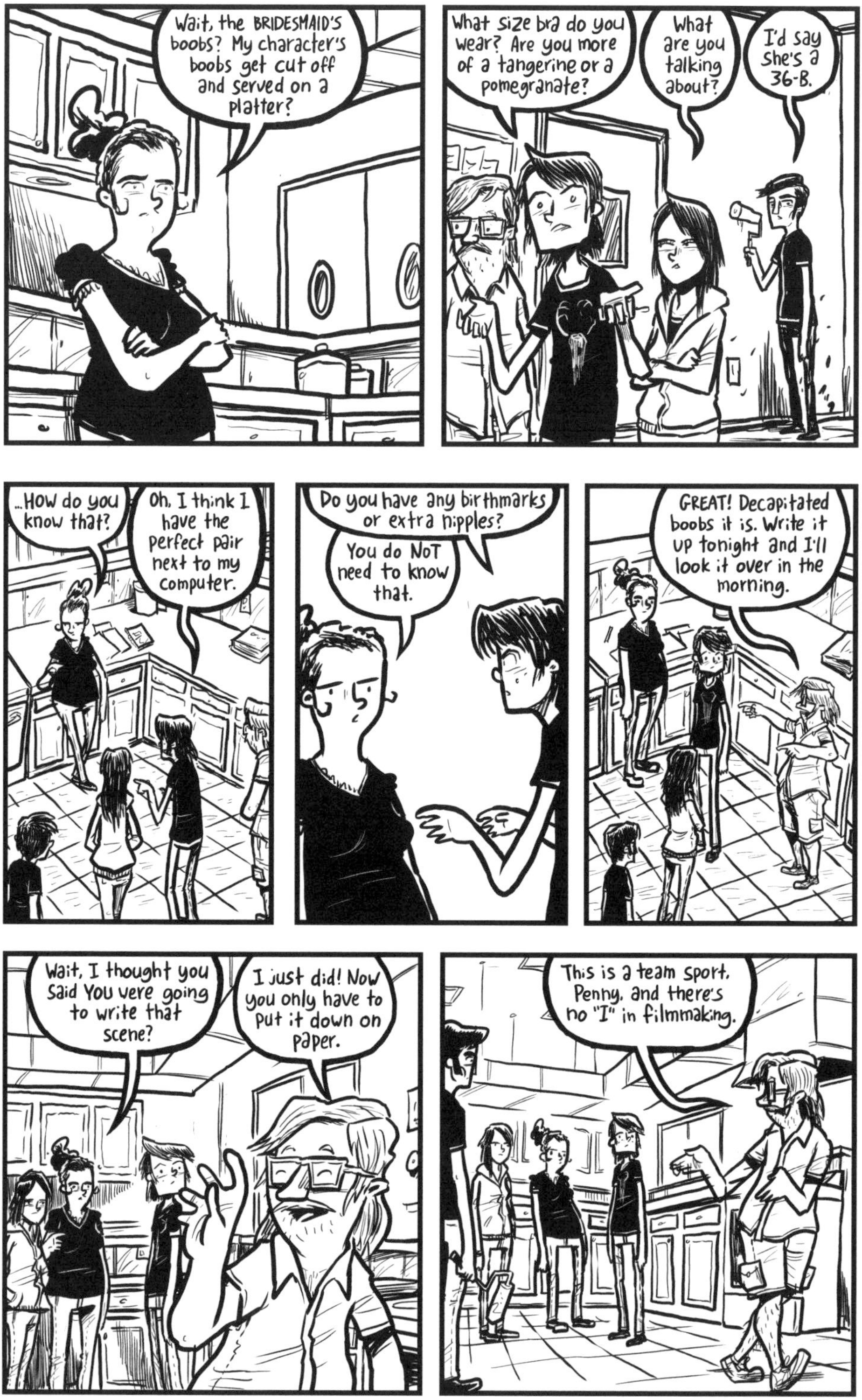
Wait, the BRIDESMAID'S boobs? My character's boobs get cut off and served on a platter?
What size bra do you wear? Are you more of a tangerine or a pomegranate?
What are you talking about?
I'd say she's a 36-B.
...How do you know that?
Oh, I think I have the perfect pair next to my computer.
Do you have any birthmarks or extra nipples?
You do NOT need to know that.
GREAT! Decapitated boobs it is. Write it up tonight and I'll look it over in the morning.
Wait, I thought you said you were going to write that scene?
I just did! Now you only have to put it down on paper.
This is a team sport, Penny, and there's no "I" in filmmaking.

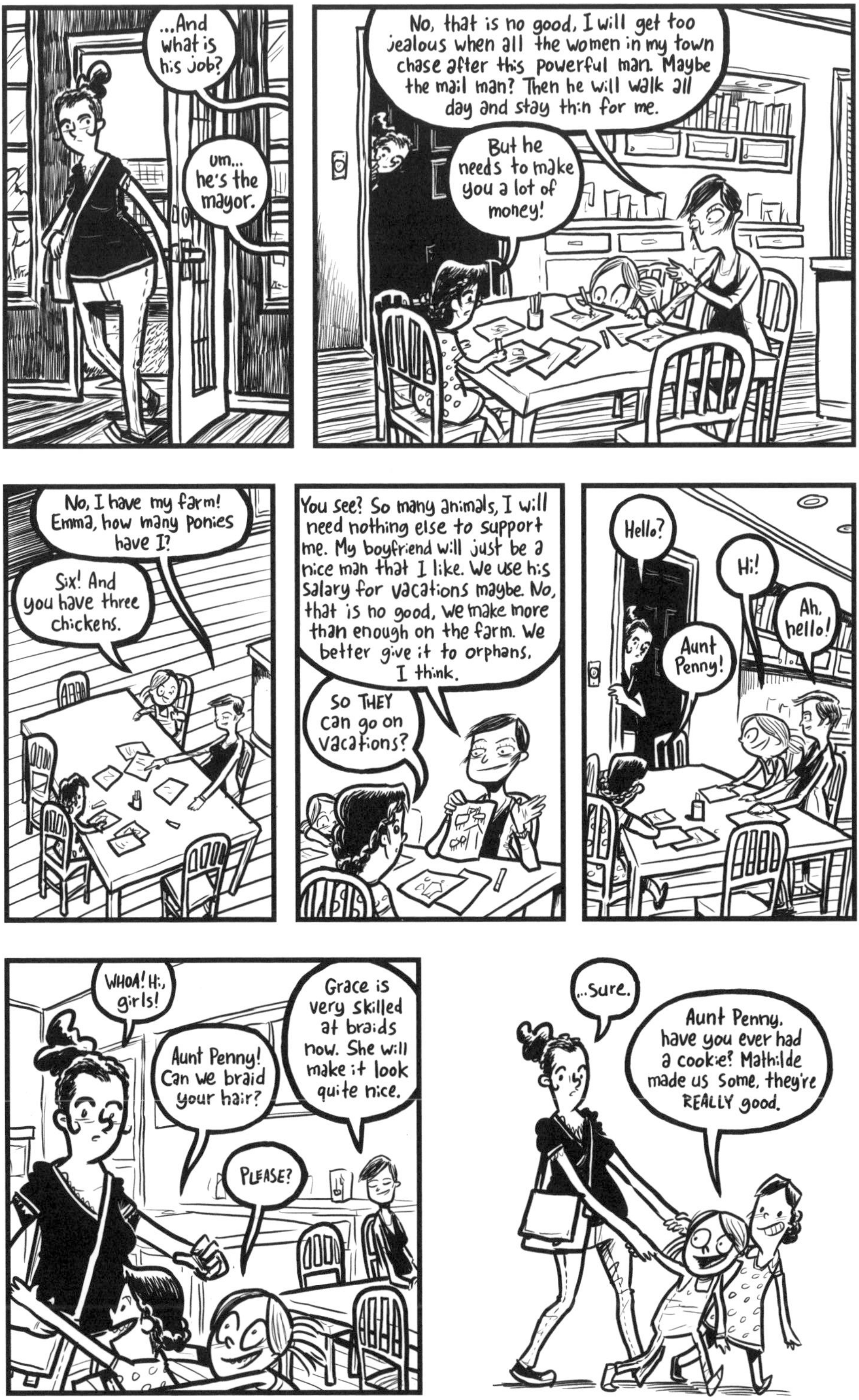
...And what is his job?
um... he's the mayor.
No, that is no good, I will get too jealous when all the women in my town chase after this powerful man. Maybe the mail man? Then he will walk all day and stay thin for me.
But he needs to make you a lot of money!
No, I have my farm! Emma, how many ponies have I?
Six! And you have three chickens.
You see? So many animals, I will need nothing else to support me. My boyfriend will just be a nice man that I like. We use his salary for vacations maybe. No, that is no good, we make more than enough on the farm. We better give it to orphans, I think.
SO THEY can go on vacations?
Hello?
Hi!
Ah, hello!
Aunt Penny!
WHOA! Hi, girls!
Aunt Penny! Can we braid your hair?
Grace is very skilled at braids now. She will make it look quite nice.
PLEASE?
...sure.
Aunt Penny, have you ever had a cookie? Mathilde made us some, they're REALLY good.

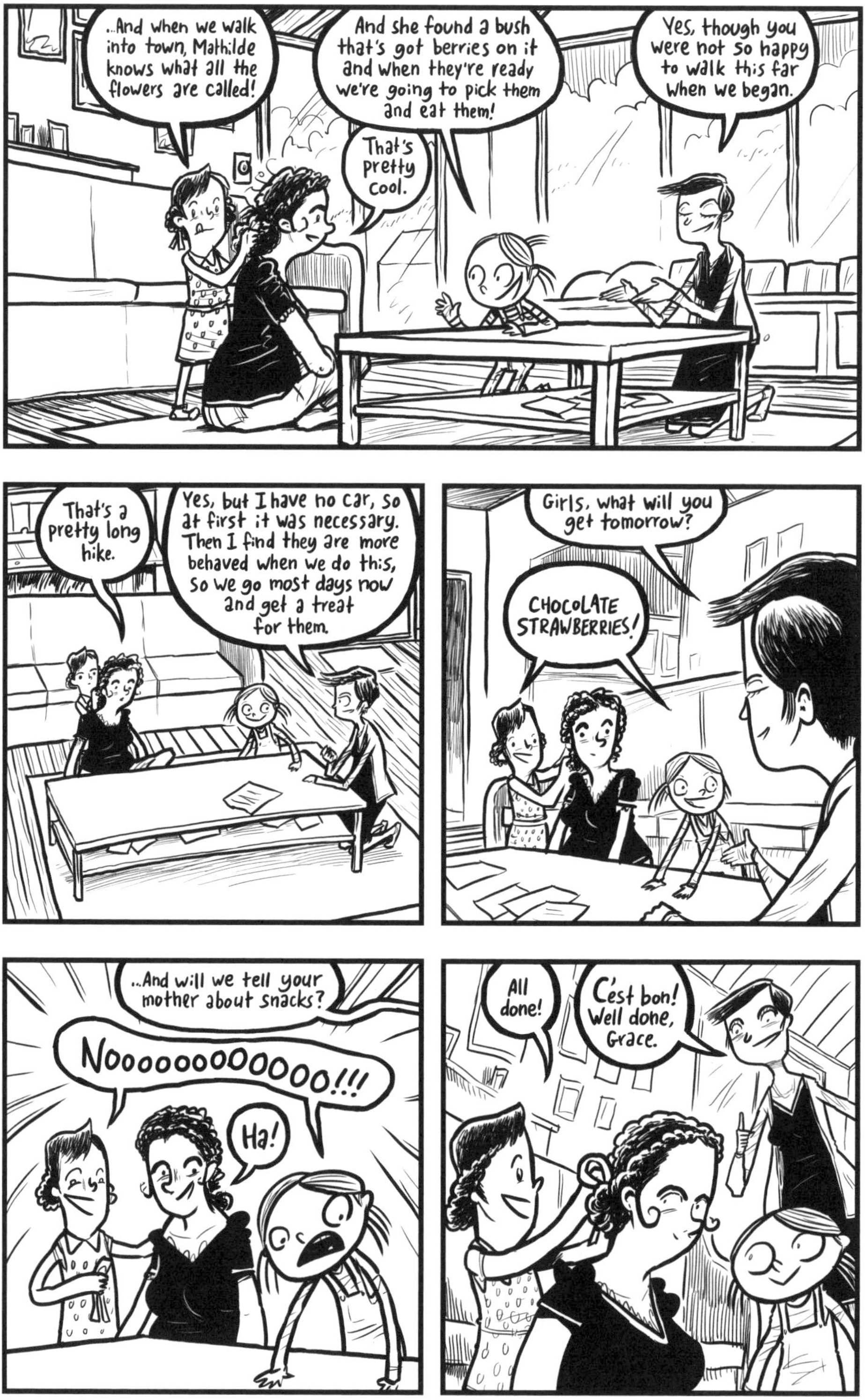
..And when we walk into town, Mathilde knows what all the flowers are called!
And she found a bush that's got berries on it and when they're ready we're going to pick them and eat them!
That's pretty cool.
Yes, though you were not so happy to walk this far when we began.
That's a pretty long hike.
Yes, but I have no car, so at first it was necessary. Then I find they are more behaved when we do this, so we go most days now and get a treat for them.
Girls, what will you get tomorrow?
CHOCOLATE STRAWBERRIES!
..And will we tell your mother about snacks?
NoooooooOOOOO!!!
Ha!
All done!
C'est bon! Well done, Grace.

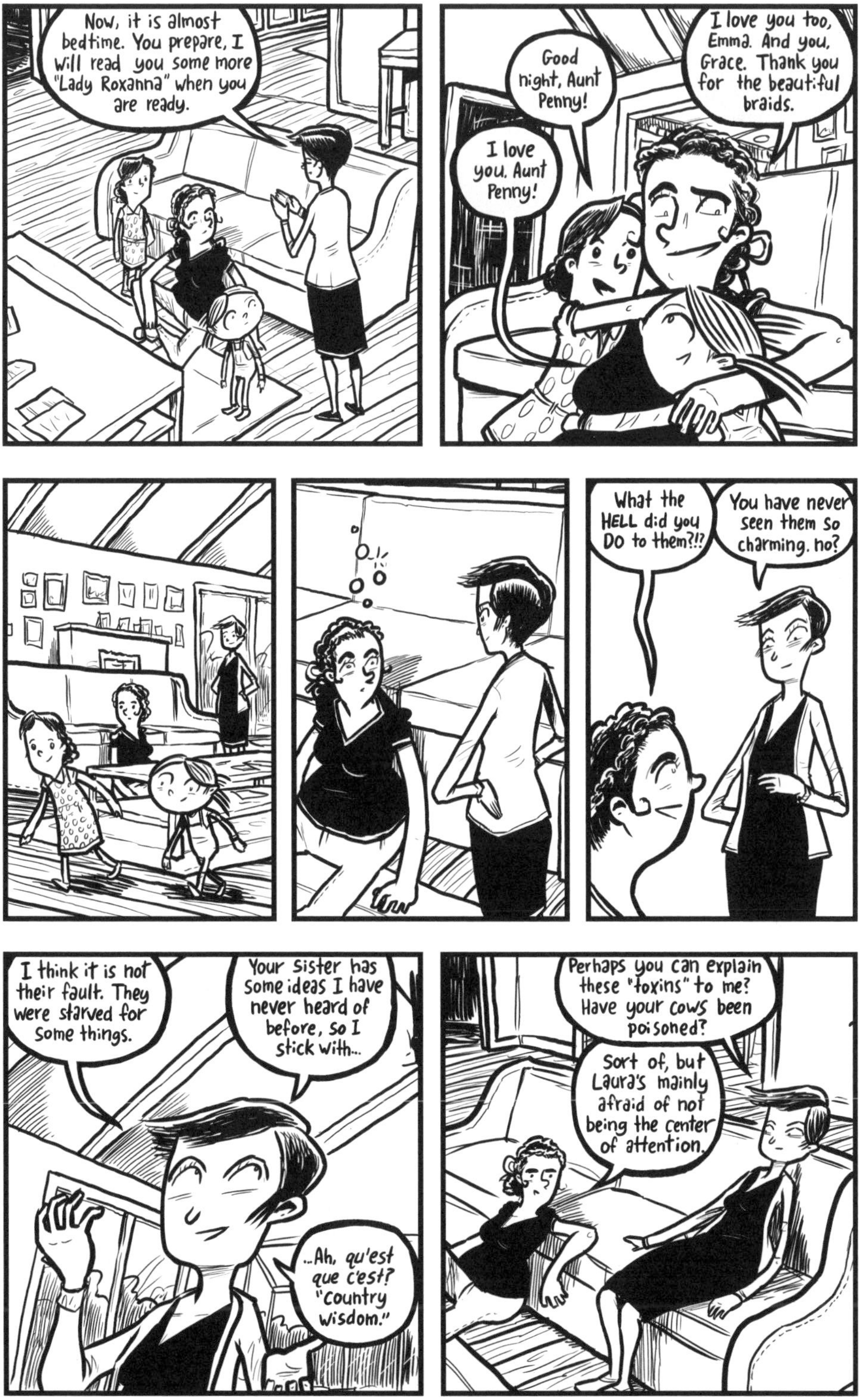
Now, it is almost bedtime. You prepare, I will read you some more "Lady Roxanna" when you are ready.
Good night, Aunt Penny!
I love you, Aunt Penny!
I love you too, Emma. And you, Grace. Thank you for the beautiful braids.
What the HELL did you DO to them?!?
You have never seen them so charming, no?
I think it is not their fault. They were starved for some things.
Your sister has some ideas I have never heard of before, so I stick with...
...Ah, qu'est que c'est? "Country wisdom."
Perhaps you can explain these "toxins" to me? Have your cows been poisoned?
Sort of, but Laura's mainly afraid of not being the center of attention.

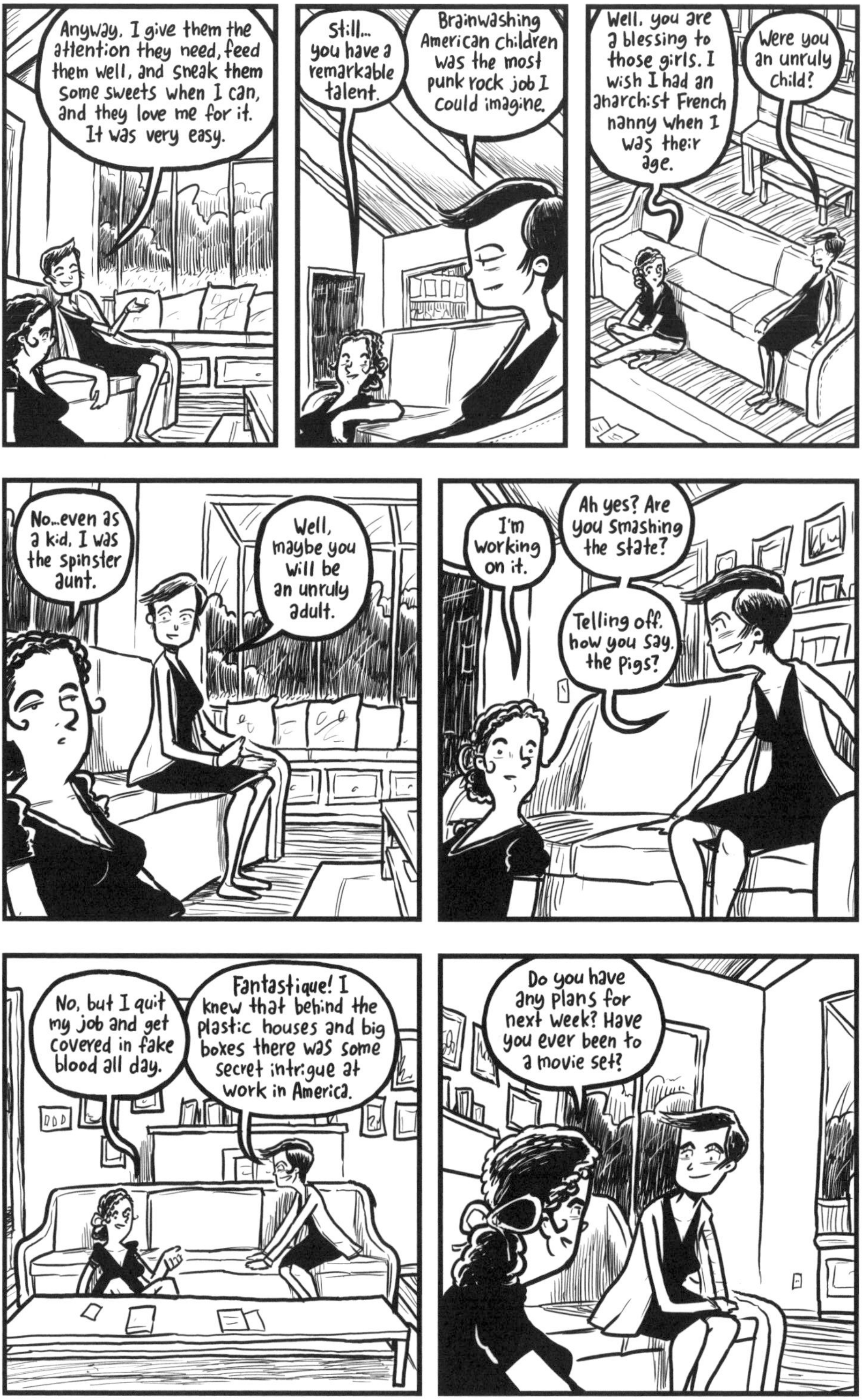

Anyway, I give them the attention they need, feed them well, and sneak them some sweets when I can, and they love me for it. It was very easy.
Still... you have a remarkable talent.
Brainwashing American children was the most punk rock job I could imagine.
Well, you are a blessing to those girls. I wish I had an anarchist French nanny when I was their age.
Were you an unruly child?
No...even as a kid, I was the spinster aunt.
Well, maybe you will be an unruly adult.
Ah yes? Are you smashing the state?
I'm working on it.
Telling off, how you say, the pigs?
No, but I quit my job and get covered in fake blood all day.
Fantastique! I knew that behind the plastic houses and big boxes there was some secret intrigue at work in America.
Do you have any plans for next week? Have you ever been to a movie set?

CHAPTER SIX

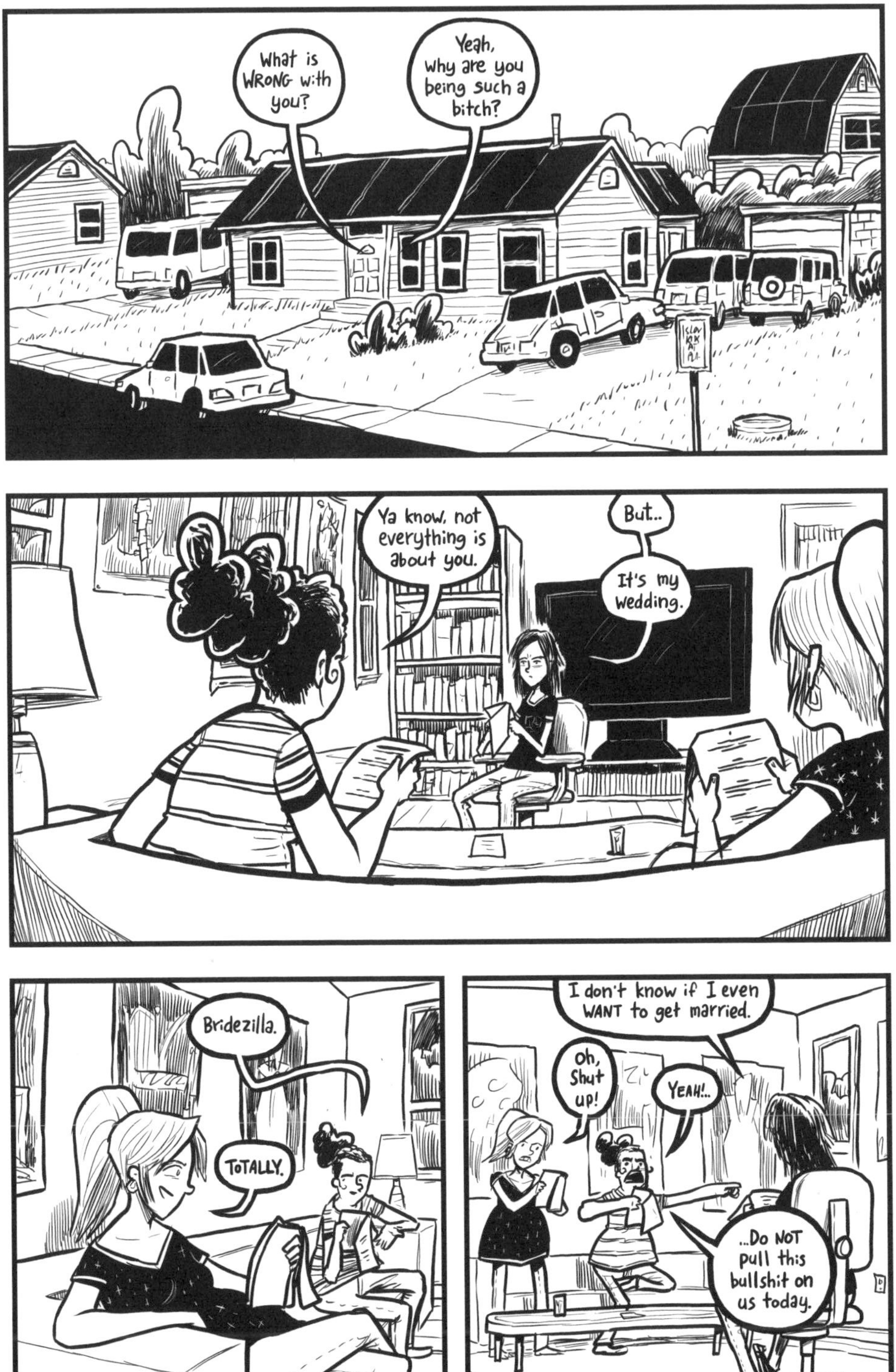
What is WRONG with you?
Yeah, why are you being such a bitch?
Ya know, not everything is about you.
But...
It's my wedding.
Bridezilla.
TOTALLY.
I don't know if I even WANT to get married.
Oh, Shut up!
YEAH!..
...Do NOT pull this bullshit on us today.

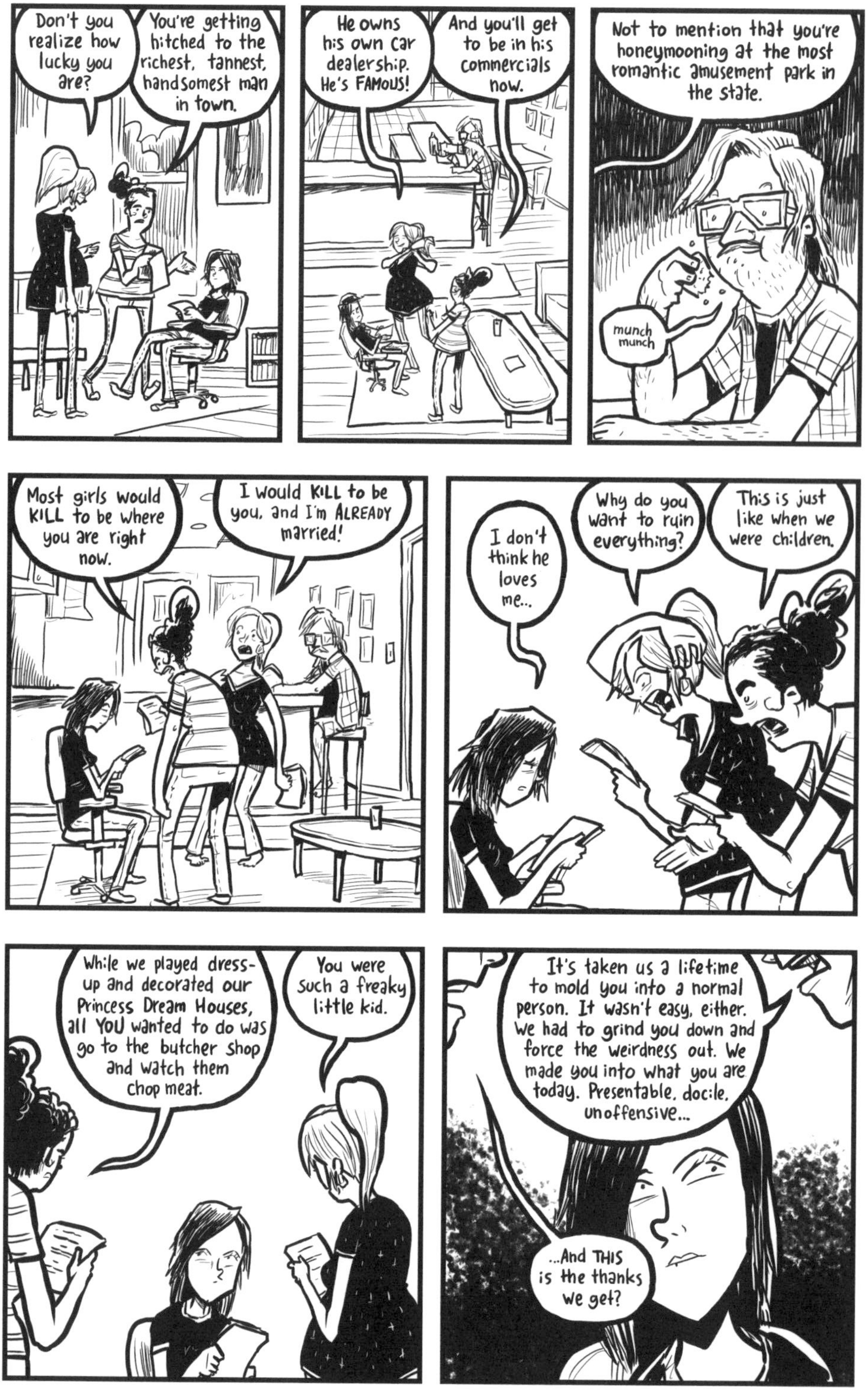
Don't you realize how lucky you are?
You're getting hitched to the richest, tannest, handsomest man in town.
He owns his own car dealership. He's FAMOUS!
And you'll get to be in his commercials now.
Not to mention that you're honeymooning at the most romantic amusement park in the state.
munch munch
Most girls would KILL to be where you are right now.
I would KILL to be you, and I'm ALREADY married!
I don't think he loves me...
Why do you want to ruin everything?
This is just like when we were children.
While we played dress-up and decorated our Princess Dream Houses, all YOU wanted to do was go to the butcher shop and watch them chop meat.
You were such a freaky little kid.
It's taken us a lifetime to mold you into a normal person. It wasn't easy, either. We had to grind you down and force the weirdness out. We made you into what you are today. Presentable, docile, unoffensive...
...And THIS is the thanks we get?

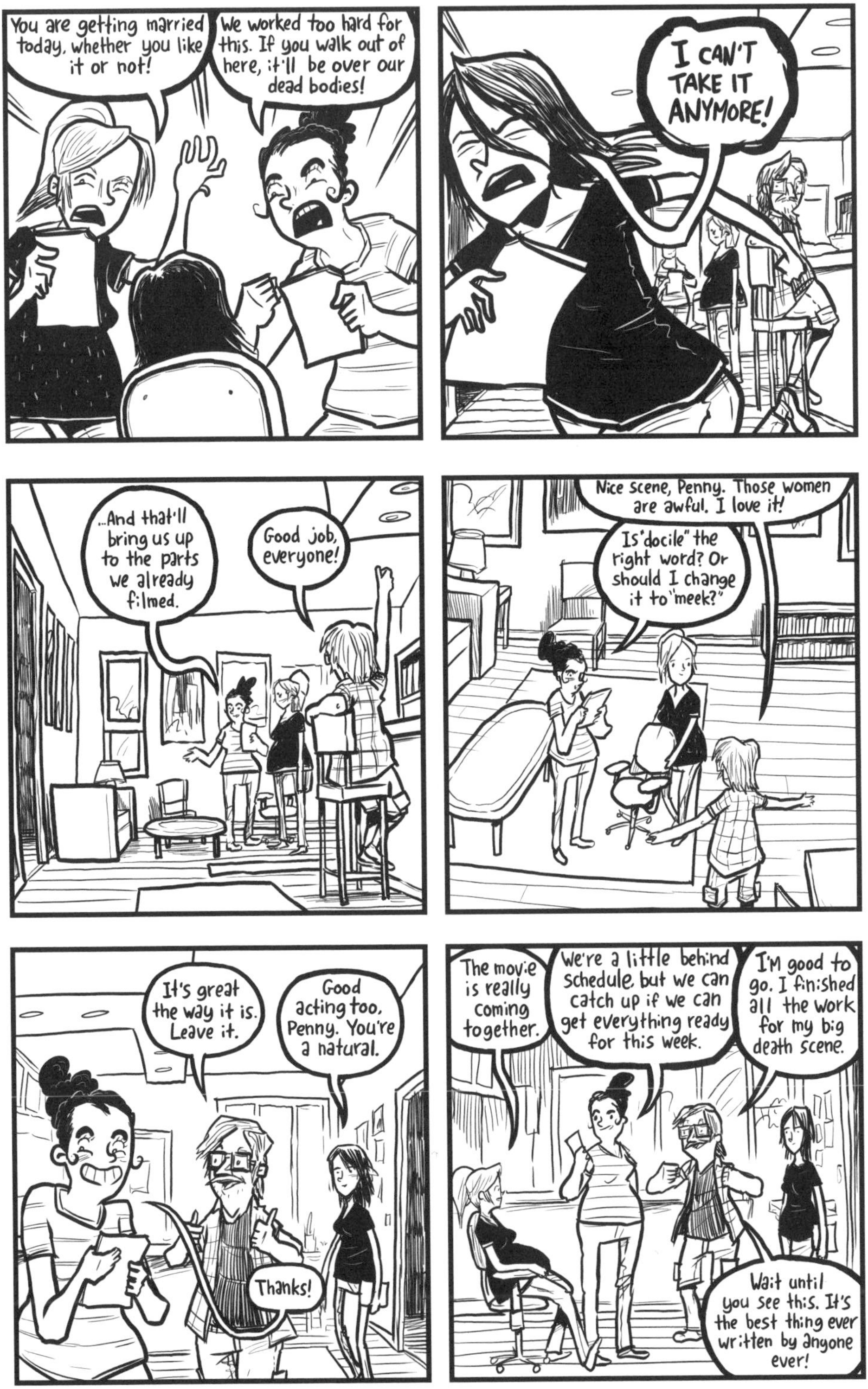
You are getting married today, whether you like it or not!
We worked too hard for this. If you walk out of here, it'll be over our dead bodies!
I CAN'T TAKE IT ANYMORE!
...And that'll bring us up to the parts we already filmed.
Good job, everyone!
Nice scene, Penny. Those women are awful. I love it!
Is "docile" the right word? Or should I change it to "meek?"
It's great the way it is. Leave it.
Good acting too, Penny. You're a natural.
Thanks!
The movie is really coming together.
We're a little behind schedule, but we can catch up if we can get everything ready for this week.
I'm good to go. I finished all the work for my big death scene.
Wait until you see this. It's the best thing ever written by anyone ever!

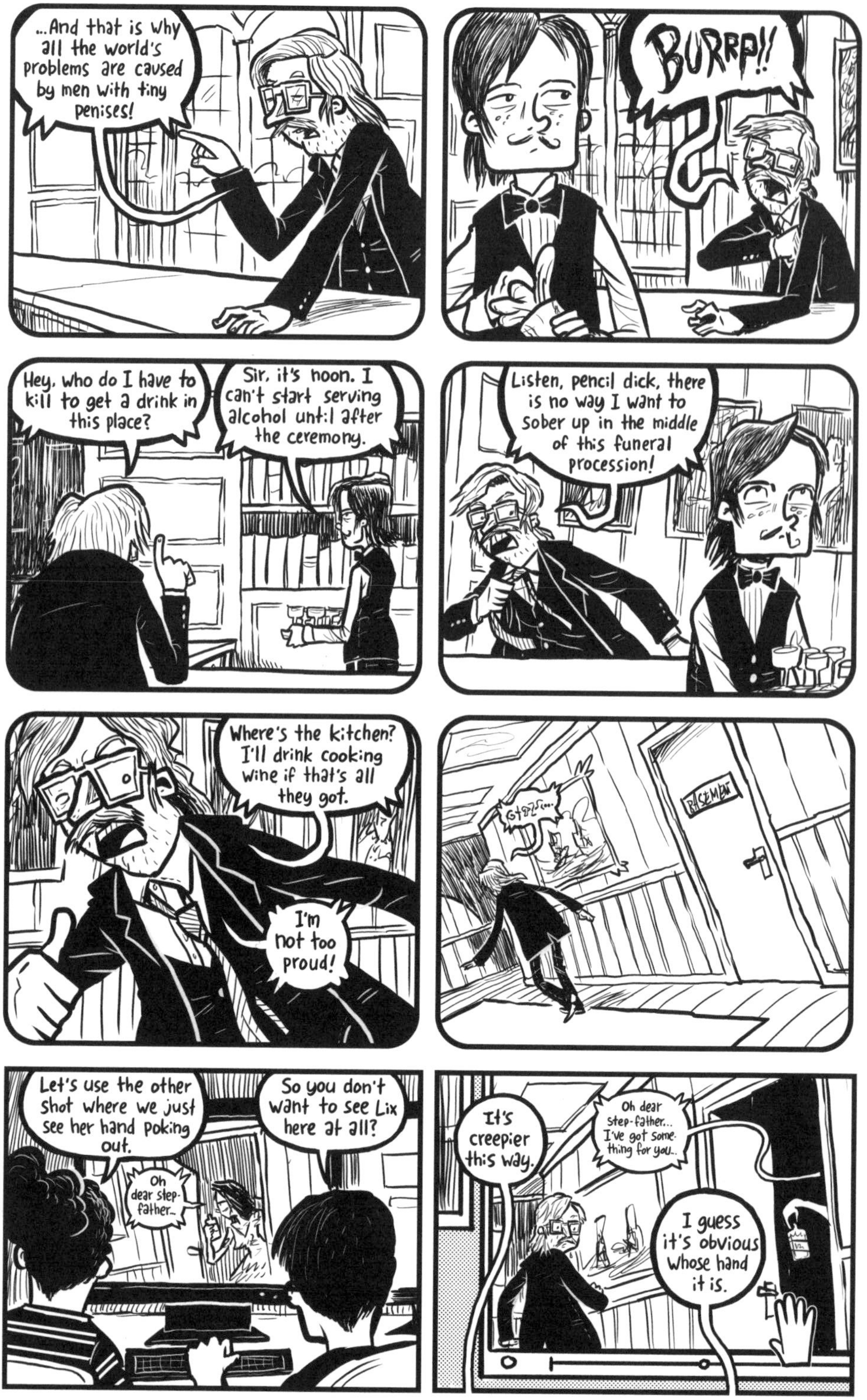
...And that is why all the world's problems are caused by men with tiny penises!
BURRP!!
Hey, who do I have to kill to get a drink in this place?
Sir, it's noon. I can't start serving alcohol until after the ceremony.
Listen, pencil dick, there is no way I want to sober up in the middle of this funeral procession!
Where's the kitchen? I'll drink cooking wine if that's all they got.
I'm not too proud!
BASEMENT
Let's use the other shot where we just see her hand poking out.
Oh dear step-father...
So you don't want to see Lix here at all?
It's creepier this way.
Oh dear step-father... I've got some-thing for you...
I guess it's obvious whose hand it is.

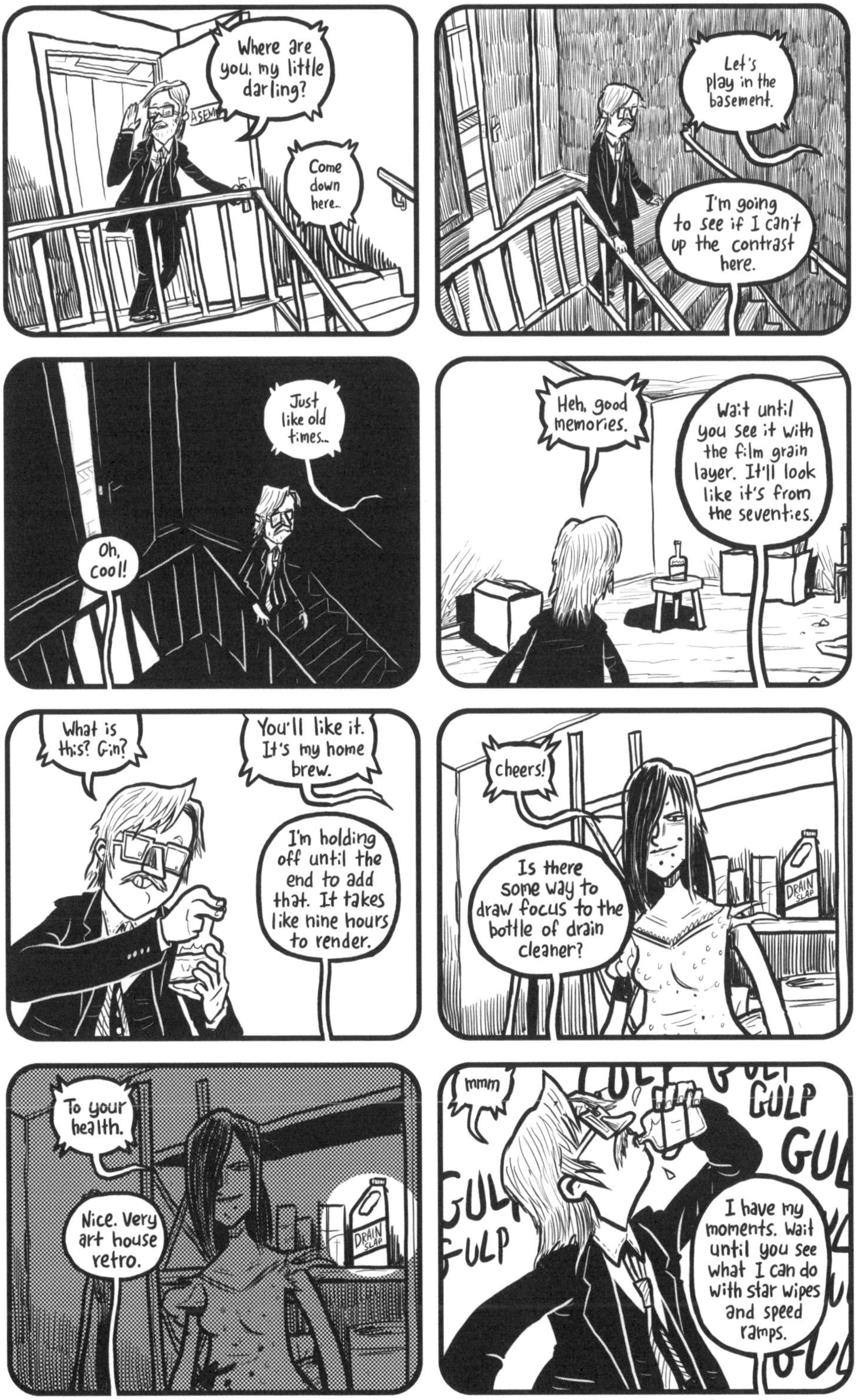
Where are you, my little darling?
Come down here...
Let's play in the basement.
I'm going to see if I can't up the contrast here.
Just like old times...
Oh, cool!
Heh, good memories.
Wait until you see it with the film grain layer. It'll look like it's from the seventies.
What is this? Gin?
You'll like it. It's my home brew.
I'm holding off until the end to add that. It takes like nine hours to render.
cheers!
Is there some way to draw focus to the bottle of drain cleaner?
DRAIN SLAP
To your health.
Nice. Very art house retro.
DRAIN SLAP
mmm
GULP
GULP
I have my moments. Wait until you see what I can do with star wipes and speed ramps.

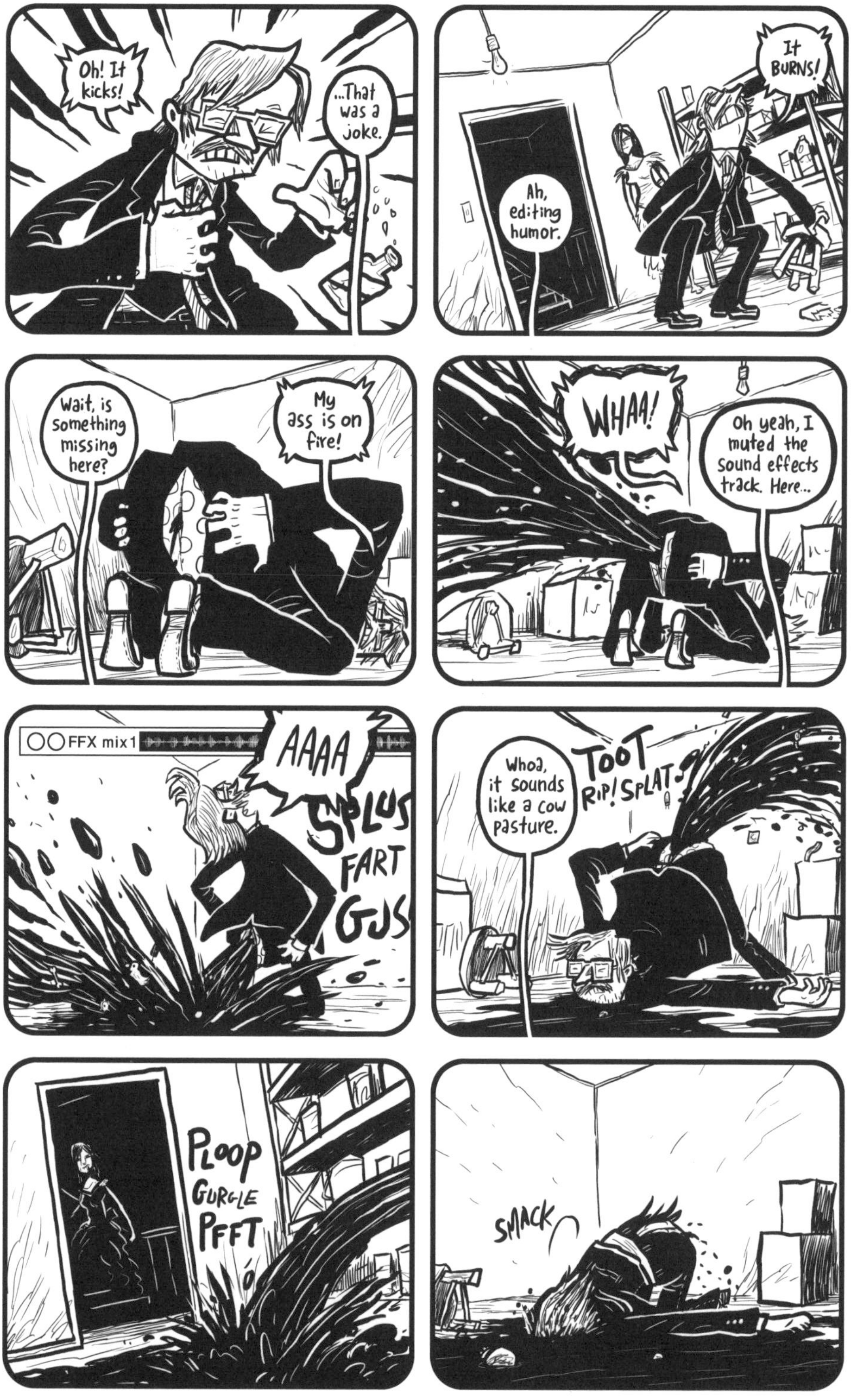
Oh! It kicks!
...That was a joke.
It BURNS!
Ah, editing humor.
Wait, is something missing here?
My ass is on fire!
WHAA!
Oh yeah, I muted the sound effects track. Here...
FFX mix1
AAAA
SPLUS
FART
GJS
Whoa, it sounds like a cow pasture.
TOOT
RIP! SPLAT
PLOOP
GURGLE
PFFT
SMACK

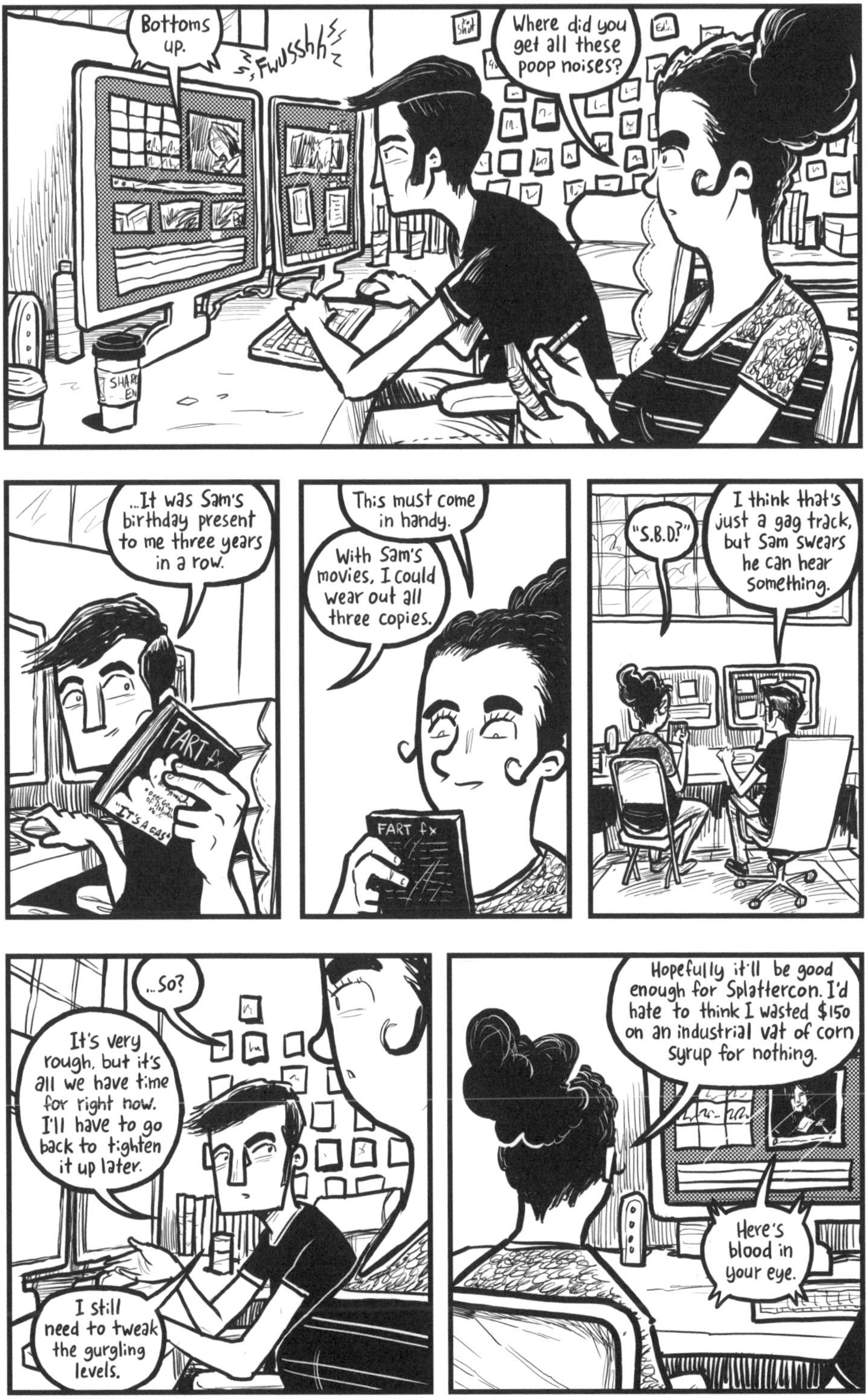
Bottoms up.
FWUSSHH
Where did you get all these poop noises?
...It was Sam's birthday present to me three years in a row.
FART fx
"IT'S A GAS"
This must come in handy.
With Sam's movies, I could wear out all three copies.
FART fx
"S.B.D.?"
I think that's just a gag track, but Sam swears he can hear something.
...So?
It's very rough, but it's all we have time for right now. I'll have to go back to tighten it up later.
I still need to tweak the gurgling levels.
Hopefully it'll be good enough for Splattercon. I'd hate to think I wasted $150 on an industrial vat of corn syrup for nothing.
Here's blood in your eye.

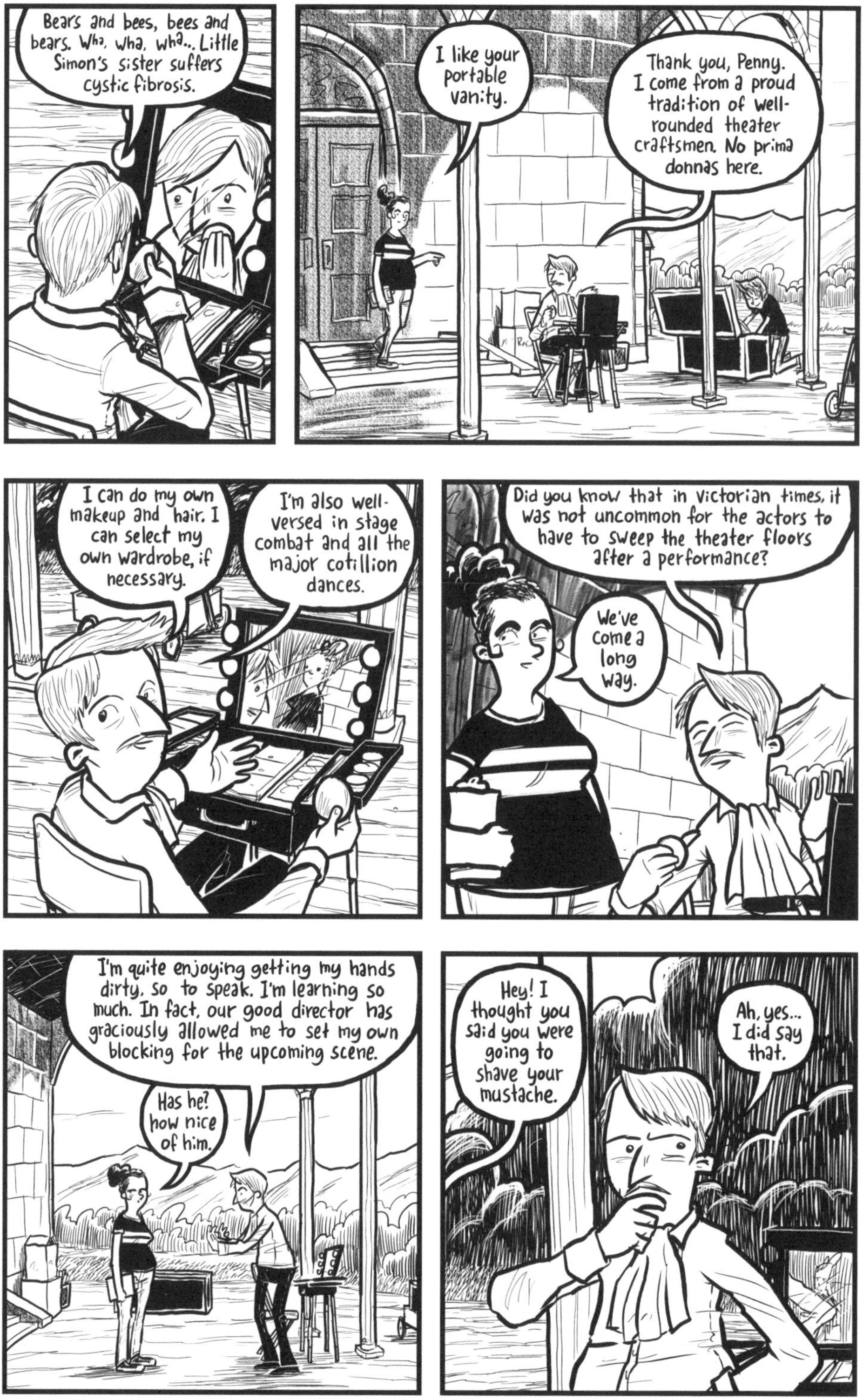
Bears and bees, bees and bears. Wha, wha, wha... Little Simon's sister suffers cystic fibrosis.
I like your portable vanity.
Thank you, Penny. I come from a proud tradition of well-rounded theater craftsmen. No prima donnas here.
I can do my own makeup and hair. I can select my own wardrobe, if necessary.
I'm also well-versed in stage combat and all the major cotillion dances.
Did you know that in victorian times, it was not uncommon for the actors to have to sweep the theater floors after a performance?
We've come a long way.
I'm quite enjoying getting my hands dirty, so to speak. I'm learning so much. In fact, our good director has graciously allowed me to set my own blocking for the upcoming scene.
Has he? how nice of him.
Hey! I thought you said you were going to shave your mustache.
Ah, yes... I did say that.

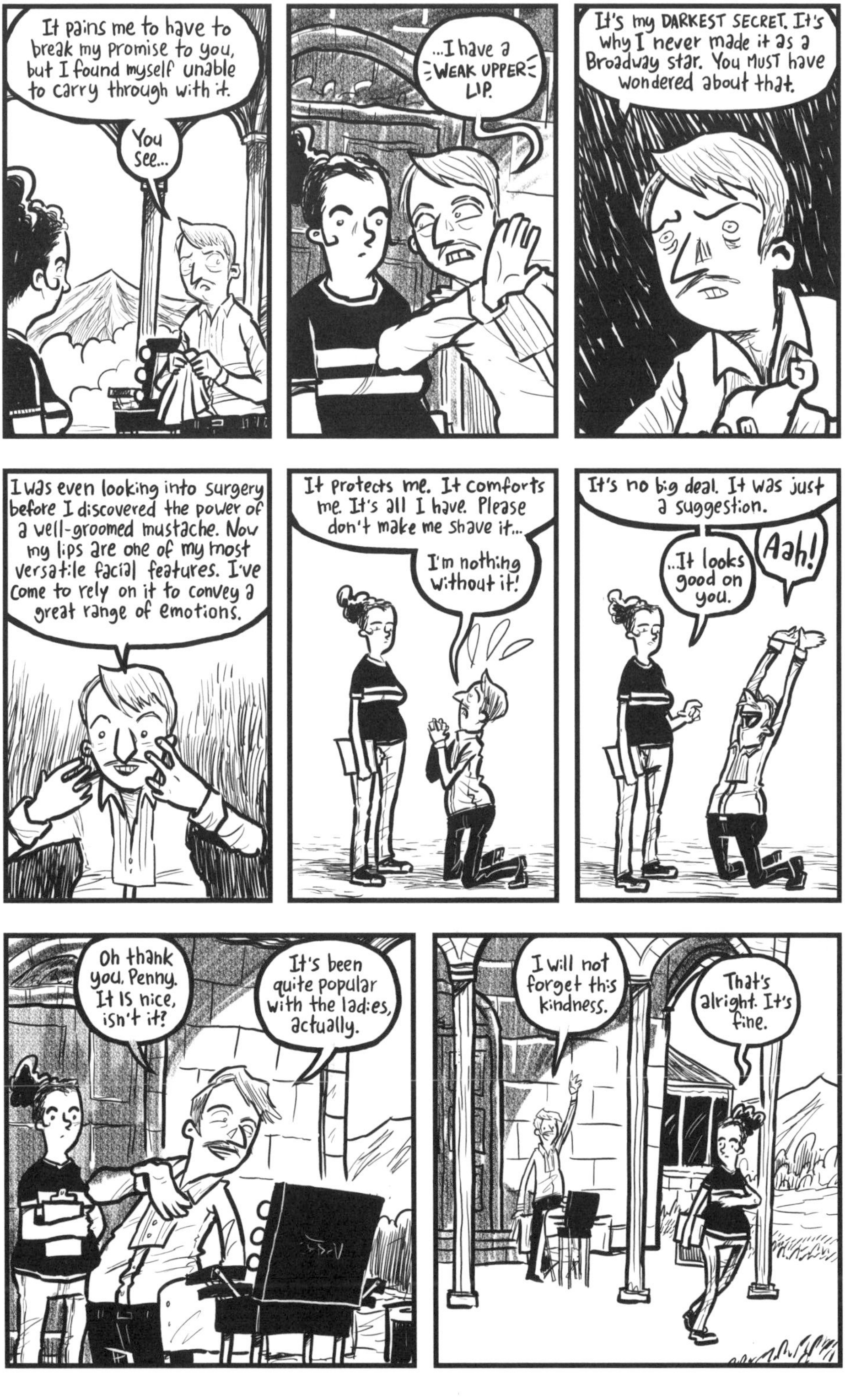
It pains me to have to break my promise to you, but I found myself unable to carry through with it.
You see...
...I have a WEAK UPPER LIP.
It's my DARKEST SECRET. It's why I never made it as a Broadway star. You MUST have wondered about that.
I was even looking into surgery before I discovered the power of a well-groomed mustache. Now my lips are one of my most versatile facial features. I've come to rely on it to convey a great range of emotions.
It protects me. It comforts me. It's all I have. Please don't make me shave it...
I'm nothing without it!
It's no big deal. It was just a suggestion.
...It looks good on you.
Aah!
Oh thank you, Penny. It IS nice, isn't it?
It's been quite popular with the ladies, actually.
I will not forget this kindness.
That's alright. It's fine.

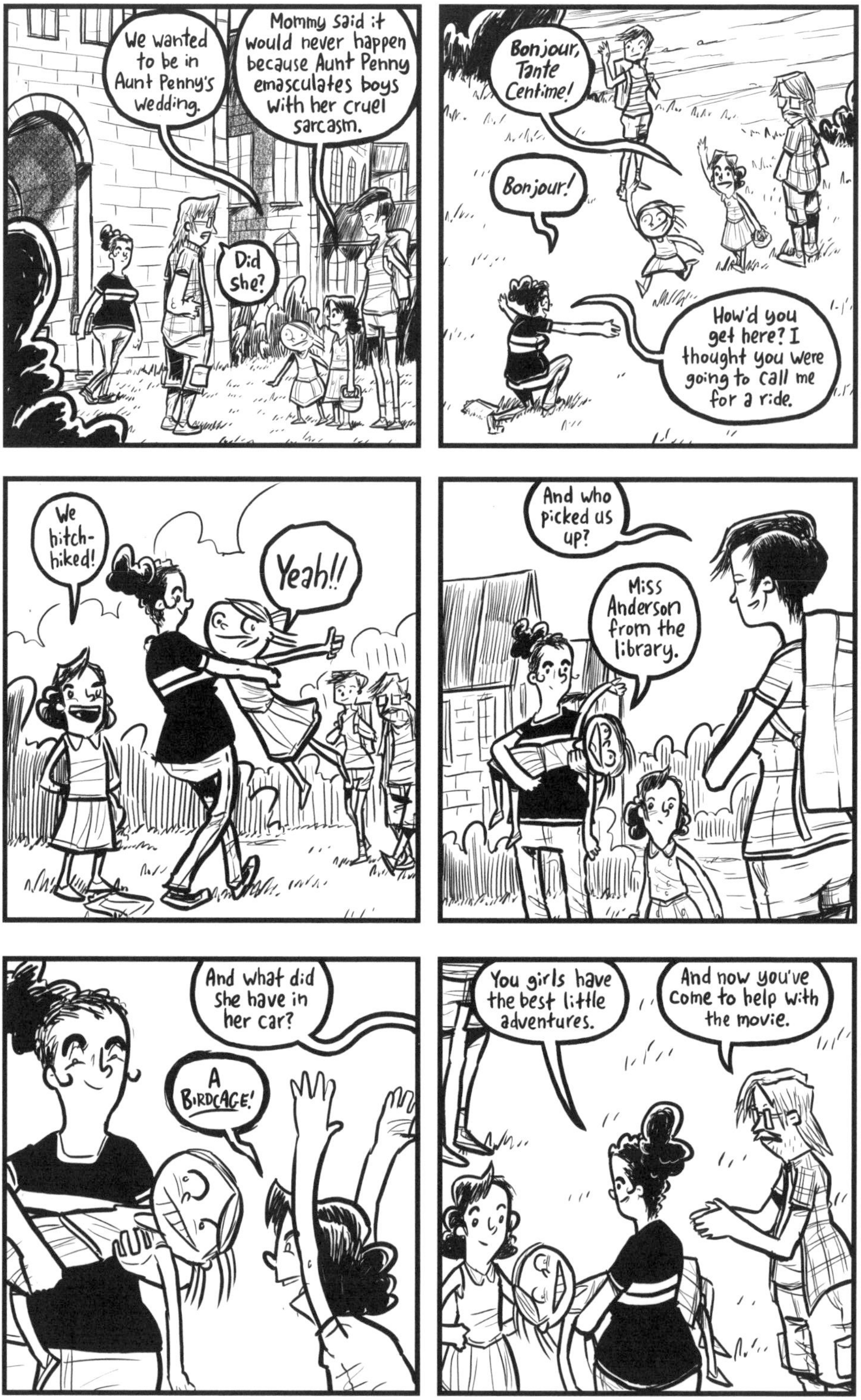
We wanted to be in Aunt Penny's wedding.
Mommy said it would never happen because Aunt Penny emasculates boys with her cruel sarcasm.
Did she?
Bonjour, Tante Centime!
Bonjour!
How'd you get here? I thought you were going to call me for a ride.
We hitch-hiked!
Yeah!!
And who picked us up?
Miss Anderson from the library.
And what did she have in her car?
A BIRDCAGE!
You girls have the best little adventures.
And now you've come to help with the movie.

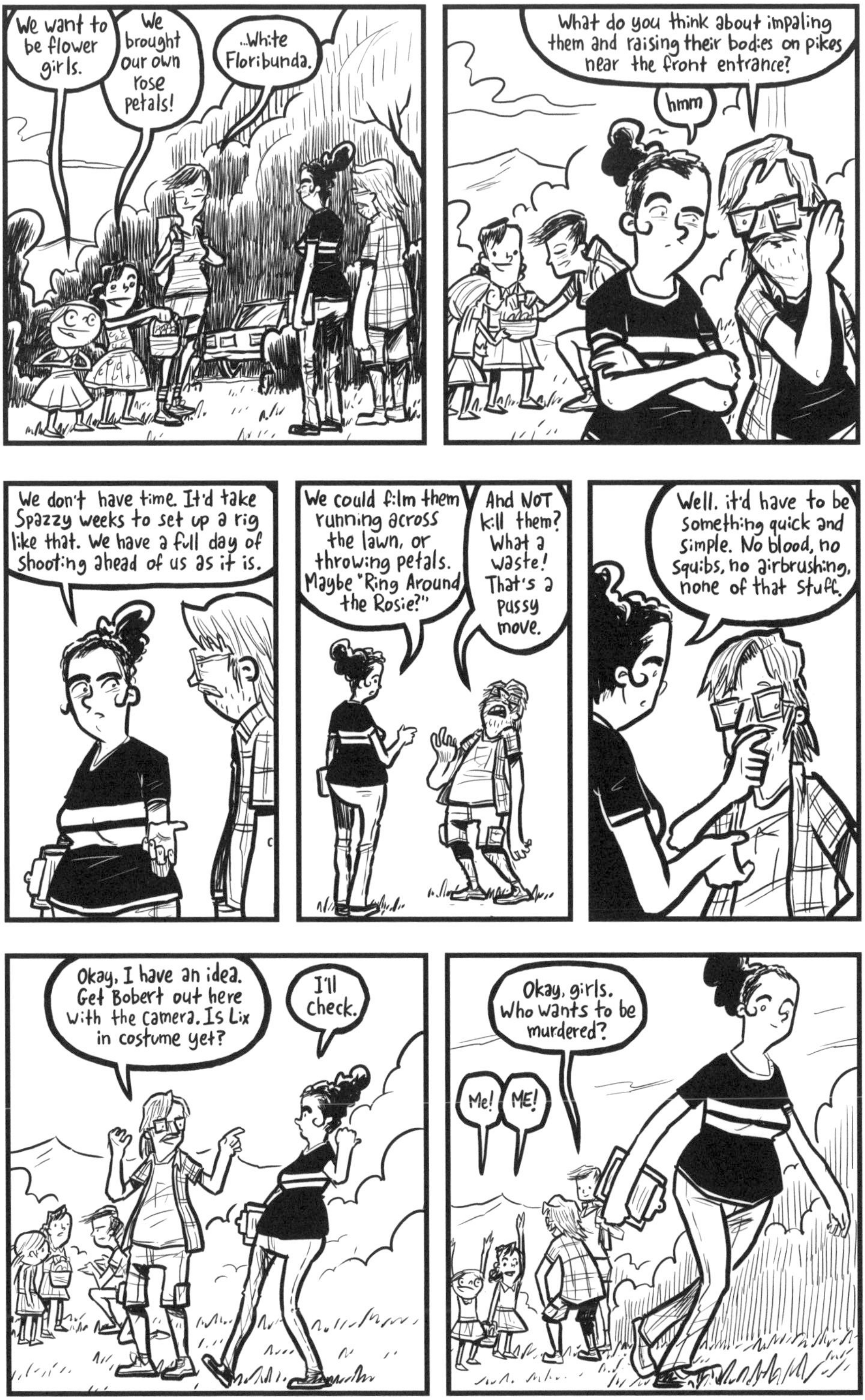
We want to be flower girls.
We brought our own rose petals!
..White Floribunda.
What do you think about impaling them and raising their bodies on pikes near the front entrance?
hmm
We don't have time. It'd take Spazzy weeks to set up a rig like that. We have a full day of shooting ahead of us as it is.
We could film them running across the lawn, or throwing petals. Maybe "Ring Around the Rosie?"
And NOT kill them? What a waste! That's a pussy move.
Well. it'd have to be something quick and simple. No blood, no squibs, no airbrushing, none of that stuff.
Okay, I have an idea. Get Bobert out here with the camera. Is Lix in costume yet?
I'll check.
Okay, girls. Who wants to be murdered?
Me!
ME!

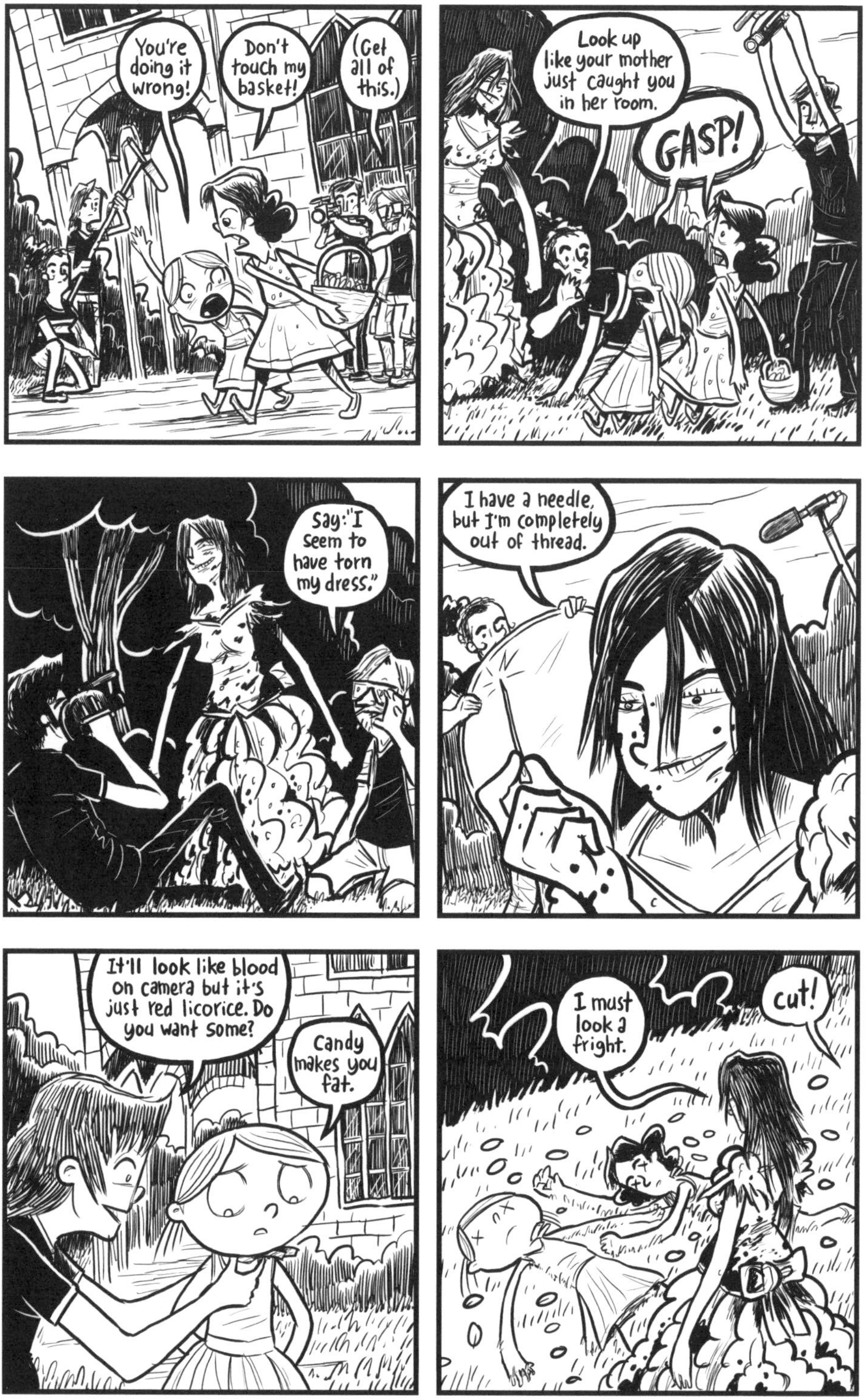

You're doing it wrong!
Don't touch my basket!
(Get all of this.)
Look up like your mother just caught you in her room.
GASP!
Say: "I seem to have torn my dress."
I have a needle, but I'm completely out of thread.
It'll look like blood on camera but it's just red licorice. Do you want some?
Candy makes you fat.
I must look a fright.
cut!

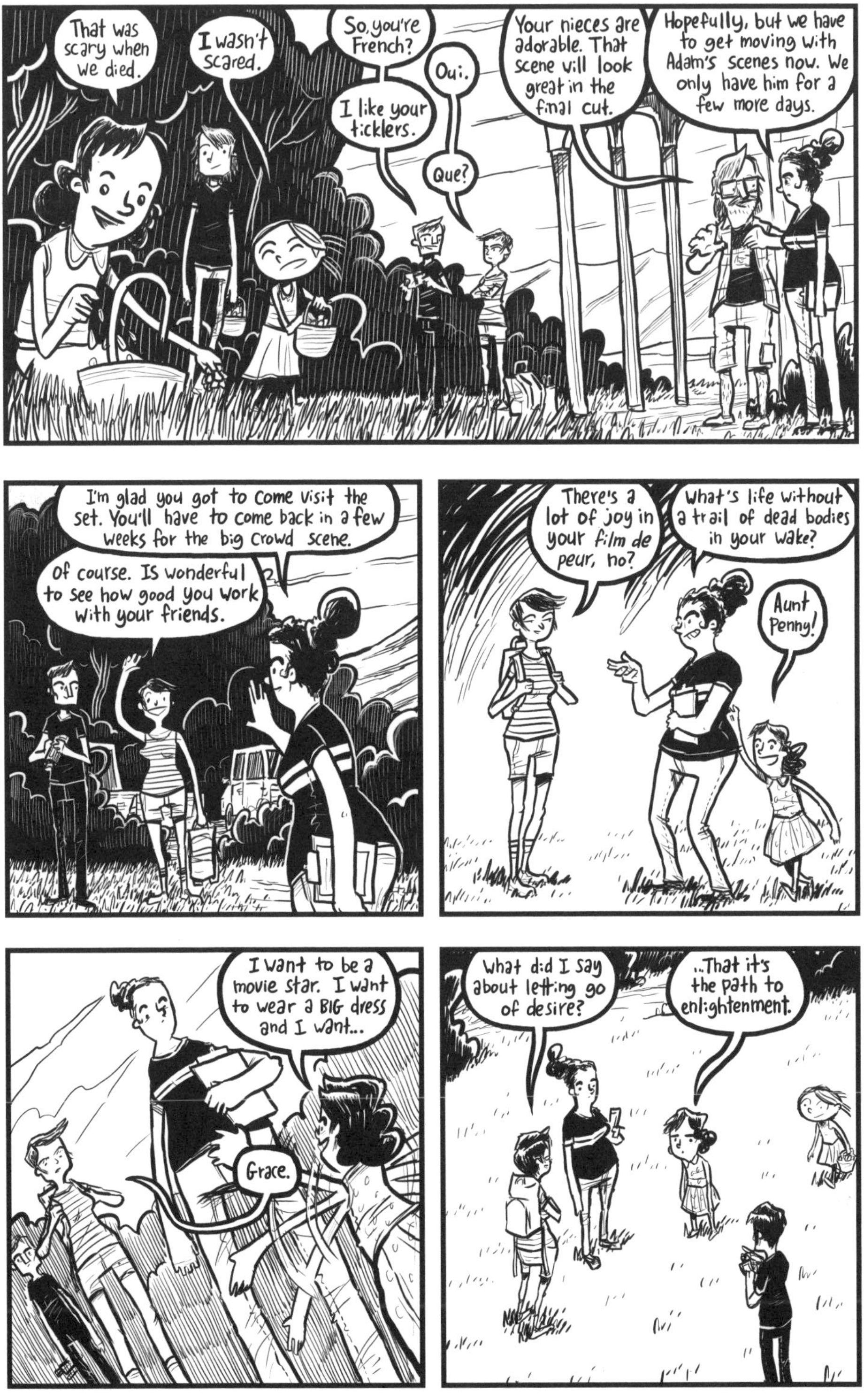
That was scary when we died.
I wasn't scared.
So, you're French?
I like your ticklers.
Oui.
Que?
Your nieces are adorable. That scene vill look great in the final cut.
Hopefully, but we have to get moving with Adam's scenes now. We only have him for a few more days.
I'm glad you got to come visit the set. You'll have to come back in a few weeks for the big crowd scene.
Of course. Is wonderful to see how good you work with your friends.
There's a lot of joy in your film de peur, no?
What's life without a trail of dead bodies in your wake?
Aunt Penny!
I want to be a movie star. I want to wear a BIG dress and I want...
Grace.
What did I say about letting go of desire?
...That it's the path to enlightenment.

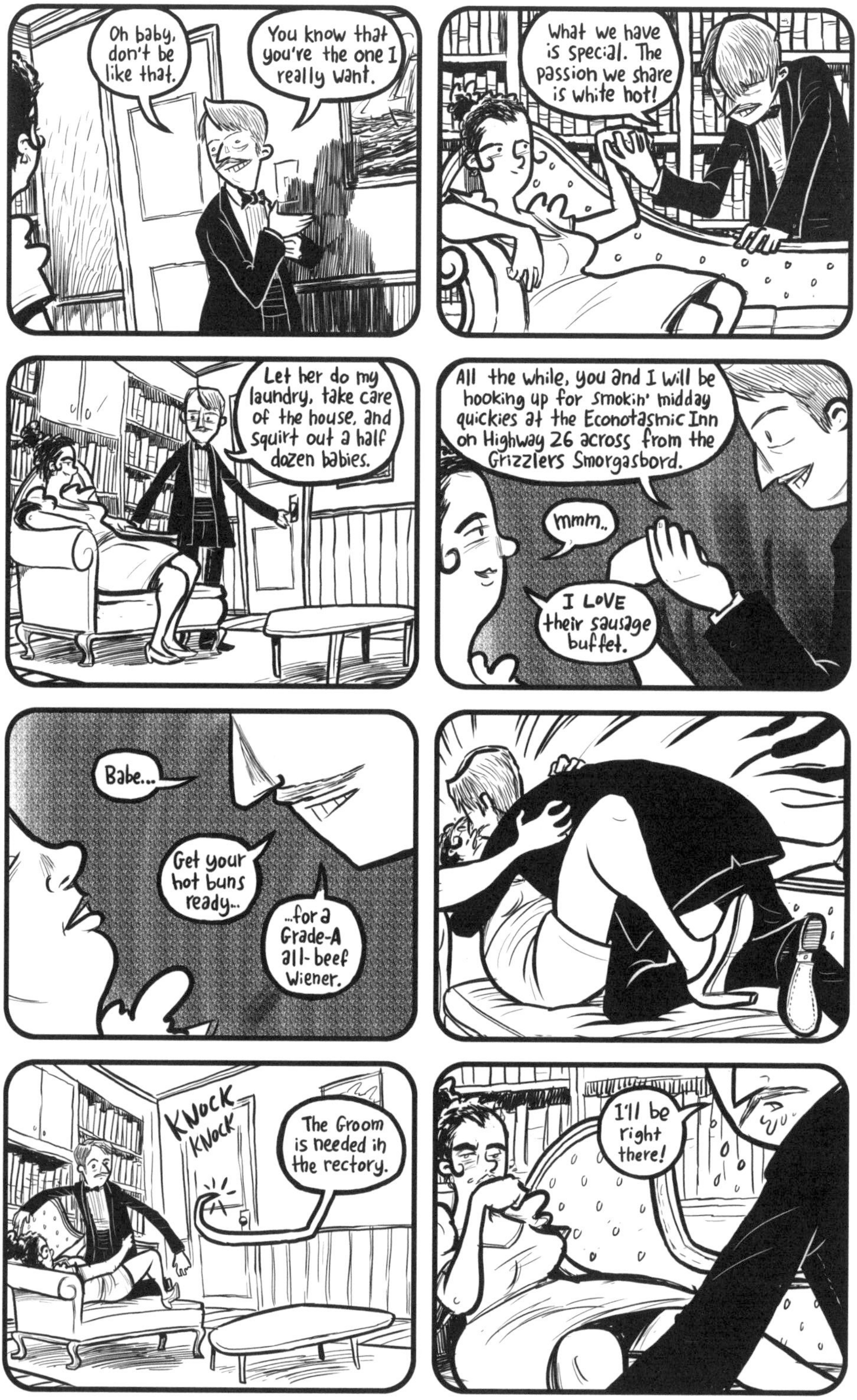
Oh baby, don't be like that.
You know that you're the one I really want.
What we have is special. The passion we share is white hot!
Let her do my laundry, take care of the house, and squirt out a half dozen babies.
All the while, you and I will be hooking up for smokin' midday quickies at the Econotasmic Inn on Highway 26 across from the Grizzlers Smorgasbord.
mmm..
I LOVE their sausage buffet.
Babe...
Get your hot buns ready..
...for a Grade-A all-beef Wiener.
KNOCK KNOCK
The Groom is needed in the rectory.
I'll be right there!

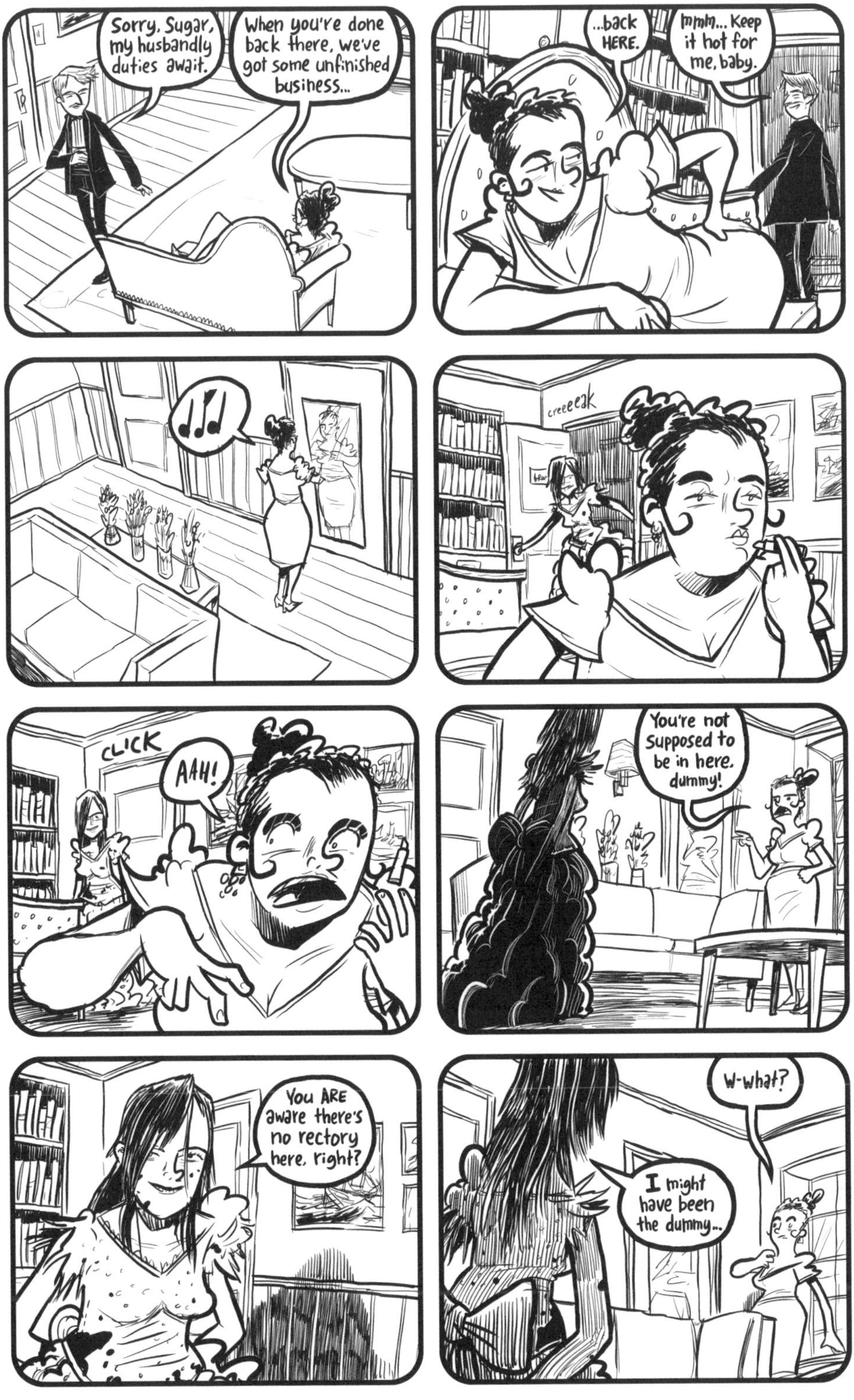
Sorry, Sugar, my husbandly duties await.
When you're done back there, we've got some unfinished business...
...back HERE.
mmm... Keep it hot for me, baby.
creeeeak
CLICK
AAH!
You're not supposed to be in here, dummy!
You ARE aware there's no rectory here, right?
W-what?
I might have been the dummy...

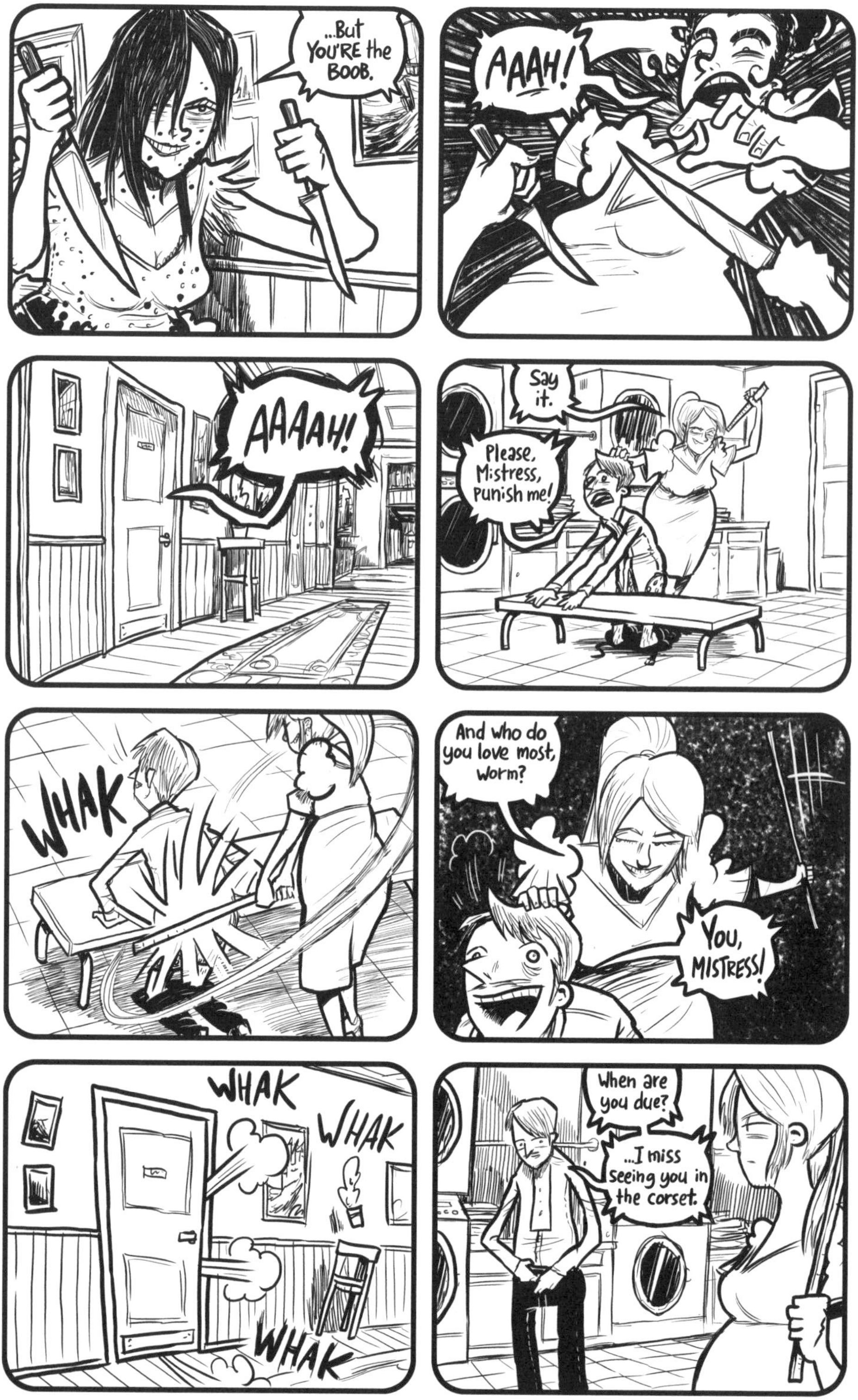
...But YOU'RE the BOOB.
AAAH!
AAAAH!
Say it.
Please, Mistress, punish me!
WHAK
And who do you love most, worm?
YOU, MISTRESS!
WHAK
WHAK
WHAK
When are you due?
...I miss seeing you in the corset.

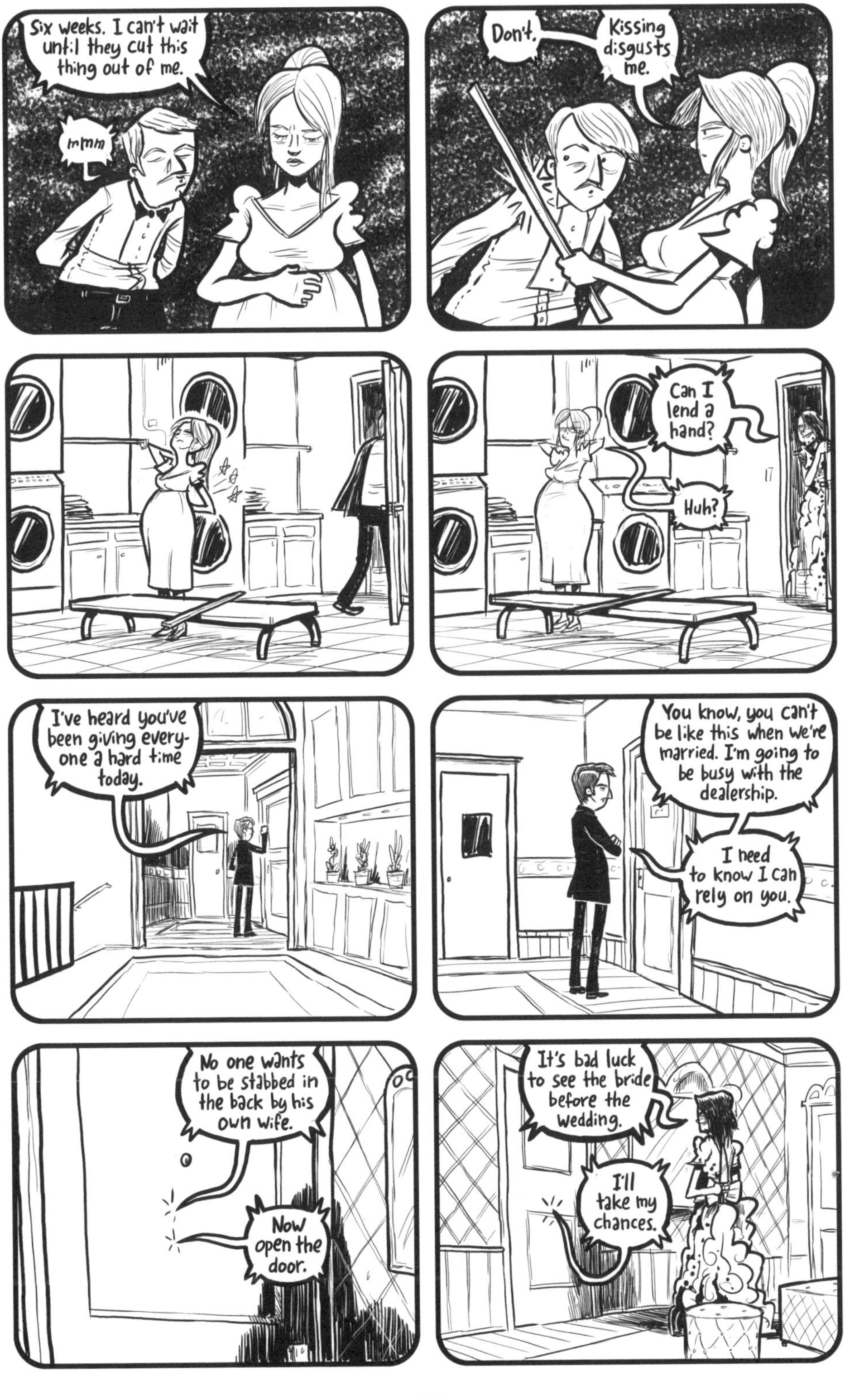
Six weeks. I can't wait until they cut this thing out of me.
mmm
Don't.
Kissing disgusts me.
Can I lend a hand?
Huh?
I've heard you've been giving every-one a hard time today.
You know, you can't be like this when we're married. I'm going to be busy with the dealership.
I need to know I can rely on you.
No one wants to be stabbed in the back by his own wife.
Now open the door.
It's bad luck to see the bride before the wedding.
I'll take my chances.

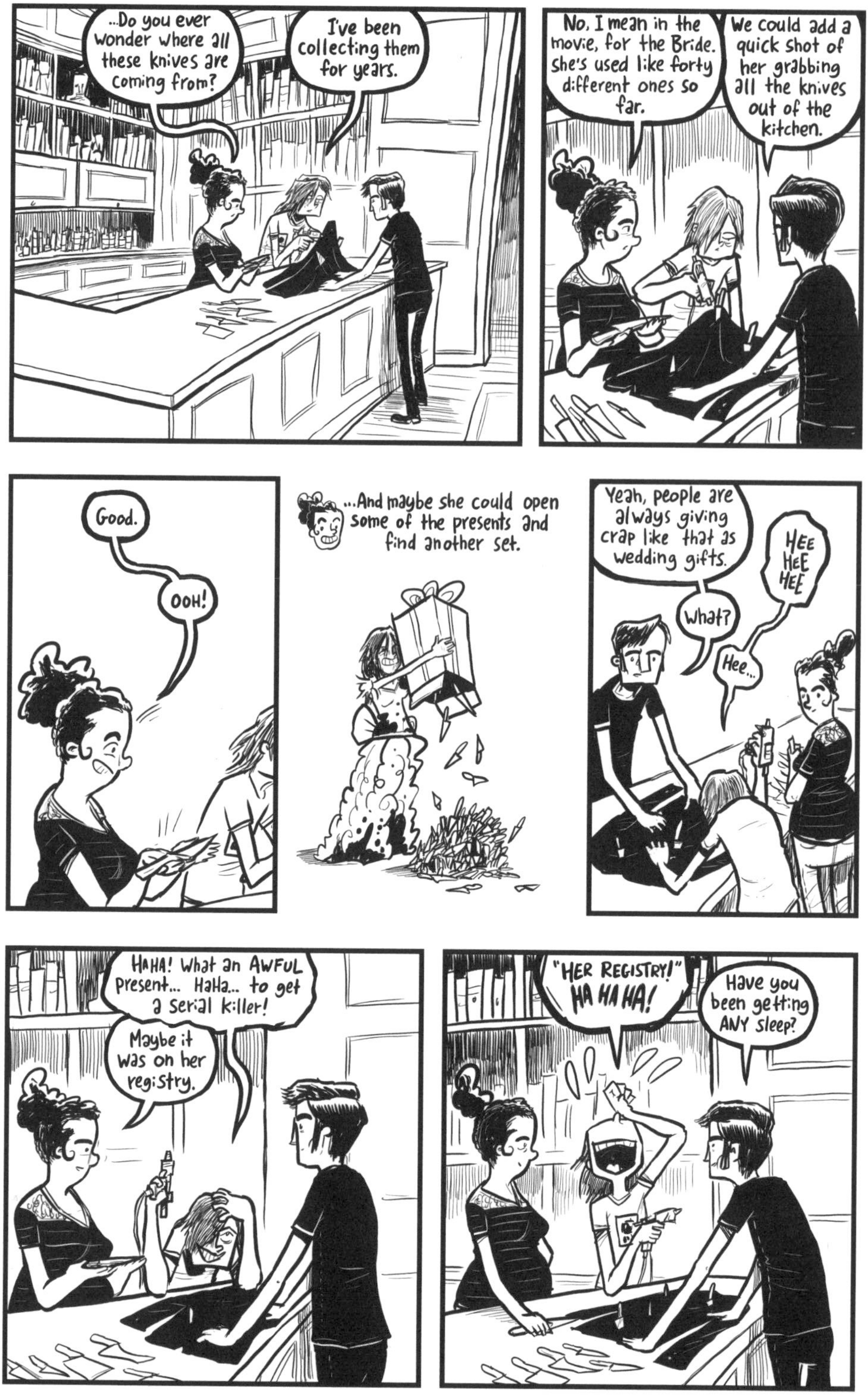
...Do you ever wonder where all these knives are coming from?
I've been collecting them for years.
No, I mean in the movie, for the Bride. She's used like forty different ones so far.
We could add a quick shot of her grabbing all the knives out of the kitchen.
Good.
OOH!
...And maybe she could open some of the presents and find another set.
Yeah, people are always giving crap like that as wedding gifts.
HEE HEE HEE
What?
Hee...
HAHA! What an AWFUL present... HaHa... to get a serial killer!
Maybe it was on her registry.
"HER REGISTRY!" HA HA HA!
Have you been getting ANY sleep?

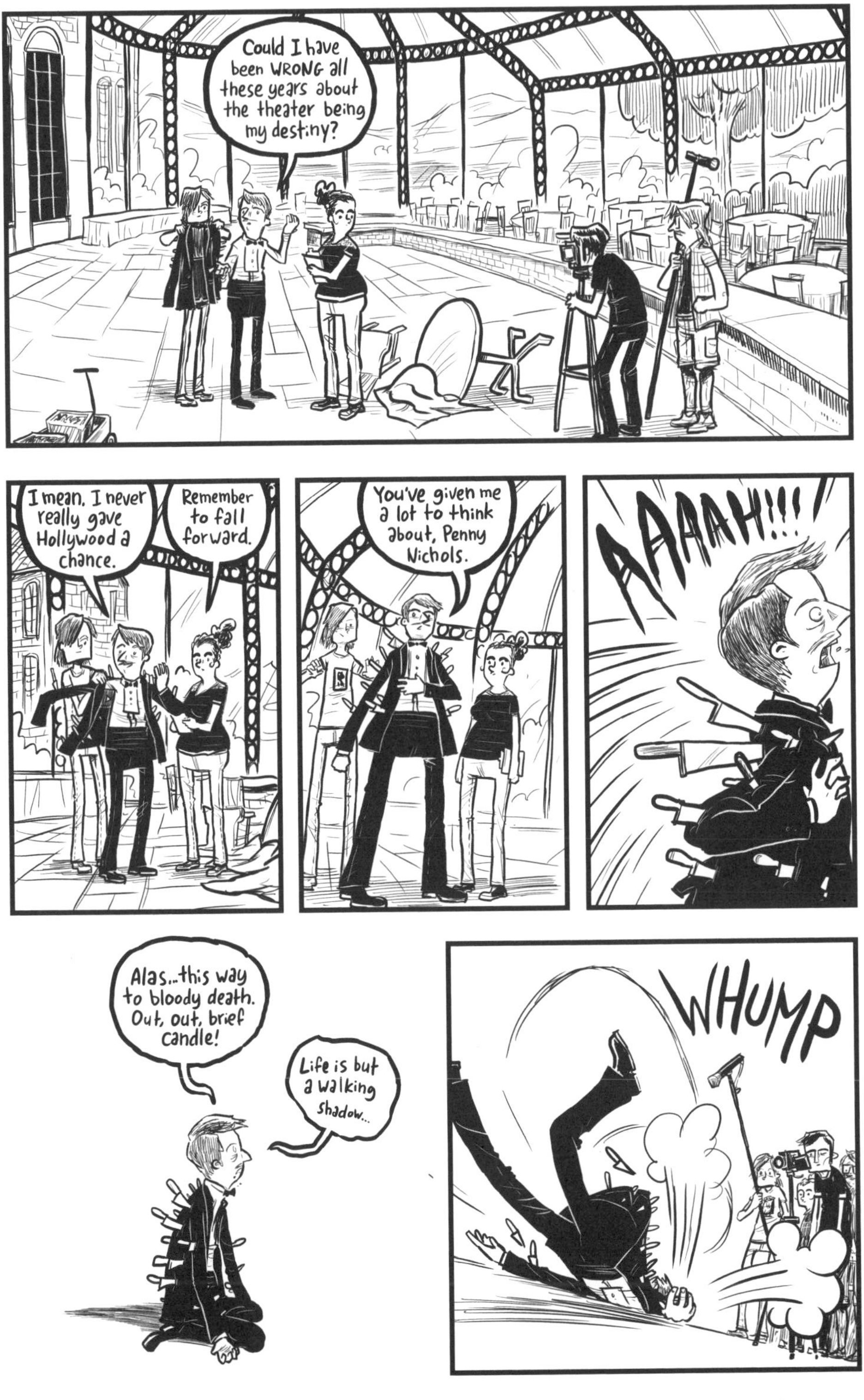
Could I have been WRONG all these years about the theater being my destiny?
I mean, I never really gave Hollywood a chance.
Remember to fall forward.
You've given me a lot to think about, Penny Nichols.
AAAAH!!!...
Alas...this way to bloody death. Out, out, brief candle!
Life is but a walking shadow...
WHUMP

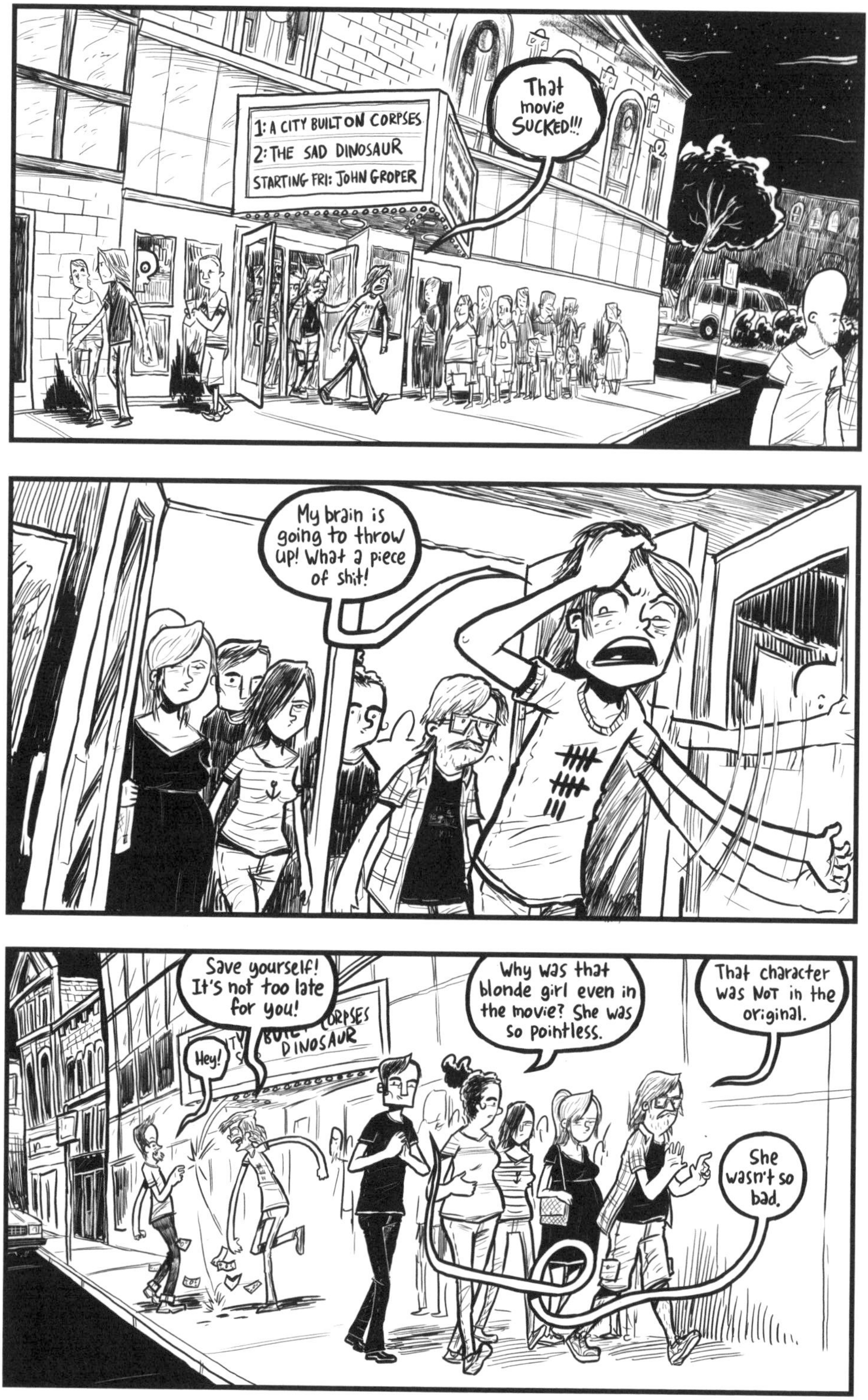
1: A CITY BUILT ON CORPSES
2: THE SAD DINOSAUR
STARTING FRI: JOHN GROPER
That movie SUCKED!!!
My brain is going to throw up! What a piece of shit!
Save yourself! It's not too late for you!
Hey!
Why was that blonde girl even in the movie? She was so pointless.
That character was NOT in the original.
She wasn't so bad.

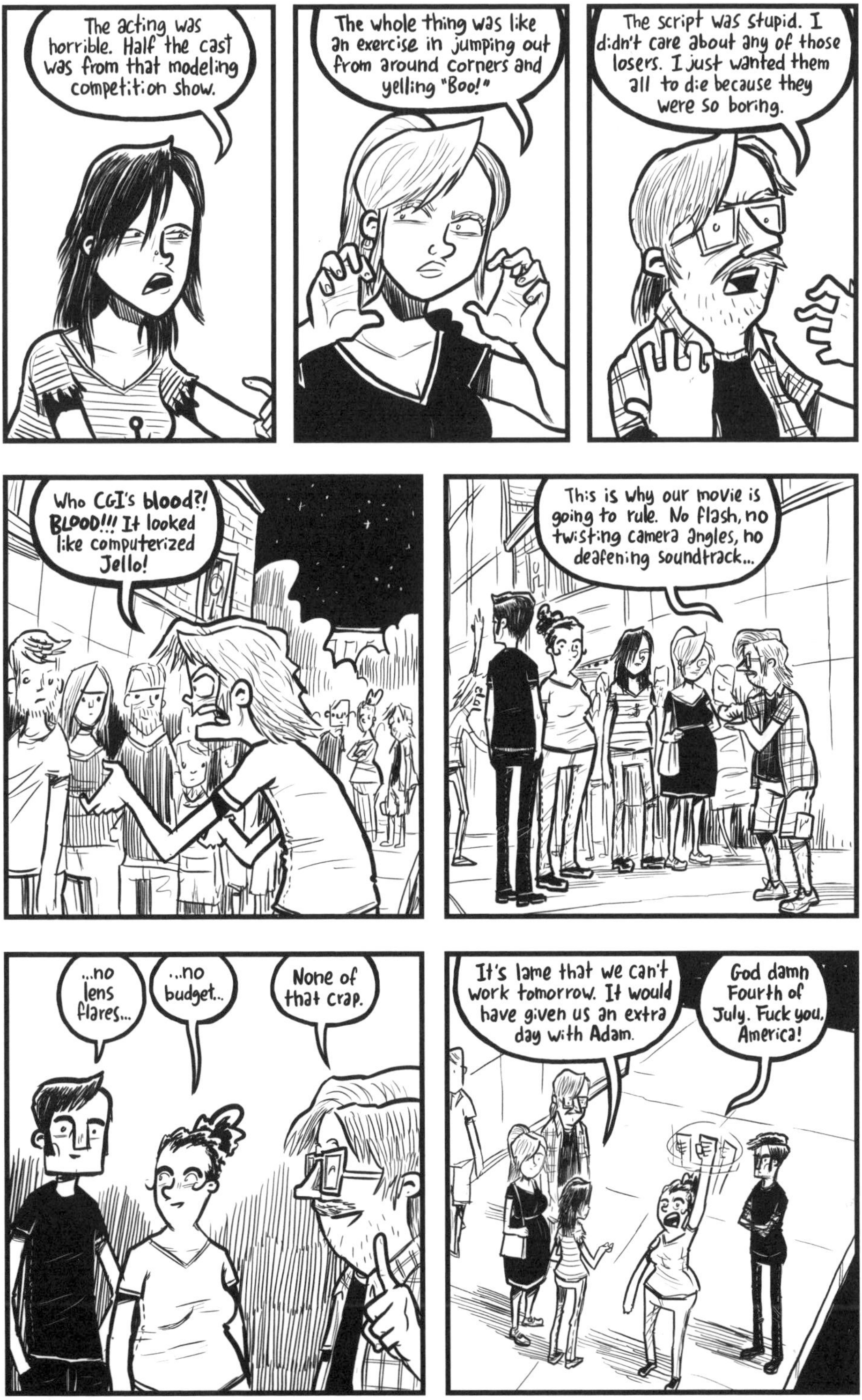
The acting was horrible. Half the cast was from that modeling competition show.
The whole thing was like an exercise in jumping out from around corners and yelling "Boo!"
The script was stupid. I didn't care about any of those losers. I just wanted them all to die because they were so boring.
Who CGI's blood?! BLOOD!!! It looked like computerized Jello!
This is why our movie is going to rule. No flash, no twisting camera angles, no deafening soundtrack...
...no lens flares...
...no budget...
None of that crap.
It's lame that we can't work tomorrow. It would have given us an extra day with Adam.
God damn Fourth of July. Fuck you, America!

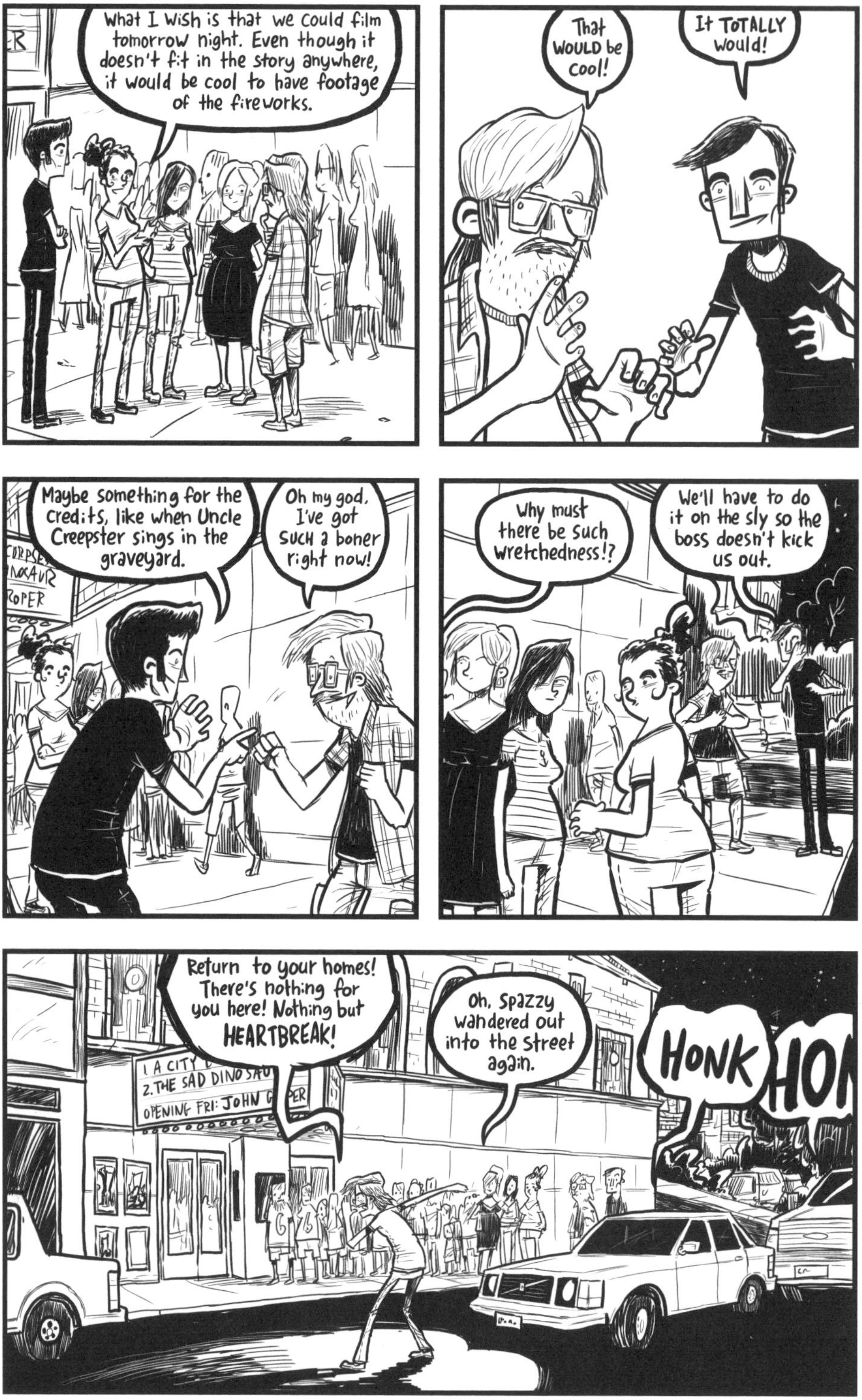
What I wish is that we could film tomorrow night. Even though it doesn't fit in the story anywhere, it would be cool to have footage of the fireworks.
That WOULD be cool!
It TOTALLY would!
Maybe something for the credits, like when Uncle Creepster sings in the graveyard.
Oh my god, I've got SUCH a boner right now!
Why must there be such wretchedness!?
We'll have to do it on the sly so the boss doesn't kick us out.
Return to your homes! There's nothing for you here! Nothing but HEARTBREAK!
Oh, Spazzy wandered out into the street again.
HONK

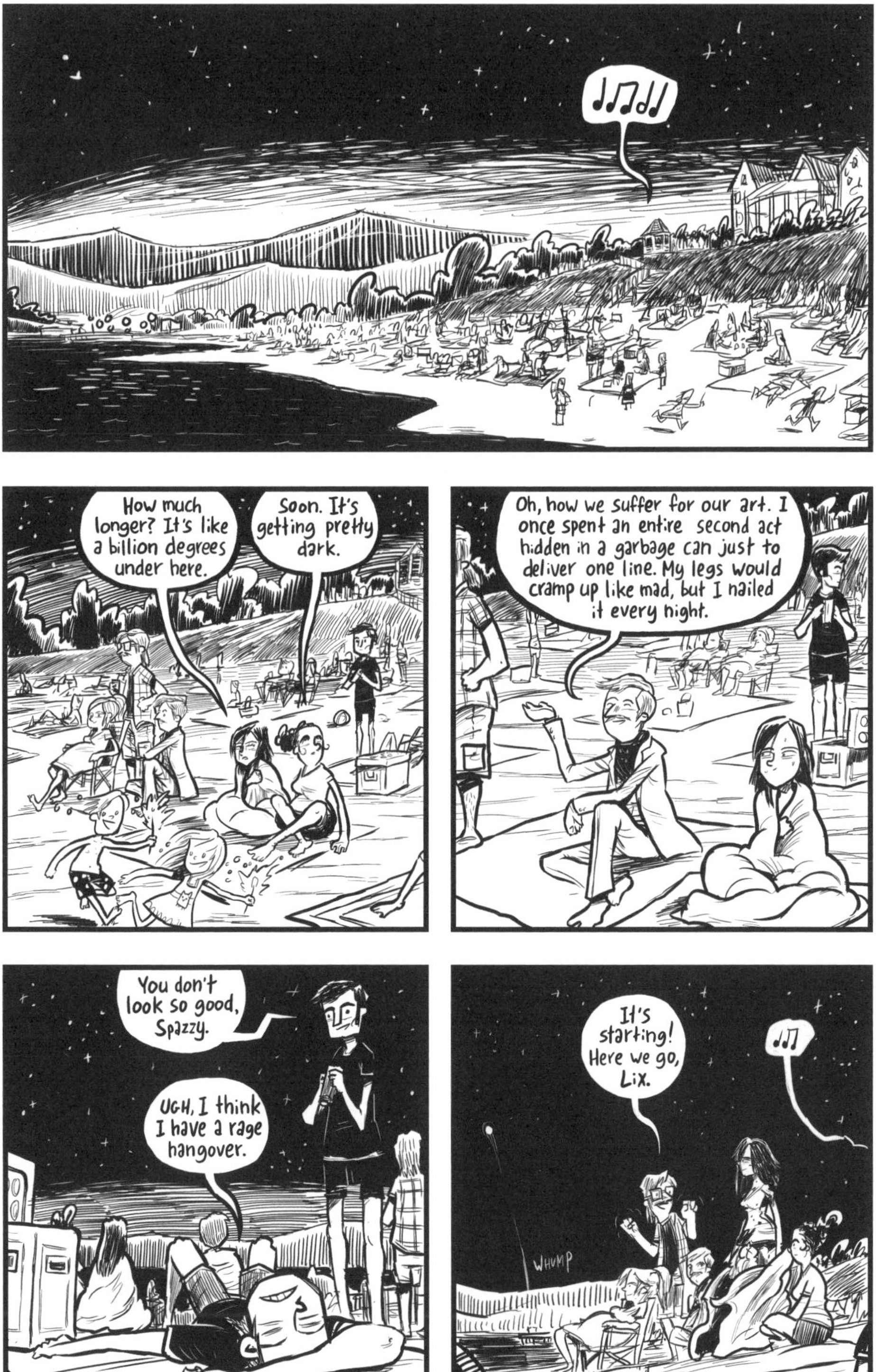
How much longer? It's like a billion degrees under here.
Soon. It's getting pretty dark.
Oh, how we suffer for our art. I once spent an entire second act hidden in a garbage can just to deliver one line. My legs would cramp up like mad, but I nailed it every night.
You don't look so good, Spazzy.
UGH, I think I have a rage hangover.
WHUMP
It's starting! Here we go, Lix.

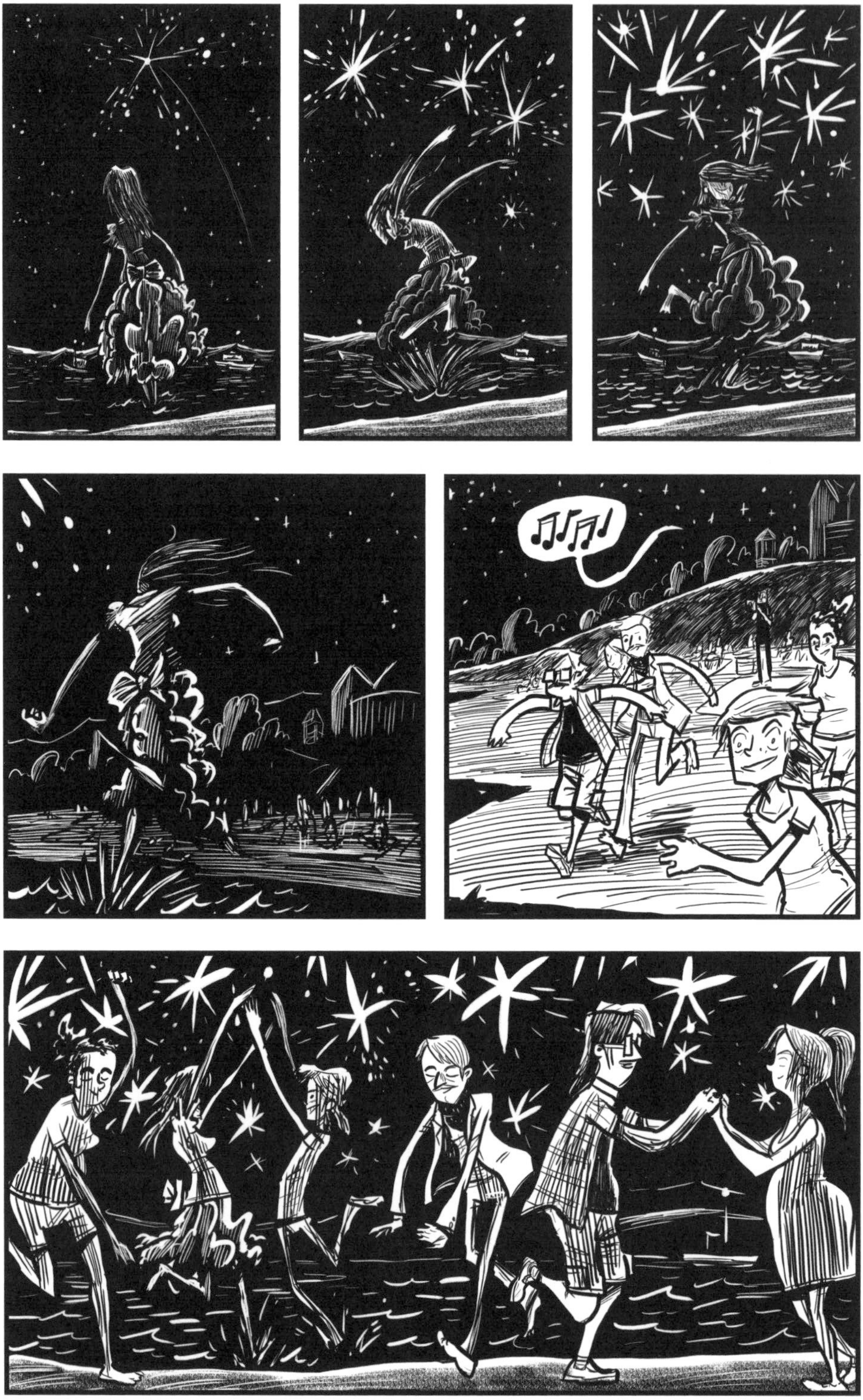

CHAPTER SEVEN

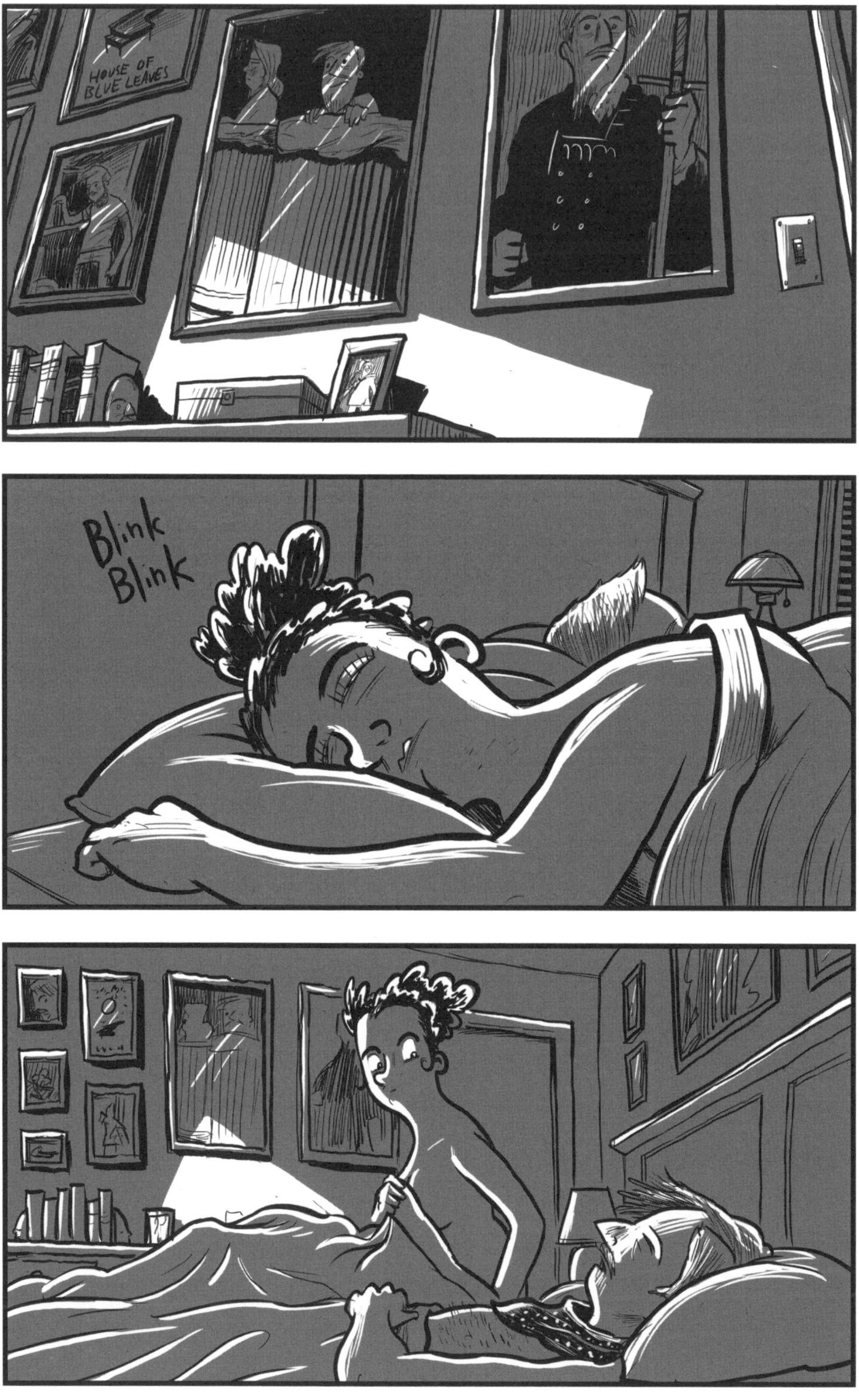
HOUSE OF BLUE LEAVES
Blink
Blink

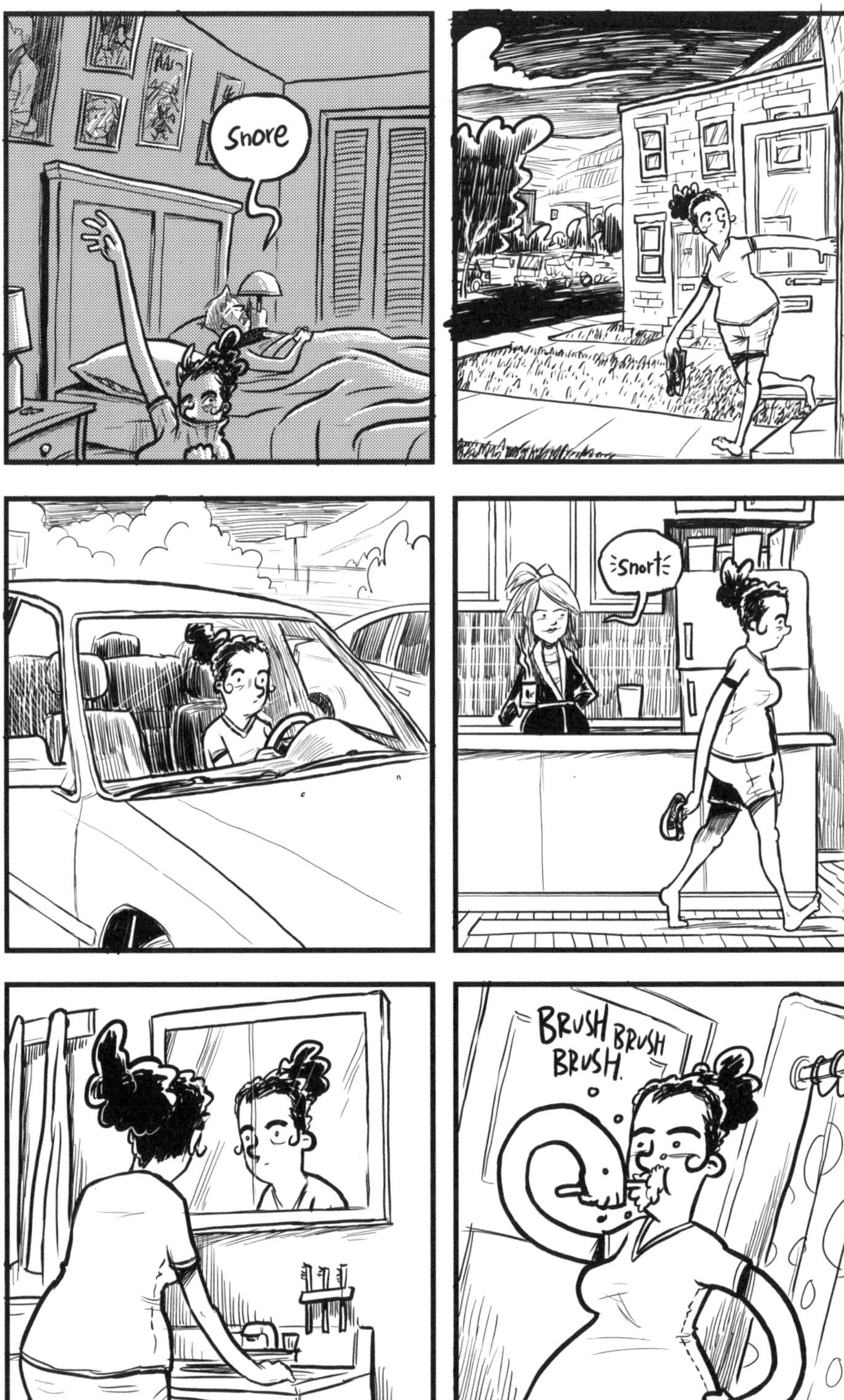
snore
snort
BRUSH BRUSH
BRUSH.

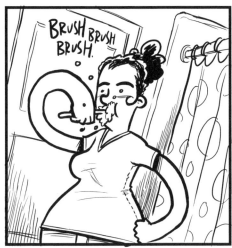

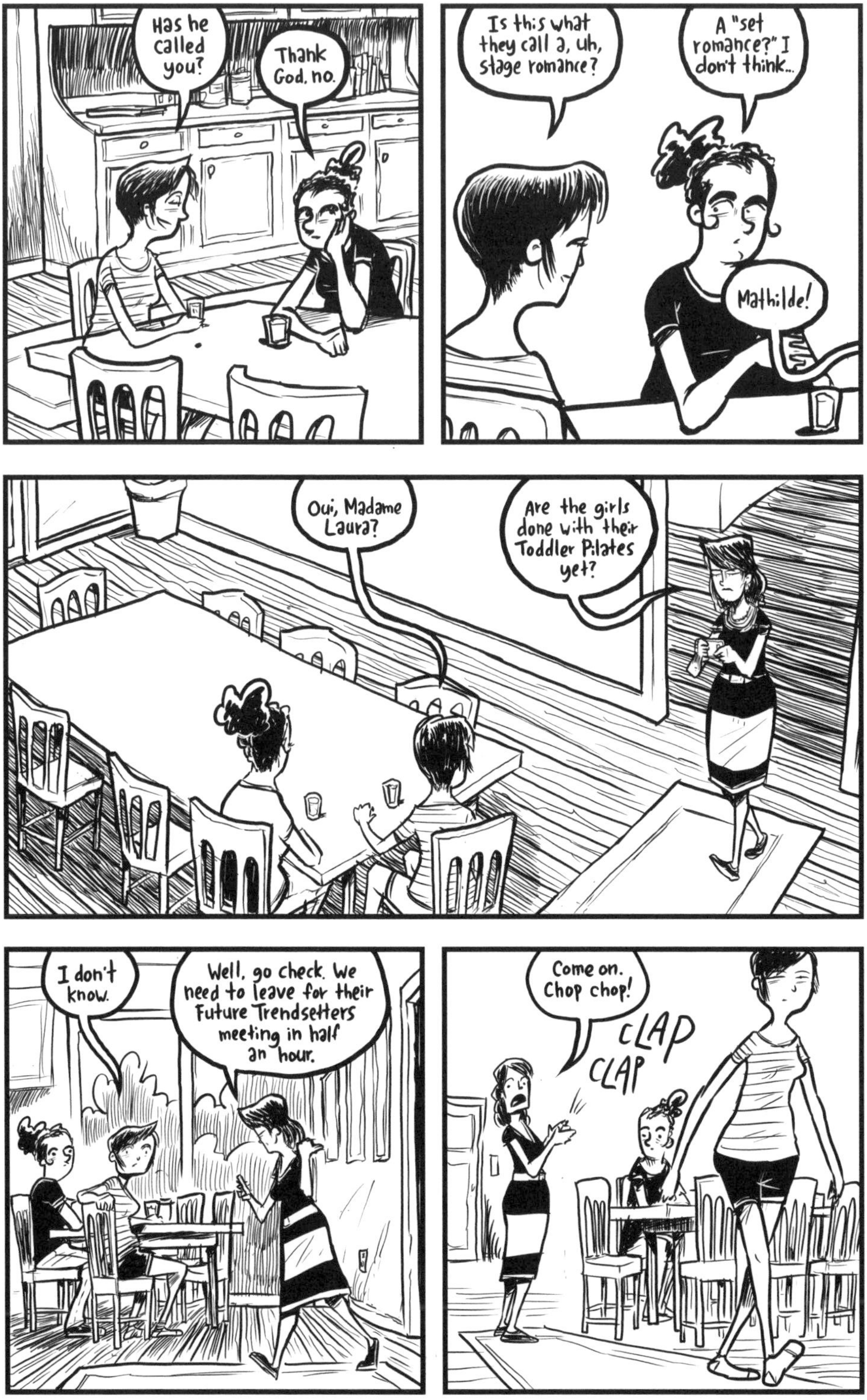
Has he called you?
Thank God, no.
Is this what they call a, uh, stage romance?
A "set romance?" I don't think...
Mathilde!
Oui, Madame Laura?
Are the girls done with their Toddler Pilates yet?
I don't know.
Well, go check. We need to leave for their Future Trendsetters meeting in half an hour.
Come on. Chop chop!
CLAP CLAP

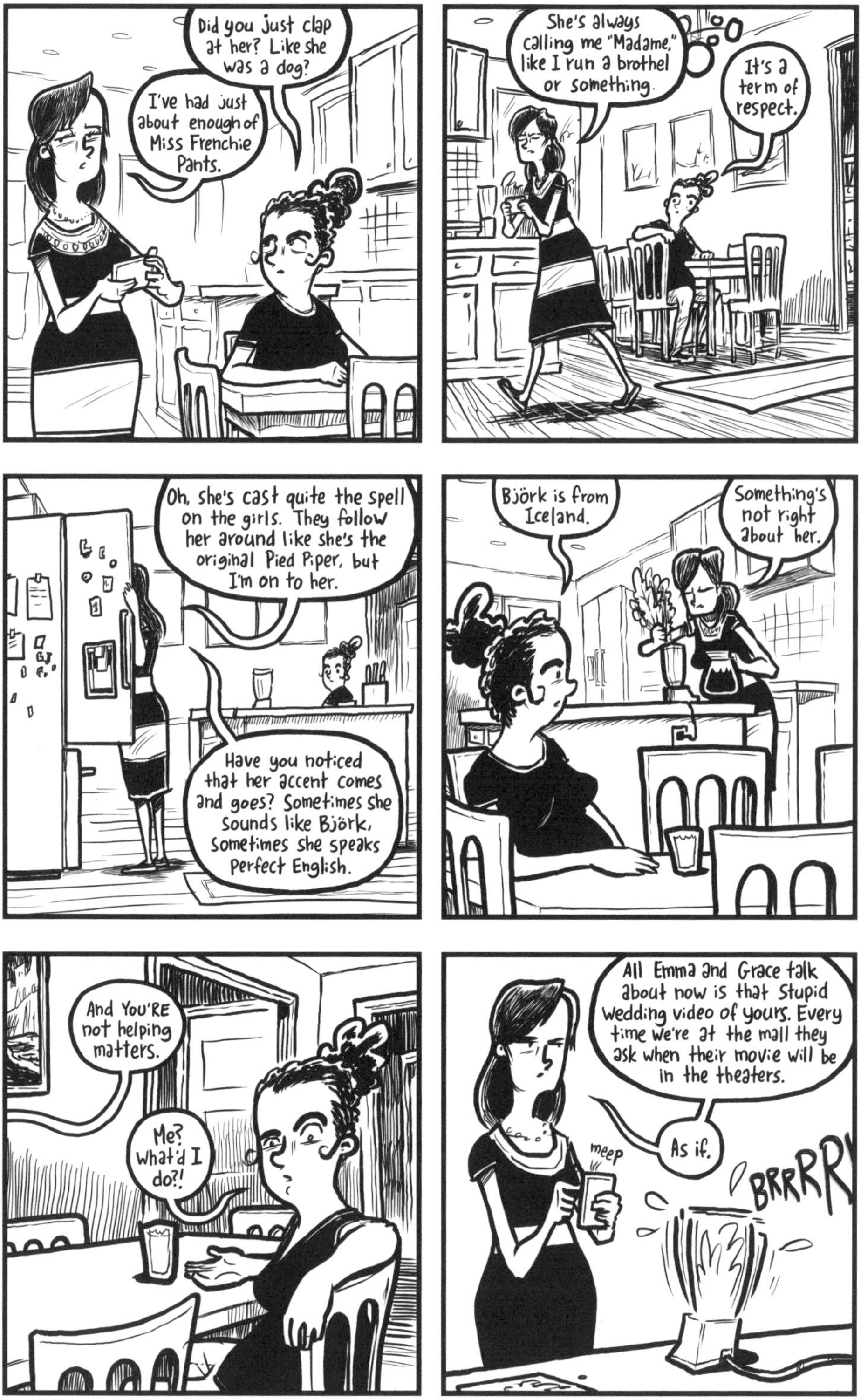

I've had just about enough of Miss Frenchie Pants.
Did you just clap at her? Like she was a dog?
She's always calling me "Madame," like I run a brothel or something.
It's a term of respect.
Oh, she's cast quite the spell on the girls. They follow her around like she's the original Pied Piper, but I'm on to her.
Have you noticed that her accent comes and goes? Sometimes she sounds like Björk, sometimes she speaks perfect English.
Björk is from Iceland.
Something's not right about her.
And YOU'RE not helping matters.
Me? What'd I do?!
All Emma and Grace talk about now is that stupid wedding video of yours. Every time we're at the mall they ask when their movie will be in the theaters.
As if.
meep
BRRRR

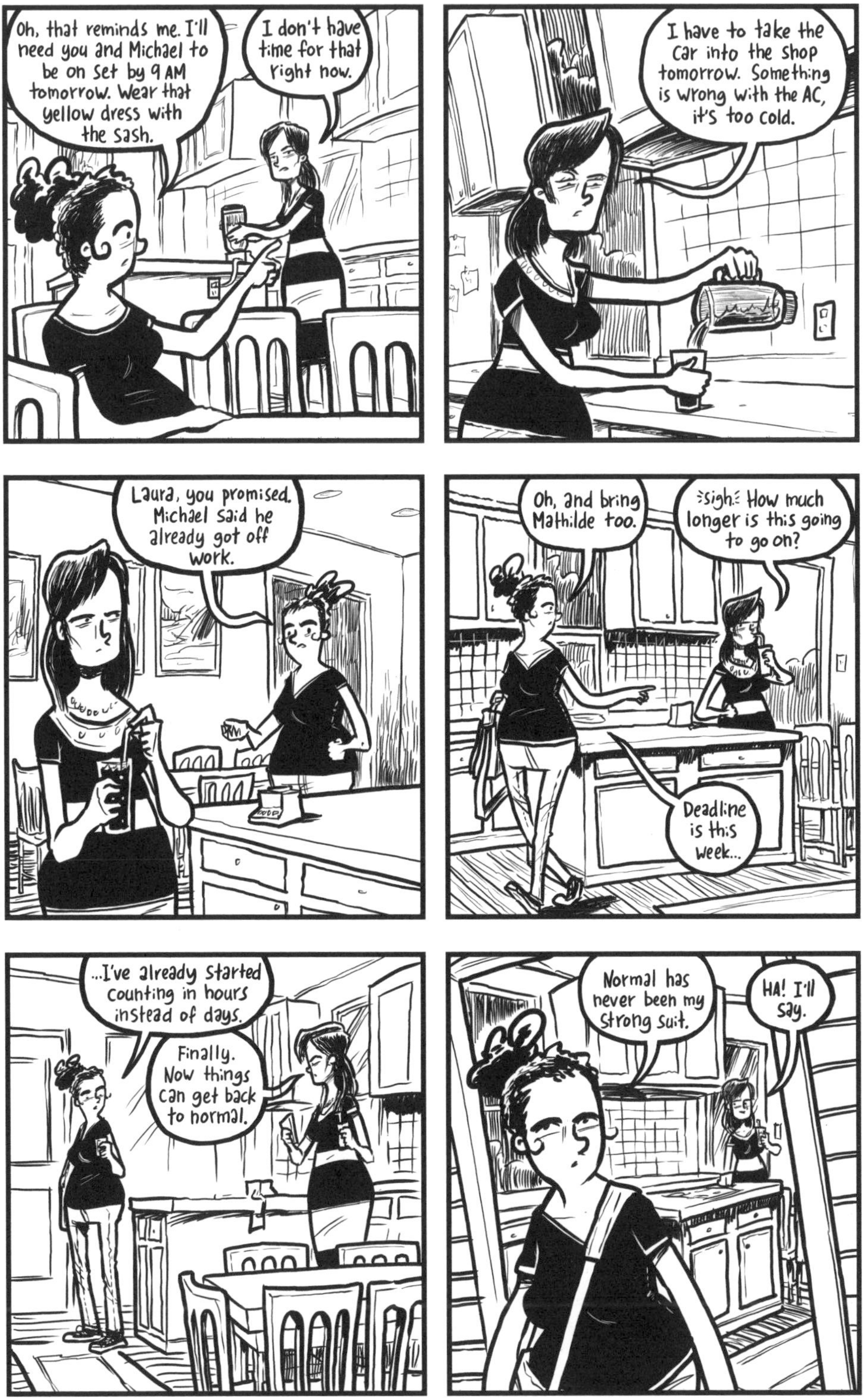
Oh, that reminds me. I'll need you and Michael to be on set by 9 AM tomorrow. Wear that yellow dress with the sash.
I don't have time for that right now.
I have to take the car into the shop tomorrow. Something is wrong with the AC, it's too cold.
Laura, you promised. Michael said he already got off work.
Oh, and bring Mathilde too.
sigh. How much longer is this going to go on?
Deadline is this week...
...I've already started counting in hours instead of days.
Finally. Now things can get back to normal.
Normal has never been my strong suit.
HA! I'll say.

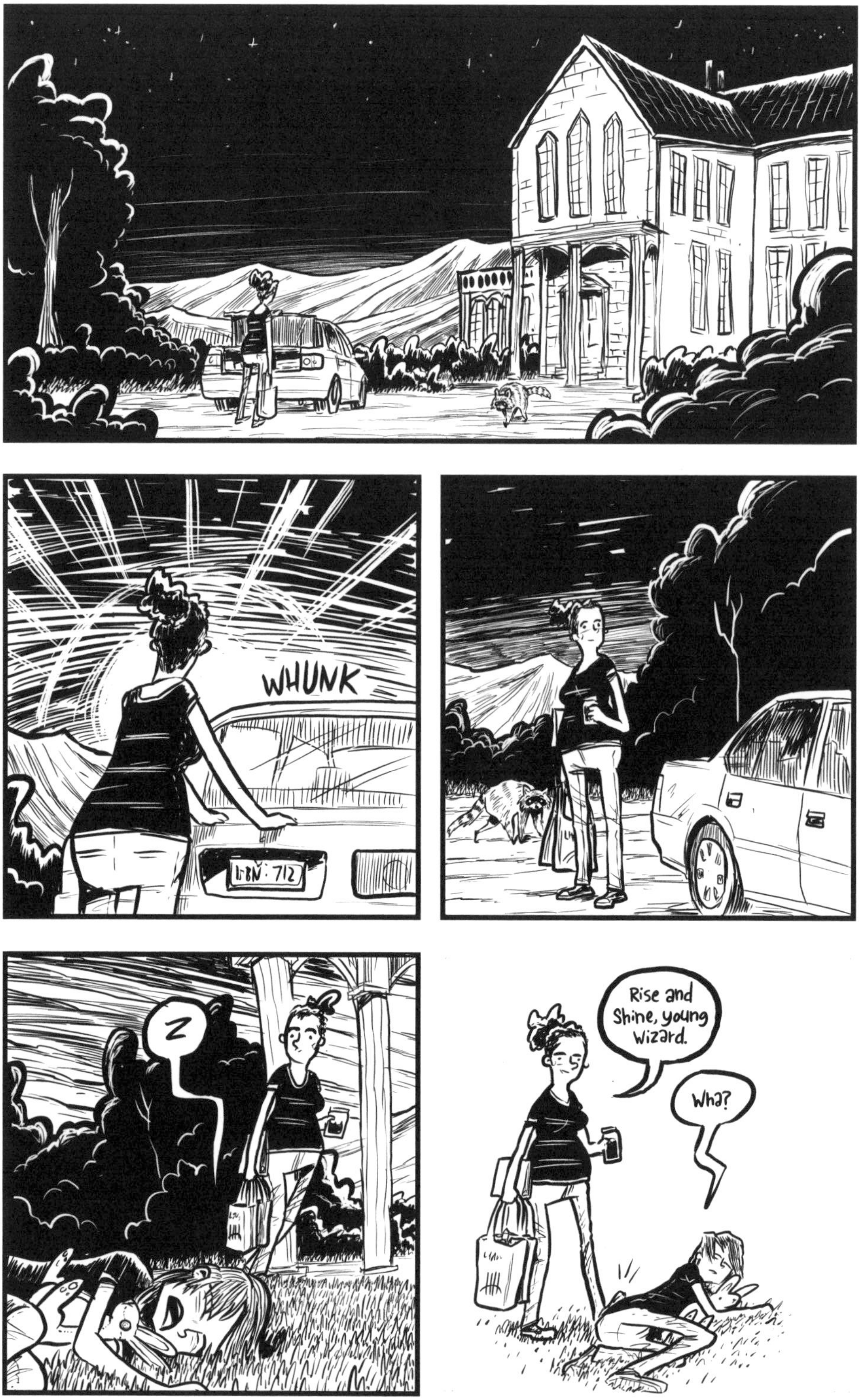
WHUNK
LBN 712
Z
Rise and Shine, young wizard.
Wha?

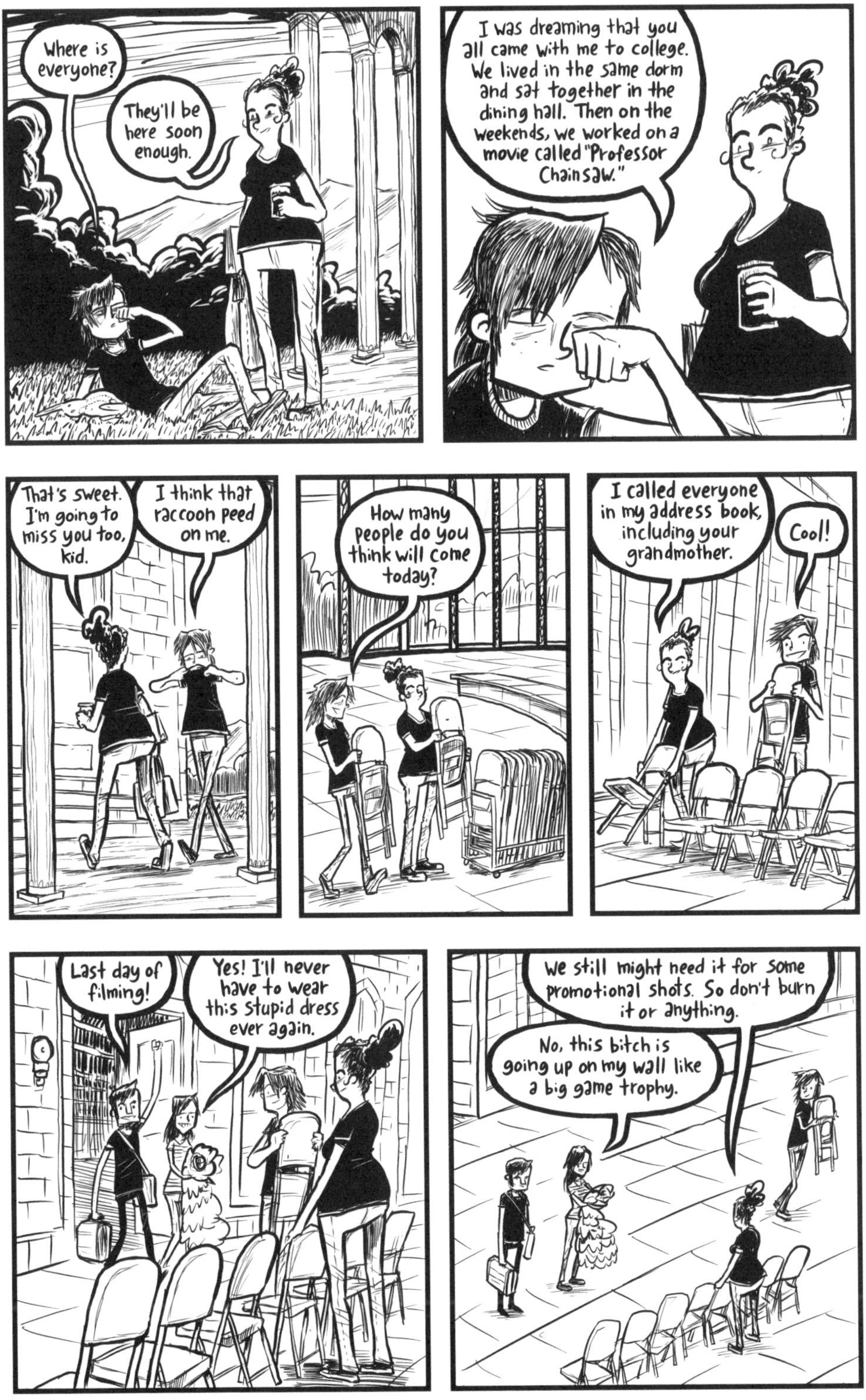
Where is everyone?
They'll be here soon enough.
I was dreaming that you all came with me to college. We lived in the same dorm and sat together in the dining hall. Then on the weekends, we worked on a movie called "Professor Chainsaw."
That's sweet. I'm going to miss you too, kid.
I think that raccoon peed on me.
How many people do you think will come today?
I called everyone in my address book, including your grandmother.
Cool!
Last day of filming!
Yes! I'll never have to wear this stupid dress ever again.
We still might need it for some promotional shots. So don't burn it or anything.
No, this bitch is going up on my wall like a big game trophy.

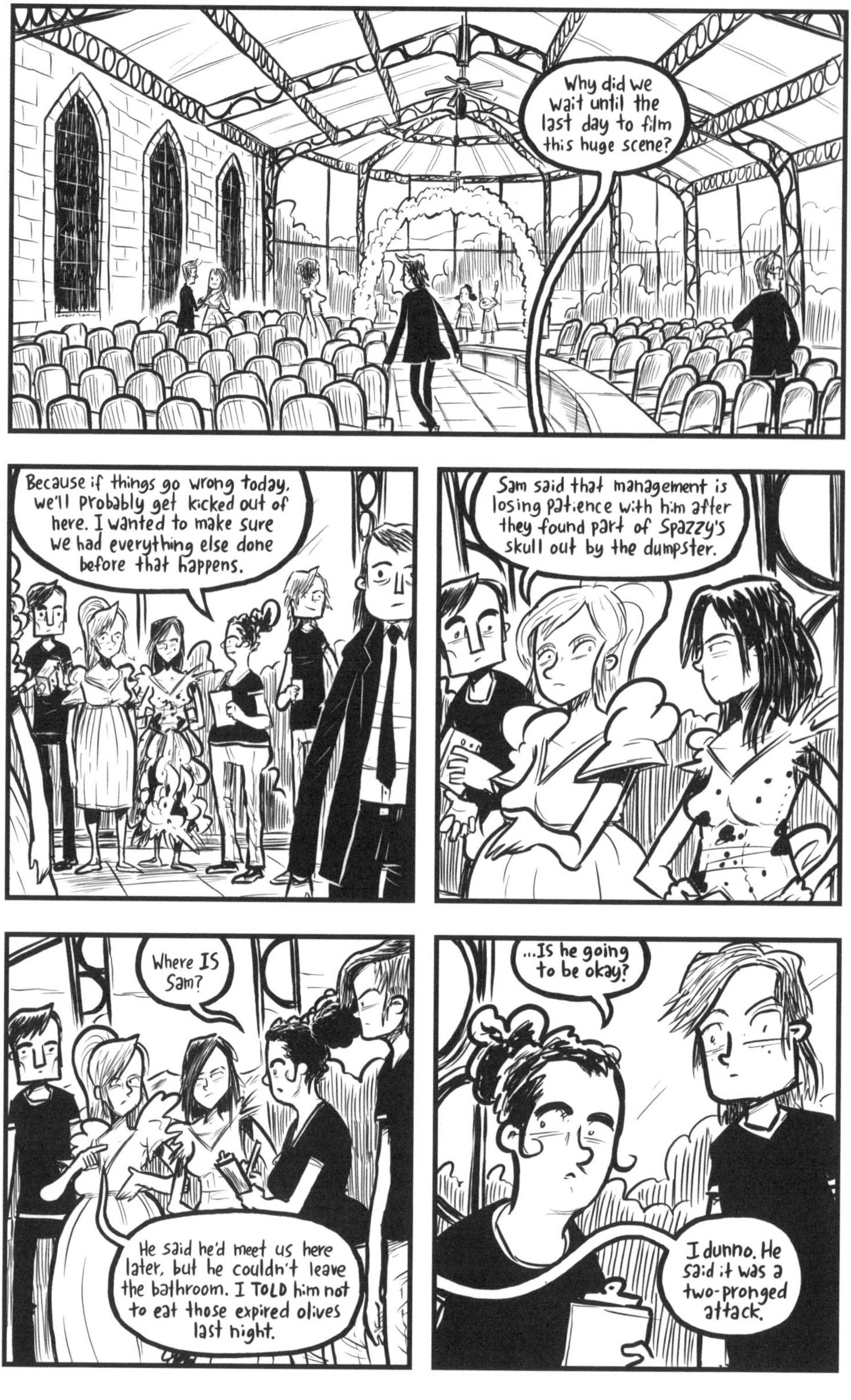

Why did we wait until the last day to film this huge scene?
Because if things go wrong today, we'll probably get kicked out of here. I wanted to make sure we had everything else done before that happens.
Sam said that management is losing patience with him after they found part of Spazzy's skull out by the dumpster.
Where IS Sam?
He said he'd meet us here later, but he couldn't leave the bathroom. I TOLD him not to eat those expired olives last night.
...Is he going to be okay?
I dunno. He said it was a two-pronged attack.

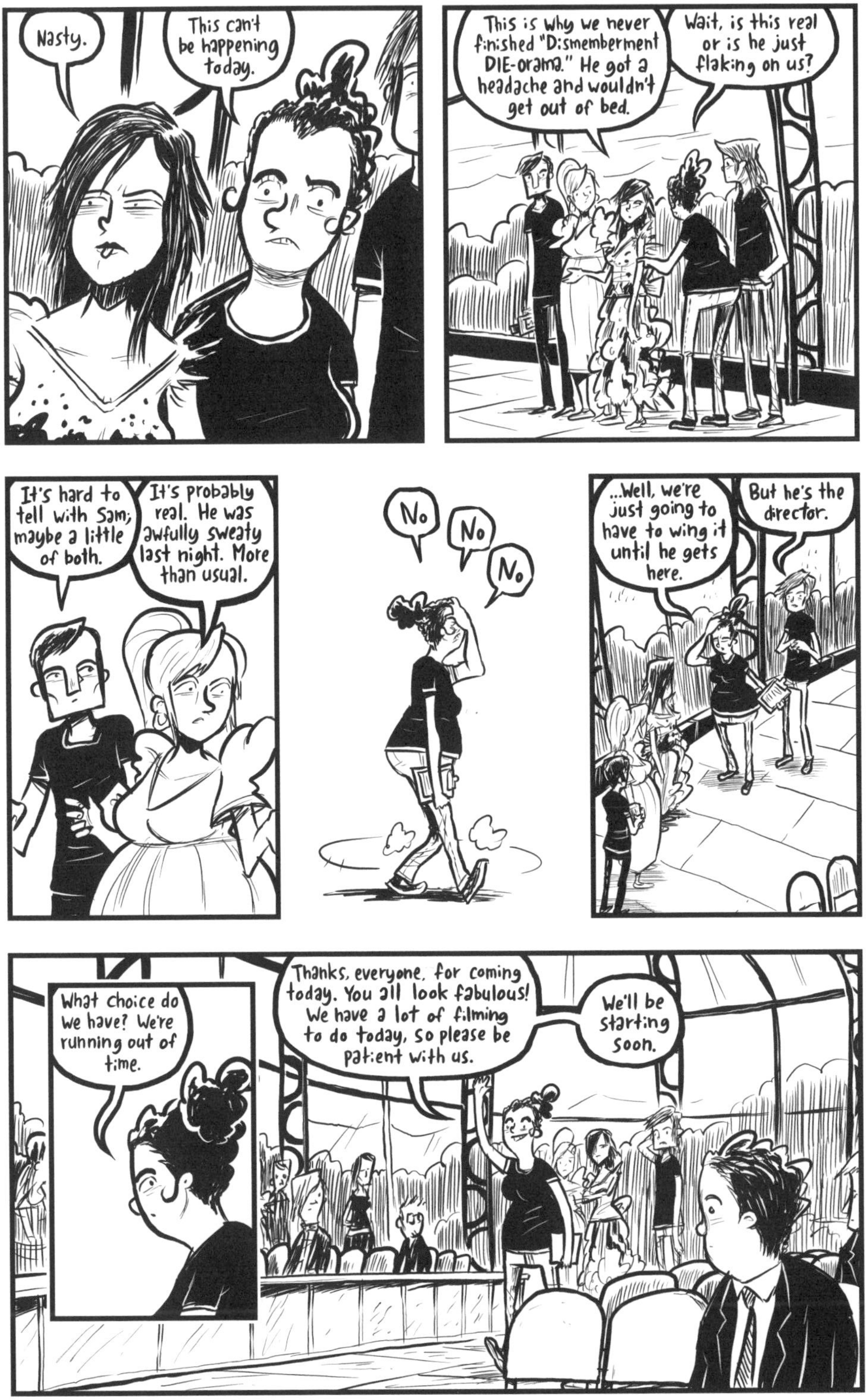
Nasty.
This can't be happening today.
This is why we never finished "Dismemberment DIE-orama." He got a headache and wouldn't get out of bed.
Wait, is this real or is he just flaking on us?
It's hard to tell with Sam; maybe a little of both.
It's probably real. He was awfully sweaty last night. More than usual.
No
No
No
...Well, we're just going to have to wing it until he gets here.
But he's the director.
What choice do we have? We're running out of time.
Thanks, everyone, for coming today. You all look fabulous! We have a lot of filming to do today, so please be patient with us.
We'll be starting soon.

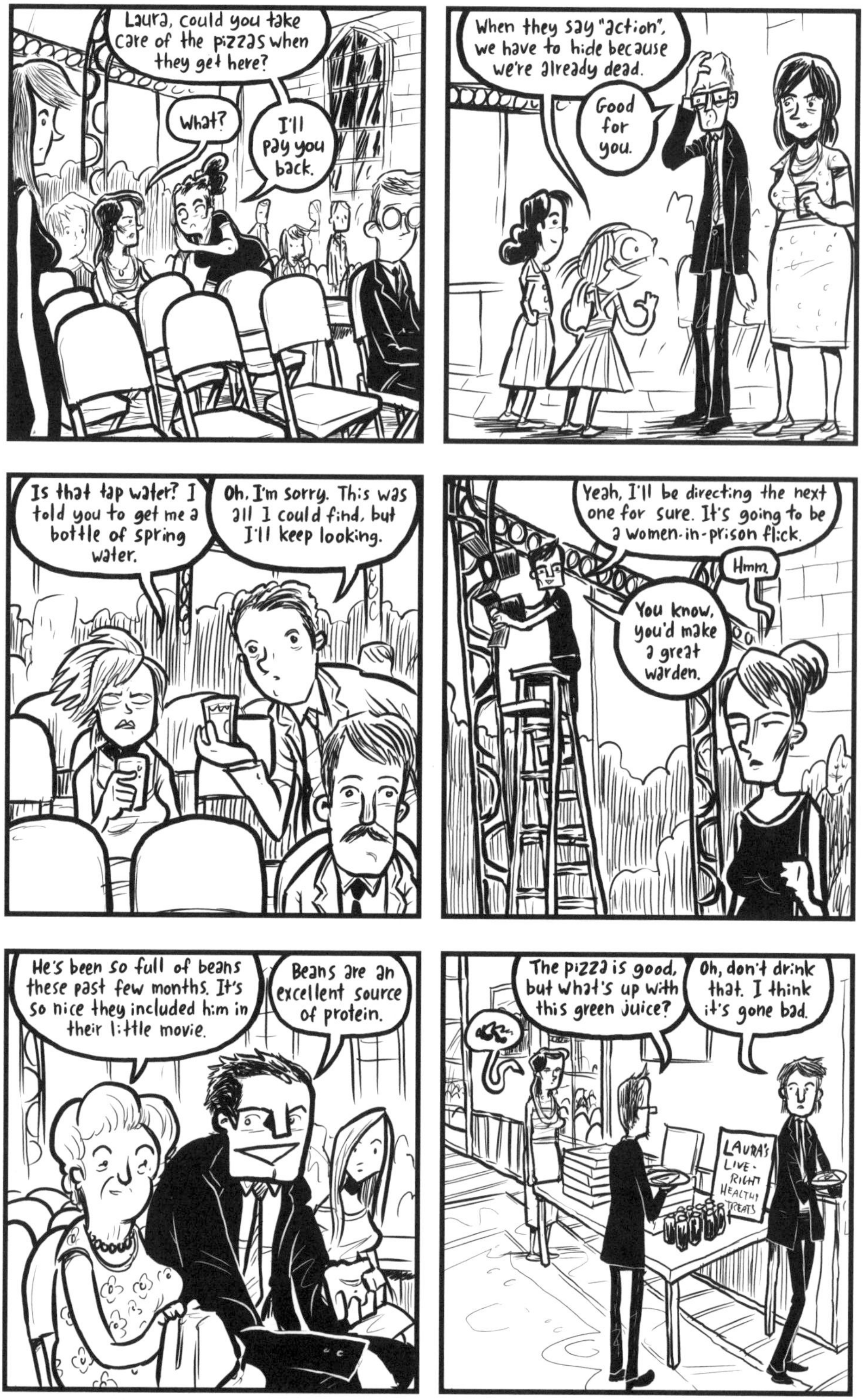
Laura, could you take care of the pizzas when they get here?
What?
I'll pay you back.
When they say "action", we have to hide because we're already dead.
Good for you.
Is that tap water? I told you to get me a bottle of spring water.
Oh, I'm sorry. This was all I could find, but I'll keep looking.
Yeah, I'll be directing the next one for sure. It's going to be a women-in-prison flick.
Hmm.
You know, you'd make a great warden.
He's been so full of beans these past few months. It's so nice they included him in their little movie.
Beans are an excellent source of protein.
The pizza is good, but what's up with this green juice?
Oh, don't drink that. I think it's gone bad.
LAURA'S LIVE-RIGHT HEALTHY TREATS

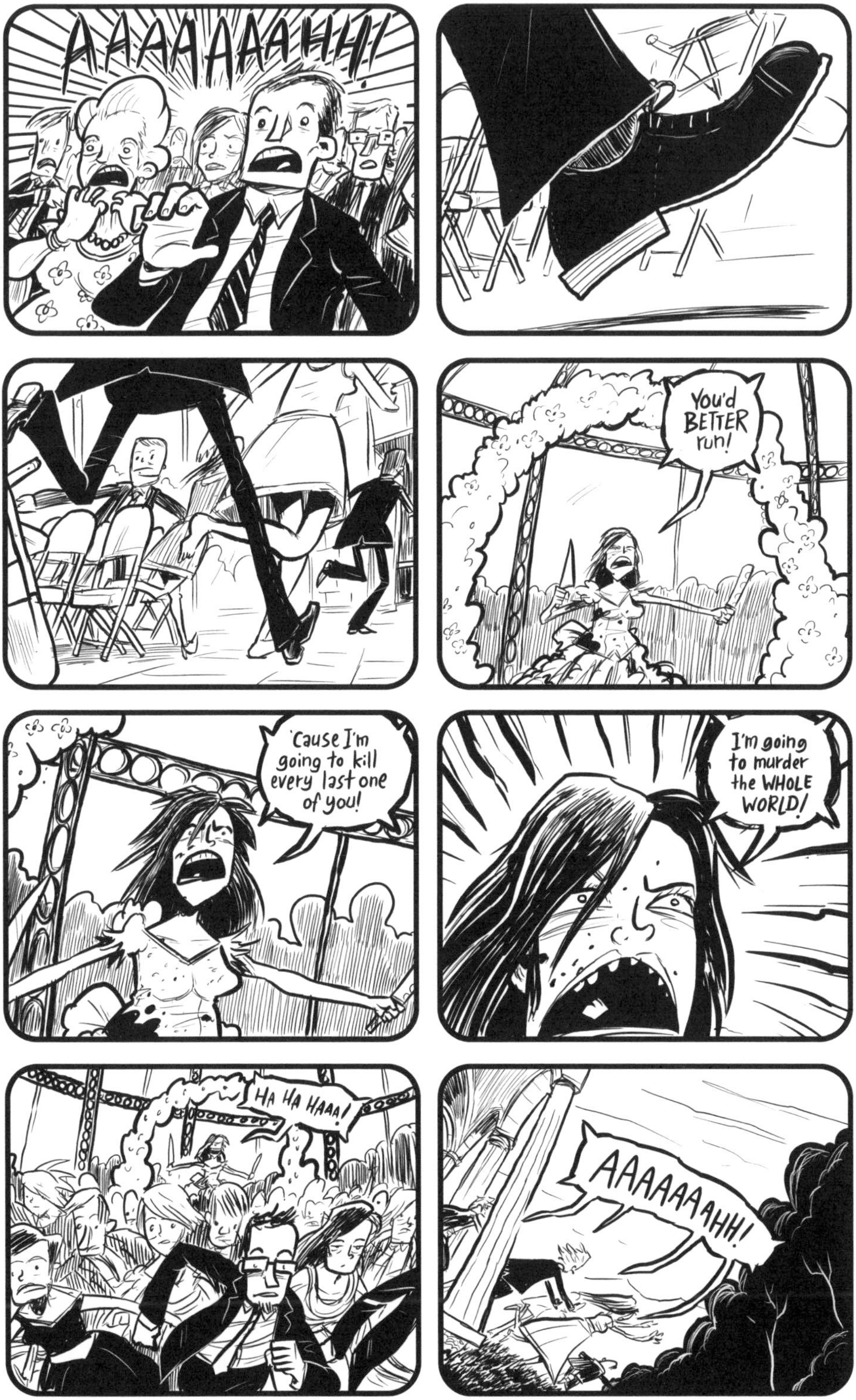
AAAAAAAHH!
You'd BETTER run!
'Cause I'm going to kill every last one of you!
I'm going to murder the WHOLE WORLD!
HA HA HAAA!
AAAAAAAHH!

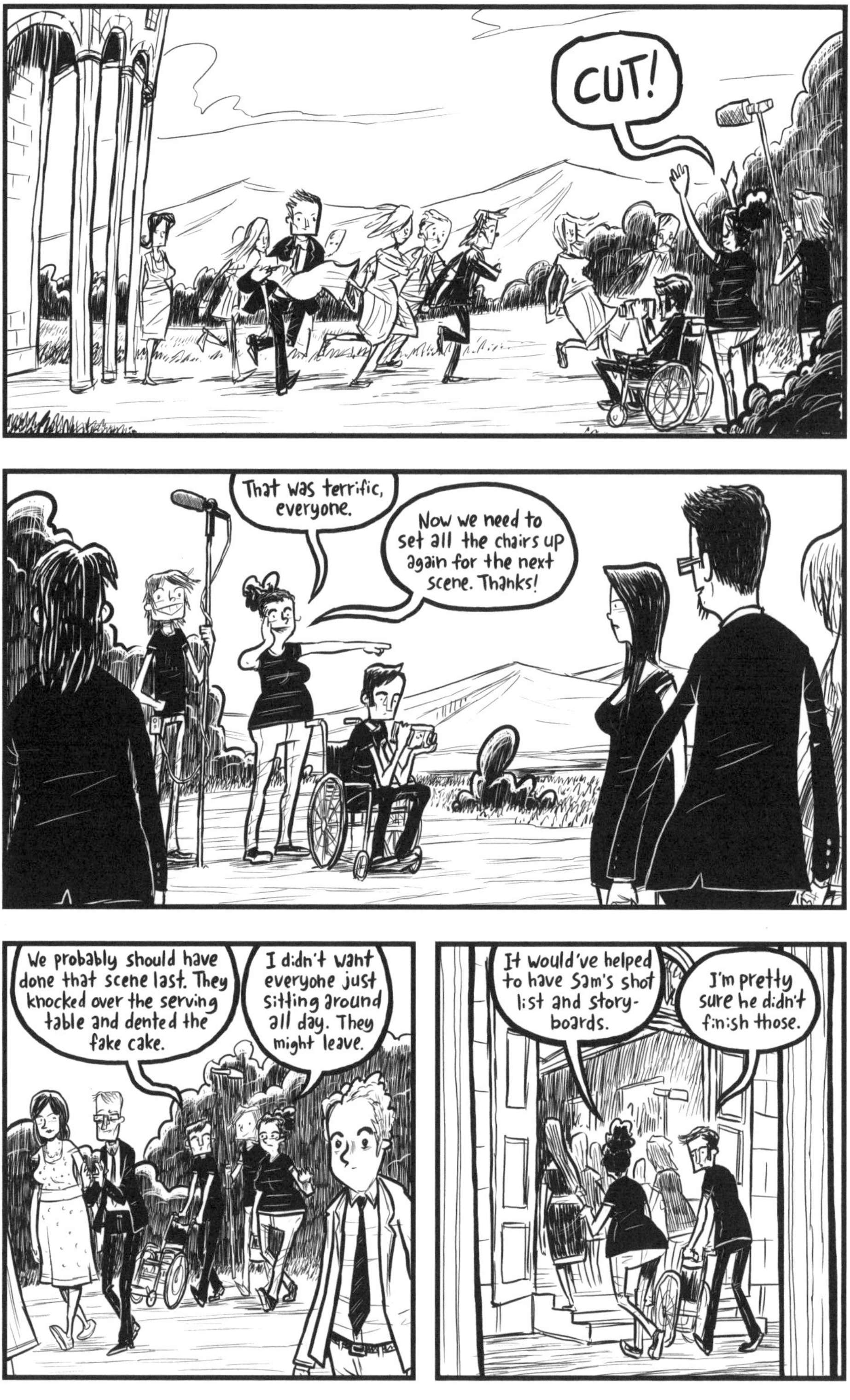
CUT!
That was terrific, everyone.
Now we need to set all the chairs up again for the next scene. Thanks!
We probably should have done that scene last. They knocked over the serving table and dented the fake cake.
I didn't want everyone just sitting around all day. They might leave.
It would've helped to have Sam's shot list and story-boards.
I'm pretty sure he didn't finish those.

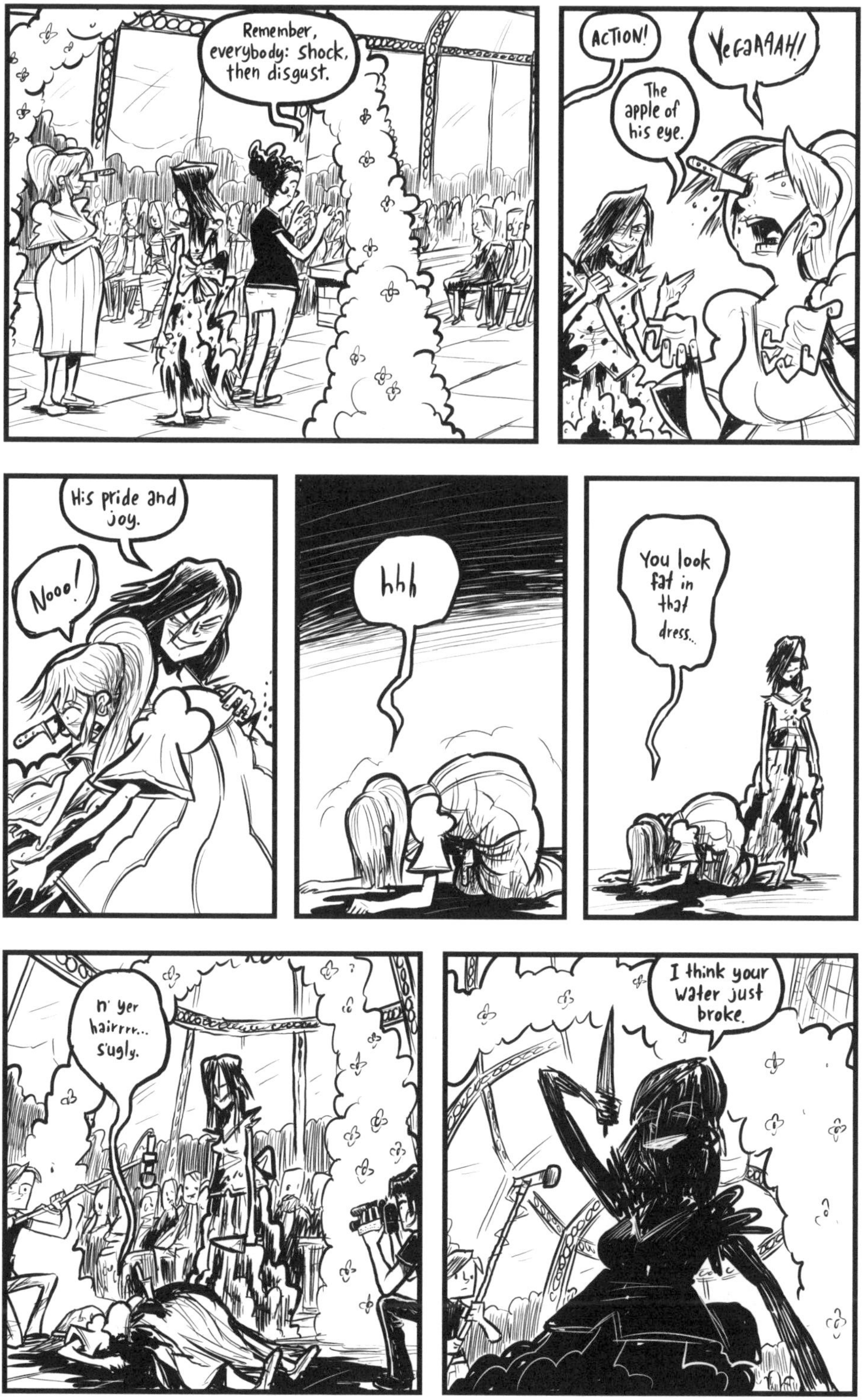
Remember, everybody: shock, then disgust.
ACTION!
YEGAAAAH!
The apple of his eye.
His pride and joy.
Nooo!
hhh
You look fat in that dress...
n' yer hairrrr... s'ugly.
I think your water just broke.

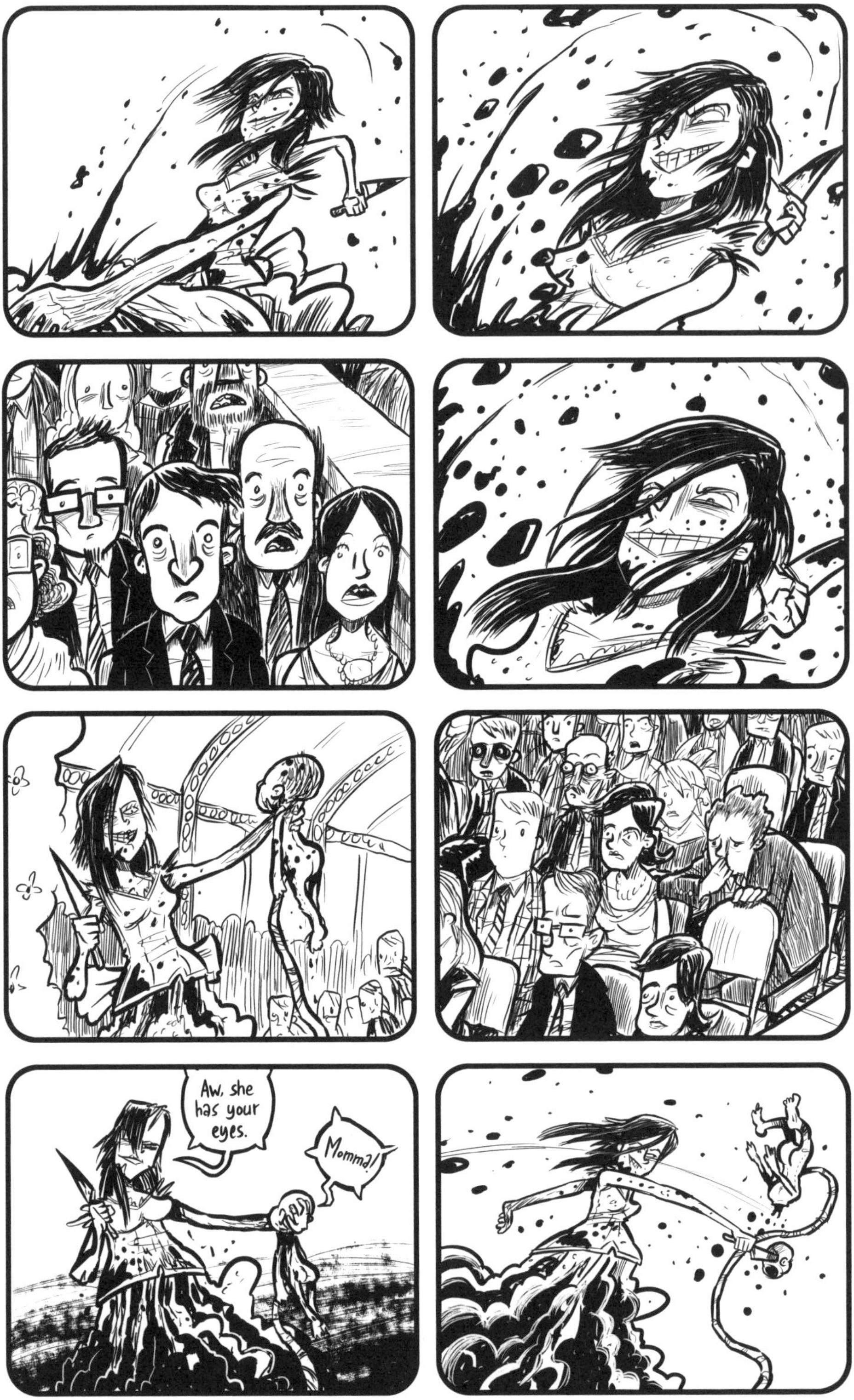
Aw, she has your eyes.
Momma!

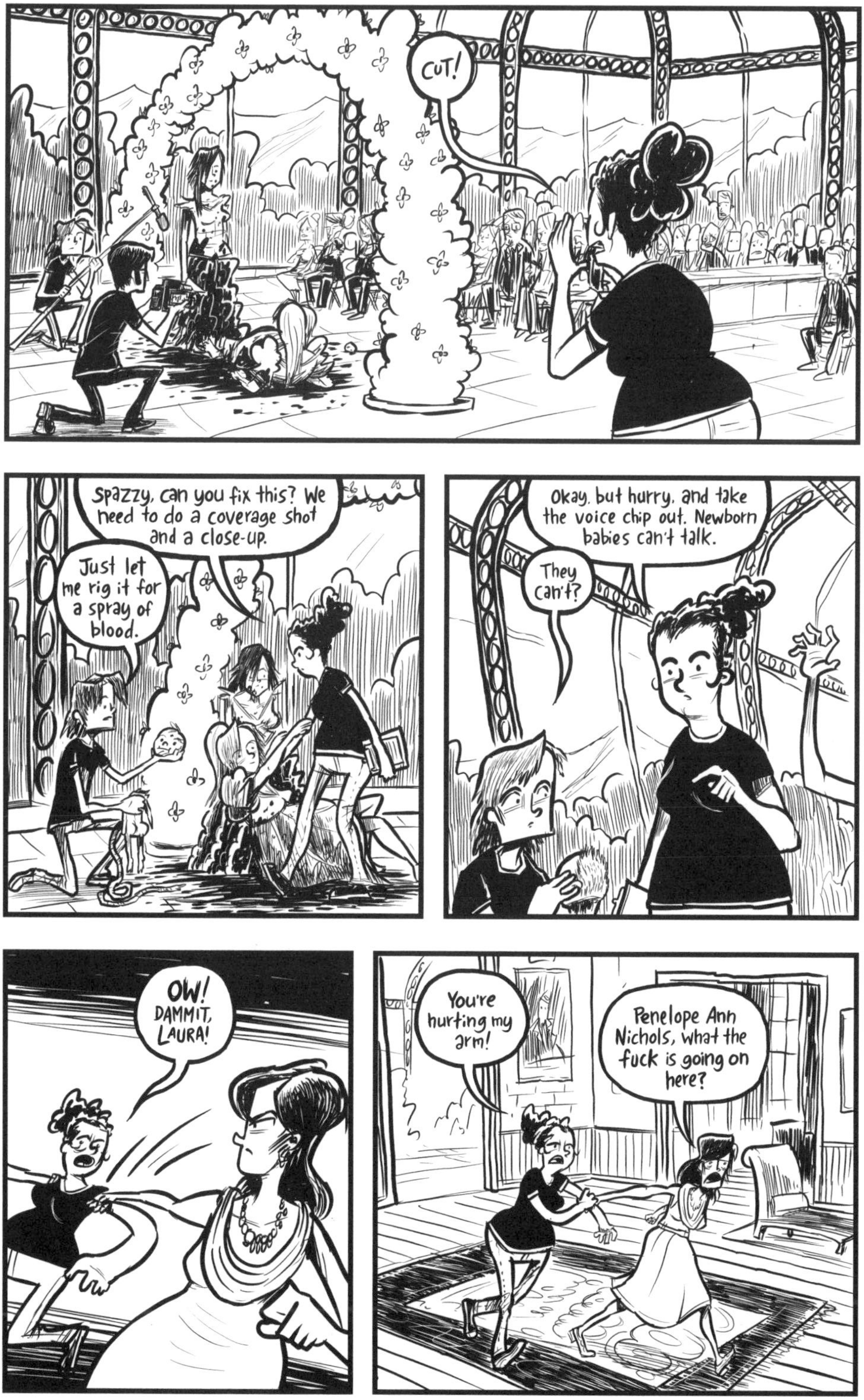
CUT!
Spazzy, can you fix this? We need to do a coverage shot and a close-up.
Just let me rig it for a spray of blood.
Okay, but hurry, and take the voice chip out. Newborn babies can't talk.
They can't?
OW! DAMMIT, LAURA!
You're hurting my arm!
Penelope Ann Nichols, what the fuck is going on here?

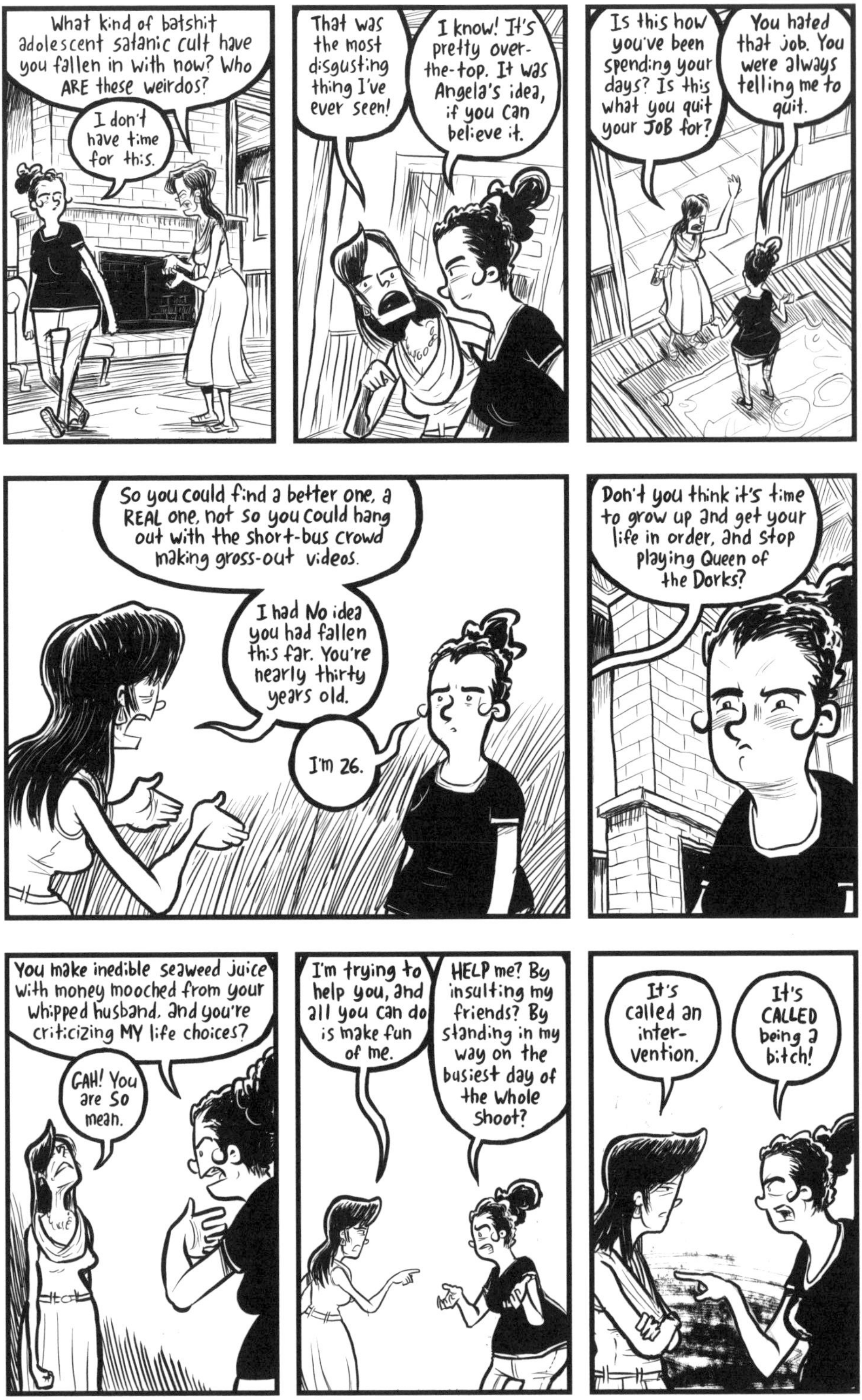
What kind of batshit adolescent satanic cult have you fallen in with now? Who ARE these weirdos?
I don't have time for this.
That was the most disgusting thing I've ever seen!
I know! It's pretty over-the-top. It was Angela's idea, if you can believe it.
Is this how you've been spending your days? Is this what you quit your JOB for?
You hated that job. You were always telling me to quit.
So you could find a better one, a REAL one, not so you could hang out with the short-bus crowd making gross-out videos.
I had NO idea you had fallen this far. You're nearly thirty years old.
I'm 26.
Don't you think it's time to grow up and get your life in order, and stop playing Queen of the Dorks?
You make inedible seaweed juice with money mooched from your whipped husband, and you're criticizing MY life choices?
GAH! You are SO mean.
I'm trying to help you, and all you can do is make fun of me.
HELP me? By insulting my friends? By standing in my way on the busiest day of the whole shoot?
It's called an inter-vention.
It's CALLED being a bitch!

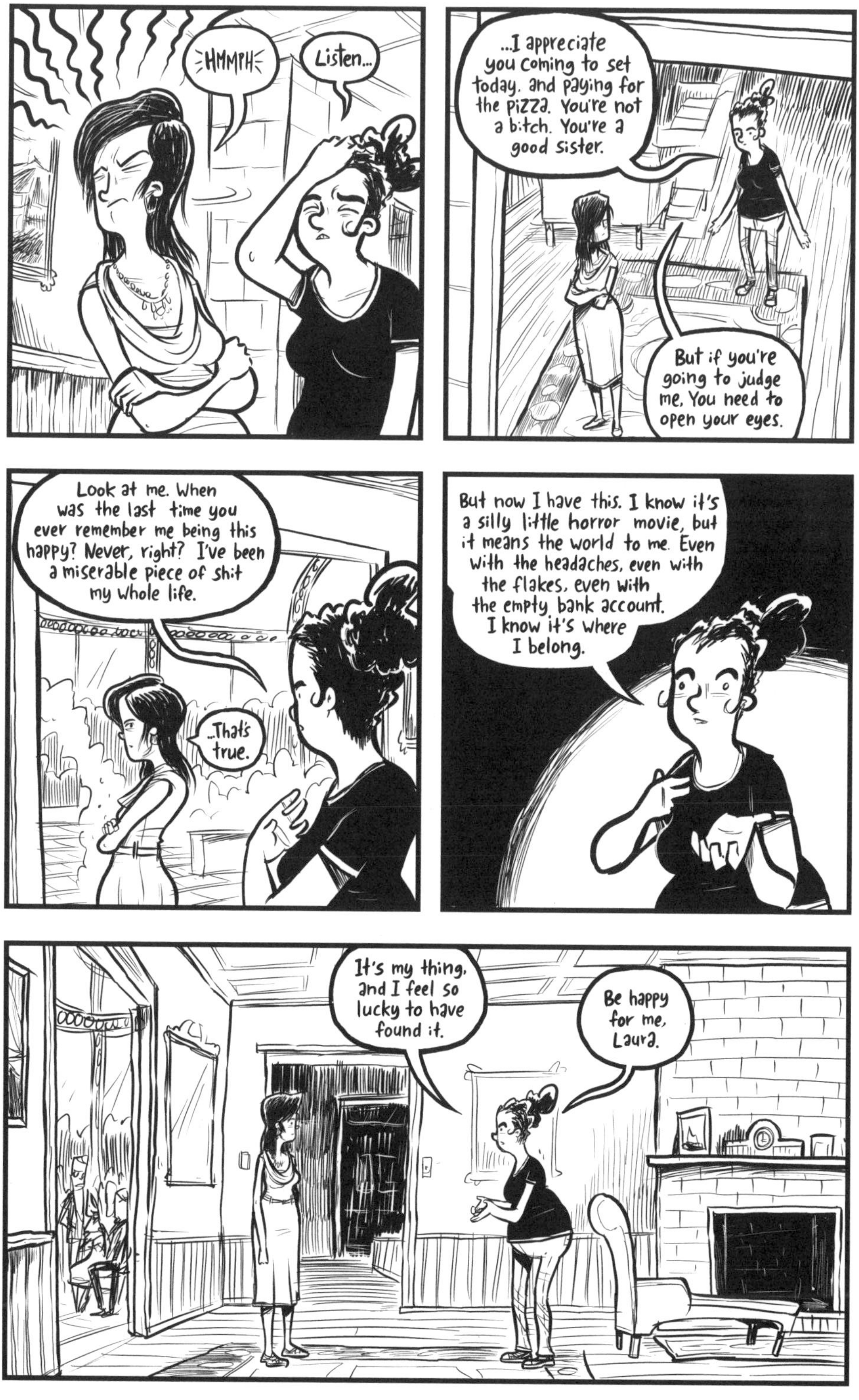
HMMPH
Listen...
...I appreciate you coming to set today, and paying for the pizza. You're not a bitch. You're a good sister.
But if you're going to judge me, you need to open your eyes.
Look at me. When was the last time you ever remember me being this happy? Never, right? I've been a miserable piece of shit my whole life.
...That's true.
But now I have this. I know it's a silly little horror movie, but it means the world to me. Even with the headaches, even with the flakes, even with the empty bank account. I know it's where I belong.
It's my thing, and I feel so lucky to have found it.
Be happy for me, Laura.

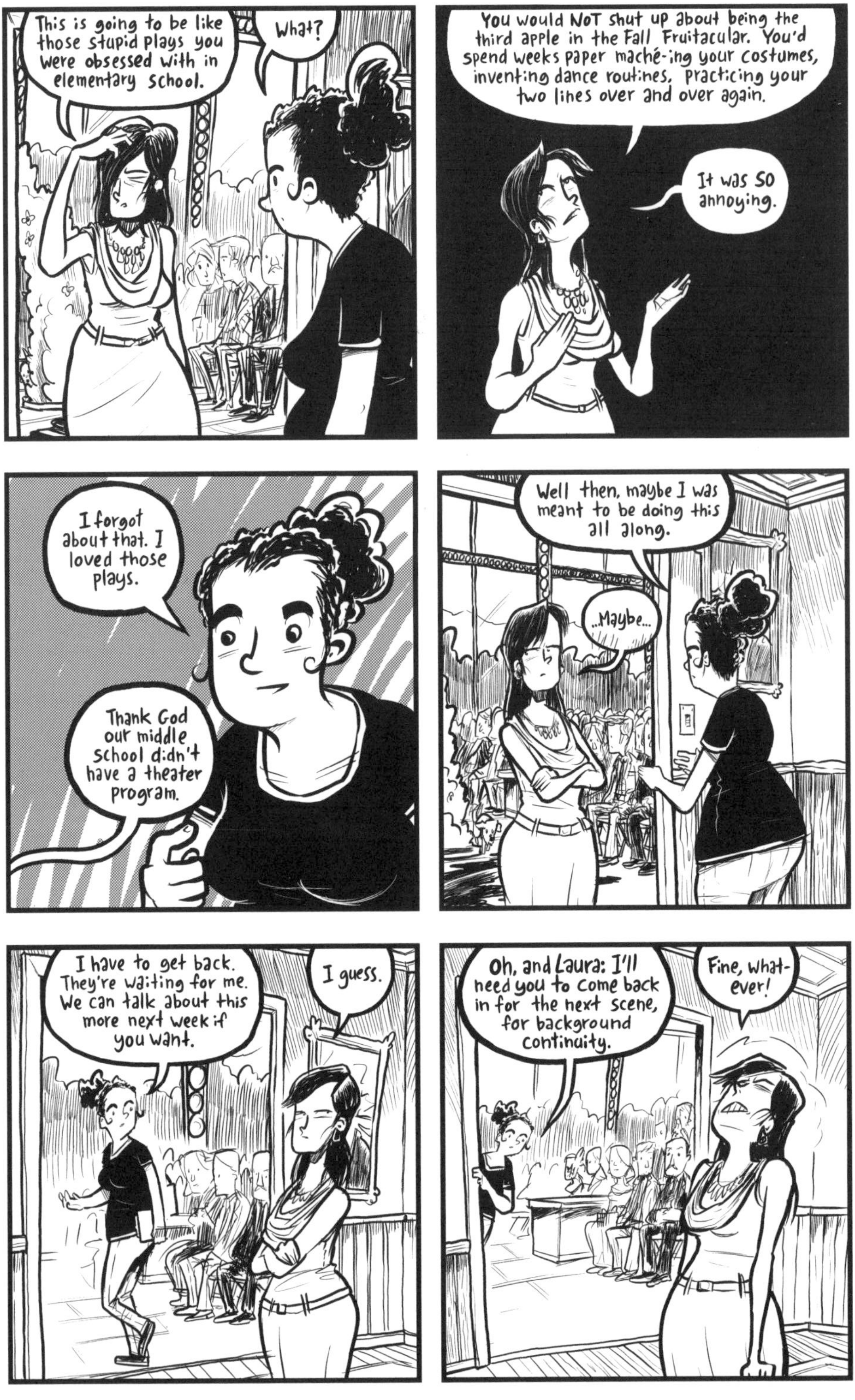
This is going to be like those stupid plays you were obsessed with in elementary school.
What?
You would NOT shut up about being the third apple in the Fall Fruitacular. You'd spend weeks paper maché-ing your costumes, inventing dance routines, practicing your two lines over and over again.
It was SO annoying.
I forgot about that. I loved those plays.
Thank God our middle school didn't have a theater program.
Well then, maybe I was meant to be doing this all along.
...Maybe...
I have to get back. They're waiting for me. We can talk about this more next week if you want.
I guess.
Oh, and Laura: I'll need you to come back in for the next scene, for background continuity.
Fine, whatever!

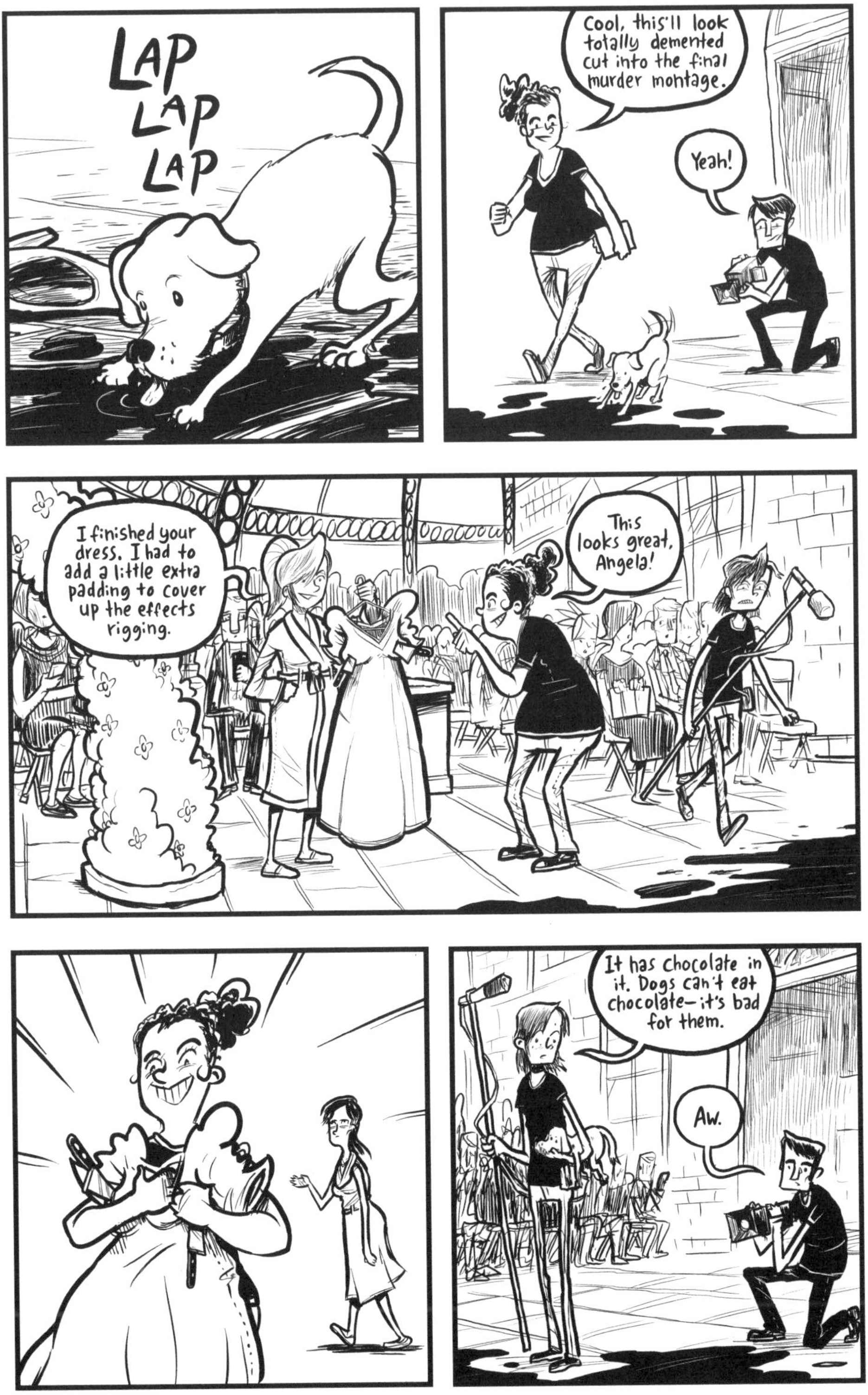
LAP LAP LAP
Cool, this'll look totally demented cut into the final murder montage.
Yeah!
I finished your dress. I had to add a little extra padding to cover up the effects rigging.
This looks great, Angela!
It has chocolate in it. Dogs can't eat chocolate— it's bad for them.
Aw.

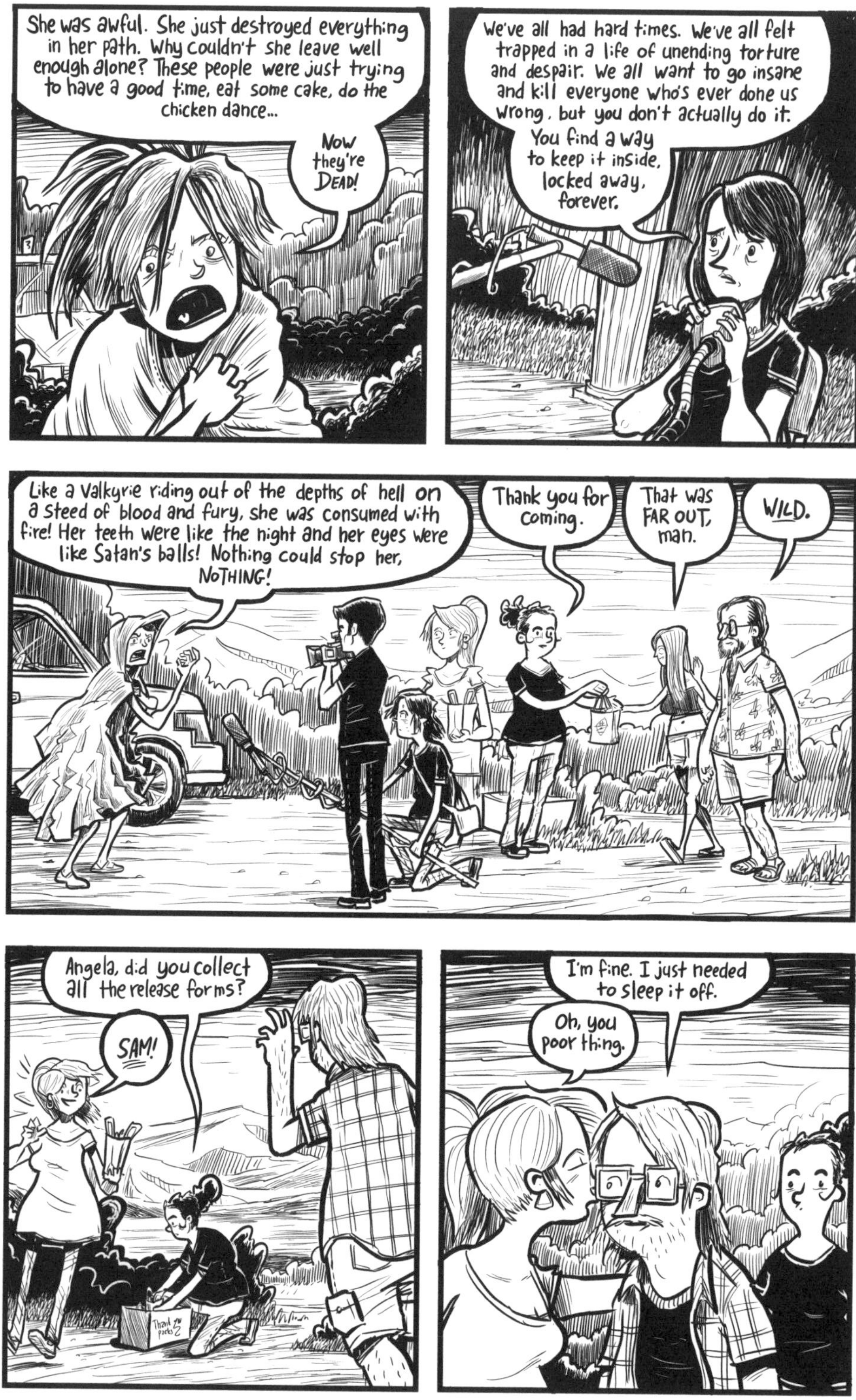
She was awful. She just destroyed everything in her path. Why couldn't she leave well enough alone? These people were just trying to have a good time, eat some cake, do the chicken dance...
Now they're DEAD!
We've all had hard times. We've all felt trapped in a life of unending torture and despair. We all want to go insane and kill everyone who's ever done us wrong, but you don't actually do it.
You find a way to keep it inside, locked away, forever.
Like a Valkyrie riding out of the depths of hell on a steed of blood and fury, she was consumed with fire! Her teeth were like the night and her eyes were like Satan's balls! Nothing could stop her, NOTHING!
Thank you for coming.
That was FAR OUT, man.
WILD.
Angela, did you collect all the release forms?
SAM!
I'm fine. I just needed to sleep it off.
Oh, you poor thing.

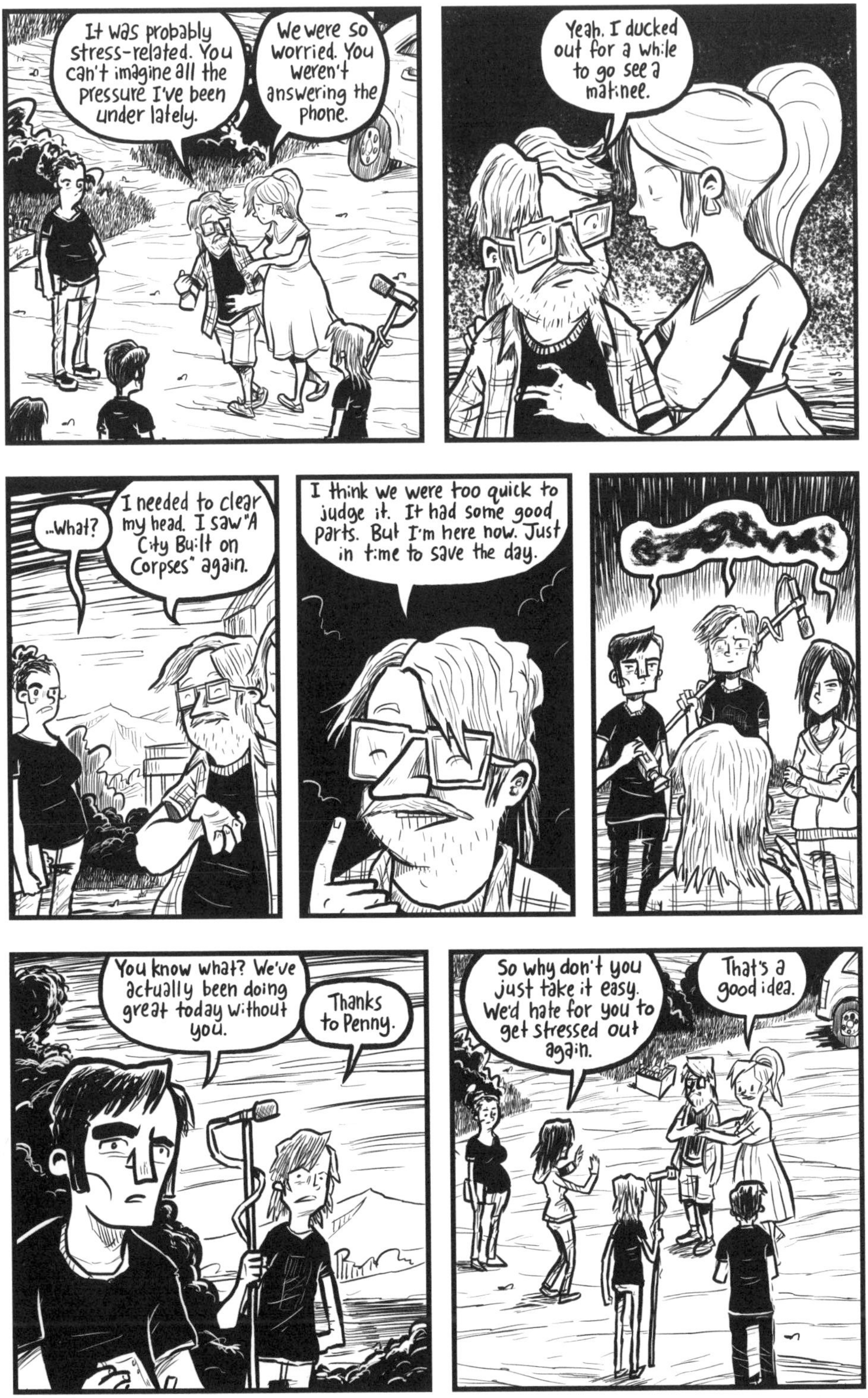
It was probably stress-related. You can't imagine all the pressure I've been under lately.
We were so worried. You weren't answering the phone.
Yeah. I ducked out for a while to go see a matinee.
..What?
I needed to clear my head. I saw "A City Built on Corpses" again.
I think we were too quick to judge it. It had some good parts. But I'm here now. Just in time to save the day.
You know what? We've actually been doing great today without you.
Thanks to Penny.
So why don't you just take it easy. We'd hate for you to get stressed out again.
That's a good idea.

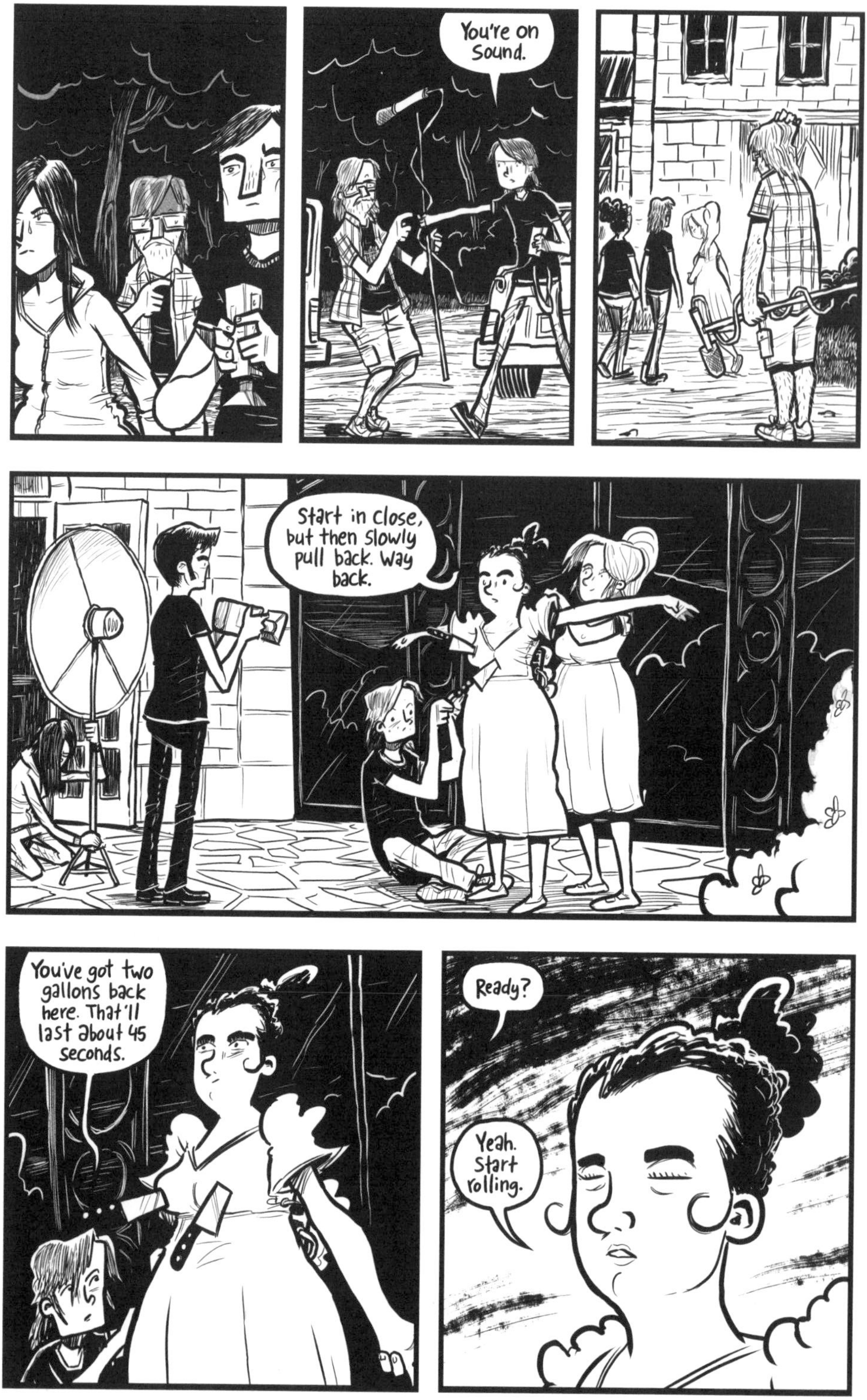
You're on sound.
Start in close, but then slowly pull back. Way back.
You've got two gallons back here. That'll last about 45 seconds.
Ready?
Yeah. Start rolling.

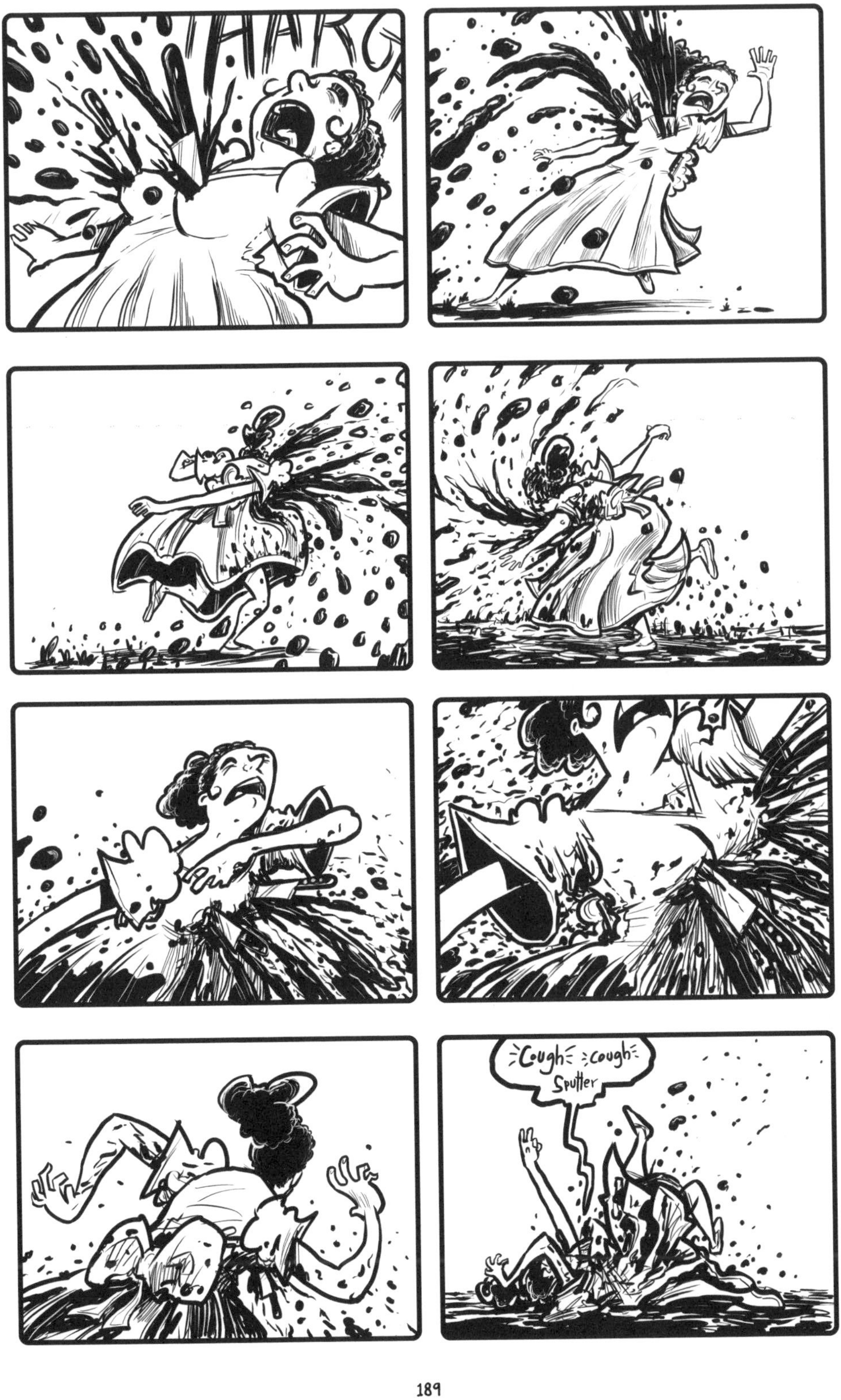
HARG
Cough cough
Sputter

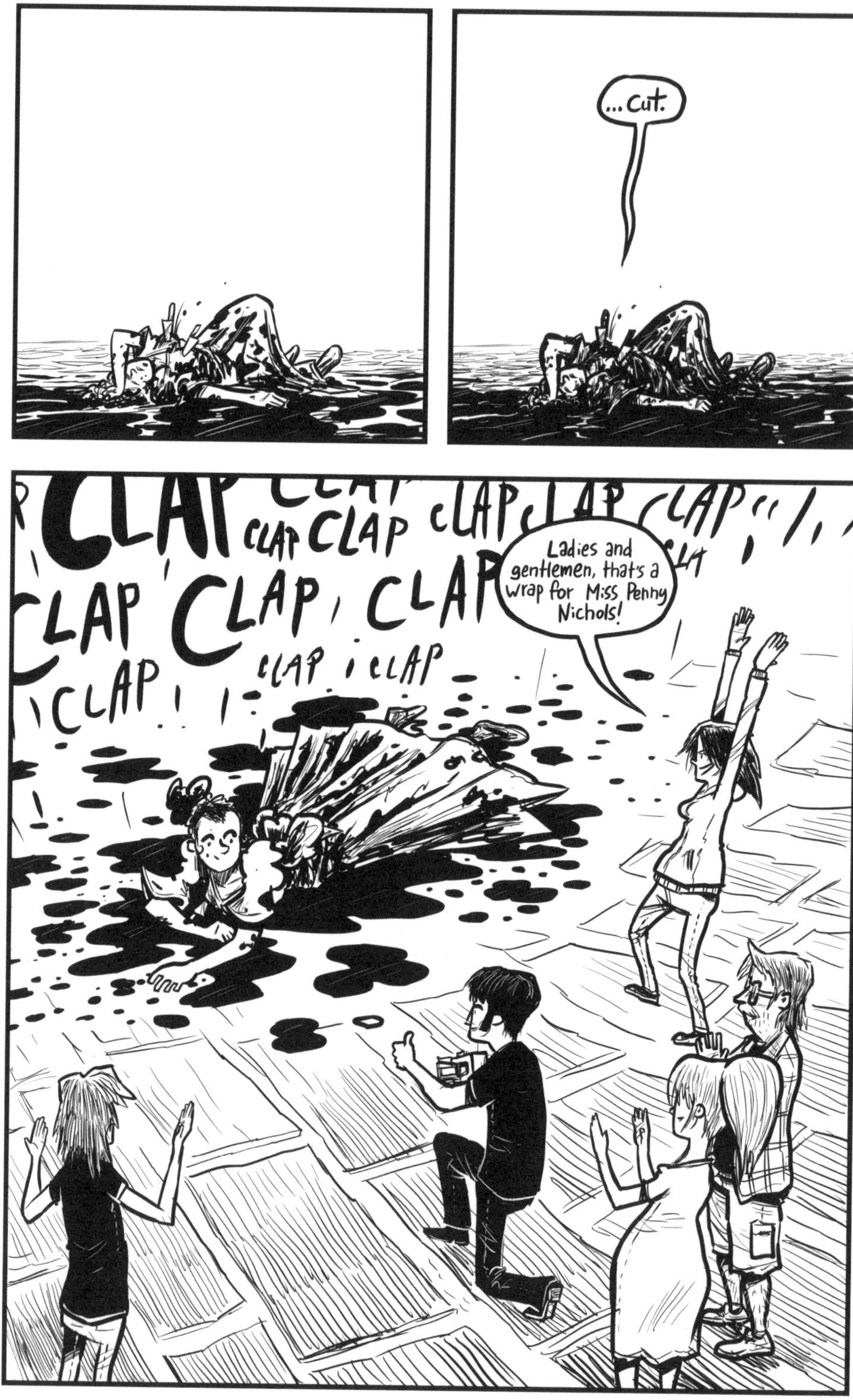
...cut.
CLAP CLAP CLAP CLAP CLAP CLAP CLAP CLAP CLAP CLAP CLAP CLAP CLAP CLAP
Ladies and gentlemen, that's a wrap for Miss Penny Nichols!

CHAPTER EIGHT

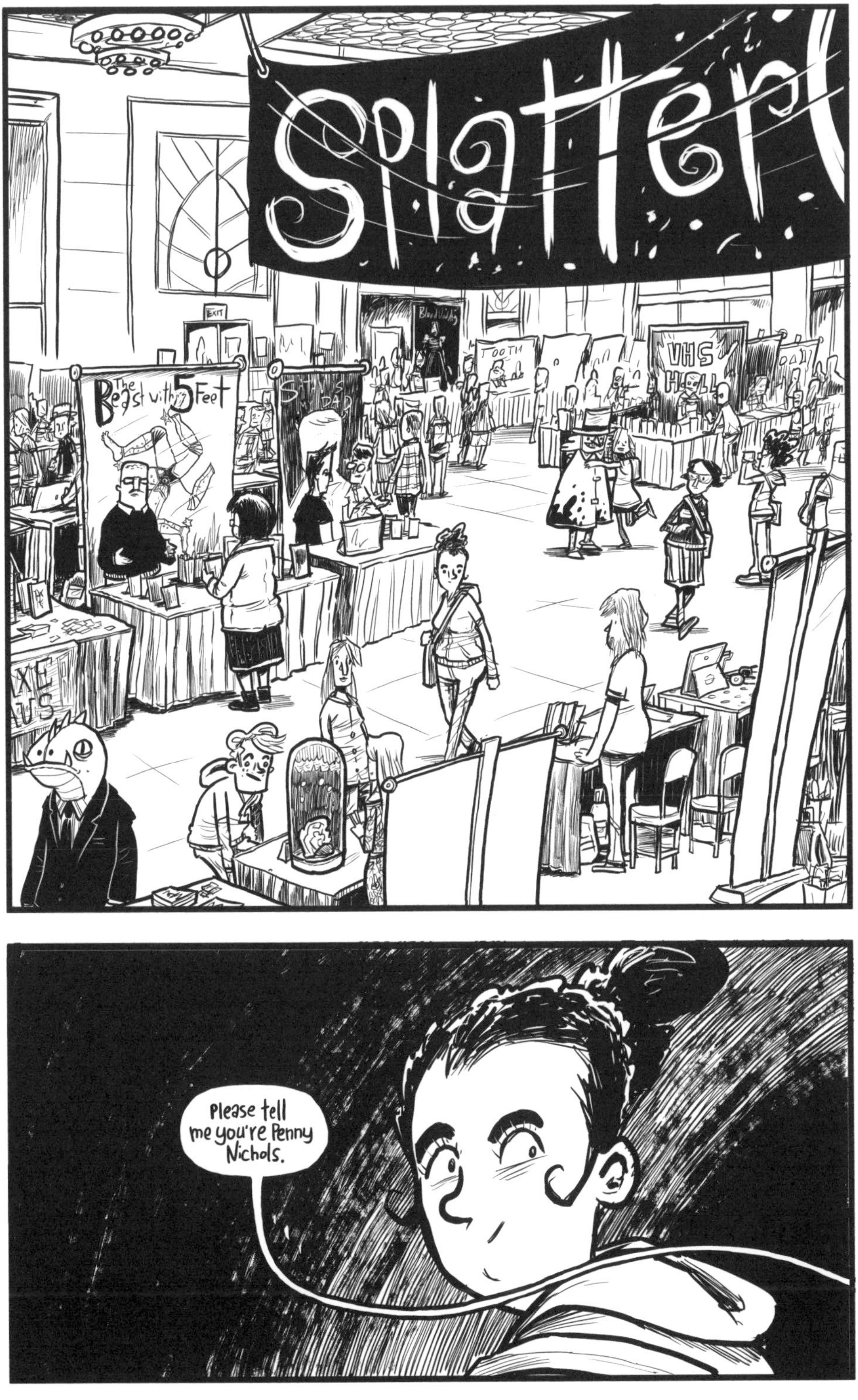
Splatter
EXIT
The Beast with 5 Feet
TOOTH
VHS
Please tell me you're Penny Nichols.

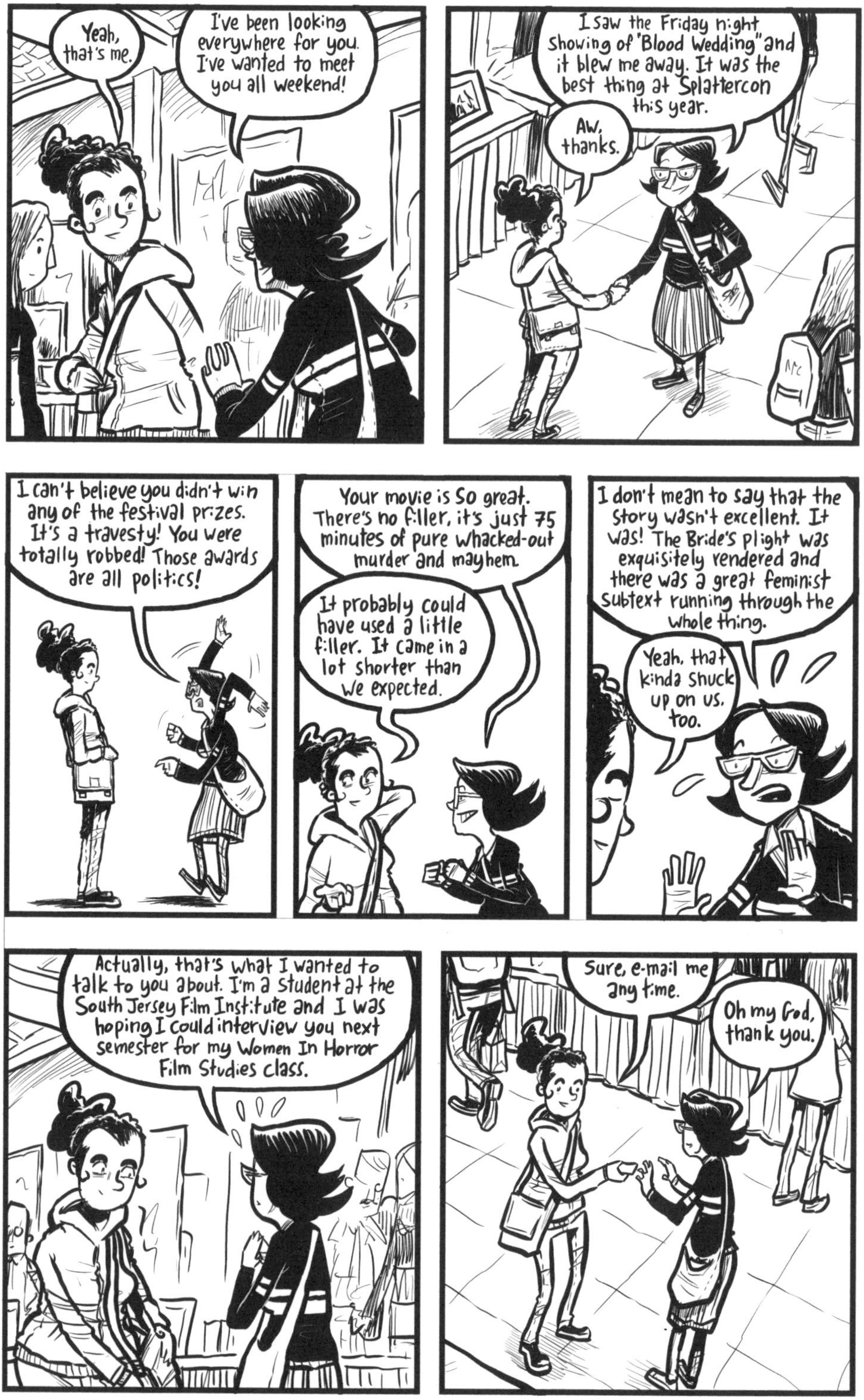
Yeah, that's me.
I've been looking everywhere for you. I've wanted to meet you all weekend!
I saw the Friday night showing of "Blood Wedding" and it blew me away. It was the best thing at Splattercon this year.
Aw, thanks.
I can't believe you didn't win any of the festival prizes. It's a travesty! You were totally robbed! Those awards are all politics!
Your movie is so great. There's no filler, it's just 75 minutes of pure whacked-out murder and mayhem.
It probably could have used a little filler. It came in a lot shorter than we expected.
I don't mean to say that the story wasn't excellent. It was! The Bride's plight was exquisitely rendered and there was a great feminist subtext running through the whole thing.
Yeah, that kinda snuck up on us, too.
Actually, that's what I wanted to talk to you about. I'm a student at the South Jersey Film Institute and I was hoping I could interview you next semester for my Women In Horror Film Studies class.
Sure, e-mail me any time.
Oh my God, thank you.

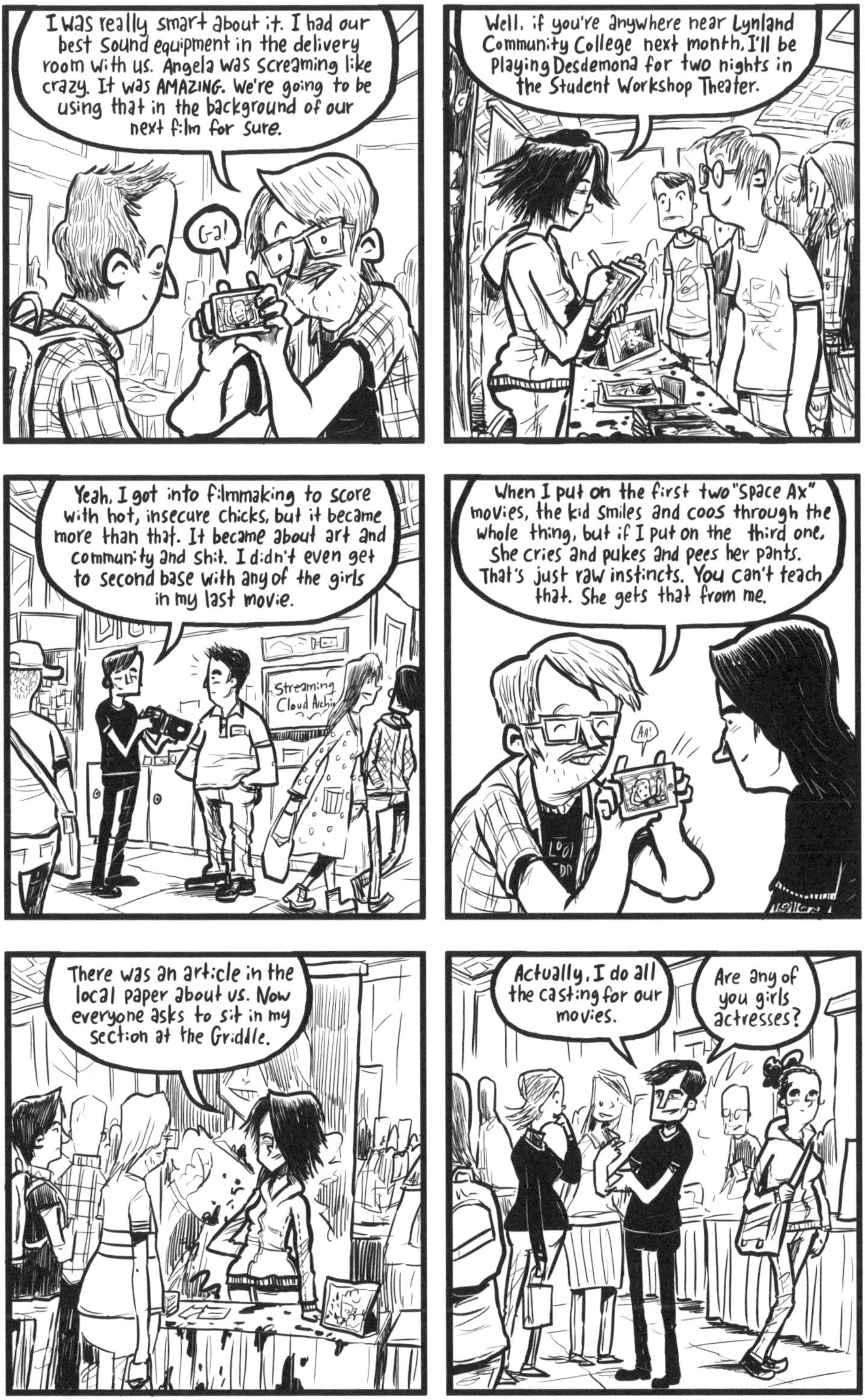
I was really smart about it. I had our best sound equipment in the delivery room with us. Angela was screaming like crazy. It was AMAZING. We're going to be using that in the background of our next film for sure.
Ga!
Well, if you're anywhere near Lynland Community College next month, I'll be playing Desdemona for two nights in the Student Workshop Theater.
Yeah, I got into filmmaking to score with hot, insecure chicks, but it became more than that. It became about art and community and shit. I didn't even get to second base with any of the girls in my last movie.
Streaming Cloud Archi
When I put on the first two "Space Ax" movies, the kid smiles and coos through the whole thing, but if I put on the third one, she cries and pukes and pees her pants. That's just raw instincts. You can't teach that. She gets that from me.
AA!
There was an article in the local paper about us. Now everyone asks to sit in my section at the Griddle.
Actually, I do all the casting for our movies.
Are any of you girls actresses?

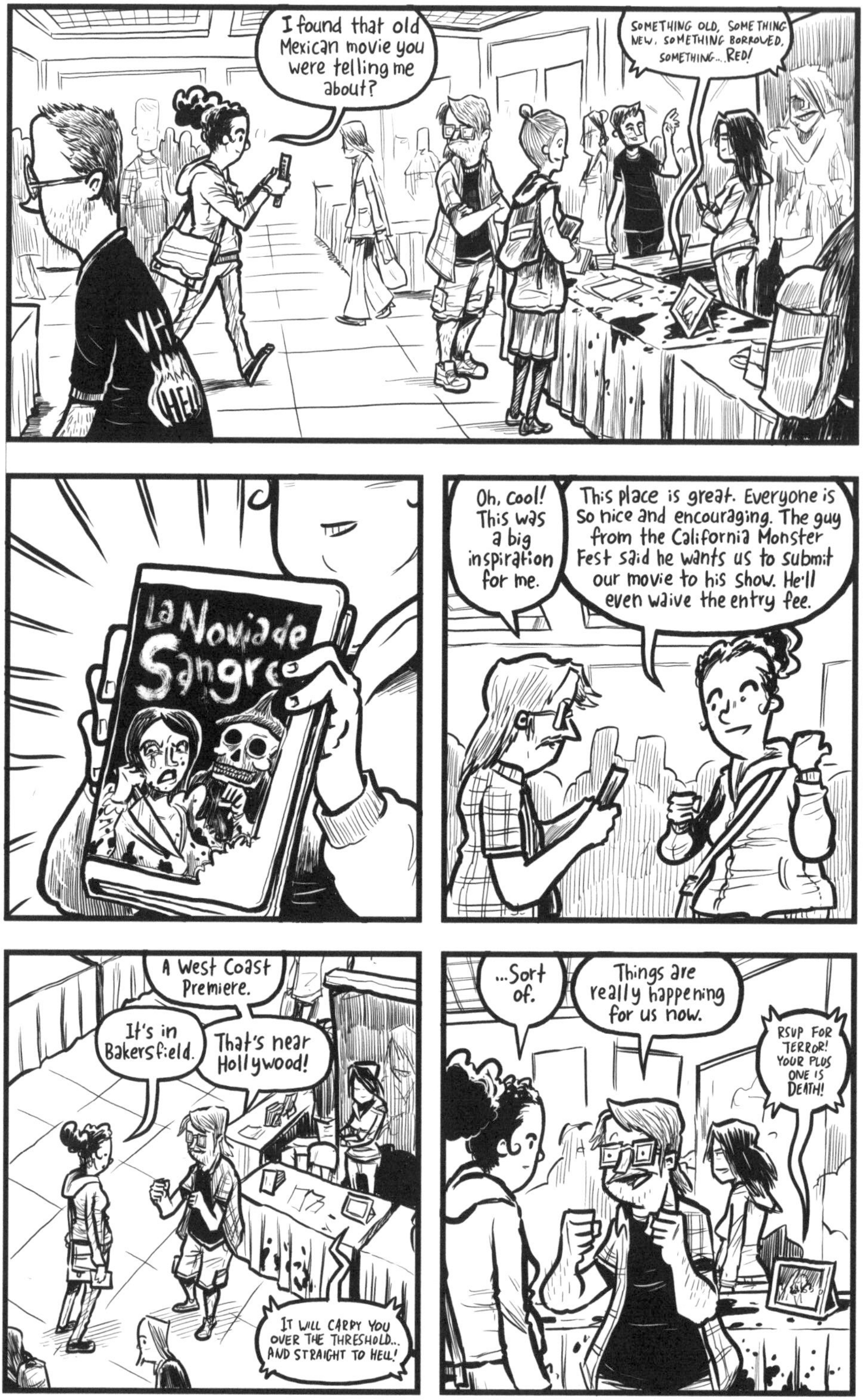
I found that old Mexican movie you were telling me about?
SOMETHING OLD, SOMETHING NEW, SOMETHING BORROWED, SOMETHING... RED!
La Novia de Sangre
Oh, cool! This was a big inspiration for me.
This place is great. Everyone is so nice and encouraging. The guy from the California Monster Fest said he wants us to submit our movie to his show. He'll even waive the entry fee.
A West Coast Premiere.
It's in Bakersfield.
That's near Hollywood!
IT WILL CARRY YOU OVER THE THRESHOLD... AND STRAIGHT TO HELL!
...Sort of.
Things are really happening for us now.
RSVP FOR TERROR! YOUR PLUS ONE IS DEATH!

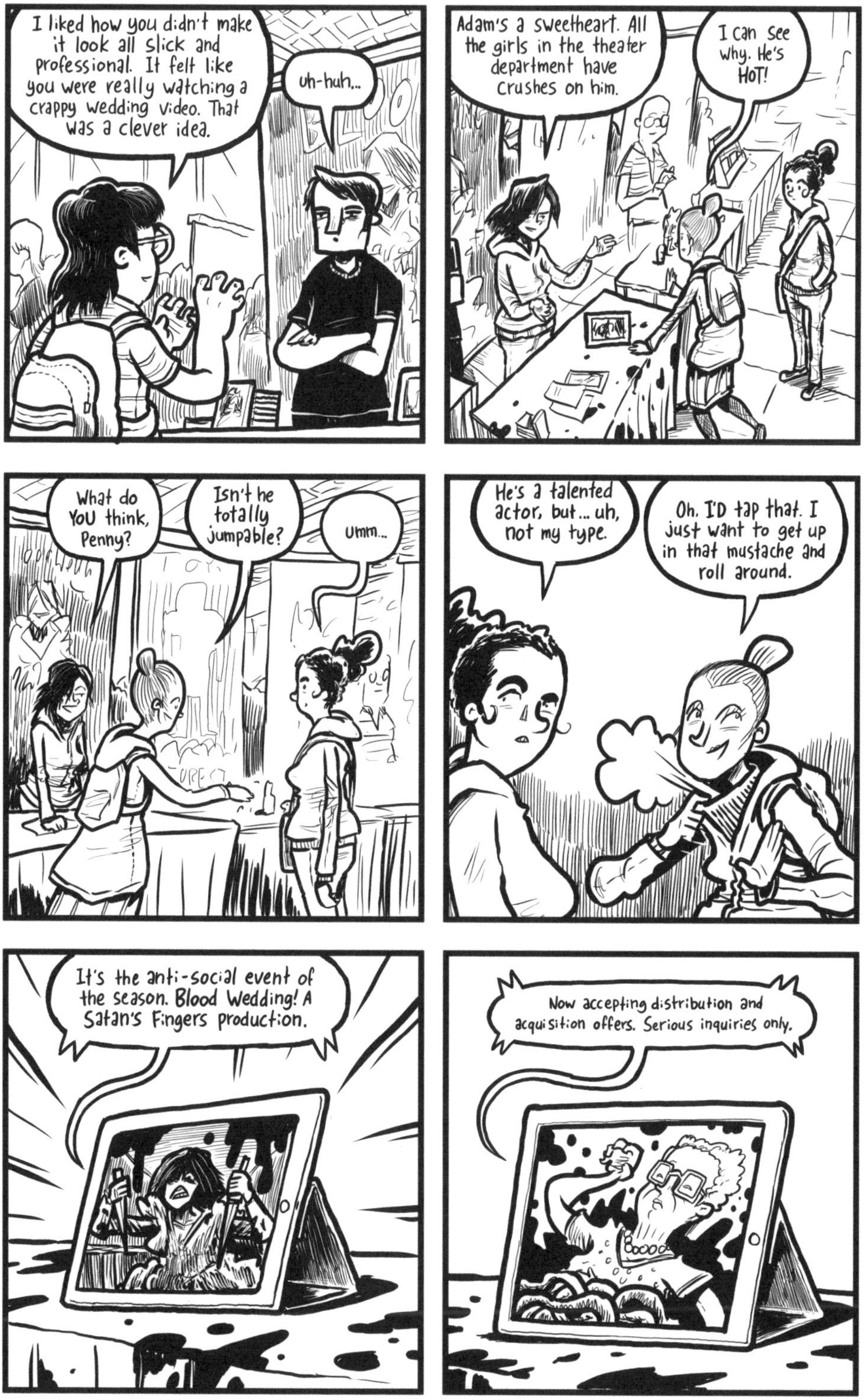
I liked how you didn't make it look all slick and professional. It felt like you were really watching a crappy wedding video. That was a clever idea.
uh-huh...
Adam's a sweetheart. All the girls in the theater department have crushes on him.
I can see why. He's HOT!
What do YOU think, Penny?
Isn't he totally jumpable?
umm...
He's a talented actor, but... uh, not my type.
Oh. I'D tap that. I just want to get up in that mustache and roll around.
It's the anti-social event of the season. Blood Wedding! A Satan's Fingers production.
Now accepting distribution and acquisition offers. Serious inquiries only.

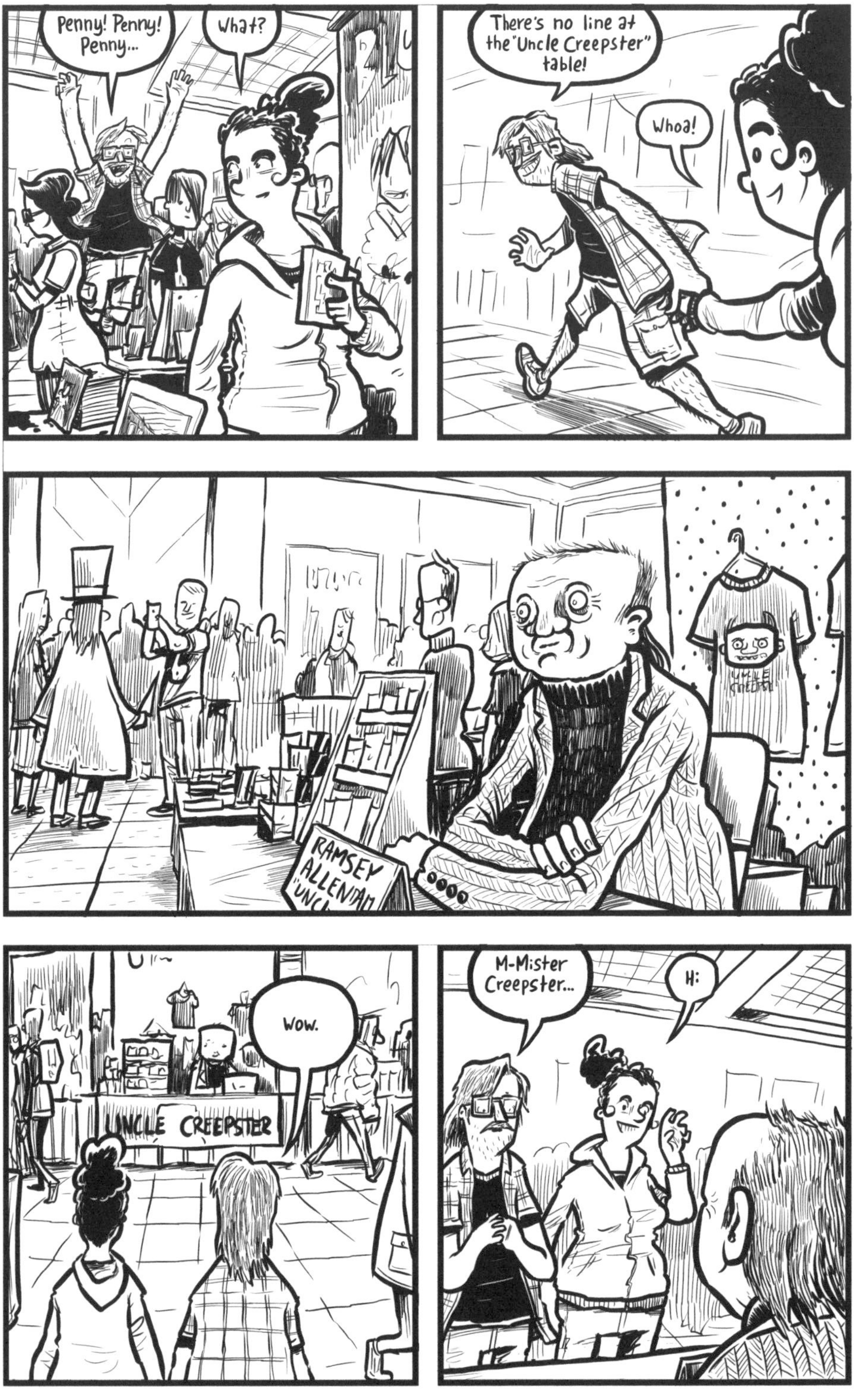
Penny! Penny! Penny...
What?
There's no line at the "Uncle Creepster" table!
Whoa!
RAMSEY ALLENDAM
UNCLE CREEPSTER
Wow.
M-Mister Creepster...
H:

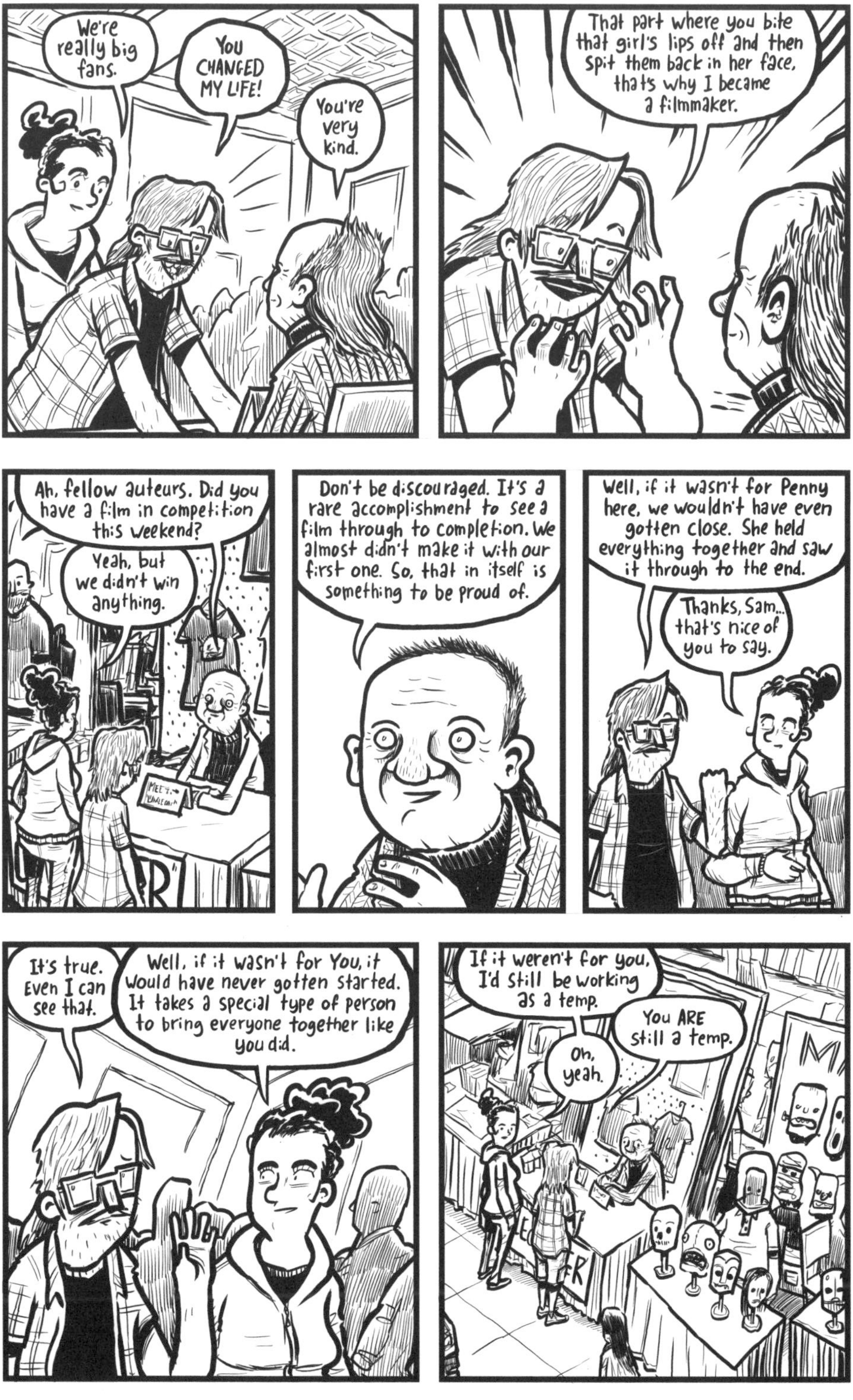
We're really big fans.
YOU CHANGED MY LIFE!
You're very kind.
That part where you bite that girl's lips off and then spit them back in her face, that's why I became a filmmaker.
Ah, fellow auteurs. Did you have a film in competition this weekend?
Yeah, but we didn't win anything.
Don't be discouraged. It's a rare accomplishment to see a film through to completion. We almost didn't make it with our first one. So, that in itself is something to be proud of.
Well, if it wasn't for Penny here, we wouldn't have even gotten close. She held everything together and saw it through to the end.
Thanks, Sam... that's nice of you to say.
It's true. Even I can see that.
Well, if it wasn't for You, it would have never gotten started. It takes a special type of person to bring everyone together like you did.
If it weren't for you, I'd still be working as a temp.
Oh, yeah.
You ARE still a temp.

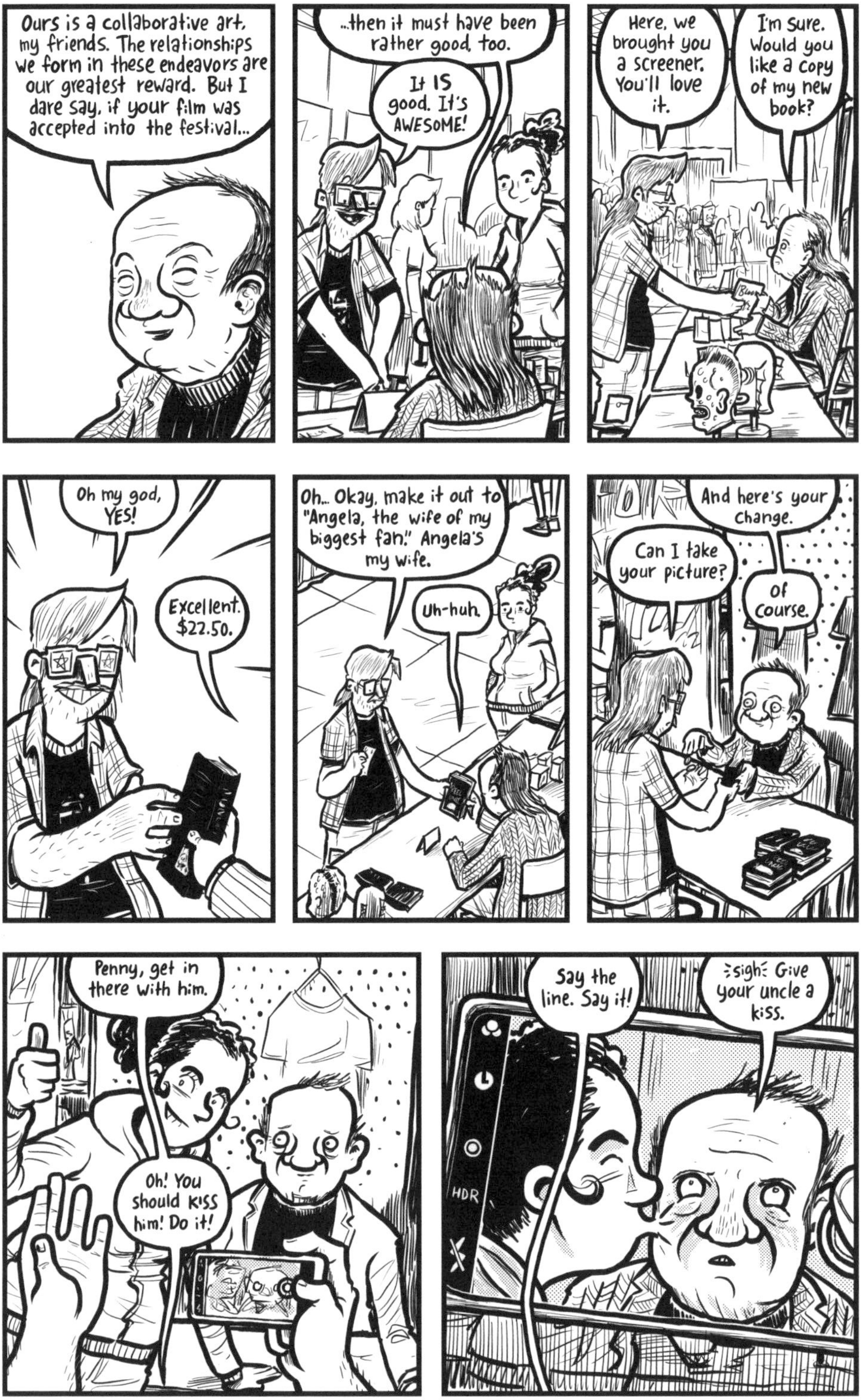
Ours is a collaborative art, my friends. The relationships we form in these endeavors are our greatest reward. But I dare say, if your film was accepted into the festival...
...then it must have been rather good, too.
It IS good. It's AWESOME!
Here, we brought you a screener. You'll love it.
I'm sure. Would you like a copy of my new book?
Oh my god, YES!
Excellent. $22.50.
Oh... Okay, make it out to "Angela, the wife of my biggest fan." Angela's my wife.
Uh-huh.
And here's your change.
Can I take your picture?
Of course.
Penny, get in there with him.
Oh! You should KISS him! Do it!
Say the line. Say it!
:sigh: Give your uncle a kiss.
HDR

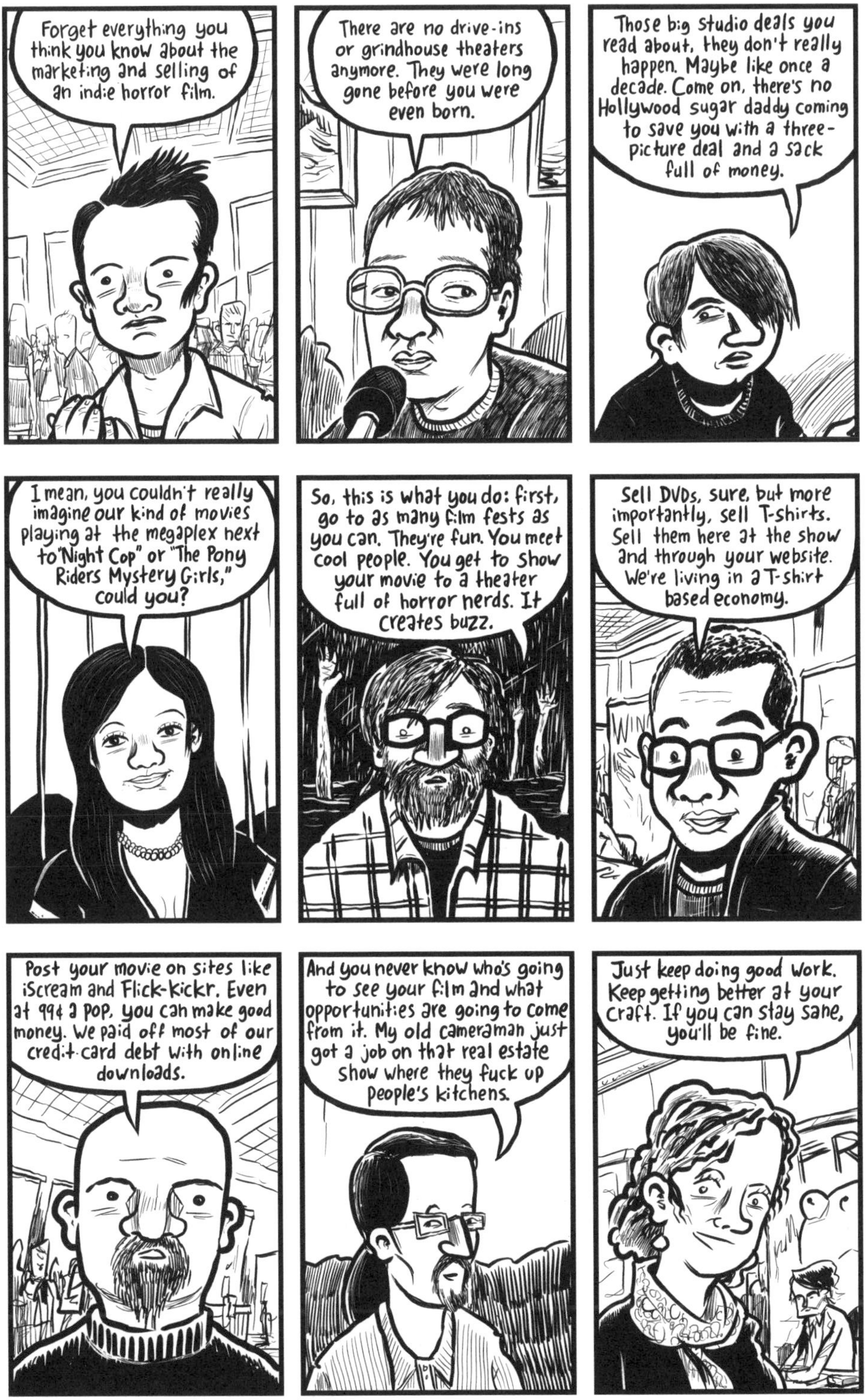
Forget everything you think you know about the marketing and selling of an indie horror film.
There are no drive-ins or grindhouse theaters anymore. They were long gone before you were even born.
Those big studio deals you read about, they don't really happen. Maybe like once a decade. Come on, there's no Hollywood sugar daddy coming to save you with a three-picture deal and a sack full of money.
I mean, you couldn't really imagine our kind of movies playing at the megaplex next to "Night Cop" or "The Pony Riders Mystery Girls," could you?
So, this is what you do: first, go to as many film fests as you can. They're fun. You meet cool people. You get to show your movie to a theater full of horror nerds. It creates buzz.
Sell DVDs, sure, but more importantly, sell T-shirts. Sell them here at the show and through your website. We're living in a T-shirt based economy.
Post your movie on sites like iScream and Flick-Kickr. Even at 99¢ a pop, you can make good money. We paid off most of our credit-card debt with online downloads.
And you never know who's going to see your film and what opportunities are going to come from it. My old cameraman just got a job on that real estate show where they fuck up people's kitchens.
Just keep doing good work. Keep getting better at your craft. If you can stay sane, you'll be fine.

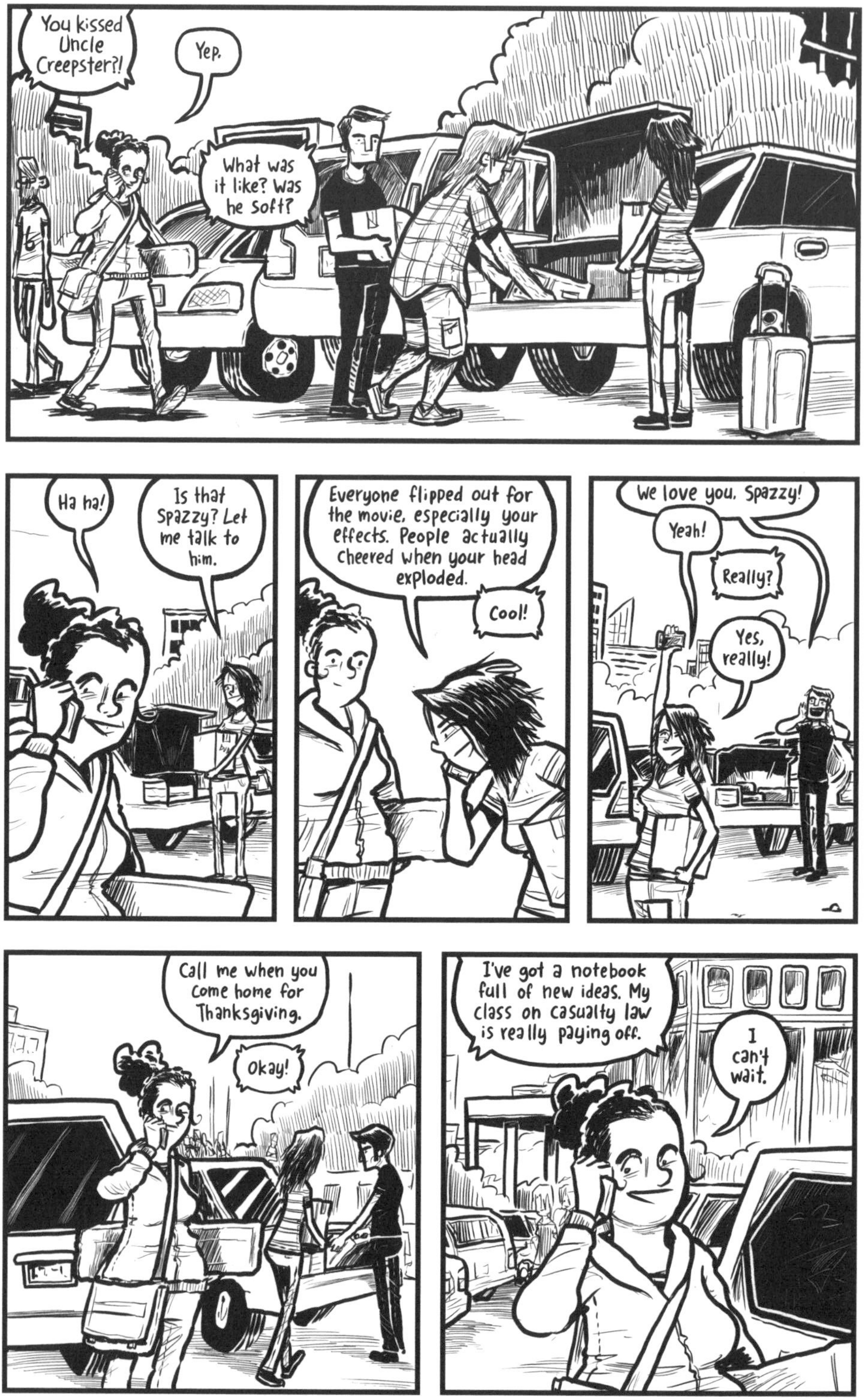
You kissed Uncle Creepster?!
Yep.
What was it like? Was he soft?
Ha ha!
Is that Spazzy? Let me talk to him.
Everyone flipped out for the movie, especially your effects. People actually cheered when your head exploded.
Cool!
We love you, Spazzy!
Yeah!
Really?
Yes, really!
Call me when you come home for Thanksgiving.
Okay!
I've got a notebook full of new ideas. My class on casualty law is really paying off.
I can't wait.

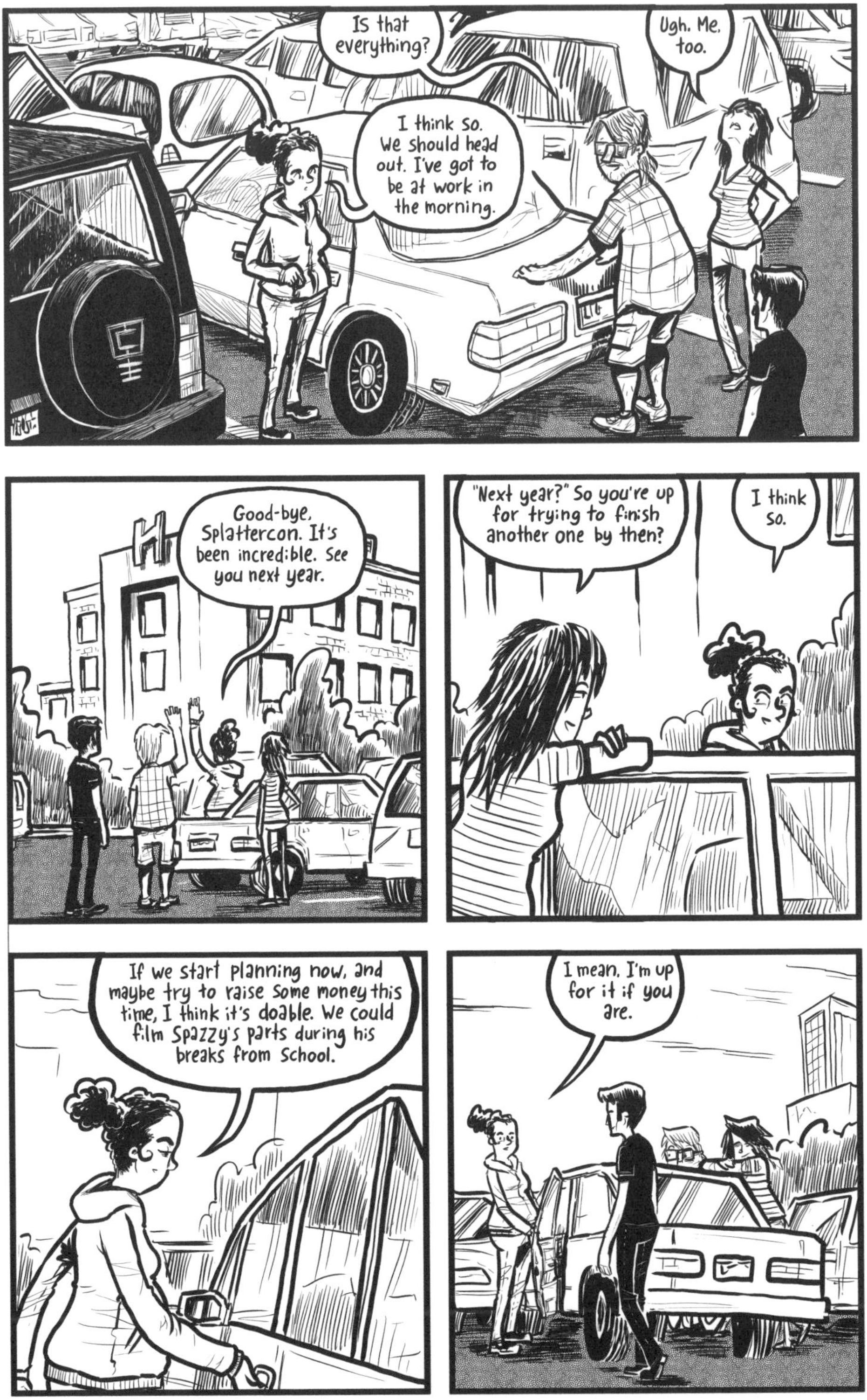
Is that everything?
I think so. We should head out. I've got to be at work in the morning.
Ugh. Me, too.
Good-bye, Splattercon. It's been incredible. See you next year.
"Next year?" So you're up for trying to finish another one by then?
I think so.
If we start planning now, and maybe try to raise some money this time, I think it's doable. We could film Spazzy's parts during his breaks from school.
I mean, I'm up for it if you are.

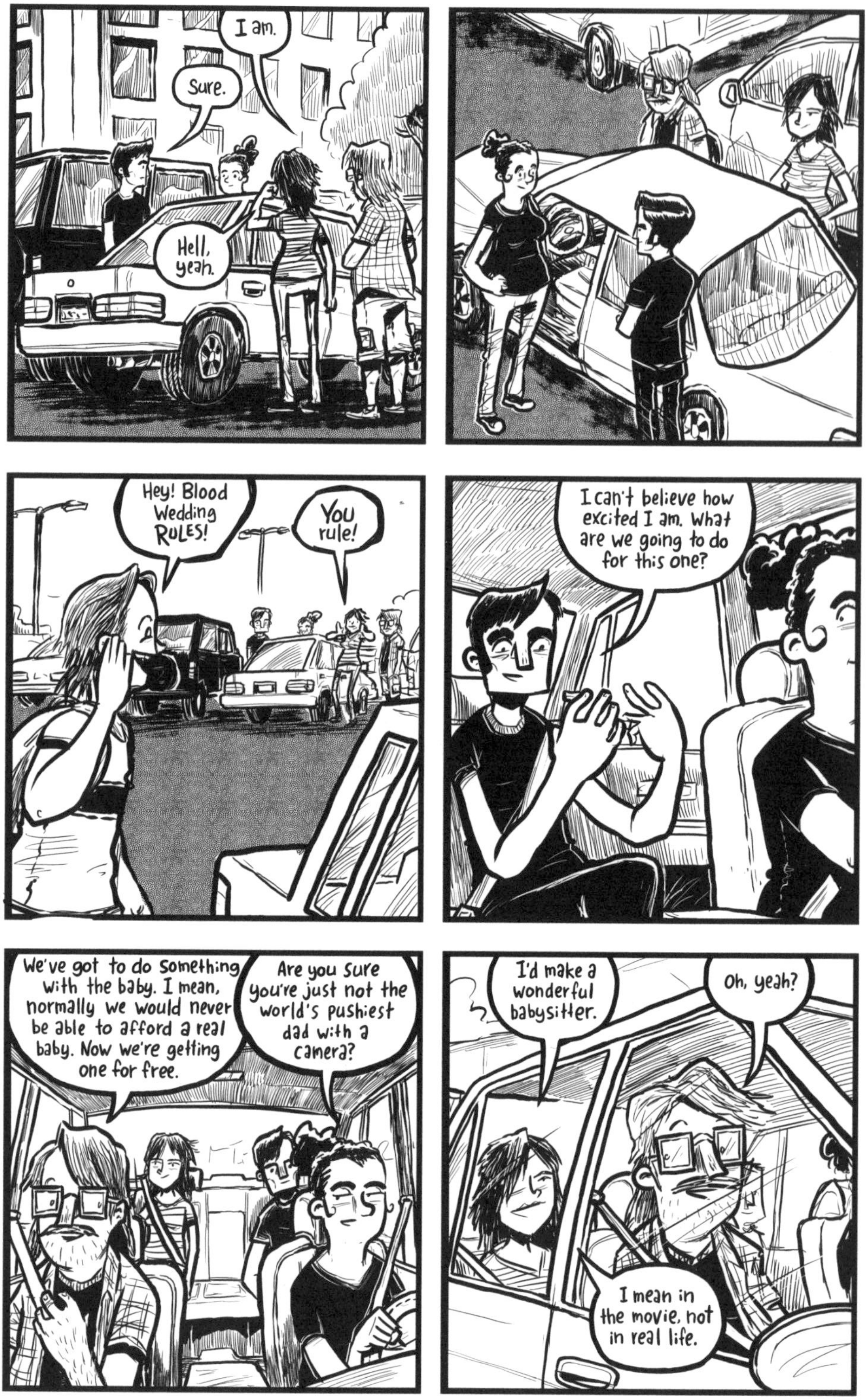
I am.
Sure.
Hell, yeah.
Hey! Blood Wedding RULES!
You rule!
I can't believe how excited I am. What are we going to do for this one?
We've got to do something with the baby. I mean, normally we would never be able to afford a real baby. Now we're getting one for free.
Are you sure you're just not the world's pushiest dad with a camera?
I'd make a wonderful babysitter.
Oh, yeah?
I mean in the movie, not in real life.

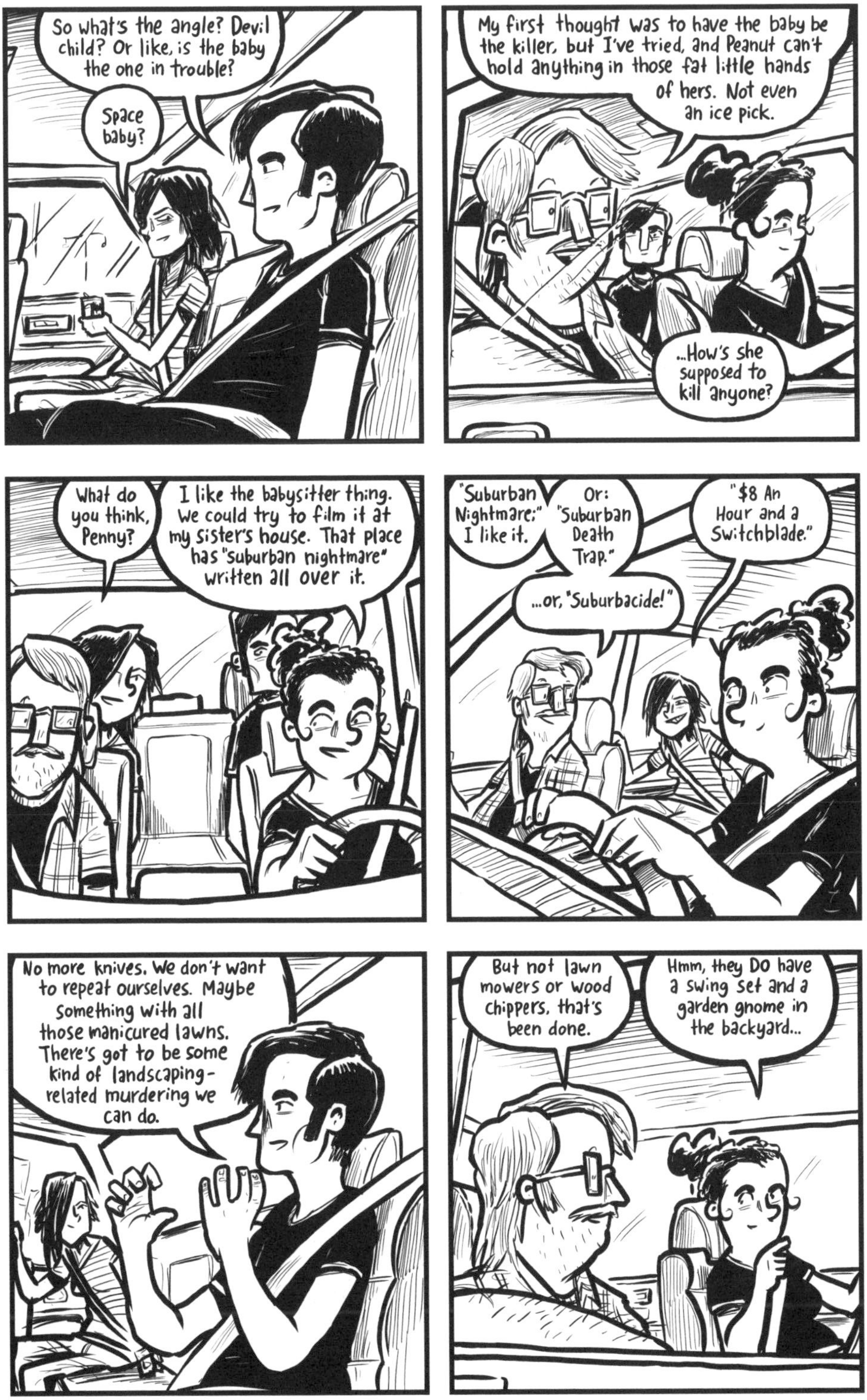
So what's the angle? Devil child? Or like, is the baby the one in trouble?
Space baby?
My first thought was to have the baby be the killer, but I've tried, and Peanut can't hold anything in those fat little hands of hers. Not even an ice pick.
...How's she supposed to kill anyone?
What do you think, Penny?
I like the babysitter thing. We could try to film it at my sister's house. That place has "suburban nightmare" written all over it.
"Suburban Nightmare;" I like it.
Or: "Suburban Death Trap."
...or, "Suburbacide!"
"$8 An Hour and a Switchblade."
No more knives. We don't want to repeat ourselves. Maybe something with all those manicured lawns. There's got to be some kind of landscaping-related murdering we can do.
But not lawn mowers or wood chippers, that's been done.
Hmm, they DO have a swing set and a garden gnome in the backyard...

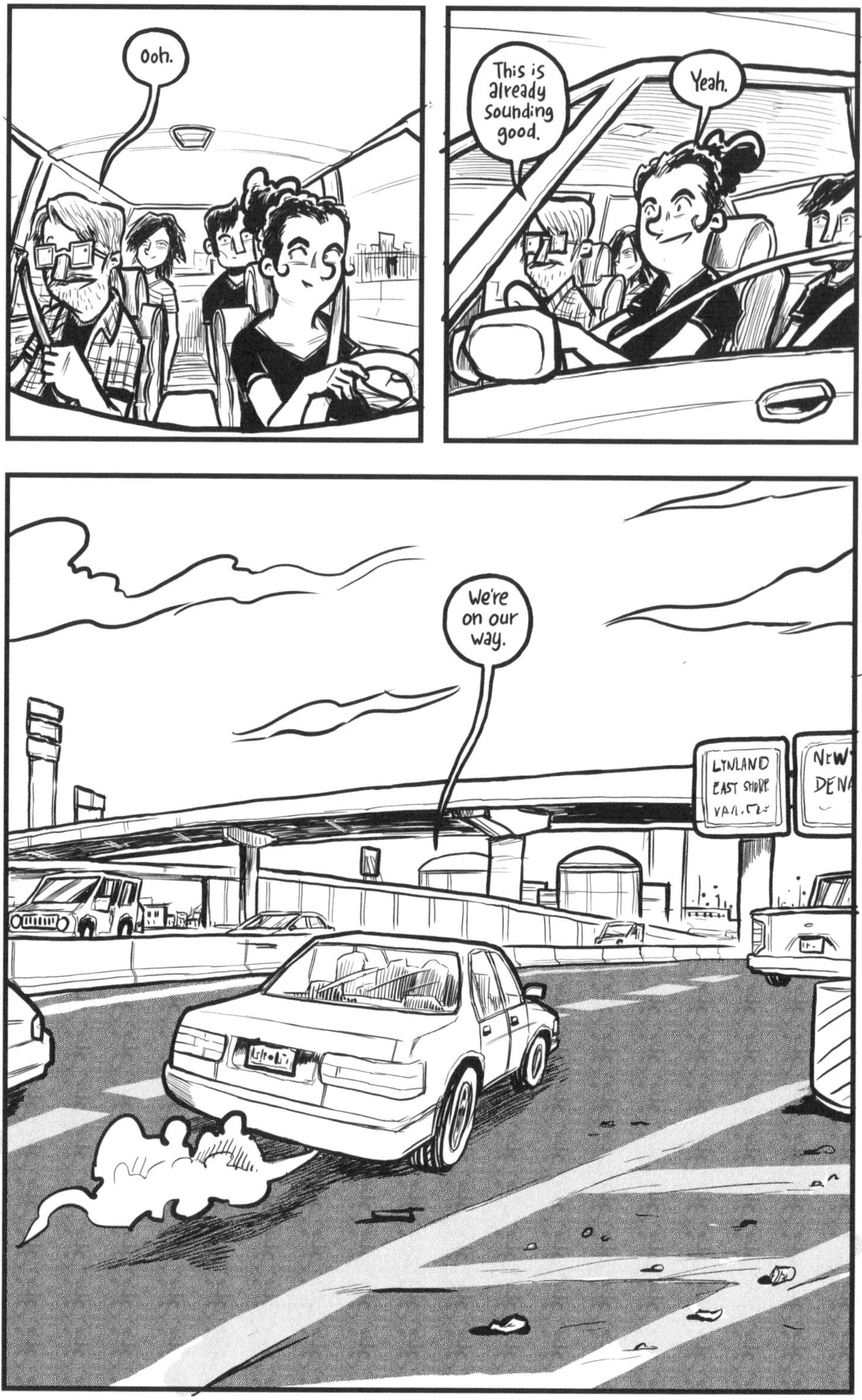
Ooh.
This is already sounding good.
Yeah.
We're on our way.
LYNLAND
EAST SHORE

ABOUT THE AUTHORS

MK REED IS THE EISNER AWARD-NOMINATED AUTHOR OF SEVERAL GRAPHIC NOVELS AND COMIC SERIES, ON SUBJECTS RANGING FROM PALEONTOLOGY, TO ROMANCE, TO FIRST AMENDMENT RIGHTS. HER LATEST SERIES, *THE CASTOFFS*, IS ABOUT TEEN GIRL WIZARDS WHO FIGHT ROBOTS.

GREG MEANS IS A WRITER AND EDITOR FROM PORTLAND, OREGON. HE WAS THE EDITOR OF THE IGNATZ AWARD-WINNING ANTHOLOGY SERIES *PAPERCUTTER* AND IS THE CO-AUTHOR OF THE GRAPHIC NOVEL *THE CUTE GIRL NETWORK* (WITH MK REED AND JOE FLOOD).

MATT WIEGLE IS THE ARTIST OF THE WEBCOMIC *DESTRUCTOR* (WITH SEAN COLLINS) AND DREW THE *ROMEO & JULIET* ADAPTION FOR SPARKNOTES. HE CURRENTLY WORKS AS AN INDUSTRIAL DESIGNER IN PHILADELPHIA.